Black Commu~~nities~~
and Learning to Read
Building on Children's Linguistic and Cultural Strengths

Black Communications and Learning to Read

Building on Children's Linguistic and Cultural Strengths

Terry Meier

LEA Lawrence Erlbaum Associates
Taylor & Francis Group

New York London

KH

Lawrence Erlbaum Associates
Taylor & Francis Group
270 Madison Avenue
New York, NY 10016

Lawrence Erlbaum Associates
Taylor & Francis Group
2 Park Square
Milton Park, Abingdon
Oxon OX14 4RN

Printed in the United States of America on acid-free paper
10 9 8 7 6 5 4 3 2 1

International Standard Book Number-13: 978-0-8058-5760-3 (Softcover) 978-0-8058-5759-7 (Hardcover)

Library of Congress Cataloging-in-Publication Data

Meier, Terry.
    Black communications and learning to read : building on children's linguistic and cultural strengths / Terry Meier.
       p. cm.
    Includes bibliographical references and index.
    ISBN-13: 978-0-8058-5760-3 (alk. paper) 1. Black English--United States. 2. Reading (Primary)--United States. 3. English language--Study and teaching--African American students. 4. African American children--Education--United States. I. Title.

PE3102.N42M45 2008
427'.973--dc22
                                      2007016033

Visit the Taylor & Francis Web site at
http://www.taylorandfrancis.com

12/20/07

To my own two shining stars,
Peter Joefish and Anya Michèle,
and to
my husband, Peter Murrell,
without whose love and support I could
not have completed this book

Contents

Preface

This book is about effective literacy instruction for children who use the language variety many linguists currently call African American English, but which, for the reasons I detail in the Introduction, I refer to as Black Communications (BC). The book is organized in four parts, whose themes center on effective literacy instruction for BC speakers in grades K through 4.

Part 1, "What Is Black Communications?," presents an overview of the BC system. It does not focus specifically on children's language, as the title of this volume may have led some readers to expect, but rather on the adult communicative system. This is because I believe that in order to build productively on the linguistic strengths children bring to school, teachers must first possess some understanding of, and respect for, the language used by the adult caregivers and role models in children's homes and communities. Children's ways of using language become more understandable, meaningful, and predictable when viewed within the context of the rules and expectations that govern language use in the speech community(ies) where they are being socialized. I do not attempt a complete description of the adult BC system, a task considerably beyond the scope of this work. Rather, my intention in part 1 is to provide readers unfamiliar with BC with a basic introduction to the major components of the language and to illustrate how these various components—phonology, grammar, lexicon, and pragmatics—work in synchrony to create a coherent whole. Using examples drawn from these four components, I make the point that in using BC, speakers follow systematic rules. Throughout part 1, and in the book as a whole, I try to show (drawing on the insights and research of many scholars) that Black Communications is more than just a "nonstandard dialect of English" as some would have it, but rather a language that, in Morgan's (2002) words, is "part and parcel of social, cultural, and political survival" and that is "about ideas, art, ideology, love and memory" (p. 7). Thus I devote considerable attention in part 1 to discussing the integral and complex interconnections among African American language, culture, and history. In doing so, I draw significantly on examples from African American historical and literary sources.

Chapter 2, "A Whole Communicative System," highlights the stylistic/ rhetorical (what's often called the *pragmatic*) component of the language. Discussing one pragmatic feature that has been identified in the linguistic literature as characteristic of some BC users—the preference for formal terms of address, especially when talking to and about African American elders—I illustrate how this particular feature connects both with other features of the BC system as well as with important aspects of African American cultural and historical experience.

Chapter 3, "Other Important Aspects of the System," focuses on the lexicon, phonology, and grammar. Whenever possible, throughout part 1, I illustrate various features of the language with examples drawn from African American children's literature.

Part 2, "Language Socialization in the African American Discourse Community," consists of two chapters that examine existing research on African American children's language socialization. Chapter 4, "Language in the Air," focuses on the various ritual spaces in which African American children are likely to be exposed to adult rhetorical models. To illustrate the importance of these models in shaping children's language abilities, I draw on the reflections of African Americans from a variety of fields as well as on examples of how these ritual spaces are portrayed in African American children's literature. In chapter 5, "Children Using Language," I examine research on African American children's language socialization through the lens of their participation in key communicative events in their communities including Sunday school lessons, ritualized language routines such as playing the dozens, conflict talk that occurs in peer and sibling interactions, and storytelling. Throughout, I make hypotheses about specific linguistic abilities children are likely to develop as a result of their participation in these events.

Part 3, "Using African American Children's Literature to Teach Essential Comprehension Strategies," consists of four chapters. In chapter 6, "Drawing on Children's Strengths," I discuss ways in which teachers can build on the linguistic abilities discussed in chapter 5 in teaching reading comprehension to BC speakers. I discuss the significance of teacher read-alouds in the early literacy curriculum and also argue for the importance of incorporating African American literature into the curriculum.

Collectively, chapters 7, 8, and 9 focus on five major comprehension strategies discussed in the reading literature: *connecting, visualizing, inferring, questioning and summarizing/retelling*. I explain each of these reading strategies in detail, drawing on examples from African American children's literature. Throughout these chapters, I draw connections between strategy instruction and the linguistic and rhetorical abilities discussed in part 2. Each chapter ends with suggestions for using African American literature to help children develop their speaking and writing abilities.

Part 4, "Learning to Decode," moves from a focus on teaching comprehension strategies to a focus on helping BC speakers learn to decode text. In chapter 10, "Emergent Literacy," I discuss the key components of an effective emergent literacy curriculum, emphasizing the importance of helping children develop a strong foundation for phonics instruction. I highlight alphabet knowledge in particular in this chapter and suggest strategies for teaching it effectively. In chapter 11, "Fostering Phonological and Phonemic Awareness," I focus on specific teaching strategies for helping children to develop phonological and phonemic awareness, placing special emphasis on the importance of drawing children's attention to the ending sounds in words. In chapter 12, "Black Communications and Phonics Instruction," I present an overview of research on the relationship between BC and phonics instruction, reviewing various arguments that have been made about the possible effects of speaking BC on the process of learning to read. I also consider in detail various pedagogical suggestions that have been made over the past 30 years for improving reading instruction for BC speakers. Finally, in chapter 13, "Implications for Research and Practice," I discuss implications of existing research on BC and decoding for researchers, teacher educators, and teachers working in early elementary classrooms.

Acknowledgments

This is a book that has grown out of my thinking and experience over almost three decades. Thus, a major portion of the book could easily be the names of all the individuals who have contributed in some way to its creation. My biggest debt of gratitude is to the bright, talented, and energetic students I have worked with over the years, from whom I have learned so much more than I have ever taught, and to the many generous teachers who have allowed me access to their classrooms and to their ideas about the complex task of teaching children to read. My debt is beyond measure.

I have benefited from the ideas and support of many thoughtful friends, colleagues, and mentors. Special thanks to Tony Baéz, Rhonda Berkower, Wilma Bonaparte, Cheryl Render Brown, Courtney Cazden, Joan May Cordova, Michèle Foster, Albie Johnson, James LaGoo, Robert Lowe, Anne Lehman, Shirley Malone-Fenner, Theresa Perry, Judith Richards, and Eddneata Thompson. I am grateful for the life and work of Dr. Mary Rhodes Hoover, scholar and educator, who worked tirelessly on behalf of the educational well-being of African American children. Her passing is a great loss, but her passion and commitment provide an enduring model. I thank those who have offered me much-needed encouragement, prayers, and inspiration during the process of writing, especially Ester Benros, Elana Berkower, Lillian Buckley, Maggie and Cornelius Dorsey, Sister Mary Hart, Irene Hiller, Sister Joanne McGovern, James Murrell, Ruth and Peter Murrell, the Sisters of the Good Shepherd, and Patricia Willot.

I thank my colleagues in the Language and Literacy Department at Wheelock College—Susan Harris-Sharples, Lowry Hemphill, and MaryAnn Johnson—for their encouragement and their willingness to sometimes carry more that their share of departmental responsibilities so that I could have time to write. I am grateful for having received the Gordon Marshall Fellowship Award at Wheelock College to support this project. I thank Rhonda Berkower for her thoughtful reading of the manuscript and for her careful editing of part 3. I thank Albie Johnson for her help in tracking down sources and for her unfailing encouragement. My thanks as well to Naomi Silverman and the editorial team at Lawrence Erlbaum Associates. I am also grateful for the meticulous proofreading skills and warm support of my production editor, Christine Andreasen.

Finally, I acknowledge my family on whose love and support I constantly rely: my husband, Peter; my children, Peter and Anya; my nephew/child, Michael Murrell; my daughter-in-law, Aimee; my siblings, Mary, Heidi, Patty, Tim, and Peter; my much-loved nieces and nephews; and my parents, Mary Susens Ryan and Terence Matthew Ryan, who live in my heart.

Chapter 1
Introduction

This is a book about effective literacy instruction for children who use the language variety many linguists currently call African American English (AAE), but which I refer to as Black Communications (BC). After much deliberation, I have chosen to use this term because I think it conveys in a very clear way the important point, made by Geneva Smitherman (2000a) and others, that this language variety includes both a linguistic component (i.e., pronunciation and grammar rules as well as distinctive vocabulary) and a stylistic/pragmatic component (i.e., ways of using the language effectively and appropriately). As I argue throughout this book, knowledge about both of these components is essential for teachers to be successful in teaching BC speakers to read.

I realize of course that many people would strongly disagree with this view. Indeed, popular consensus on this subject seems to be that as long as teachers have respect for the language variety children bring from home, it is not really necessary for them to possess detailed knowledge about specific features of that variety. After all, so proponents of this position argue, the goal of literacy instruction is proficiency in reading and writing standard English (SE). Surely, this argument continues, the particulars of Black Communications, or of any other "nonstandard variety of English," are largely irrelevant to achieving that goal.

As an education professor who teaches courses in language and literacy and who frequently conducts workshops with teachers on the topic of linguistic diversity, I have heard this position articulated literally hundreds of times. In many cases, I have found that even bringing up the topic of Black Communications raises strong emotions in teachers and prospective teachers. This was particularly the case during the period following the Oakland, California School Board's widely publicized decision in 1996 to recognize what they termed *Ebonics* as the home language of many of its students and to build upon that linguistic foundation in designing literacy instruction. At that time

I frequently heard education students and workshop participants express the view, often in advance of any actual discussion of the subject, and often in heated tones, that they were "against Ebonics."

But as educator Lisa Delpit (1998) points out, in actuality, "[one] can be neither for Ebonics or against Ebonics any more than [one] can be for or against air. It exists" (p. 17). Like all languages, Black Communications/ Ebonics resides in the minds of its users and therefore cannot be summarily dismissed from the classroom by teachers who consider it irrelevant to instruction. Black Communications not only finds expression in the sounds, sentences, words, and gestures its users produce when they communicate, but is present as well in the assumptions they make about the meaning of other people's utterances and in the ways they make sense of events, including, of course, what happens in school.

Perhaps not surprisingly, given the technical nature of much of the literature about BC, for the most part it has been linguists, not educators, who have had the most to say about the relationship between BC and literacy instruction. With few exceptions, linguists who study BC have been strong proponents of the position that teachers need to take BC into account in teaching literacy effectively to BC speakers (e.g., Ball, 1992; Baratz & Shuy, 1969; Baugh, 1981, 1999; Green, 2002; Labov, 1972, 1995, 2001; Lee, 1993; Rickford, 1999; Smitherman, 2000a; Wolfram, Adger, & Christian, 1999). In the words of linguist John Rickford (1999), "The undeniable fact . . . is that most African American children come to school speaking the vernacular. It will emerge in the classroom, and how teachers respond to it can crucially affect how the students learn to read, and how well they master standard English" (pp. 337–338).

The Oakland Ebonics Resolution

The linguistic community's position on the importance of building literacy instruction on the foundation of students' native language abilities was evident in its support of the Oakland Ebonics resolution. Some readers may recall the Oakland, California School Board's decision in 1996 to recognize Ebonics (BC) as the home language of a large percentage of its students and to utilize that language as a means of helping students develop proficiency in standard English (SE). In terms of classroom instruction, the Oakland School Board basically advocated two measures: (a) that teachers acknowledge and celebrate the legitimacy and beauty of Ebonics/BC, and (b) that teachers use the method of contrastive analysis to draw students' conscious attention to systematic differences between the phonological (sound) and grammatical rules of Ebonics/ BC and those of SE.

In essence, the goal was for Ebonics/BC speakers to become bilingual/ bidialectal, proficient in both Ebonics/BC (the language variety they presumably already knew) and SE (the language variety they were acquiring in school). In addition, the educators and community activists who developed the Oakland resolution, in close collaboration with linguist Ernie Smith, envisioned professional development opportunities for teachers to learn more about African American language, culture, history, and literature so that they could incorporate this knowledge into the design of motivating and intellectually challenging curriculum for students.

Given the fact that in 1996 African American students comprised over half the Oakland school district population and that the pedagogical strategies advocated by the Board were entirely consonant with what is arguably the most fundamental principle of learning—that is, that new knowledge is most easily acquired in the context of familiar knowledge—the Oakland resolution was hardly revolutionary. Yet public reaction to it was swift and condemnatory, erupting with what linguist William Labov (1999) aptly characterized as "all the force of madness mixed with racism" (in foreword to Rickford, J. R., 1999). For months following announcement of the resolution, the media, and the public influenced by it, went wild, vilifying the Oakland School Board and ridiculing the notion that Ebonics was anything more than slang and "bad English."

At its annual meeting in January, 1997, the Linguistic Society of America issued a resolution in support of the Oakland Board's position, characterizing the Board's decision to recognize children's vernacular (i.e., Ebonics/BC) in teaching them SE as both "linguistically and pedagogically sound" (reprinted in Perry & Delpit, 1998, p. 161). However, the Linguistic Society of America's endorsement was hardly the stuff of front-page headlines for a media industry enamored of its own negative version of the Ebonics story. J. M. Rickford (1999) recalls how during this period he and other linguists submitted Op-Ed articles on the issue to major national newspapers, only to have their offerings declined:

> Sometimes the newspapers would say, "Well, the issue is passé." But the next weekend you would see another editorial or Op-Ed piece ranting and raving about the horror that Ebonics represents or the wrongness of the Oakland resolutions, so it was clearly not the timeliness of the issue that was in question but the take on it which linguists represented. (p. 342)

Also missing from the discussion . . .

What was missing from the public discourse about the Ebonics resolution was not only informed discussion about the linguistic and pedagogical legitimacy of the Oakland Board's position, but also any real discussion about the educational conditions that had motivated the Board to act in the first place: namely, the low levels of literacy and the high academic failure rate of African American students in Oakland schools—and, indeed, in schools across the country.

In an article responding to critics of the resolution, written shortly after the story about it broke in the press, Oakland school superintendent Carolyn Getridge describes what she terms the "dire situation" prompting the Oakland Board's initial formation of a task force to study African American achievement in Oakland schools: an aggregate grade point average of 1.8 for African American students compared to the district average of 2.40 as well as vastly disproportionate rates of truancy, suspension, and referral to special needs compared to other children in the district. Getridge writes:

> These statistics are both mind-numbing and a cause for moral outrage. The situation has not improved itself during the decade of reform launched by the landmark report, *A Nation at Risk*, and yet there has been little public reaction to the failure of our public schools to educate minority children. . . . The question is not whether or not we must act; rather we are confronted by questions of how best to act, and how quickly can we act? (reprinted in Perry and Delpit 1998, p. 174)

The same sense of moral urgency echoes in the words of Oakland School Board member Toni Cook as she describes for a reporter an older man from the community who would regularly attend board meetings: ". . . he would stand with those trembling hands and talk about the performance of African American kids—test scores, truancy—and he said, 'I see having four black board members has made no difference in what these kids are doing'." "And we hung our heads," Cook tells the reporter, "because it was true! We had a crisis situation and we kept coming up with old ways. Or ways that were so homogenized they didn't really wake anybody up" (Asimov, 1997, reprinted in Perry and Delpit, 1998, p. 174).

African American Children and Literacy Achievement

Tragically, the language these two women use to express their anguish over the educational plight of their community's children (e.g., statistics that are "mind-numbing" and "cause for moral outrage"; the urgent need to wake somebody up) held then (in 1996/97), and holds now, little possibility of waking up the consciousness of a public long since numb to the underachievement of African American students. Elaine Richardson opens her book *African American Literacies* (2003) with her own sense of moral outrage as she analyzes the messages encoded in a bookmark produced by the organization Teach for America. This bookmark, which is reproduced in Richardson's book, highlights the image of a young African American male with the following words: "He is in the eighth grade but he's reading at the fourth grade level. Will you change this?" As Richardson rightly observes, without major changes in current pedagogical practices, persuading young college graduates to commit to spending 2 years teaching in low-income communities is hardly likely to make a significant difference in literacy outcomes for poor children in this country. Even more germane to the discussion here, however, is Richardson's observation of how the image of the young Black male body in the bookmark is used to symbolize illiteracy (p. 6). Indeed, for many people, low literacy outcomes for African American students, especially males, are so taken-for-granted as to be hardly worth comment, let alone cause for public alarm.

We have abundant evidence that, overall, African American children, particularly those from low-income backgrounds, perform less well on standardized measures of reading achievement than do their European American counterparts (Bankston & Caldas, 1998; Entwisle & Alexander, 1988; Hedges & Nowell, 1998; NAEP, 1997; Singham, 1998). Furthermore, these performance differences actually increase as children proceed through school, creating the anomalous phenomenon discussed by Steele (1992) that the longer African American students spend in school, the worse they do (see also Rickford, J. R., 1999). In the area of literacy, this is a phenomenon made all the more anomalous by 30 years of ethnographic research whose findings suggest that children socialized in the African American speech community enter school with extremely sophisticated linguistic abilities (Goodwin, 1990; Haight, 2002; Heath, 1983; Labov, 1972; Vernon-Feagans, 1996).

This phenomenon becomes less puzzling, however, when one considers the fact that neither the literacy curriculum, nor anything else about most schools, has been designed with the aim of fostering African American achievement. It is in fact a tribute to the intellectual and linguistic resourcefulness of African American children that in spite of most teachers not knowing anything about the systematic, rule-governed ways in which they use language, in the absence of school curricula that draw to any significant extent upon African American cultural practices, literature or history, and in the face of teachers' pervasive, poisoning underestimation of their intellectual potential, the majority somehow manage to emerge as literate from our schools. The reality is that many BC speakers become literate not because of, but in spite of, what happens in our classrooms. It is they, not their teachers, who end up figuring out the connections between old and new knowledge. If children were not so resourceful, if African American children in particular were not so alert to linguistic nuance, so skilled in reading social context, then we would have a great deal more literacy failure to account for than we already have.

If BC speakers have the inner resources to survive in our schools, there is no question of their potential to thrive, given teachers who recognize their intellectual potential and know how to build on their strengths. This is the conviction that has guided me in writing this book and that has fueled my work as a teacher and teacher educator over the past 30 years.

My interest in the topic of Black Communications is a long-standing one. It began in the 1970s when, as a young White teacher, I took a job in a community college teaching writing to a student population that was predominantly

African American. Although I believed fervently in my students' potential and was committed to their success, I quickly discovered that I lacked the linguistic and cultural knowledge I needed to actually help them achieve. As a result, in addition to talking with students about their lives and perspectives, I began to read from an African American canon I had previously known little about—the autobiography and speeches of Malcolm X, the sermons of Dr. Martin Luther King, and the work of Frederick Douglass, W. E. B. DuBois, Toni Morrison, and Toni Cade Bambara, just to name some of the many writers whose work I eagerly devoured.

Soon after its initial publication in 1977, I read Geneva Smitherman's now classic *Talkin and Testifyin: The Language of Black America* (1977). This book, written in a style that mixes academic English and what was then termed Black English, was my first real introduction to a comprehensive view of Black language. What made the book so compelling, in addition to its creative style, was that Smitherman not only provided a description of the linguistic system—its sound patterns, grammar, and vocabulary—but also discussed the language's stylistic features and its relationship to Black culture and the Black oral tradition. My community college students found Smitherman's ideas and descriptions as exciting as I did. *Talkin and Testifyin* led me to other books about Black language and, with its intriguing pedagogical possibilities, was part of my inspiration for eventually returning to graduate school to learn more about language development, literacy, and linguistics. Eventually, I moved from teaching writing to become the director of a community college/university partnership program designed to recruit and prepare teachers of color. As part of my work, I began spending significant amounts of time in urban elementary schools, observing and working with teachers on issues of literacy. This work quickly became my passion.

Over the past 13 years, I have had the good fortune to teach and work with preservice and practicing teachers in two very different geographical areas of the United States, one a large metropolitan city in the Northeast and the other the largely rural Sea Island area of South Carolina. Much of my practical knowledge about BC and literacy instruction in the primary and elementary grades has grown out of my experiences working with some of these very talented and committed individuals. I am grateful for all that they have shared with me—their insights, dilemmas, exciting curricular ideas, and especially the opportunities many have provided to spend time observing, working, and learning in their classrooms. I draw significantly on their wisdom in this book.

The relationship between BC and literacy education is a subject about which there has been considerable, and sometimes passionate, scholarly and popular discussion over the last 30 years. At least since the 1970s, linguists focused on BC and educational issues—Beryl Bailey, Geneva Smitherman, William Labov, John Baugh, and John Rickford, to name just some of the most prominent over the years—have taken a strong and vocal stand on the importance of building literacy instruction on the foundation of students' BC abilities. The scholarly discussion about BC and literacy instruction has also extended beyond a sole focus on BC's phonological and grammatical patterns. This part of the discussion has been going on for a long time, beginning, for many people, with the publication of Smitherman's influential book *Talkin and Testifyin* in 1977. Since then, many scholars have argued, often with great eloquence and many examples from classroom practice, for the importance of incorporating stylistic and rhetorical aspects of BC into literacy instruction. Among these scholars are Arnetha Ball, Evelyn Dandy, Lisa Delpit, Michèle Foster, Mary Rhodes Hoover, Carol Lee, Jabari Mahiri, and Elaine Richardson, again, to name only some. Quite clearly, we do not lack for excellent scholarship on this topic. Nor, in what Smitherman has recently described as "this late hour in the history of the African-centered Educational Movement," do we lack models of successful schools or of exemplary teachers whose curricula and pedagogical strategies draw heavily on knowledge about Black Communications. As Smitherman notes, some of the schools incorporating curricula and pedagogical strategies built upon Black students' linguistic and cultural abilities have been successful for almost 3 decades (Smitherman in foreword to Richardson, 2003, p. x).

Yet in spite of substantial scholarship and many examples of effective practice, we cannot claim widespread acceptance among teachers of even the most basic assumptions represented in this body of work—for example, that Black Communications is a rule-governed linguistic system instead of just "standard English with mistakes," or that BC speakers come to school with a rich repertoire of linguistic resources for literacy learning. Little wonder that literacy outcomes for African Americans in our schools continue to be so problematic. Like many of my colleagues in this field, I write in the belief that the majority of teachers truly want to be effective with all of their students. I also write with the knowledge that most teacher preparation programs do not offer courses on Black Communications or even on linguistic diversity in general. It is my hope that this book will be a useful introduction to the topic of BC and literacy instruction for teachers and future teachers and that it will inspire readers to further exploration of the issues raised.

Part 1
What Is Black Communications?

Chapter 2
A Whole Communicative System

An Opening Vignette

A number of years ago, I was teaching a course on language and culture to a group of preservice and practicing teachers who live and work in the Sea Island area of South Carolina. Except for me, all of the people in the class were African American, and the majority were bilingual BC/SE speakers. On this particular evening, we had been engaged in a lively discussion about the relationship between BC and Gullah, a Creole language spoken by many African American people living in the Sea Islands, including quite a few people in our class. At one point, I interrupted the discussion to show a portion of a videotape about "Black English" that was part of a PBS television series entitled *The Story of English* (1986). Although the series was somewhat dated, I thought the class might find the video interesting, especially since it contained several short episodes featuring people from the Sea Islands, including a number of elderly people. After the video clip was over, however, I found it difficult to re-engage the class in conversation. The energy and enthusiasm so palpable during our earlier discussion seemed to have suddenly evaporated. "What was wrong?" I wondered. Were the students just tired, anxious for the four-hour class to be over?

Finally, one student volunteered that she hadn't liked the video much. The White narrator, she said, was "offensive." Surprised, I listened as she described her anger over the fact that the narrator had referred to the older African American people who appeared in the video using only their first names (e.g., "Janie") instead of including a formal title with the name (e.g., "Ms. Janie" or "Ms. Hunter). Suddenly, heads began to nod around the room, and soon the air was once again filled with the sounds of animated conversation as many class members shared that they, too, had been offended by what they also perceived as the narrator's display of disrespect toward African American elders. Several people even admitted that after the first time the narrator referred to an elder by first name alone, they had simply tuned the rest of the video out. Clearly, from these students' perspectives, the narrator of the video had violated an important, if uncodified, rule about appropriate verbal behavior.

Three Important Points

I begin the discussion of Black Communications with this anecdote because I think it illustrates three important points about the language:

1. BC is a whole communicative system that includes not only vocabulary, grammar and phonology (rules for pronouncing words), but also rules or patterns for using the language appropriately in different communicative situations.
2. As is the case with every other language variety in the world, BC speakers use language in ways that are inextricably linked to culture.
3. Many aspects of BC are deeply rooted in the historical experiences of African Americans.

Each of these points will now be discussed at length.

A Whole Communicative System

In my experience, when people are asked to think about what comprises a language, they almost invariably come with the same three linguistic components: vocabulary, grammar, and ways of pronouncing words (i.e., phonology). Black Communications, for example, is often characterized by its speakers' use of distinctive grammatical patterns, pronunciation features, and vocabulary items. Typically, these are described, by lay people and linguists alike, in terms of the way they differ from usages characteristic of other varieties of English, most notably SE. For instance, unlike SE (but similar to other varieties of English as well as to a number of other languages), BC has a grammatical rule that allows for the use of multiple negatives in a sentence (e.g., *They don't have no business doing that*). Similarly, distinctive ways of pronouncing certain words, such as *DE-troit* (not *De-TROIT*), *summAHtime* (not *summERtime*) and *thang* (not *thing*) have been cited in the linguistic literature as characteristic BC pronunciations, different from the way these words are pronounced in SE, as well as in most other varieties of English (Morgan, 2002; Smitherman, 2000b). And in terms of vocabulary, the word *homey* to describe a friend or the word *stupid* to mean good are examples of lexical usages that originated among BC speakers and that are not considered part of the formal SE lexicon.

But as the anecdote about my class suggests, BC is in fact made up of more than just the distinctive grammar features, pronunciation rules, and vocabulary items previously illustrated briefly. As linguist Lisa Green (2002) points out, "it is necessary to look to expressive language and verbal strategies and not just to syntactic and phonological patterns to find salient patterns of AAE" (p. 160). Like all language varieties, BC includes rules for using the language appropriately in different social situations, rules that are as systematic as its grammatical rules. These "rules of use" are often referred to as *pragmatic rules*. For the BC speakers in my class in South Carolina, one pragmatic rule for using language appropriately appeared to be a preference for using formal terms of address when talking to or about African American elders. In an interesting study that sheds light on what happened in my class, Lee Baker (1999) examined forms of address managers and staff used with one another in two different kinds of organizational settings: organizations run primarily by African Americans and those run predominately by White Americans. Baker found that in those settings where African Americans were in charge, interactions between managers and staff were characterized by what he calls "title + name reciprocity" (p. 120). That is, all employees in those settings, regardless of their job position or ethnicity, addressed one another using formal titles (e.g., *Mr.* Martin, *Dr.* Harper). In contrast, in White-run settings, "first name reciprocity" (e.g., Carol, Tom) characterized communication among employees, again, regardless of position or ethnicity. Commenting on the significance of these findings, Baker writes:

> The important issue here is that the traditional African American form of address is a different cultural and language pattern than the general pattern employed at corporations imbued with hegemonic prestige. If African American forms of address are used at a work site, then at the cultural level, we can assume that African Americans have power. (p. 120)

Baker's findings lend support to the notion that for many BC speakers, forms of address may be more formal than those typically used by members of White mainstream speech communities, at least in some social situations and with some interlocutors. Does this mean that all African Americans, or even all BC speakers, display a preference for using more formal terms of address in certain social situations than do SE speakers? Of course not. There is great diversity within the BC discourse community as there is in all speech communities. Just as not every BC speaker uses multiple negation or refers to his or her friends as *homies*, we should not expect an individual BC speaker to use every one of the pragmatic rules that have been identified in the literature as characteristic of the BC speaking community. This variability among speakers, however, does not negate the fact that the ways in which members of a particular speech community use language to accomplish various social purposes follow systematic, recognizable patterns, just as much as does their use of phonological and grammatical features. Thus, while not all BC speakers may follow it, in Baker's study, the BC pragmatic rule specifying a preference for formal terms of address in certain social situations is clearly widespread enough among BC speakers that it could be used to reliably distinguish African American-led work sites from White-led work sites. As well, the fact that all of the students in my South Carolina class had a similarly negative reaction to the narrator's use of first names to describe African American elders was not a random coincidence, but an indication of the fact that as members of the BC speech community, they shared certain assumptions about what constitutes appropriate linguistic behavior.

It is sometimes the case that different pragmatic rules—that is, different notions of how to use language appropriately in a specific social situation—can end up causing, or contributing to, misunderstandings between speakers from different linguistic communities. This point is well illustrated in the anecdote from my class. According to their own self-reports, some students' negative reactions to the narrator's speech behavior caused them to actually tune the narrator out, to stop paying attention to the content of his message. As a further example of how a difference in pragmatic rules can lead to misunderstanding between speakers, consider another pragmatic feature that has been associated with BC in the linguistic literature: a strong emphasis on speaker accountability (Kochman, 1981; Morgan, 2002). According to Marcyliena Morgan (2002), BC is a communicative system that involves what she calls "an exacting sense of speaker agency" in which people in a communicative interaction are held accountable for what they say, rather than for what they intend by their statements (p. 64). This contrasts with a common assumption held by many White mainstream SE speakers that what matters most in communication is not one's actual words, but rather one's intended meaning. Consider the following example.

Several years ago, an African American friend of mine unexpectedly found herself on the same airline flight as one of her White colleagues. As their seats were not near each other—my friend was sitting toward the back of the plane and her colleague toward the front—they agreed to meet in the terminal after the flight. When my friend emerged from the plane into the gate area, her colleague was waiting for her, and evidently impatiently, as she greeted her with the words: "Oh my God, X, I felt like I was waiting for you to get off the back of the bus!" In addition to voicing her indignation at her colleague's choice of words, my friend, ever the teacher, tried to explain that for many African Americans, the expression "the back of the bus" conjured a set of historical events that were not to be referenced lightly, particularly by a White person. Thus the colleague's use of this expression was highly disrespectful, at best.

The colleague, however, did not view the situation in the same way. Although she expressed regret over the fact that my friend was upset, she went on to imply that everything my friend had just explained didn't apply in this case because she hadn't *meant* to be disrespectful. The colleague was asserting the right to have her remarks interpreted not on the basis of what she said, but on the basis of her intentions, what she meant by what she said. In other words, because the colleague did not intend to insult my friend, no insult had in fact occurred. On the other hand, from my friend's perspective, as she explained it to me, if her colleague did not realize that her use of the term "the back of the bus" in that particular context was disrespectful and insulting, she should have.

The last point seems to me particularly significant in terms of possible miscommunication between African American BC speakers and White SE speakers. In my experience, many White people know very little about the historical or present day experiences of African Americans, nor have they thought very much about their own (albeit perhaps unwitting) complicity in continuing systems of racial oppression in this society. Thus, for example, a White student teacher I worked with who described her class of predominantly African American kindergartners as "acting like a bunch of monkeys" one afternoon professed to be shocked by a Black parent's negative reaction when she heard this description. The student teacher said that she had "no idea" that the image of a monkey had a symbolic significance for many African Americans that could be traced back through centuries of racist portrayals in popular fiction, art, vaudeville shows, cartoons, jokes, movies, and other forms of media. And in our conversations about this issue, it was clear that because she claimed not to have known any of this, the student teacher didn't view herself as responsible in any way for the parent being upset by her description of the class. Nor did she feel as though she owed the parent an apology or even a further conversation. From her point of view, it wasn't "fair" to be held accountable for something she didn't mean. Viewed from the perspective of many BC speakers, however, this young woman's profession of ignorance did not absolve her from accountability for the racialized implications of her words. According to Morgan and others, in the BC communicative system, to cite ignorance about "that which you should know but do not" as a reason for why you shouldn't be held responsible for the implications of your words is not acceptable.

In my experience, many White people find this strong emphasis on speaker accountability among BC speakers difficult to deal with, even threatening, when they are challenged by a Black person around something they have said. Oftentimes in this situation, the White person becomes defensive, denying the validity of the Black person's interpretation of his or her statements in ways similar to those described in the previous examples. This typically results in shutting down further meaningful communication about the issue at hand. When this happens between White teachers and BC speaking students in a classroom setting, the context in which I have most often seen it occur, the results can be costly in terms of student-teacher relationships and, as a result, also in terms of student achievement and learning.

Thus, as I have attempted to illustrate throughout this section, pragmatics—that is, ways of using language appropriately in different social situations—are an essential component of any communicative system, including, of course,

BC. Evelyn Dandy's (1991) model of the Black Communications system, reproduced in Figure 2.1, is useful for visualizing something of the complexity of this communicative system. The circle labeled *Speech Code* that appears in the upper left of the model encompasses the phonological, grammatical, and lexical aspects of the system, those parts of the language that are sometimes referred to as the linguistic component. Dandy's model enables us to clearly see that these three aspects represent only one part of the larger communicative system. All of the other circles in Dandy's model—*speech acts, style, nonverbal behavior, special speaking behaviors, sociolinguistic rules for speaking,* and *moral teachings*—represent aspects of the communicative system that could be characterized as pragmatic features. Thus Dandy's model illustrates in a vivid way how much more there is to BC than just the lexical, phonological, and grammatical features most people associate with this language variety.

Obviously, Dandy's model does not include all of the details that would be necessary to specify every single feature of the system. Note, for instance, that one of the lines extending from the circle labeled *Speech Acts* says "others,"

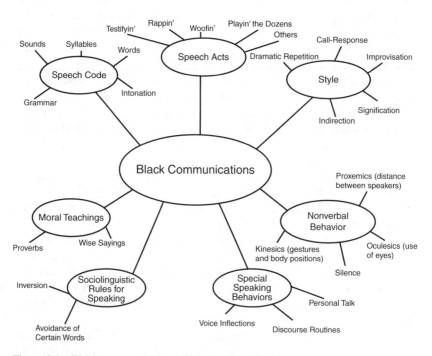

Figure 2.1   Black communications from Dandy (1991).

indicating that had she so chosen, Dandy might have included many more examples of BC speech acts, including loud talking, sounding, capping, signifying, and reading dialect, just to name some that have been discussed in the literature. Similarly, if we wished to locate the BC pragmatic rule about use of formal titles on Dandy's model, we would have to add another line extending from the circle labeled *Sociolinguistic Rules for Speaking*. (And, of course if we wanted to include all the sociolinguistic rules for speaking in the system, we would need to draw many more lines from this circle.)

Perhaps it also goes without saying that in actual practice (e.g., conversation, oral performance), the components of BC represented by the circles in the diagram are not stand-alone entities, but are utilized by speakers in complex and interlocking ways. Thus, for example, a speaker engaged in a *speech act* such as signifying (i.e., making a point about someone/something in an indirect, often metaphorical way) might make use of BC *nonverbal behaviors* (e.g., characteristic gestures or facial expressions), as well as certain features of BC *style* (e.g., dramatic repetition, call-response) in executing that speech act. Similarly, for a speaker familiar with both BC and SE phonological and grammatical patterns features (see circle labeled *Speech Code* in Figure 2.1), the speech act of signifying might involve code-switching between the two systems in order to create a particular effect upon the listener.

The way in which BC speakers draw simultaneously, and often strategically, on different components of the system is illustrated next in excerpts from a sermon entitled "Holding on to Your Song" that was delivered by the Reverend W. Franklin Richardson (2002) in the aftermath of the Rodney King beating and trial in Los Angeles in the 1990s. In this sermon, Reverend Richardson begins his sermon by describing the United States as a "hostile land" for Black people, comparing their situation in the United States to that of the Israelites in exile in Egypt. How can African Americans survive, how can they hold onto their song, in a strange and hostile land? Reverend Richardson tells his congregation:

> . . . You've got to somehow have the ability to rise above what you're going through. There's no short answer, there's no short cut, but if we are going to survive, if we are going to make it, we've got to have the capacity to rise above our circumstance and be all that we can be.

> *Benjamin Mays once said that he got on the bus and the bus driver told him to get to the back of the bus. Told him to take his place, so, one of the college students came and he said Dr. Mays do you mean you gonna let a bus driver—you are a president of a university, have all that education—and you gonna let a bus driver insult you. He said, young man the bus driver can't insult me. He said, he told me to sit in the back of the bus and the only way I was able to sit there, my mind never got in the back of the bus, my body was in the back of the bus and I knew that one day my body would join my mind in the front of the bus . . .*

. . . How do you hold on to your purpose? How do you hold on to your joy? How do you hold on to the quality of life in your journey when everything around you is pulling you down and denying your personhood? The first thing we have to do is to understand that we must never allow our location and our situation to obscure our destination. We must never allow, no matter how bad things get, no matter how mean the folk get, we must not ever allow them, like Benjamin Mays, to help us to obscure the fact that we have a more noble destination to which we are moving and we cannot allow temporary and present frustration cause us to fail to understand where we are. You and I must not allow it. (Richardson, 2002, pp. 69–70)

In the previous excerpt, Reverend Richardson draws on a number of *stylistic features* of BC, including alliteration, repetition (of words, phrases and parallel structures), rhythmic building to a point, use of dramatic dialogue (what Smitherman, 2000a, calls "narrativizing"), and the skillful juxtaposition of opposites (e.g., mind/body; back/front; our location and situation/our destination). In dramatizing the story about Benjamin Mays, Reverend Richardson not only recounts a story likely familiar to some in his congregation, but at the same time evokes the centuries-old African and African American belief that one's body might be enslaved, but not necessarily one's mind and spirit, a distinction that allowed enslaved African Americans to gather together in secret and sing, "Before I'd be a slave I'd be buried in my grave" (in Jones, 1993, p. 11). Thus Reverend Richardson draws in this excerpt on traditional *Moral Teachings* (see Figure 2.1) within the African American speech community. He also uses a number of expressions—for example, the ability/capacity "to rise above," "be all that we can be," and "the back of the bus"—that are resonant of African American historical experience and the moral wisdom and accomplishments of the community. He draws as well on *Sociolinguistic Rules for Speaking* in the Black preaching tradition (as well as in the larger community) as he alternates throughout his sermon between use of the pronouns *you* and *we* (e.g., "How do *you* hold on to . . ." "The first thing *we* have to do . . ."). This usage serves to break down the distinction between speaker and listener and to emphasize the unity of all Black people.

Although Reverend Richardson employs primarily SE grammatical forms in the portion of his sermon excerpted previously, like many African Americans, he is also able to employ BC grammatical features (*Speech Code* in Dandy's model) and can code-switch effectively between the two systems, as illustrated in the closing portion of his sermon:

. . . Folks who don't know Jesus, they don't know how we can do it. They say how you do that, how you all can sing when folk messing with you, how you all keep on smiling when folk putting you down, how is it that you keep on feeling good when everything around you ought to make you feel bad, how is it Christian that you can be happy with cancer and high blood pressure and children that won't do right, how is it Christian that you can keep on singing?

Well, we got an answer for them: I sing, oh I sing because I'm happy, I sing because I'm free, His eye is on the sparrow, now if He watching over the sparrow you know He's watching over me. I sing because I'm happy, I sing because I'm free, ain't gonna let nobody steal my song. Turn to somebody and tell them: "I ain't gonna let nobody steal my song." The doors of the church open. Somebody here ought to join the church. Come on now don't let nobody steal your song. (Richardson, p. 74)

In this portion of the sermon, Reverend Richardson uses a number of grammatical patterns characteristic of BC. These include the following:

1. Use of appositive pronoun (i.e., using both a noun and pronoun for the same person or object)—for example, *"Folks who don't know Jesus, they don't know . . ."*
2. Formation of a "wh" question without an auxiliary or with an auxiliary immediately following the subject—for example, *". . . how you do that . . .";* *"how you can sing. . .";* *". . . how you all keep on smiling. . ."*
3. Zero copula or auxiliary—for example, *". . .when folk messing with you . . .";* *". . . if he watching over the sparrow . . .";* *"The doors of the church open."*
4. Use of "got" for SE "have"—for example, *". . . we got an answer."*
5. "Ain't " as a negative auxiliary—for example, *". . . I ain't gonna. . ."*
6. Multiple negation—for example, *". . . I ain't gonna let nobody steal my song."*

Perhaps the most important point to be made about Reverend Richardson's use of BC grammatical patterns here is that, in using them, he is following rules. Like all language varieties, BC is systematic and rule-governed. Thus while the BC patterns Reverend Richardson uses here do not conform to the grammatical rules of SE, they are correct and well-formed structures in BC. The fact that he is able to switch so easily between SE and BC grammatical forms in his sermon is not unusual. Reflecting specifically on the importance of the Black preacher's ability to use both SE and BC, Rickford and Rickford (2000) write: "The preacher who uses Standard English exclusively, without any of the motifs, rhythms, and gestures of the soulful preaching style (as rare as he or she would be to come across) is in serious risk of appearing detached or 'uppity,' and thereby of losing the interest of a good portion of the congregation" (p. 56). Research by Piestrup (1973) and Foster (1987, 1989, 1997, 2001) suggests that the ability to use both language varieties effectively is a major asset in teaching African American children as well.

Although not captured in the written transcription of the sermon, it is likely that considerable call-response interaction (*Style* in Figure 2.1) occurred between Reverend Richardson and the congregation in the actual delivery of the sermon, as such interaction is characteristic of the traditional Black church. (Note Reverend Richardson's directive to the congregation to "turn to somebody and tell them . . . .") The transcript also does not convey any of the pronunciation features or variations in inflection, cadence, and voice quality (all aspects of *Speech Code* on Dandy's model) that may have marked his speech or any of his *nonverbal behaviors*, a highly important aspect of BC. Nonetheless, the excerpts from Reverend Richardson's sermon do succeed in capturing some sense of how the various components of the BC system represented in Dandy's model work together to create language in use in the everyday world.

The Inseparable Connection Between Language and Culture

The second point about Black Communications suggested by the anecdote from my class in South Carolina is its integral connection to culture. As is true for every language and its community of speakers, BC constitutes a set of cultural practices that are closely linked to other cultural practices and beliefs within African American communities.

It is no accident, for example, that the BC pragmatic rule about using formal titles in addressing adults applies with special force to elderly adults, reflecting the deep respect accorded the elderly in traditional African American culture. Scholars concur that the esteem in which elders have traditionally been held throughout African American history has its spiritual and cultural roots in west and central Africa (e.g., Gutman, 1976; Mbiti, 1990; Nobles, 1991; Rawick, 1972; Stuckey, 1987). A number of historians have discussed the key role played by elders in passing down traditional knowledge to young people in enslaved communities, thus reinforcing and preserving many traditional African values (e.g., King, 1995; Schwartz, 2000; Stuckey, 1987). Also significant, as King (1995) points out, were:

> . . . chances for the children and elderly slaves, serving in loco parentis, to develop relationships. Children became attached to caregivers and entered into fictive associations. . . . In the absence of relatives, surrogates or fictive families were valuable. Related or not, older slaves often showed kindness to children. The plethora of "aunts" and "uncles" indicates that children learned early on to show deference to their elders in keeping with a traditional African custom. (p. 15)

Literary scholar Farah Jasmine Griffin (1995) has suggested that the ancestor is a recurring image or trope within African American narratives about Black migration from the South to urban centers in the North that were produced in various forms (musical, visual, and literary) throughout the twentieth century. Within literary narratives, Griffin argues, the ancestor, often an elder, is represented as either an actual character or a metaphorical presence in the text (e.g., symbolized in food, music, memory, song, dreams, spirituality, religion).

In a number of literary works, this ancestral presence functions as a potential source of guidance, strength, and wisdom in helping characters cope with the challenges of an urbanized Northern environment.

That reverence for elders and for the wisdom they impart continues to be an essential African American cultural value is in evidence everywhere one looks in the Black community—in traditional Black churches where elders have a special and highly respected position, in the "everyday" interactions among extended family members living in close proximity to one another; in the prevalence of "fictive kin" and mentoring relationships between the old and young; in the lyrics of rap songs that pay homage to musical ancestors; in the "elder knowledge" passed on in ritual settings like barbershops and beauty shops, Sunday school classes and after school programs, bars and pool halls, family reunions and storytelling events; and in the pages of African American literature that narrate and celebrate the generative role of the elderly in African American life. Thus the BC pragmatic rule specifying that elders be addressed by formal titles reflects, and is illustrative of, deeply held cultural values within African American communities.

One of the reasons this connection to culture is so significant is that, for most of us, culture is, at least in part, what we have grown up taking for granted about the world, what we assume to be true, and what we *do* without ever stopping to think very much about it. I doubt, for example, that the White narrator in the video I showed my class intended to communicate disrespect toward the people he interviewed in the video when he referred to them by their first names. One plausible explanation for the narrator's choice of words is that he was simply following the pragmatic rules for using language appropriately in his speech community. Perhaps his use of the African American elders' first names was intended to signify the narrator's liking for these individuals or perhaps a sense of camaraderie, or even intimacy, with them (e.g., "As a result of our interaction around this video, we're on a 'first name basis.'"). Or perhaps his choice of words was intended to convey some sort of belief on the narrator's part that, as adult human beings, he and the elders featured in the video shared equal status in the world and therefore didn't have need of formal titles in referring to one another. These meanings are difficult to specify with certainty because they are taken for granted and seldom articulated. It is probably safe to assume, however, that in the moment of speaking, the narrator did not stop to think about the linguistic form he was using (i.e., first name or title + name). As is the case for all of us in most communicative circumstances, the narrator's rules for using language appropriately in this situation were likely operating below the level of conscious awareness.

On the surface at least, this notion of two different cultural/linguistic patterns for addressing others, operating at least partly outside the speaker's conscious awareness, easily lends itself to a "cultural relativity" kind of analysis—that is, it's not that one pattern is "superior to" or "better than" the other; these patterns simply posit two different linguistic forms for accomplishing similar communicative purposes. Viewed from this lens, as a professor of language and culture, I might have responded to my students' objections to the narrator's use of people's first names by making just that point. I might have pointed out to students, for example, that they were obviously reacting to the narrator's choice of words on the basis of its significance from their cultural perspective, without taking into consideration what the words might have meant from the narrator's cultural frame of reference. This is a classic case of cross-cultural miscommunication, one might be tempted to conclude, and seemingly a good object lesson for a course in language and culture.

But in fact there was more involved in my students' reaction to the narrator's words than a cross-cultural misunderstanding based on different rules for using language appropriately. That something much deeper was at issue was signaled by several students' assertion, mentioned earlier, that the narrator's first use of an elder's first name led them to effectively "tune out" the rest of the tape. These were all thoughtful, highly motivated students who, before the videotape was shown, had been animatedly engaged in our conversation about the very topic discussed in the video. One has to conclude, therefore, that these adult students must have been very strongly affected by the narrator's words in order to suddenly close their minds to further discussion about a subject in which they were so clearly interested. Attempting to understand the depth and significance of these students' reaction leads to consideration of another important point about Black Communications: it is a language that cannot be meaningfully discussed without reference to the historical experience of African Americans, including the history of their interactions with and relationship to White people in this country.

The Significance of History

A pivotal scene in Mildred Taylor's children's novel *Roll of Thunder, Hear My Cry*, set in Mississippi in the 1930s, occurs when the eight-year-old narrator Cassie accidentally bumps into a White girl named Lillian Jean on the sidewalk one afternoon in the little town of Strawberry. Although Cassie apologizes, her apology is not enough for Lillian Jean, who insists that Cassie step off the sidewalk and walk in the road. "'You can't watch where you going, get in the road,'" she tells Cassie. "'Maybe that way you won't be bumping into decent white folks with your little nasty self'" (p. 114). As the girls begin to argue and a crowd gathers around them, Lillian Jean's father intervenes, shoving Cassie into the road and insisting that she apologize again in front of everyone watching. Although Cassie's grandmother, Big Ma, is present, she is powerless to protect her granddaughter in the racist context of 1930s

Mississippi. Humiliated, Cassie is not only forced to apologize again, but also to address Lillian Jean as "Miz":

> "I'm sorry," I mumbled.
> "I'm sorry, *Miz* Lillian Jean," demanded Mr. Simms.
> "Big Ma!" I balked.
> "Say it, child."
> A painful tear slid down my cheek and my lips trembled. "I'm sorry . . . M-Miz . . . Lillian Jean."
> When the words had been spoken, I turned and fled crying into the back of the wagon. No day in all my life had ever been as cruel as this one.
> (pp. 115–116)

Taylor here dramatizes a scene enacted thousands upon thousands of times in African American history, in which a Black person is forced, under threat of grave injury, even death, to outwardly express agreement with the notion that she or he is inferior to the White person(s) with whom she or he is interacting. During the interaction in Strawberry, Lillian Jean's father refers to Cassie as a "little nigger"; he addresses her as "gal" and her beloved grandmother as "Aunty" (pp. 114–115). Nonetheless, Cassie must call Lillian Jean "Miz." She literally has no other choice, as the consequences of not doing so are potentially life-threatening for her family.

This scene depicting the (attempted) humiliation of a Black person around "terms of address" was doubtless prefigured in countless interactions between Black and White people during the 250 years of African American enslavement in this country. Most of these interactions can only be imagined. Some, however, were recorded in the ex-slave narratives collected by Works Progress Administration (WPA) workers and Fisk University students during the 1930s. Ms. Rebecca Jane Grant, for example, 92 years old at the time she was interviewed in South Carolina, recalls being whipped with a cowhide strap at the age of eight for failing to address a White toddler as "marster": "Marster Henry was just a little boy about three or four years old. Come about halfway up to me. Wanted me to say marster to him—a baby!" (in Hurmence, 1989, p. 57). Another formerly enslaved African American interviewed by a Fisk University student remembers that whenever the "marster's" family had a new baby, all the enslaved people on the plantation would be called in and told to "'see your new marster.' We had to call them babies 'Mister' and 'Miss,' too" (in Sutcliffe, 2000, p. 97).

In her book *Language, Discourse, and Power in African American Culture* (2002), Marcyliena Morgan includes an excerpt from a story told by Mary Walker, a folk artist in Los Angeles, in which she describes how she first met her husband in New Orleans in 1927. A significant point in the story is that when she first saw him, Mrs. Walker thought her husband was White. Her realization that he was in fact Black is not communicated directly in the story, but conveyed through reference to cultural knowledge and symbols that may not be decipherable to a cultural outsider:

> And when I got there he says are you
> **Miss Mary Cooper**? And then I knew it was him, you
> know (laughs). (p. 49)

As Morgan explains: "In Louisiana in 1927, White men did not refer to young Black women as *Miss* (p. 50). Thus, when her future husband spoke to her for the first time using the respectful title *Miss*, Mrs. Walker immediately recognized him as Black ("And then I knew it was him . . ."").

What is important about this example for the discussion here is that it illustrates how linguistic behavior—here choice of address form—can be symbolic of cultural meanings that grow out of shared historical experience. In the 1920s, the symbolic significance of this particular linguistic behavior—that is, addressing a Black woman as *Miss*—was so great that simply on the basis of its occurrence, Mrs. Walker could confidently identify the race of the speaker. References to cross-racial interactions involving the use/misuse of terms of address abound in the oral and written narratives of African American people. One example is the following interaction between a White policeman and Dr. Alvin Pouissant, an eminent African American psychiatrist and author:

> "What's your name, boy?" the policeman asked.
> "Dr. Pouissant. I'm a physician."
> "What's your first name, boy?"
> "Alvin." (Pouissant, 1967, reprinted in Smitherman, 2000a, p. 97)

On one level, traditional African American rules of address reflect no more than one particular cultural pattern among many stylistic possibilities in this increasingly diverse society. On another, deeper level, however, these rules of address, like everything about BC, tell a story about the historical experience of African Americans. Throughout most of that experience, White people have addressed Black people, not in terms that had anything to do with general stylistic preferences, but in terms that were deliberately aimed at disrespecting and terrorizing them. It was across this history that my students in South Carolina likely heard the White narrator in the video refer to elderly African American people by their first names.

A Complex Tapestry

Looking again at Figure 2.1, we can see that one thing missing from Dandy's model is any representation of the relations between linguistic practices and cultural-historical processes. In truth, the relations between these would be difficult to represent in a diagram like Figure 2.1 because these entities are so intricately intertwined with one another. To capture this dimension of the BC system—the ways in which linguistic practices are enmeshed in culture and history—we might usefully think of BC not as an array of circles representing different components of the system as in Figure 2.1, but, more metaphorically, as a complex weave of linguistic, cultural, and historical threads not easily separable from one another. Difficult as these threads may be to separate, gaining an appreciation for the rich complexity of the BC system requires an effort to do just that—to tease apart and examine in more detail some of the most prominent cultural and historical threads woven into the larger linguistic design.

Consider once again, for example, the BC sociolinguistic rule for speaking identified at the beginning of this chapter: the preference for using formal titles in addressing and referring to adults, especially elders. Try for a moment to envision this rule not as a line extending from the circle labeled *Sociolinguistic Rules for Speaking* in Figure 2.1, but as a single, colorful thread woven tightly into the fabric of the African American English (AAE) system. Let us imagine that we are concentrating all of our attention on this single thread, trying to trace its intricate pathways through the field of cloth of which it is a part. What we are interested in discovering is a picture of how this single linguistic rule, this tiny thread in a huge whole tapestry, is interwoven with the threads of African American history and culture as well as how it is intertwined with other components of the language represented in Dandy's model. This picture will help in gaining a better understanding of how the various linguistic, cultural, and historical threads woven together in the fabric of the BC system work together to create a coherent and meaningful whole.

In attempting to describe this picture in the rest of this chapter, I will only be able to touch on a tiny portion of the myriad interconnections whose full explication could easily constitute a book in itself. Thus, in the next sections, I rely heavily on a small number of examples to suggest the broad contours of areas of history, culture, language, and literature well deserving of much fuller and richer exploration. More specifically, I use the BC pragmatic rule about use of formal titles as an entry point into an examination of three other aspects of the BC communicative system: use of kinship terms, proverbs and wise sayings, and cultural stories. My goal in doing so is to further illuminate the systematicity and complexity of BC. As alluded to earlier and as illustrated in Dandy's model, readers should bear in mind that the three aspects of the system I focus on in the rest of this chapter—use of kinship terms, proverbs and wise sayings, and cultural stories—represent only a very small portion of the larger BC system. Because this book as a whole centers on the relationship between BC and literacy instruction, whenever possible, both here and in subsequent chapters, I draw on examples from African American children's literature that could be incorporated into literacy teaching.

Use of Kinship Terms

In examining connections between the BC pragmatic rule about use of formal titles and other aspects of the BC system, I turn now to a consideration of other commonly used terms for describing and addressing people in the BC system. Specifically, I focus here on the prevalent use of kinship terms within the African American speech community. Like a number of other aspects of the BC communicative system, the use of kinship terms leads back to consideration of spiritual beliefs and cultural practices that enslaved Africans brought with them to America from their Central and West African homelands. Among the most central of these was the importance attached to kinship connections. According to psychologist Wade Nobles, traditional African kinship systems:

> Stretched laterally (horizontally) in every direction as well as vertically. Hence, each member of the tribe was related not only to the tribal ancestors (both living-dead and spirits) but also to all those still unborn. In addition, each was a brother or sister, father or mother, grandmother or grandfather, cousin or brother-in-law, uncle or aunt, or some relation to everybody else. (quoted in Jones, 1993, p. 5)

Kinship ties remained integral to the lives of enslaved Africans living in America despite persistent efforts by White enslavers to rupture those ties. Writing about Black cultural life in Virginia and South Carolina during the eighteenth century, historian Phillip Morgan (1998) maintains that "by the end of the eighteenth century, the building and rebuilding of kin ties had produced dense kin networks for some Piedmont slaves in both town and countryside" (p. 511), a circumstance that sometimes aided runaways who were able to enlist the aid of extended family members in their escape (p. 529). Morgan also notes "the slave practice of naming children for extended kin" (p. 549). In addition to offering one another practical aid and emotional support when these were possible, enslaved African Americans also remained connected to one another on a deeper, more spiritual level. As a number of historians have described (e.g., Creel, 1988; Jones, 1993; Levine, 1977; Raboteau, 1978; Rawick, 1972; Stuckey, 1987), continuing connections to the ancestors and to one another were celebrated, often secretly, in spiritual/cultural rituals such as the ring shout ceremony, singing, and storytelling.

In discussing the spirituals in his classic work *Black Culture and Black Consciousness* (1977), historian Lawrence Levine writes the following:

> The world described by the slave songs was a black world in which no reference was ever made to any white contemporaries. The slave's positive reference group was composed entirely of his own peers: his mother, father, sister, brother, uncles, aunts, preacher, fellow "sinners" and "mourners" of whom he sang endlessly, to whom he sent messages via the dying, and with whom he was reunited joyfully in the next world. (p. 37)

Children were beloved members of the enslaved community. In her historical account of the lives of enslaved children and youth, Wilma King (1995) describes the tenacious efforts enslaved parents and grandparents made to stay connected with and to protect and influence the lives of their children and grandchildren (see also Douglass, 1845/1968; Gutman, 1976; Jacobs, 1861/1987; Morgan, 1998; Schwartz, 2000; Stuckey, 1987; Yellin, 2004, as well as published collections of the WPA and Fisk University ex-slave narratives). Morgan (1998) writes: "Slave parents assiduously bequeathed the few things they had to their children—their knowledge, their skills, their names. They cared for their infants in the fields, made sure they got enough food, grieved over their death, and feared separation from them" (p. 548).

Significantly, according to Morgan, the bond between siblings was especially strong: "Brothers and sisters played a significant role in some slaves' lives well into adulthood. . . . Even slaves well advanced in years retained close ties to brothers and sisters" (p. 548). A poignant illustration of the importance of kin, including brothers and sisters, is captured in the reminiscences of Mr. W. L. Bost, age 87 when he was interviewed in 1937. He recalled a song that he and others had often sung during enslavement, the first three lines of which were the following:

> Oh, Mother, let's go down,
> Let's go down, let's go down, let's go down.
> Oh, Mother, let's go down, down in the valley to pray.

After reciting the entire first stanza, Mr. Post told the interviewer: "Then the other part was just like that, except it said 'father' instead of 'mother,' and then 'sister' and then 'brother'" (in Hurmence, 1984/2001, p. 96).

For many children, parents, and families, enslavement's cruelest face was the constant fear and, for some, the reality of being sold away from one another. King (1995) writes: "The trauma of separation and the fear of never seeing each other again were pervasive" (p. 104). In an effort to cope with the almost unimaginable horror and grief accompanying children's separation from their parents, enslaved African American communities embraced the "orphaned" youngsters in their midst, becoming "fictive kin" for children to whom they were not biologically related. Deborah Hopkinson captures this historical reality in the fictional children's book *Sweet Clara and the Freedom Quilt* (1993). Separated from her mother and sent to work at another plantation at the age of 12, Sweet Clara, the story's narrator, tells the reader: "When I got there, I cried so much they thought I was never gon' eat or drink again. I didn't want to leave my momma" (unnumbered pages). The chain of events that eventually leads Clara to reunion with her mother and to freedom is set in motion by an enslaved woman at the new plantation who essentially "adopts" the grieving Clara. Describing a relationship that historical accounts suggest was common in the antebellum South (in addition to references previously cited, see also Guthrie, 1996, 2001), Clara says: "Aunt Rachel was raising me now. She wasn't my for-real blood aunt, but she did her best to care for me" (unnumbered pages). The concept and practice of fictive kinship has remained central to African American survival in the United States up to this very day.

The historical background I have presented here, though very brief, provides some context for appreciating the pervasive use and cultural/historical significance of kinship terms within the African American speech community. *Brother/brotha/bro* and *sister/sista*, for example, are frequently occurring forms of address for Black males and females, regardless of biological kinship. Use of these terms emphasizes the unity and interrelatedness of the entire Black community. The importance of kinship ties and the closeness that traditionally exists among extended family members finds expression, for example, in the words Maya Angelou chooses to describe the proximity of two geographic spaces in her autobiographical novel, *I Know Why the Caged Bird Sings* (1969/1993): "the little garden that lay *cousin-close* to the store . . ." (p. 24).

Describing the use of kinship terms within the traditional Black church, Smitherman (1977/1986) writes:

> Conceiving of the church as the human family in microcosm, church folk typically address one another in this fashion (i.e., as brother and sister). Older women are addressed as "Mother," and older men are the church family "Elders." The term *soul-brother* is simply an extension of this concept. (p. 57)

In her 2000 dictionary, Smitherman (2000b) includes an entry for *play* as an adjective preceding the words *brother, sister, cousin, aunt* with the following definition: "A person who is not one's biological kin but who is so close and shares so much history and experience that he/she attains the status of biological kin." She includes the example of an interview story in which one rapper refers to another as his "play cousin" (pp. 230–231). Although the word *play* does not precede it, the use of *aunt* in the title of Faith Ringgold's well-known children's book *Aunt Harriet's Underground Railroad in the Sky* (1992) conveys the historical and cultural connection between the nineteenth-century Harriet Tubman and the twentieth and twenty-first century children who are her spiritual, if not her direct biological, descendants.

Listing BC terms for referring to males, linguist Lisa Green (2002) includes three that clearly evoke a "fictive kinship" connection: *cuz, homes,* and *kinfolk* (p. 28). Smitherman (2000b) defines *cuz* as "a form of address (and reference) to your *homey*" (p. 102), and describes *homey* (and its variant forms *homegirl/homeboy, homes, home, home slice* and *homefolks*) as a word that can be used generically to describe a Black person (p. 168), just like the more traditional terms *brother* and *sister* can. Exemplifying the longevity of variants on the terms home(s)/homey within the Black discourse community, Smitherman notes that "Black soldiers during World Wars I and II used the terms *Homes* or *Home Slice* to greet new Black soldiers joining the ranks" (p. 34).

In an article on Black women's discourse, linguist Denise Troutman (2001) discusses (among other things) terms of address used to express solidarity among African American women. She refers to these terms as "culturally-toned diminutives" and provides a list that includes *girl, sistah, sistah friend, honey, honey child, child, baby, baby girl, precious*, and *muh-dear*. Describing their use, Troutman writes the following:

> For generations, African American women have used culturally-toned diminutives. The diminutive *girl*, for example, is a highly visible and popular word used by many African American females to show solidarity in all spheres of their existence, public and private, and in all age groups. If they view themselves as peers, one African American female can and will call another African American female *girl*. Thus an African American five-year-old girl may say to her eight-year-old sister, 'Girl, you beda stop dat' or 'Girl, you crazy.' These same sentences can be used by older African American females of any age. The females involved do not have to be blood relatives in order for the diminutive to be used appropriately, although they may be. The females could be cousins, neighbors, classmates, playmates, co-church members or colleagues. (p. 217)

Of particular note is Troutman's observation that it isn't necessary that the females involved be biologically related in order to use these diminutives appropriately with one another. Here, again, we see the importance of the notion and practice of "fictive kin" within the Black community.

Perhaps not surprisingly, Troutman's culturally-toned diminutives appear frequently in children's literature written by African American authors. Their use not only adds to the cultural authenticity of this literature, but is also likely to strike a responsive chord with many African American children, who, like all children, benefit greatly when the literature used in school includes culturally familiar language and experiences. Following I provide three examples of children's books that include these culturally-toned diminutives.

In Irene Smalls's children's book *Irene and the Big, Fine Nickel* (1991), set in 1950s Harlem, seven-year-old Irene refers to her two best friends' mother with the polite form of address "Miss Sally," and also addresses her friend Lulabelle with the diminutive *girl* described by Troutman. When Lulabelle suggests that the girls play hide-and-seek, for example, Irene responds, "'Girl, first let me tell you about Charlene'" (unnumbered pages). Both Miss Sally, Lulabelle's mother, and Miss Susie, the woman who runs the West Indian bakery on the corner, address the children in the story with the diminutives *chillun* and *chile*.

Patricia McKissack's book *Ma Dear's Aprons* (1997) is set in rural Alabama in the early 1900s. In the Author's Note that begins the book, McKissack explains that the diminutive *Ma Dear* (a variant spelling of Troutman's *muh' dear* in the previous list) is a short form of "mother dear" (unnumbered pages). In the book, little David Earl's "Ma Dear" is a domestic worker who wears a different color apron every day of the week except Sunday. Sunday is "the no-work-day," when she "never wears an apron" and mother and son go to church and then to have a picnic supper at Sutter's Mill Creek (unnumbered pages).

Finally, in *Jewels* (1998) by Belinda Rochelle, Lea Mae, the young narrator of the story, travels with her parents every summer to visit her great-grandparents, 'Ma Dear and Pop Henry, who tell her stories about their lives and about African American history. Talking about her great-grandmother, Lea Mae explains that "''Ma dear is my mother's grandmother. Mom calls her Grandmother dear, but I call her 'Ma dear for short'" (unnumbered pages).

It is easy to underestimate the potential significance for the young reader of such a seemingly small detail as an author's decision to use a culturally resonant term like *girl* or *honey child* in the text. Relevant here is an essay in which Toni Morrison (1970/1993) reflects upon her decision to open her novel *The Bluest Eye* with the phrase "Quiet as it's kept." She explains how this simple phrase conjures for her—as she assumes it does for many of her African American readers—multiple childhood memories of "black women conversing with one another, telling a story, an anecdote, gossip about some one or event within the circle, the family, the neighborhood" (p. 212). "Quiet as it's kept" is a phrase chosen by Morrison for "how it speaks and bespeaks a particular world and its ambience" (p. 212) and thus establishes an immediate intimacy between the text and the reader who is also familiar with that world. Just so, one can imagine how the use of culturally toned diminutives and other culturally familiar words and phrases in African American children's literature might also speak and bespeak "a particular world and its ambience" for young Black children and thus help draw them into intimate connection with the text.

Proverbs and Wise Sayings

As indicated in Dandy's model (see Figure 2.1) one of the ways in which the wisdom of the elders surfaces in BC is in proverbs and wise sayings. "'Speak the truth and shame the devil,'" Mama advises Libby Louise in *The Honest-to-Goodness Truth* (2000) by Patricia McKissack. "'Respect yo elders and do what's right,'" Grandma Waters keeps reminding her mischievous grandson in *Little Muddy Waters* by Ronald Daise (1997). "'God don't love ugly,'" Irene remembers her godmother always telling her in *Irene and the Big, Fine Nickel* (Smalls, 1991).

Sometimes described as "the daughters of experience" (Smitherman, 2000a, p. 236), according to Jackson-Lowman (1997), "proverbs contain the narrative wisdom of the people from whom they are derived. Stored in them are truth, wisdom, experiences, values, customs, and traditions" (p. 74). Proverb traditions have a long and continuing history among diverse cultural groups in

Africa, and in the view of a number of scholars, the use of proverbs within African American culture reflects continuity with an African past (e.g., Jackson-Lowman, 1997; Levine, 1977; Smitherman, 2000a). As Smitherman (2000a) points out, however, this continuity with African proverb traditions does not imply that the proverbs in use among African Americans today are the same ones used by their African ancestors. Rather, Smitherman says, the cultural continuity with Africa lies in "the use of proverbs as a rhetorical tradition infusing every aspect of African diasporic life" (p. 240). In a study conducted among Black residents of Detroit, Smitherman and her colleagues (2000a) collected a corpus of over 800 proverbs from 80 informants, leading Smitherman to conclude, along with evidence from other studies, that "proverbs are significant in the continuing development and survival of African descendants" (p. 247).

The uses of proverbs are multiple. Some that have been described in the literature include teaching a moral lesson, making and/or reinforcing a point in an argument by appealing to shared knowledge and beliefs, socializing children, making a point or confronting someone in an indirect way, suggesting a strategy for dealing with a problematic situation, teaching life skills, resolving a conflict, and teaching critical thinking. Throughout African American history, proverbs have been used to teach ways of dealing with a racially oppressive system. Historian Lawrence Levine (1977), for example, lists a number of proverbs that taught "the advantages and necessity of reticence and caution" in dealing with White people, both during and after enslavement. Among the proverbs included on Levine's list are the following: "'A smart redbird don't have much to say'"; "'De fox wants to know how de rabbit's gittin on'"; "'De mousetrap don't go to sleep'"; and "'Everything good to hear is not good to talk'" (p. 101). Perhaps reflecting the truth of the adage that "the more things change, the more they stay the same," at least as it applies to the workings of racism in our society, Levine reports that "as late as the 1950s and 1960s, Roger Abrahams was able to collect cautionary proverbs that paralleled exactly those the slaves had told: 'That's why a dog has so many friends—he wags his tail and keeps his mouth shut.' 'A fish would never get caught if he kept his mouth shut'" (p. 372).

Also emphasizing the role that "proverbial wisdom" has historically played in helping African Americans to deal with various forms of societal oppression, educator Janice Hale (1994) recommends that proverbs, songs, and stories from African and African American traditions be incorporated into instruction. About proverbs in particular she writes:

> Proverbs teach African American children the folk wisdom and life skills drawn from the African culture. Teachers and parents should realize that these skills played an important part in the resilience African Americans displayed against overwhelming oppression and should help preserve the foundation of this faith and perseverance. (p. 151)

Smitherman (2000a) suggests the usefulness of proverbs in teaching critical thinking, a suggestion that some people might initially view with skepticism given the popular view that proverbs reflect a kind of simplistic thinking at odds with the complexity of most life situations. This view of proverbs as essentially simplistic is reflected in the assumption that one can specify in the abstract what a particular proverb "means." Not so. A proverb does not have a literal, or fixed, meaning. Instead, its meaning has to be derived by applying the proverb to the context in which it is used, a task that often requires a good deal of rigorous thinking. A wonderful example is contained in Patricia McKissack's *The Honest-to-Goodness Truth*, cited earlier. As the book opens, despite her mother's admonition to "tell the truth and shame the devil," Libby Louise tells her mother a lie anyway and is duly punished for it. Repentant, Libby resolves that very night to be done with lies. From that moment on, she will "tell the truth and shame the devil," no matter what. But what that proverbial statement actually means is not as clear as Libby initially thinks it is. At first, she makes the mistake of taking the statement literally, pointing out "truths" and tattling on friends until no one will speak to her anymore. As the story continues, Libby has to dig deep and think hard to figure out the true meaning of her mother's words.

The role that proverbs and wise sayings passed down from the elders played in helping African Americans to rise above the racism and limiting circumstances surrounding them is powerfully illustrated in another McKissack book, *Goin' Someplace Special* (2001), set in Nashville, Tennessee in the 1950s. On her way to the public library, almost-twelve-year-old 'Tricia Ann not only has to sit in the "colored section" in the back of the bus, but also faces Jim Crow signs and racist comments at every turn. But, as McKissack explains in the Author's Note and illustrates throughout the story, 'Tricia Ann has been "fortified with enough love, respect, and pride to overcome any situation [she] encountered" (unnumbered pages). As she sets out on her journey, her grandmother tells her, in the exact words uttered by countless Black parents, grandparents, teachers and other elders to the young people in their care: "'hold yo' head up and act like you b'long to somebody'" (unnumbered pages). Squaring her shoulders to walk to the back of the bus later in the story, 'Tricia Ann recalls her grandmother's words: "'Those signs can tell us where to sit, but they can't tell us what to think,'" again, words that literally became a refrain during the Jim Crow era in the South and that also, not surprisingly, conjure up Reverend Richardson's story about Benjamin Mays and the back of the bus. At one point on her journey, when she is almost ready to give up and return home, recalling her grandmother's often-echoed reminder that "you are somebody . . ." renews 'Tricia Ann's determination and sets her back on her way toward the library, a place that her grandmother calls "a doorway to freedom," wisdom also handed down from generation to generation in African American communities (unnumbered pages).

Smitherman's (2000a) Detroit data, still being analyzed at the time of her writing, reveal that among the most popular of the 800 proverbs offered by her Detroit informants are the following five:

1. What goes around comes around—the most frequently given proverb of all;
2. A bird in the hand is worth two in the bush;
3. You reap what you sow;
4. What goes up must come down;
5. What happens in the dark must come to light. (p. 244; for a more extensive list, see Smitherman, 2000a)

Interestingly, Smitherman and her colleagues (2000a) found that despite the predictable finding that older informants knew more proverbs than younger informants, all of the informants knew some proverbs, including those in the 17–20 age group. In the introduction to *Black Talk* (2000b), described previously, Smitherman notes that:

> Old proverbs, popular for decades in the Black language community, like "Actions speak louder than words" (recorded by Chocolate Milk, 1975) and "Smiling faces sometimes tell lies" (recorded by Undisputed Truth, 1971), were turned into hit song titles in the Rhythm 'n' Blues era of the 1950s to the 1970s. In 1990s Hip Hop, the old proverb "The blacker the berry, the sweeter the juice" was incorporated into Tupac Shakur's repertoire of self-esteem raps. That old saying "tryin to make a dolla outa fifteen cent" found its way into MC Lyte's 1998 album *Seven & Seven*, as well as into raps by Tupac and Master P who remind us that that they are "Just another Black man caught up in the mix, tryin' to make a dollar outa fifteen cent." (p. 24)

In her dictionary entry for *the blacker the berry, the sweeter the juice*, Smitherman (2000b) also notes its recent use in a slogan to support historically Black colleges: "'The Blacker the college, the sweeter the knowledge'" (p. 71). Clearly, proverbs are alive and well in the African American speech community, and their use has many pedagogical possibilities as Hale, Smitherman, and others have suggested.

The proverbs and wise sayings discussed in this section are connected to the pragmatic rule about use of formal titles in the sense that both have special applicability to elders and are related to the reverence accorded elders in African American culture. In the next section, I discuss cultural stories, another aspect of BC that bears a special relationship to elders because it is through African American elders that many such stories are passed on from one generation to another. (Readers may want to note that in Figure 2.1, "cultural stories" would likely be represented as part of the circle Dandy labels as *Moral Teachings*.) Given constraints of space, in the discussion that follows, I focus on only one representative story among many in the African American oral tradition.

Cultural Stories

In the seventeenth and eighteenth centuries, African American storytellers, sometimes referred to as griots, helped enslaved Africans maintain a spiritual connection to their past. Literary scholar Genevieve Fabre (1999) describes the storytelling session as a "ceremonial space" for early enslaved African Americans, one that provided an opportunity to "symbolically (stage) the reunion with countrymen, the travel back to the motherland and home of the ancestors" (p. 40). Like the West African griots from whom they were descended, African American storytellers preserved an oral record of kinship connections and, under the cruel and barbaric conditions of enslavement in America, kept alive memories of African beliefs and traditions.

For any group of people, storytelling is more than a means of preserving a record of historical experience, that is, recalling "what happened." It is also a means of both ascribing meaning to that experience and of deriving precepts and lessons for how to conduct one's life in the present. Stories passed down from the period of enslavement chronicle enslaved Africans' experiences in America at least partially through the lens of African spiritual beliefs and meaning systems. To the extent that these stories remain alive, they become part of what the writer Toni Cade Bambara (1992) has referred to as the "historical persistent past" (p. xii), shedding interpretative light on the present. One such story focuses on "what happened" over two centuries ago at a place called Ibo Landing, located, so legend has it, on one of the Sea Islands off the coasts of Georgia and South Carolina, the islands where the majority of enslaved Africans first set foot in America. There are three versions of the Ibo Landing story. In one version, a group of Ibo tribesmen, enslaved and transported from their homeland in Africa to Ibo Landing in America, walked on water all the way back to Africa rather than live in slavery. In the second version of the story, these same Ibo sprouted wings and flew to Africa. In the third version of the story, the Ibo walked into the water and drowned themselves in front of the ship's crew rather than remain enslaved (Dash, 1992).

According to historian Michael Gomez (1998), a theme that emerges in interviews conducted in the 1930s with formerly enslaved African Americans living in coastal Georgia focuses on Africans who could fly. Paul Singleton, for example, told an interviewer: "'Muh daddy use tuh tell me all duh time bout folks wut could fly back tuh Africa. Dey could take wing and jis fly off.'" Gomez writes: "That this was an important topic is evinced by the number of times it is mentioned in the Georgia coastal collection, which is many, and by Singleton's use of the phrase 'all duh time'" (p. 117).

That this centuries-old story of mythical/historical resistance, passed down orally from one generation to the next, retains its narrative power and symbolic significance in African American culture is evidenced in both the everyday expressions and the oral "testimony" of individual African Americans, as well as in the pages of African American literature. Thus, for example, Bambara remembers her great-grandmother's advice:

> Great grandmama, encouraging the mind to leap, taught that we can indeed walk on the water, so long as we know where we're going and why. "Course, fear of sinking stops many folk from taking necessary steps," she'd say. "And too, we're trained in this land to distrust the journey entirely." (p. xi)

While doing research in the 1980s for the critically acclaimed film *Daughters of the Dust*, set in a mythic Ibo Landing on a South Carolina Sea Island in 1902, director and writer Julie Dash discovered that the story of Ibo Landing was so important to African American people living in the Sea Islands that people living in virtually every community claimed an area of their island as the site of the actual Ibo Landing. The story figures prominently as well in Paule Marshall's novel *Praise Song for the Widow,* in which the protagonist's Great Aunt Cluny recalls her grandmother's recitation of the story and her statement, almost an echo of Bambara's "real-life" great-grandmother quoted herein, "My body may be here, but my mind's long gone with the Ibos" (quoted in Bambara, 1992, p. xii).

Toni Morrison also draws on this mythohistorical story in *Song of Solomon* (1977/1987), a novel in which the key to the protagonist Milkman's identity, and his spiritual awakening, lies "hidden" in the lyrics of a children's play song, which, when decoded, reveal that Milkman's great-great-grandfather was, as one character in the novel puts it, "one of those flying African children" (p. 321). More important of course than any literal interpretation of this centuries-old story about flying Africans are its symbolic possibilities, a realization Milkman comes to as his Aunt Pilate is dying: "Now he knew why he loved her so. Without even leaving the ground, she could fly." Indeed, flying is a central metaphor, or trope, within African American literature, including literature written for children. In just one example of the latter, *Tar Beach* (1991), Faith Ringgold creates the story of a little girl named Cassie Louise Lightfoot whose dreams of freedom lift her over the roof of her family's tenement building in Harlem one night and carry her off on a magical journey high above the city of New York. On her journey, Cassie envisions a truly "new" city, one infinitely more just and humane than the one she and her family currently inhabit. "It's very easy," Cassie later tells her little brother, Bebe, "anyone can fly. All you need is somewhere to go that you can't get to any other way" (unnumbered pages).

That the story of Ibo Landing should be so often recalled and imaginatively refigured in African American literature is powerful evidence of its significance in African American culture. Of its oral recitations—the literally thousands of times over two centuries that this story must have been recalled and refigured in ordinary, and extraordinary, conversations—and of the possible effects of its tellings upon its listeners—how sustaining it might have been, for instance, and under what horrific circumstances—we of course have no records. These can only be imagined. The story of Ibo Landing is but one of many stories from an African American oral tradition that have extended for over three-and-a-half centuries. It is a tradition still very much alive today. As Smitherman (2000a) points out, it is within this tradition, "through song, story, folk sayings and rich verbal interplay among everyday people" that "lessons and precepts about life and survival are handed down from generation to generation" (p. 199).

Using the BC pragmatic rule about use of formal titles as an entry point, I have briefly examined three other components of the BC system: kinship terms, proverbs and wise sayings, and, in this section, cultural stories. As can be seen by looking back at Figure 2.1, these particular components comprise only a small portion of the overall BC system. Providing a full description of this system is clearly beyond the scope of a single chapter. My more modest goal in examining these three components has been to give the reader some sense of both the complexity of the BC system and its inextricable connections to history and culture. I turn in chapter 3 to consideration of several other important points about the BC system and about the African American speech community in general.

Chapter 3
Other Important Aspects of the System

To Begin, a Word About "Slang" and the BC Lexicon . . .

Perhaps the most widely shared misconception about BC is its popular characterization—and scornful dismissal—as "just slang." This characterization sells short both the complexity of the BC system (which, as the discussion so far has illustrated, includes much more than simply vocabulary) and, just as importantly, the verbal sophistication reflected in the ongoing generation of new slang terms. Slang, of course, is not the exclusive property of Black Communications, or of any other language variety for that matter. In his dictionary of key linguistic concepts, R. L. Trask (1999) defines slang as "informal and often ephemeral linguistic forms" and as "informal but colorful words and expressions" (p. 279). Every language variety includes some slang words and expressions, typically used not only by speakers in relatively informal contexts, as Trask's definition suggests, but also more often by young people than by older speakers.

What distinguishes slang words and expressions in BC from those found in other varieties of English is their abundance, their energy and creativity, and the incisive social commentary they often embed. Speaking specifically to the energy and creativity that characterize BC slang, Geneva Smitherman (1998), who is the foremost authority on the Black lexicon, writes:

> The dynamism and creativity in the lexicon revitalizes and re-energizes bland Euro-talk. There's electricity and excitement in *playas* "flamboyant, flashy, highly desirable men or women, with the power to have multiple relationships." The metaphors, images, and poetry in Black talk make the ordinary *all that, and then some* "excellent, fantastic, superb." AAVE [i.e., BC] is a dramatic, potent counterforce to verbal deadness and emptiness. One is not merely accepted by a group, she is *in like Flin.* Fraternities and sororities don't merely march; they perform a *step show* "intricate marching patterns and steps performed in a group formation." And when folk get *amp* "stirred up, in a heightened emotional state," they don't fight the feeling, they *testify*

"give testimony to, speak about the power of something or someone in a high-spirited, emotional way." (p. 217)

Although it is not technically correct to categorize the entire BC lexicon under the rubric of *slang*, one of the prominent lexicographers of the language, Clarence Major, entitled his 1994 dictionary *Juba to Jive: A Dictionary of African American Slang* with the avowed intention of "bring[ing] to the language we call slang a better name, a better reputation" (p. xxvii). Provocatively, Smitherman (2000b) suggests that "the underlying tone of resistance" embedded in the BC lexicon may account for its easy dismissal as "just slang," conjuring up that term's popular connotations of short-livedness and nonseriousness. She writes:

> Slang, after all, is rather lighthearted and harmless, and it's usually short-lived—here today, gone tomorrow—but the social critique embodied in Black slang is SERIOUS AS A HEART ATTACK. For 1990s Hip Hoppers, fed up with the oppressive treatment of PEOPLE OF COLOR in the nation's major cities, it's not *New* York, it's *Zoo* York; it's not Los *Angeles*, it's Los *Scandalous*. In the 1960s, Malcolm X shocked white America by dubbing northern cities UP SOUTH, contending that these supposedly progressive areas were just a variation on the theme of racial domination that Blacks were experiencing DOWN SOUTH. In these and many other examples, Africans in America flipped the script, making an alien tongue their own by imbuing "ole massa's" language with their unique, African semantics. (p. 3)

Primarily the argot of young people, slang is, without question, the most vibrant, creative, and constantly evolving component of the BC system. Its endless production evidences the verbal sophistication as well as the political and social consciousness of African American young people from a diversity of social class backgrounds and educational levels.

Despite its prominent use among young Black people (and its prominence in popular stereotypes about Black language), however, slang actually comprises, as stated previously, only one portion of the BC lexicon. Linguist Lisa Green (2002) divides this lexicon into two major components: (a) words and phrases that cross generational and regional boundaries and that have been used in Black communities for a long time, and (b) the kind of current slang items (used primarily by adolescents and young adults) that we have been discussing in this section so far. Frequently cited examples of the first type of lexicon are the words *ashy* and *saddity* (sometimes spelled *siditty*), which, as Green points out, are used by all age groups (p. 15). Smitherman defines *ashy* as "the whitish or grayish appearance of skin due to exposure to wind and cold, which shows up more on African Americans than European Americans due to Black people's darker skin pigmentation" (p. 56) and *saddity* as "snooty, uppity-acting," noting that *dichty* is an older term for the same concept (p. 251).

Green points out that the word *ashy* is not widely used, or even known, outside the Black community. Yet its use among African Americans extends back many generations, as evidenced in the following example from one of the ex-slave narratives. Describing the arrival of Yankee soldiers during the Civil War, Ms. Sarah Debro, age 90 at the time she was interviewed, said: "I was scared and my hands was *ashy* . . ." (in Hurmence, 2001, p. 58). At one point in *I Know Why the Caged Bird Sings* (1969/1993), which describes Maya Angelou's coming of age during the 1930s and 40s, Angelou provides the following description of her brother: "It was summer and his pants were short, so the pickle juice made clean streams down his *ashy* legs . . ." (p. 23). And in the children's book *Irene and the Big, Fine Nickel* (1991), set in the 1950s, Smalls writes: "Irene rubbed the Vaseline from her face and neck onto her legs. Godmother told her to do that to keep her skin from getting *ashy* . . ." (unnumbered pages).

Illustrating more contemporary use of this word, Smitherman (2000b) offers the following from the late rapper Notorious B.I.G.'s 1997 album *Life After Death*: "'I went from *ashy* to classy,'" that is, Smitherman explains, "from being an unsophisticated, rough, country-bumpkin type who let his 'ash' show to an up-scale, well-groomed, no-ash showing BIG WILLIE PLAYA (i.e., 'a person who is affluent, accomplished, powerful . . . '; [p. 68])" (p. 56). Green (2002) cites another example of the term's contemporary use from a 2000 pamphlet about skin care featuring an article entitled "Get ASHY SKIN Glowing Again" (p. 15).

Like ashy, *saddity/siddity* is a word that has been in use for a long time and that is still used today by African Americans from different age groups. Angelou (1969/1993), for example, describes the St. Louis teachers of her youth as acting "very *siddity*" . . . "talk[ing] down to their students from the lofty heights of education and white folks' enunciation" (p. 64), while Toni Morrison uses the more old-fashioned term *dichty/dicty* for a character's description of Northern Black people during the 1920s in her novel *The Bluest Eye* (1970/1993): "'Northern colored folk was different too. *Dicty*-like. No better than whites for meanness'" (p. 117). A friend of mine, who grew up in Kentucky during the 1960s, recalls that whenever her mother's aunt came to visit, she would straighten my friend's hair and that of her four sisters with a hot comb. As she finished with each girl's hair, she would always say, "There you go, little Miss *Saddity*," suggesting both that term's association with "good (i.e., straight) hair" and the fact that my friend and her sisters looked so good in their new "dos" that they had reason to act stuck-up. Evidence that the term *saddity* is still in use today comes from a television sitcom, "Half and Half," a program that has an almost all-Black cast; during an episode that aired in September 2003, one character accounts for her actions by explaining: "I did it to beat those *saddity* Dee Dees." As another example of this word's contemporary use, at one point in *Pushkin and the Queen of Spades* by Alice Randall, a novel published in 2004 and set in the 1990s, the narrator describes her young son's propensity for throwing up on the pretentious: "Pushkin didn't seem to aim, but he had a way of reaching out and touching whatever or whoever was most *seddity* in a room" (p. 35).

Many more examples could be offered of words from the BC lexicon that have a long history in the Black community, are still in use today, and are not widely known or used outside the Black community (interested readers should consult Major [1994] and Smitherman (2000b), as well as other sources listed in the bibliography). I will provide only one more example here: the expression *ain studying you/him/her/that*. Smitherman (2000b) defines this expression as "a dismissal of the person or matter at hand, no intention of dealing with the person, object or situation" and provides the following example of contemporary usage: "'I done tol you I *ain studying bout* that old car'" (p. 52). Another example of contemporary usage comes from Dana Johnson's 2001 short story collection *Break Any Woman Down*. At one point in the story "Melvin in the Sixth Grade," Owen tells his younger sister: "'I'm graduating this year, Ave. I *ain't stuttin* these white folks'" (p. 16). Later, Ave, the narrator, reflects on the fact that she'd "heard that word [i.e., stuttin/studying] my whole life from my grandmamas, mama, Daddy, everybody" (p. 16). As still another example of fairly contemporary usage, at one point, Pilate, a character in Toni Morrison's novel *Song of Solomon* (1977/1987), says to her brother, Macon: "'But you should of known better than to think I'd go back there for them little old bags. I *wasn't stuttin 'em* when I first laid eyes on 'em, I sure wasn't thinking about them three years later'" (p. 208). And in McKissack's *Goin' Someplace Special* (2001), a discouraged 'Tricia Ann hears her grandmother's voice telling her "... *don't study on quittin',* just keep walking straight ahead and you'll make it" (unnumbered pages).

Some notion of the longevity of this expression within the BC speech community can be gleaned from its use in one of the ex-slave narratives. In the following, Ms. Vergie (interviewed in the 1930s) is talking about a bus driver who insisted that she pay the regular fare even though she was in possession of a "book" that allowed her to travel for free: "He let me go on by to my seat, 'cause I *wasn't studying about* paying my fare after I had handed him the book" (in Sutcliffe, 2000, p. 41).

As indicated in Smitherman's entry and as illustrated in the previous examples, the phrase *ain studying you/him/her/that* is expressed in the negative form (i.e., *ain't* studying/*wasn't* studying) and carries a definite implication of dismissal—that is, as Smitherman says, the speaker has no intention of dealing with the situation or person at hand. Thus, Owen, in this example ("'I ain't stuttin' these white folks'"), clearly does not possess the slightest degree of interest in the white folks at his school, and Ms. Vergie, in the last example, had <u>no</u> intentions of paying the unfairly demanded bus fare. To gain a better sense of the unique meaning attached to this phrase in the BC lexicon, it is useful to compare a sentence like *I ain't studying calculus this semester* with the example sentence contained in Smitherman's entry for this phrase: "... *I ain studying bout that old car.*" The words *"ain('t) studying ..."* have a different meaning in the two examples. For one, the meaning of the word *studying* is not the same in both: in the first example, *studying* has the meaning of systematically pursuing a body of knowledge, whereas in the second example, *studying* has the meaning of giving attention to or thinking about something, a meaning that is specifically associated with the BC lexicon (Major, 1994, p. 454). Secondly, in the first example, the words *ain't studying calculus* do not carry the same implication of dismissal that is essential to the meaning of *ain studying you/him/her/that* in the BC lexicon and to the meaning of this phrase as it is used in the second example. As a matter of fact, in the first example, the words *ain't studying calculus* do not even comprise a meaningful unit in the same sense that *"ain studying bout that old car"* do in Smitherman's example. What makes the phrase *ain studying you/him/her/that* specific to the BC lexicon and not part of the more general mainstream English lexicon, then, is that *ain studying you/him/her/that* is a phrase with a particular cultural meaning and one that is seldom, if ever, used outside of the Black speech community. And, as the example of its use by Ms. Vergie, an African American elder in the 1930s, makes clear, this still-current phrase has way too long a history of use in that community to be classified as *slang*.

As I hope the examples of *ashy, saddity,* and *ain studying you/him/her/that* have illustrated, the BC lexicon is comprised of more that just the current words and expressions in use among African American young people (as creative and linguistically sophisticated as that portion of the lexicon is). As suggested by the examples discussed here, much of the lexicon consists of words and phrases that have been in use for a long time, that cross geographical space and social class, and whose meanings reflect the unique cultural and historical experiences of African American people. Perhaps no single word or expression illustrates this last point more powerfully than does the word *cool*.

Unlike words such as *ashy* and *saddity* (and expressions like *ain't studying that*) that aren't used much, if at all, outside the Black speech community, *cool*—like many other words in the BC lexicon—is used by speakers of other varieties of English as well. What makes the word *cool* specific to the BC lexicon are the unique cultural meanings attached to it. Smitherman (1998) explains:

> . . . at first glance it [i.e., *cool*] might not seem to be a race-conscious idea. However, a disempowered group daily forced to face the possibility of its destruction can ill-afford to be "hot." Lynch mobs in the old days, police brutality in this new day—any heat generated by rage and anger could literally be dangerous to a Black person's health. Hence the value of calmness, suppressing one's rage and anger, that is, maintaining one's *cool* as a survival strategy. 1990s African American youth talk about *chillin*, their middle-aged parents still refer to it as *keep yo cool*, and an eighty-five-year-old Black man recently used the term *copasetic* to refer to the state of being *cool*. (p. 206)

In the novel *Mama Day* (1988/1993), Gloria Naylor has one of her central characters give voice to the cultural and historical significance attached to the word *cool* in African American experience:

> "Now I'm gonna tell you about *cool*. It comes with the cultural territory: the beating of the bush drum, the rocking of the slave ship, the rhythm of the hand going from cotton sack to cotton row and back again. It went on to settle into the belly of the blues, the arms of Jackie Robinson, and the head of every ghetto kid who lives to a ripe old age. You can keep it, you can hide it, you can blow it—but even when your ass is in the tightest crack, you must never, ever LOSE it." (p. 102)

And testifying to the continuing relevance of *cool* in the lives of African American young people, Marcyliena Morgan (2002) quotes the rapper Kool Moe Dee from his 1991 hit "How Kool Can One Black Man Be?":

> But cool ain't a mood/It's an attitude dude/It's a tone/It's a tempo/A mind set/A rhythm/Lifestyle/Religion/It's just how ya livin'/I'm righteously cool/ While here and hereafter/I'm so cool/That I have to ask ya'/How cool?/How cool?/How cool can one black man be? (p. 40)

Morgan connects the concept of *cool* to social face; a *cool* social face, she writes, "is the ability to act on symbolic incidents and subtle varieties of cultural practice with eloquence, skill, wit, patience and precise timing" (p. 40). This ability is perfectly illustrated by the young heroine, 'Tricia Ann, in McKissack's book *Goin' Someplace Special,* referred to earlier. Reminded by two White children that if she wanted to attend a performance at the Grand Music Palace, she would have to sit in the "buzzard's roost," the last three rows of the balcony reserved for Black patrons, 'Tricia Ann demonstrates total *cool* as she responds scornfully, hand on hip, "In the last three rows of the balcony? Why, I wouldn't sit up there even if watermelons bloomed in January" (unnumbered pages).

As mentioned earlier, *cool* is only one of many words in the BC lexicon that are also used by speakers of other varieties of English, but that are used by African Americans with unique or special meanings attached. Hence, they are considered part of the BC lexicon. Some words acquire unique meaning in the BC lexicon through a process, described earlier, that linguists describe as *semantic inversion*, whereby a word comes to mean the opposite of at least one of its meanings in the general, mainstream English lexicon. Oft-cited examples include *bad* to mean "good," *cold* (pronounced *coal*) to mean "superb," *stupid* to mean "excellent", *phat* (fat) to mean "great," and *shut up* to mean "keep talking" (Smitherman, 2000a). Although most of the words included in the preceding examples are relatively recent additions to the lexicon, the process of semantic inversion, like so much about BC, can be traced back to a much earlier period in African American history and perhaps even to West and Central

African linguistic practices that included the use of double entendre, punning, word play, and various other forms of verbal indirection. I found the following example of semantic inversion in one of the ex-slave narratives collected in the 1930s. Ms. Delia Buckley, age unknown at the time she was interviewed, recalled: "I married right here in my own house in they backyard; married Pretty. That's what they calls him, 'cause he's so ugly, I reckon" (in Waters, 2002, pp. 49–50).

Perhaps the ultimate irony about the popular dismissal of the whole BC communicative system as "nothing but slang" is how quickly slang words and expressions in BC get adopted—some would say "stolen"—by the mainstream culture and used, not only to express individual speakers' sense of themselves as "hip" and urbane, but to sell all kinds of products in the popular media. Commercials for Kentucky Fried Chicken provide a case in point. Some readers may recall a 1990 television commercial whose "punch" comes from the supposed naivety of an older, obviously un-hip, White person who doesn't realize that describing chicken as *bad* actually means that it's "good" (also cited in Dandy, 1991). More recently, a radio advertisement suggested that the same bad chicken is *so* good that KFC should give out "*phat* degrees" (cited in Smitherman, 2000b, p. 29). It's a safe bet, of course, that in neither case did the chicken conglomerate pay either homage or royalties to the Black discourse community whose creativity with language helped earn them millions.

Examples of the popular culture's embrace of BC slang abound. A Revlon lipstick commercial appearing on television in fall, 2003 urges consumers to *"Get your glide on,"* while an article entitled *"Get Your Drink On"* in the Boston *Metro Weekend* magazine (1/28–30/05) "invites" readers to attend the fourteenth annual Boston Wine Expo at a fancy, ocean-front location. In November, 2003, *Today Show* co-host Katie Couric introduces style and fashion expert Steven Cojocaro with the words: "Cojo's *in the house.*" A travel writer for *The Boston Globe*, in an article about her recent Caribbean cruise (9/14/03) describes her young son as "running with his new-found *posse.*" And an article appearing in *The Boston Globe* entitled "Just *Bling* for Room Service" (1/2/05) begins, "Whether you call it *bling bling* or that old word 'jewelry,' you can have your pick at the Ritz-Carlton New York, Central Park without leaving your room."

"I do not know what white Americans would sound like if there had never been any Black people in the United States," James Baldwin observed in a *New York Times* essay in 1979, "but they would not sound the way they sound" (reprinted in Perry and Delpit, 1998, p. 68). As examples of originally "Black" words and phrases in common use among Americans in 1979, Baldwin included—just to name some—*sock it to me, let it all hang out, right on!, uptight, get down, get with it, funky,* and *whipped.* Additions to these examples could fill many pages because, as Smitherman points out, the list of words and phrases that have "crossed over" into the mainstream is just about endless.

Again, just some of them, not previously mentioned, include the following: *homeboy; chill; hit on; twenty-four-seven; bad mouth; attitude* (as in don't give me any); *you go, girl; soulmate; nickel 'n' dime; all that; my bad; cut somebody some slack; rip off; nitty gritty; grapevine* (as in, heard it through); *kick back; sell out; light-weight; gig; dis; 4-1-1* (as in, what's the. . . ?); *high five; mess around; catch you later; get real; get on somebody's case; one-on-one; get it together; got your back; bug; got game; props; TLC; tight* (as in, we are); and *say what?*

It's not just what you say . . .

Using the BC lexicon appropriately requires not only knowledge about word meanings, but also knowledge of the rules for proper pronunciation, what linguists often refer to as *phonological rules*. These include both rules for pronouncing individual consonant and vowel sounds within words and rules governing patterns of stress and intonation (often called *prosodic features*) that affect larger linguistic units, such as whole words, phrases and sentences (Green, 2002). The way in which these two levels of the sound system work in concert to create what Smitherman (2000a) has called "the authentic Black sound" (p. xiii) is suggestively evoked in the following passage from Morrison's *The Bluest Eye* (1970/1994), although the actual sound of the words Morrison describes can, of course, only be imagined:

> They come from Mobile. Aiken. From Newport News. From Marietta. From Meridian. And the sound of these places in their mouths make you think of love. When you ask them where they are from, they tilt their heads and say "Mobile" and you think you've been kissed. They say "Aiken" and you see a white butterfly glance off a fence with a torn wing. They say "Nagadoches" and you want to say "Yes, I will." You don't know what these towns are like, but you love what happens to the air when they open their lips and let the names ease out. (p. 81)

Many African American children's writers attempt to capture characteristic BC phonological and intonational patterns in print, a practice that adds significantly to the cultural authenticity and rhetorical power of their work. One of the points that I try to impress upon students in the multicultural children's literature courses that I teach is the importance of teachers being able to do a good job of reading that literature aloud. For non-BC speakers, this requires both considerable practice and the humility to recognize the fact that no matter how much time they put into practicing, they are unlikely to ever be able to read that literature aloud with quite the same skill as a native BC speaker. This last is a point that hit me with special force when I began teaching a course on African American children's literature in South Carolina and listened, mesmerized, to the teachers in my class read some of my favorite books aloud. One of those teachers, clearly in no doubt about her elocutionary powers, turned to me after a particularly animated reading of McKissack's *Flossie and the Fox* (1986) and said: "Now, don't be hatin' on me, Dr. Meier, just 'cause I read (*reed*, not *red*) so good" (or in other words, "don't be *envious* of my superior ability," which, of course, I was).

If it is difficult for a non-native speaker to produce Smitherman's "authentic Black sound" in reading aloud well-practiced text, it is even more difficult to do so in everyday spontaneous speech. As noted earlier, many words and expressions from the BC lexicon get appropriated by people outside the African American speech community, particularly by adolescents. Sometimes what gets adopted in this process are not actually new words or phrases, or even new meanings, but pronunciations popularly associated with the Black speech community. In the late 1990s in Boston, for example, it was not uncommon to hear adolescents from a variety of linguistic and cultural backgrounds use pronunciations like the following: *Sup?* (What's up?); *Aight* (alright); and *Ah 'on' know* (I don't know). Similarly, in the early nineties, young people all over the country could be heard mimicking some of the pronunciation features and intonational patterns used by the actor Will Smith in his role as "The Fresh Prince of Bel-Air."

Being able to pronounce a few words from the BC lexicon more or less correctly, however, hardly constitutes phonological proficiency in the language. Speakers who are phonologically proficient in BC know more than list of words and their correct pronunciations. Much more significantly, they know the systematic rules governing the patterns of sounds that can occur in BC. As is true with speakers of every language variety, BC speakers did not learn these rules in a conscious way; that is, no one sat them down and explicitly taught them the BC pronunciation rules. Rather, they acquired them, effortlessly and unconsciously, as a result of being raised or spending significant amounts of time interacting in a community of BC speakers. And, again, like speakers of all languages, despite the fact that the vast majority of BC speakers probably could not articulate these phonological rules, they follow them consistently in speaking the language. Literacy teachers working with BC speakers need to know the major BC phonological rules. Here, I will examine only one of the prominent phonological patterns in the language, one that has a significant potential impact on the process of learning to read, especially for monolingual BC speakers: final consonant cluster reduction.

Many words in English end in a consonant cluster, a phonological "grouping" composed of two consonant sounds, as in the words *desk* and *test*. A systematic rule in BC allows for the reduction of this "two consonant" sound to a "single consonant" sound under certain conditions. Thus, a BC speaker may well produce *des* for *desk* and *tes* for *test*. In the children's book *Irene and the Big, Fine Nickel*, discussed earlier, the following representations of consonant cluster reduction occur:

"That's just fine, *chile*," Miss Sally said.

"Here comes *ole* skuzzy Charlene," Lulamae said.

In both of these examples, the final cluster *ld* has been reduced to the single consonant sound /*l*/. Readers should note that because there is no standard, generally accepted way of representing systematic BC pronunciations in print, different writers use different ways of approximating these in graphic form. In these examples, for instance, author Irene Smalls uses the letters *le* (*chile*, *ole*) to represent the single consonant sound /*l*/, even though the letter *e* carries no sound value in these words. In contrast, Geneva Smitherman (2000b) uses the spelling *"coal"* to approximate the spoken sound of *"cold"* in BC, while in the Smitherman example used earlier in the section on the lexicon—"I *ain* studying bout that old car"—she simply deletes the apostrophe and the final *t* to represent one BC pronunciation of *ain't*. Often writers use an apostrophe to represent a deleted sound, for example, *wil'* (*wild*). Thus in trying to make sense of literature that attempts to capture in print what (some) BC speakers sound like (in some situations), readers should keep this variability in mind. What matters are sounds, not spellings. The sounds are systematic, even if the spellings used to represent them aren't.

Studies have consistently found that BC speakers are more likely to reduce final consonant clusters when the following word begins with a consonant rather than a vowel and when the cluster ends in either *t* or *d*, both valuable pieces of information for literacy teachers. Another factor that influences whether or not a particular cluster will be reduced has to do with *voicing*, a term that is used by linguists in describing consonant sounds. As Rickford and Rickford (2000) explain, voicing refers to "whether your vocal chords are held closely together, vibrating noisily (voiced), or whether they are spread apart and not vibrating (voiceless)." To illustrate, they use the example of consonants *s* and *z*, "identical sounds except that *s* is voiceless and *z* is voiced" (p. 104). Linguistic analysis of BC speakers' speech consistently reveals that when the two consonants in a cluster share the same voicing value, the cluster is more likely to be reduced than when one consonant in the cluster is voiced and the other is voiceless. The influence of voicing on the process of consonant cluster reduction in BC provides another illustration of the rule-governed nature of this process.

As the next two chapters will discuss, children socialized in African American communities are likely to participate in many play activities involving the use of rhyme. Not surprisingly, the rhymes children produce in these situations often reflect BC pronunciation patterns, including final consonant cluster reduction. Consider the following examples, taken from two traditional African American jump-rope songs:

Teddy bear, Teddy bear, do the *twist*
Teddy bear, Teddy bear, do it like *this*.
(recorded in Jemie, 2003, p. 120)

Oh, step it, step it, step
it *down*
Oh, swing your love and
turn *around*.
(recorded in Jones and Hawes, 1972, p. 115)

In the first example, the rhyme between *twist* and *this* depends upon the reduction of the final *st* cluster in *twist* to the single consonant sound /*s*/, producing *twis*, not *twist*, and thus resulting in the rhyme *twis/this*. Similarly, in the second example, the words *down* and *around* rhyme because the process of consonant cluster reduction results in *around* being pronounced as *aroun*. Rhymes created through the process of consonant cluster reduction can be found in African American songs dating back to the period of enslavement, as exemplified in the following stanza from a song entitled "Juba," which is still sometimes sung in the Sea Islands area of South Carolina:

You sift-a the meal, you give me
the husk
You cook-a the bread, you give me
the crust.
(recorded in Jones & Hawes, 1972, p. 39)

In this example, the rhyme between *husk* and *crust* is based on the pronunciation of both final clusters *sk* and *st* as the single consonant sound /*s*/, resulting in the rhyme *hus/crus*.

Educator Elizabeth Whatley (1980) describes these kinds of rhymes as ones based on "sound-sound" patterns as opposed to the visual-sound patterns that form the basis for most rhyming activities in the early literacy curriculum. Because rhymes based on sound-sound patterns are so common in African American songs and rhyming games, Whatley advocates that teachers develop instructional strategies that recognize the validity of both patterns. I will have more to say about this issue as well as about other BC phonological patterns in part 4. Here, suffice it to say—as I hope this brief discussion of final consonant cluster reduction has illustrated—that the pronunciation patterns used by BC speakers are as systematic and rule-governed as every other component of the BC system.

Grammatically speaking . . .

Although Black Communications shares much of its grammar with Standard English, there are some notable differences between the two systems. Like many other language varieties, BC is characterized by the use of multiple negation. Thus a sentence like *They don't have no money for the movies* is grammatically correct in BC but not in SE. In some cases, BC speakers can also invert the order of a negative indefinite noun subject (e.g., *nobody, nothing*) and a negative auxiliary (e.g., *can't, don't, ain't*) to create what are known as "negative inversion" sentences, as in *Ain't nobody home* (example in Rickford, 1999, p. 8). As the last example illustrates, *ain't* is a permissible and widely used preverbal negator in BC functioning as the equivalent of SE *am not, isn't, aren't, hasn't, haven't and didn't* (Rickford, 1999, p. 8). Possession in BC can be marked solely by juxtaposition as in *the girl mama*, whereas in SE, possession is doubly marked, once by the positioning of the possessor next to the possessed (i.e., juxtaposition) and again by the use of *'s*, as in *the girl's mama*. Other areas of systematic difference between the two varieties include forms of questions, relative clause formation, and the production of sentences using existentials. (On this last difference, compare the BC sentence, *It's some coffee in the kitchen*, with its likely SE "translation," *There's some coffee in the kitchen* [example in Green, 2002, p. 80].)

By far the largest number of differences between the two varieties, however, involves the use of verbs. As John Rickford and Russell Rickford put it in *Spoken Soul* (2000), verbs are where the action is, the location where much of what is "distinctive" and "identity-affirming" about Black Communications gets marked (p. 125). Following, I briefly describe some of the most distinctive verb patterns characteristic of the BC system.

Habitual Be

Habitual be, also referred to as *aspectual be*, communicates that an action is recurring or that it takes place on different occasions (Green, 2002). In the sentence, *Those girls be hanging out after school*, for example, *be* denotes habitual or interative meaning, such that the "hanging out" event occurs on different occasions, perhaps regularly. Similarly, in the sentence, *"He be doing homework 'til 9 or 10 o'clock,"* the African American woman who used it was making the point that her grandson usually or typically does homework until 9 or 10 o'clock in the evening. Recently, in the wake of Hurricane Katrina, a young African American man working in a discount store made the following comment to me about the store managers: *"They all be throwing everything away."* He was communicating his disapproval of the managers' habit of regularly/routinely throwing away slightly damaged items that somebody could use. The recurring nature of the action conveyed by habitual *be* is well captured in the following sentence recorded in Smitherman (2000): *"This bus on time today, but most times, it be late"* (p. 273).

Habitual *be* does not occur in Standard English. To communicate the same meaning in SE, that is, that an action is performed regularly or habitually, the speaker must rely on the use of adverbs—for example, *He is usually/often/ regularly doing homework until 9 or 10 o'clock*. Habitual *be* is used frequently by BC speakers and is strongly identified with African Americans by the larger society. Rickford and Rickford (2000) refer to habitual *be* as "probably the best-known but least understood of [BC's] grammatical signposts" (p. 113). This lack of understanding about its meaning was clearly reflected in the kinds of jokes that surfaced on the Internet in the aftermath of the Oakland Ebonics controversy in 1997. One such joke went like this: *Question: What do you call Toys R Us in Harlem? Answer: We Be Toys.* This joke is a nonsensical one, as it reflects total ignorance of the meanings conveyed by the use of *be* in Black Communications.

Smitherman (2000a) provides two examples of classroom situations in which the teacher's unfamiliarity with habitual *be* caused miscommunication between the teacher and a student. The first example was recorded in an elementary school in Los Angeles and appeared originally in the work of educator Noma LeMoine (1999):

TEACHER:	Bobby, what does your mother do everyday? (Teacher apparently wanted to call Bobby's parents.)
BOBBY:	She be home!
TEACHER:	You mean, she *is* at home.
BOBBY:	No, she ain't, 'cause she took my grandmother to the hospital this morning.
TEACHER:	You know what I meant. You are not supposed to say, "she *be* at home." You are to say, "she *is* at home."
BOBBY:	Why you trying to make me lie? She ain't at home. (in Smitherman, 2000, p. 25)

As Smitherman explains, in keeping with the meaning of BC habitual *be*, Bobby was indicating that his mother is usually or typically at home during the day, not that she was there on this particular occasion. Without an understanding of the grammatical system Bobby is using, the teacher not only mistakes Bobby's meaning, but ends up confusing and frustrating him as well, likely undermining his confidence that his teacher is someone who knows what she is talking about and can be trusted.

Smitherman's second example comes from an interaction that took place in a first-grade classroom in Detroit. In this example as well, the teacher's lack of knowledge about the habitual meaning conveyed by the use of *be* caused misunderstanding:

TEACHER:	Where is Mary?
STUDENT:	She not here.
TEACHER:	(exasperatedly): She is *never* here!
STUDENT:	Yeah, she be here.
TEACHER:	Where? You just said she wasn't here. (Smitherman, 2000a, p. 25)

Copula Absence or "Zero Copula"

Copula absence, or zero copula, refers to the absence of *is* or *are* (i.e., the copula) in some present tense constructions, as in the following example from *Me and Neesie* (1975/2005), a children's book by Eloise Greenfield:

> "Janell, baby!" Aunt Bea said. *"You pretty as ever."* (unnumbered pages)

In SE, the latter sentence would be rendered either as *You are as pretty as ever*, with the copula appearing in its full form (*are*), or as *You're as pretty as ever*, with the copula in its contracted form (*'re*).

Other examples of copula absence include the following:

- *"He real little."* (In Smitherman, 2000, p. 137)
- *"She my teacher."* (Smitherman, p. 137)
- *"I don't care if they mad at me!"* (Goodwin, 1990, p. 207)
- *"People crazy."* (In Rickford & Rickford, 2000, p. 114)
- *"We tryin to get all the money, cousin."* (In Alim, 2003, p. 49)

Copula absence is an inherent variable in BC; that is, full, contracted, and deleted forms are all used. Thus as linguist H. Samy Alim (2003) explains, a BC speaker "can produce sentences like *He is the leader* (full form), *He's the leader* (contracted form) and *He the leader* (absent form), all of which have the same meaning" (p. 46). This variability is not random, but highly systematic. Studies consistently reveal, for example, that copula absence is strongly affected by the grammatical category of the following word or phrase (Labov, 1972; Rickford, 1999). The copula (i.e., *is* or *are*) is least likely to be absent in BC before a following noun phrase (*She the star*), more likely to be absent before predicate adjectives and locatives (*She pretty; She in the back*), still more likely to be absent before a verb ending in *ing* (*She looking fine*) and <u>most</u> likely to be absent before the future form *gonna* or *gon'* (*She gonna really be mad*). In addition, these same studies show that: (a) the copula is less likely to be produced following a pronoun subject (*She the diva*) than a noun subject (*Geneva the diva*), and (b) that the copula *are* is much more frequently absent than *is*.

Adding still more detail to the systematicity described herein is the BC rule dictating that, while present tense forms *is* and *are* can be absent under certain conditions, past tense copulas *was* and *were* cannot. There are also present tense copula forms that are seldom, if ever, absent. The copula must be present when the subject is the first person singular pronoun *I*. Thus *I am cold* or *I'm cold* are both acceptable in BC, but not *I cold*. Similarly, the copula used with the third person singular neuter subject, *it*, virtually always appears either in full or contracted form: *It is raining* or *It's raining*, but not *It raining*. These constraints governing copula absence in BC provide compelling evidence of the highly systematic, rule-governed nature of its grammar. Research reveals that BC speakers as young as three and four religiously observe these same constraints in producing zero copula forms in their speech (Wyatt, 2001).

No Required Subject-Verb Agreement

In Standard English there is a rule that verbs used with third person singular subjects (e.g., *he, she, the cat*) must be marked with *–s.* This is reflected in the following paradigm using the verb *walk*:

I	walk	**We** walk
You	walk	**You** (plural) walk
He/She	walks	**They** walk

In contrast, Black Communications does not require that verbs used with third person singular subjects be marked with *–s.* In BC, the same verb form may be used with all subjects (i.e., first, second and third person singular or plural). This is illustrated in the following quotation, excerpted from an interview with a young Black woman in East Palo Alto, California (Rickford & Rickford, 2000). The verbs that would include the third person singular agreement marker *–s* in SE have been underlined:

> ". . . it <u>seem</u> like, when I be driving, it <u>seem</u> like every corner I drive around, there <u>go</u> somebody you know pushing a baby . . ." (p. 110)

It is sometimes the case that the plural form of the verb is the one generalized across person and number (Green, 2002; Labov, 1972). For example, the invariant form of the verb *to be* in past tense is *was* rather than *were.* However, in the majority of cases, as Rickford and Rickford (2000) point out, it is the singular form of the verb that is generalized across person and number (p. 126).

Stressed or "Remote Past" Been/BIN

Stressed *been* (sometimes written BIN) is used to indicate that an action or a state began in the remote past and is still continuing up to the present moment. It is pronounced with emphatic stress. As linguist Lisa Green (2002) points out, the concept of *remote past* is relative and can refer to "a time period of fifteen minutes ago or fifteen years ago." "One way to put it," Green explains, "is that BIN is used to indicate that the time period referred to is longer than normal for an activity, or it can be used to affirm that a state has indeed held for a long period of time" (p. 55). Among others, she offers the following examples with accompanying SE glosses:

- *He <u>BIN running</u>.* (SE gloss: He's been running for a long time.)
- *"I <u>BIN knowing</u> he died."* (SE gloss: I've known for a long time that he died.)

- A: *"The police going bad."*
- B: *"They ain't going bad. They <u>BIN</u> bad."* (SE gloss: They aren't going bad. They have been bad for a long time; p. 56)

An example of stressed been occurs on the opening page of Andrea Davis Pinkney's *Fishing Day* (2003), a picture book about a girl who goes fishing with her mother:

> "Mama, you up?" I call. But before Mama even answers, I smell hominy cooking in the kitchen. Mama leans in the doorway of my bedroom. "I *been* up," she says. "Making sure we got us a hot breakfast." (emphasis in the text; unnumbered pages)

As with BC habitual *be*, there is no exact equivalent for capturing the meaning of stressed been in SE. As can be seen in Green's examples, SE glosses of sentences containing stressed been do not necessarily communicate the notion of a longer-than-normal time period that is implied by the use of this form in BC. In Green's examples, the running event, the state of knowing, and the state of having gone bad have all been "in play," so to speak, for a period of time that is in some sense "remarkably" long. Similarly, the little girl's mother in *Fishing Day* has been up for an unusually, a "remarkably," long time. It is this sense of a time period whose length is "worth remarking on" that is captured in stressed BEEN and that is difficult to "translate" into equivalent SE form.

In his classic work *Language in the Inner City* (1972), linguist William Labov offers the following example of an interaction between a White psychologist, Paul, and a six-year-old African American boy, Samuel, in which the adult's not knowing the meaning conveyed by stressed been resulted in confusion between them:

SAMUEL (TO PAUL):	I *been* know your name.
PAUL:	What?
SAMUEL:	I *been* know your name.
PAUL:	You better know my name?
SAMUEL:	I *been* know your name. (p. 54)

Completive Done

Done is sometimes used in BC to emphasize the completed nature of an action. Unlike stressed been/BIN, however, it is not spoken with particular stress. Green (2002) provides the following examples from the speech of an elderly African American woman: "'I *done done* all you told me to do. I *done visited* the sick'" (p. 60). She also includes this example from the speech of a nine-year-old boy: "'I *done* already *finished* that'" (p. 61).

Steady

Steady (often pronounced *study*) is a preverbal marker used to indicate that an action is occurring in an on-going, continuous, or persistent fashion. It precedes a verb in its *–ing* form and typically follows habitual *be* (Green, 2002; Rickford, 1999). This use of *steady* is pretty much unique to BC speakers; it has no direct SE equivalent. Examples from the linguistic literature include the following:

- *Ricky Bell be steady steppin' in them number nines.* (Baugh, 1984, p. 4)
- *He steady be tellin' em how to run they lives.* (Baugh, 1984, p. 4)
- *People be on them jobs for thirty years just steady working.* (In Green, 2002, p. 72)
- *She be steady typin on that computer.* (In Alim, 2003, p. 46)

Indignant Come

Come is a preverbal marker, also unique to BC, that is used to express speaker indignation about an action or state of affairs. Examples include the following:

- *He come walking in here like he owned the damn place.* (Spears, 1982, p. 854)
- *You the one come telling me it's hot. I can't believe you got your coat on.* (In Green, 2002, p. 73)
- *Don't come acting like you don't know what happened and you started the whole thing.* (Green, 2002, p. 73)
- *Don't come tellin me bout no late buses and all that; you just late and you messed up.* (In Smitherman, 2000b, p. 96)

Author Eloise Greenfield used BC indignant *come* in the title of her 1974 book, *She Come Bringing Me That Little Baby Girl*, about a boy who is upset when his new sibling turns out to be a girl. The first line of the text reads: "I asked Mama to bring me a little brother from the hospital, but she come bringing me that little baby girl wrapped all in a pink blanket" (unnumbered pages). Indignant *come* is also used in Patricia McKissack's *Flossie and the Fox* (1986) in which a fox is trying to convince Flossie that he really is a fox. At one point, Flossie tells Fox: "'You just an ol' confidencer. Come tellin' me you was a fox, then can't prove it. Shame on you!'" (unnumbered pages).

Future Forms

Just as in SE, there are basically two ways of indicating the future in BC:

- with the future marker *will*—for example, *She will (She'll) be speaking tonight;* and
- with some form of *going to*—for example, *He's gonna bring the dessert.*

But while the future is marked in essentially the same way in BC and SE in terms of grammar, because of phonological processes operative in BC, BC speakers sometimes express the future in distinctive ways. Due to the fact that the modal *will*, and its contracted form *'ll*, do not have to appear on the surface in BC (i.e., they can be deleted), future tense is often indicated in BC by the use of *be*. This use of *be* is sometimes referred to as "future *be*." Here are some examples:

- *"Wait awhile. She be right around."* (In Rickford & Rickford, 2000, p. 113)
- *I be there in a minute.* (In Smitherman, 2000, p. 23)
- *They family be gone Friday.* (In Smitherman, 1977, p. 20)
- "Don't mean nothin' cuz we be playin' together next day anyway." (Goodwin, 1990, p. 156)

Similarly, phonological processes operate on *going to/gonna* in a way that often results in the pronunciation *gon'*. Illustrating this characteristic BC pronunciation, in *The Honest-to-Goodness Truth* (2000) by Patricia McKissack, Libby Louise owns up to her lie about feeding her horse by telling her mother: "*'I was gon' do it* soon as I got back from jumping rope with Ruthie Mae'" (unnumbered pages). Later McKissack writes: "It was the first time Libby had lied to Mama, and as far as she was concerned *it was gon' be the last*" (unnumbered pages).

Recall the previous discussion of zero copula and the research finding that *is* and *are* are most often absent after the verb *gonna/gon'*. As a result, usages like the following, without *is* or *are* preceding *gonna/gon'*, are prevalent in BC as a way to express the future:

- *Yeah, there gon be some changes over here.* (From Queen Latifah's *Ladies First*, reprinted in Smitherman, 2000a, p. 273)
- *You gon' tell it in a minute.* (In Smitherman, 2000, p. 256)
- *What we gon get out the deal since we left everything?* (In Green, 2002, p. 85)
- *You better watch him cause he gon take credit for the work that you did.* (In Alim, 2003, p. 46)

Finally, the marker *finna* can also used in BC to indicate the immediate future, i.e., an action that is imminent or just about to happen. Rickford and Rickford (2000) explain that *finna* is derived from *fixing to*, a future form used by both African Americans and Whites in the South (p. 121). Examples, with SE glosses, include the following:

- *I'm finna get up out of here* . . . [I'm about to get up out of here](In Rickford & Rickford, 2000, p. 121)

- *I don't know about you, but I'm finna leave.* [SE gloss: I'm getting ready/about to leave.] (In Green, 2002, p. 70)
- *She was finna move the mattress herself when I got there.* [SE gloss: She was getting ready/about to move the mattress when I got there.] (Green, 2002, p. 70)
- *They finna do something.* [They're about to do something.] (Green, 2002, p. 71)

Needless to say, this whirlwind tour of a number of prominent BC verb patterns has captured only the surface of BC's complex grammatical system. Readers interested in exploring this system in more detail should consult the excellent references listed in the bibliography.

Some Final Points: Diversity Within the African American Speech Community

Any attempt to describe a phenomenon as complex and constantly changing as a communications system inevitably runs the risks of both overgeneralization and oversimplification. As many linguists have pointed out, Black Communications is not a single, monolithic entity used in exactly the same way by all speakers. It is likely, for example, that the BC practice of using formal titles in addressing and referring to African American elders may be more prominent among Black people in certain parts of the country and in certain age groups than in others. Similarly, BC phonological and grammatical rules are used more widely by some groups of African Americans than others, depending on such factors as socioeconomic status, age, and gender (Edwards, 1992; Labov, Cohen, Robins, & Lewis, 1968; Wolfram, 1969).

There is also considerable variation in the way BC is used by individual speakers in different social contexts and with different people (Alim, 2003; Baugh, 1983; Rickford & McNair-Knox, 1994). As pointed out earlier, some African Americans may not use *any* of the phonological and grammatical patterns typically associated with BC, yet still may use language in ways that are characteristic of BC in terms of pragmatics and style. A number of linguists (most of whom use the term African American English [AAE] rather than BC) have proposed that there are in fact a variety of AAEs, including a variety that has been described as "standard AAE" (Lewis, 1981; Taylor, 1971; Spears, 1988, 1998). Standard AAE (SAAE) is defined by Spears (1998) as a variety of AAE having "distinctly African American traits while having none of the features widely agreed upon as being non-standard, e.g., the use of *ain't* and multiple negatives within a sentence." According to Spears, "the distinctively African American features of SAAE have to do, primarily, but not solely, with prosody and language use" (p. 230). The concept of standard AAE/BC is a highly useful one for teachers to keep in mind as they work to help BC speakers develop a speaking and writing voice that conforms to SE phonological and grammatical conventions when appropriate (e.g., a formal speech, an academic paper), but that also incorporates stylistic and prosodic patterns associated with African American oral and written traditions.

In thinking about BC, readers should also bear in mind that language behavior, like all cultural practices, changes and evolves over time in response to multiple influences and circumstances. In her Detroit proverb study, for example, Smitherman found that older African Americans knew more proverbs than younger African Americans, a finding suggesting that proverbs may not be as widely used by African Americans today as they once were, at least not in the urban Midwest. Given all of this complexity, it should be clear that the overview of the BC system that has been presented here and in the last chapter provide only a general, and therefore necessarily simplified, picture of a constantly evolving, multifaceted, interactional system well worth further exploration.

Additionally, the point should be made again that some African Americans do not use BC. Facility in a particular language variety is developed in the context of cultural interaction, after all, not genetically endowed. Therefore, teachers cannot assume either (a) that all African American children will use BC, or (b) that those who do will necessarily use all of its features and/or employ them to the same extent as one another. Also, as numerous scholars have pointed out, the African American speech community has always been a bilingual one, its members valuing facility in both Black Communications and Standard English. Morgan (2002), for example, describes the African American speech community as one in which both BC and SE "function as the language of home, community, history and culture" (p. 66) as "both are considered crucial to improve life chances" (p. 67). Thus, as Morgan suggests, most adults want their children to be able to use both BC and SE and to choose appropriately between them depending upon the particular social context.

In an essay describing her experiences growing up in the largely Black town of Ocala, Florida, literary scholar Joyce Hope Scott (1998) sketches a vivid portrait of a community for whom BC and SE existed in "dialogic relationship" to one another, a relationship modeled by the adult members of that community. Scott writes:

> I learned very early, in the home, that there was a place for both languages in our communal experience. My mother taught me the beauty of both standard and Black English by reading to me when I was young, first the classic fairy tales, then later Dickens and English and American poets. I especially liked her to read the Sunday funnies aloud; sometimes she would ad lib on the characters' dialogue using the Black vernacular. My mother was, and remains, a true storyteller, with a vast repertoire. I always knew what kind of story she was about to tell by the language she slipped into. (p. 192)

Her mother's masterful use of these two language varieties was echoed in the linguistic repertoire of Scott's African American teachers. Of one particularly memorable and inspiring teacher, Scott writes:

> While I didn't think it remarkable at the time, I now find it fascinating that one of my most brilliant and articulate English teachers read Paul Laurence Dunbar's dialect poetry with a power and facility that I have not witnessed before or since. She could also bring an audience to its feet with her rendering of Edgar Allan Poe's "Annabel Lee" or Shakespeare's sonnet number twenty-nine: "When in disgrace with fortune and men's eyes/I all alone beweep my outcast state." Even those with only minimal education could sense and understand the import of an "outcast state" and its relevance to them. To me, this teacher was magic, and I wanted to be able, one day, to articulate with the artistry she possessed. (p. 194)

Research suggests that, like Joyce Hope Scott, many African American children arrive at school already able to code-switch between BC and SE with considerable adeptness (Etter-Lewis, 1985; Hester, 1996; Seymour & Ralabate, 1985; Wyatt, 2001; Wyatt & Seymour, 1990). Like Scott, they have developed these bilingual abilities as a result of their language socialization in families and communities that not only value both varieties, but whose members have had access to opportunities for learning the standard variety. Children socialized in these circumstances are not learning SE for the first time in school.

This is less likely to be the case, however, for African American children who come from poor and working-class backgrounds. Wyatt (2001) describes research by Kovac (1980) and Reveron (1978), which found that, beginning around the age of four, middle-class African American children started to use fewer BC phonological and grammatical features than their working-class counterparts. Moreover, in contrast to middle-class children, working-class children's use of BC features increased with their age, a finding supported by other studies (e.g., Labov, 1972). Wyatt sounds an important caution against overgeneralizing the connection between socioeconomic status and use of BC phonology and grammar. Obviously teachers looking at an individual child should not make assumptions about the child's language based solely on his or her family's socioeconomic status because such assumptions could very well be wrong. Wyatt's caution duly noted, however, numerous studies have found that use of BC pronunciation features and grammatical patterns is significantly more characteristic of poor and working-class speakers than of middle-class speakers (e.g., Edwards, 1992; Labov et al., 1968; Rickford & Rickford, 2000; Wolfram, 1969).

This more frequent use of BC phonology and grammar should not be interpreted to mean that poor and working-class African Americans do not want their children to learn standard English or that they underestimate the value of being bilingual. On the contrary, as discussed previously, the African American speech community clearly values facility in both BC and SE. But even though facility in both varieties is a value shared across the community, different social classes are likely to have differential access to opportunities for learning SE (see Morgan, 2002). Many poor and working-class BC speakers are far more dependent on school as a context for developing SE skills than are their middle-class peers because they are likely to participate in fewer social situations outside of school where the use of both varieties is common. Thus for children from under-resourced communities, mastery of the SE phonological and grammatical patterns necessary to be fully bilingual is likely to be much more affected by the quality of instruction offered by their teachers than is the case for many middle-class children.

But whether or not BC speakers enter school as essentially monolingual in BC or as already substantially bilingual, it is clear that they come with facility in a communicative system every bit as rule-governed and complex as SE, or as any other language variety for that matter. Socialization into that communicative system provides BC speakers with rich linguistic and cultural resources for learning to read. I turn now, in part 2, to a fuller exploration of those resources.

Part 2
Language Socialization in the
African American Discourse Community

Chapter 4
Language in the Air

A substantial body of research on language socialization and use in African American communities suggests that despite socioeconomic, geographical, and other differences among people of African descent in this country, people socialized in African American communities share many cultural values and norms (Goodwin, 1990; Haight, 2002; Heath, 1983; Labov, 1972; Mahiri, 1998; Mitchell-Kernan, 1972; Morgan, 2002; Smitherman, 2000a; Troutman, 2001; Vernon-Feagans, 1996). Among these is the extremely high value that the culture places on verbal expressiveness and rhetorical skill, linguistic abilities exhibited even by very young children growing up in Black communities. Black people's deep love for and sophisticated use of language are legendary and are represented in the countless folktales, songs, stories, proverbs, oral language rituals, sermons, speeches, narratives, novels, poems, plays, and essays that comprise the centuries-old Black oral and literary traditions. Once asked by a reporter what she thought made her writing so distinctive, the Nobel Prize winning novelist Toni Morrison famously responded: "The language, only the language . . . It's the thing black people love so much—the saying of words, holding them on the tongue, experimenting with them, playing with them. It's a love, a passion" (LeClair, 1981, p. 27).

This deep love for language and facility in using it well are passed on to children in African American communities as they participate in both the everyday and the special, celebratory activities of their families and communities. Literary scholar Henry Louis Gates, Jr. (1988) has argued that passing on Black linguistic traditions constitutes a highly conscious socialization process on the part of Black parents and caregivers. About his own father's participation in this process, Gates writes:

> My fascination with black language stems from my father's enjoyment of absolute control over its manipulation. My father has mastered black language rituals, certainly; he also has the ability to analyze them, to tell you

what he is doing, why, and how. He is a very self-conscious language user. He is not atypical. It is amazing how much black people, in ritual settings such as barbershops and pool halls, street corners and family reunions, talk about talking. Why do they do this? I think they do it to pass these rituals along from one generation to the next. They do it to preserve the traditions of "the race." (1988, p. xi)

As an illustration of how African American adults consciously instruct children in the effective use of Black linguistic traditions, Gates includes a childhood anecdote recounted by linguist Claudia Mitchell-Kernan. Though lengthy, this anecdote is worth reproducing here in full as it provides such a vivid example of the instructive process Gates is describing. In this anecdote, Mr. Waters employs the Black art of *signifying* (which can be briefly defined as the art of making a point through the use of metaphor and indirection) to instruct young Claudia in how to "hold a conversation":

At the age of seven or eight I encountered what I believe was a version of the tale of the "Signifying Monkey." In this story a monkey reports to a lion that an elephant has been maligning the lion and his family. This stirs the lion into attempting to impose sanctions against the elephant. A battle ensues in which the elephant is victor and the lion returns extremely chafed at the monkey. In this instance, the recounting of this story is a case of signifying for directive purposes. I was sitting on the stoop of a neighbor who was telling me about his adventures as a big game hunter in Africa, a favorite tall-tale topic, unrecognized by me as a tall tale at the time. A neighboring woman called to me from her porch and asked me to go to the store for her. I refused, saying that my mother had told me not to, a lie which Mr. Waters recognized and asked me about. Rather than simply saying that I wanted to listen to his stories, I replied that I refused to go because I hated the woman. Being pressured for a reason for my dislike, and sensing Mr. Water's disapproval, I countered with another lie, "I hate her because she say you were lazy," attempting, I suppose, to regain his favor by arousing ire toward someone else. Although I had heard someone say that he was lazy, it had not been this woman. He explained to me that he was not lazy and that he didn't work because he had been laid-off from his job and couldn't find work elsewhere, and that if the lady had said what I reported, she had not done so out of meanness but because she didn't understand. Guilt-ridden, I went to fetch the can of Milnot milk. Upon returning, the tale of the "Signifying Monkey" was told to me, a censored prose version in which the monkey is rather brutally beaten by the lion after having suffered a similar fate at the hands of the elephant. I liked the story very much and righteously approved of its ending, not realizing at the time that he was *signifying* at me. Mr. Waters reacted to my response with a great deal of amusement. It was several days later in the context of re-telling the tale to another child that I understood its timely telling. My apology and admission of lying were met by affectionate humor, and I was told that I was finally getting to the age where I could "hold a conversation," i.e., understand and appreciate implications. (reprinted in Gates, 1988, p. 84)

In this example, Mr. Waters's approach to teaching young Claudia how to "hold a conversation" is one of indirection. He tells her a story from the Black oral tradition whose significance, and in particular its applicability to the situation at hand, Claudia must figure out for herself. As this example makes clear, being able to hold a conversation within the African American rhetorical tradition means being able to understand and appreciate implications which are not made explicit or stated directly. One must be able to see beneath the surface or literal meaning of someone's words to uncover the fuller, deeper meanings of what is being said. This is, of course, not unlike the skill that literacy teachers struggle so hard to help their students acquire—the ability to draw inferences, to "read between the lines" of what is literally written on the page.

Linguist Marcyliena Morgan (2002) describes the way language was used in the South Side Chicago community where she grew up in terms that echo both Gates's and Mitchell-Kernan's focus on adults' self-conscious employment of Black rhetorical structures as well as their enjoyment of "talking about talk":

> When people in my childhood neighborhood talked about language and communication as they frequently did, they referred to racial, social and regional differences and the importance of style and ambiguity in conversing with those in positions of power, especially under white supremacy. They also expressed great love and respect for conversations that were deeply ambiguous. Everyday conversations were always filtered through proverbs, references to past events and people. (p. 1)

Of particular note in the previous passage is Morgan's emphasis on the concept of *ambiguity*. In a later passage, Morgan reflects on "the joy of a community that strongly believes that the most difficult aspect of communication is figuring out what someone actually means, and why they said it the way they did" (p. 3). Here again we see the importance attached to *indirection*, to conveying and deciphering meanings that are not directly stated, not made obvious, not literal. As Morgan describes in the longer passage quoted here, "everyday conversations" in her community were "filtered" through the figurative language of proverbs and references to historical/cultural knowledge not made explicit in the conversation. Morgan makes clear that while the frequent use of indirection ends up posing "the most difficult aspect of communication" within the African American speech community, its skillful use is an aesthetic accomplishment, something to be admired, respected, and reveled in. Within the African American speech community, then, verbal facility is measured not by the ability to make one's point explicit or clear, but by the ability to make one's point in a clever or unusual way and with such skill that the point does not require explicit statement. As Morgan suggests, being able to participate effectively within such a speech community requires astute powers of interpretation as well. One must be able to, in Mitchell-Kernan's terms, "understand and appreciate (the) implications" of other people's words. As Gates describes, the verbal artistry of the Black community is particularly on display in ritual settings like "barbershops and pool halls, street corners and family reunions," settings that comprise what Melissa Harris-Lacewell (2004) terms "the everyday spaces of black people's lives" (p. 1) and in which children are often eager listeners to the conversational interactions that occur around them.

Ritual Spaces

One such ritual setting is the porch, a site of African American conversation and storytelling immortalized in the fiction of Zora Neale Hurston as well as in her autobiography, *Dust Tracks on a Road* (1942/1995). In *Dust Tracks*, Hurston describes her childhood fascination with the storytelling sessions held on Joe Clarke's store porch in Eatonville, the small, all-Black Florida town in which she grew up during the late 1890s and early 1900s. For Hurston, "life took on a bigger perimeter" (p. 52) as she listened to the "menfolks" tell tales in which "God, Devil, Brer Rabbit, Brer Fox, Sis Cat, Brer Bear, Lion, Tiger, Buzzard and all the wood folk walked and talked like natural men" (p. 48). Hurston recalls how she would drag her feet going in and out of the store in order to "allow whatever was being said to hang in my ear" (p. 46). Hinting at the way in which her own later abilities as a writer may have been influenced by the stories she heard on the porch, Hurston writes: "I picked up glints and gleams out of what I heard, and stored it away to turn it to my own uses" (p. 52). In a recent biography of Hurston, Valerie Boyd (2003) writes:

> There, on the store porch, Zora learned what would become the primary language of her own literature, the vital force of her life as a storyteller. She learned this language—these phrases and stories and nuances—by heart. Which is to say she learned them irrevocably—not as memorized information to be recounted by rote, but as an essential part of who she was, and who she was to become. (p. 39)

For acclaimed children's author Patricia McKissack (1986), growing up many decades later in Nashville, Tennessee, her family's porch was the backdrop for her grandmother's "hair-raising" ghost stories, her mother's dramatizations of Paul Lawrence Dunbar's poetry, and her grandfather's humorous stories "told in the rich and colorful dialect of the rural South" (Author's Note, unnumbered pages). Like Hurston, McKissack suggests a connection between the artistry of the stories she heard as a child and the development of her own artistry as a writer: "Long before I became a writer, I was a listener" (Author's Note, unnumbered pages).

The porch as symbolic site for story and conversation also appears in some African American children's literature. In Sandra Belton's (1993) book, *From Miss Ida's Porch,* for example, young and old congregate on Miss Ida's porch because it is a "telling place," where adults not only share stories about their lives and about African American history, but also engage in playful repartee with one another and with the children who comprise their admiring and participatory audience. When one little girl in the book expresses disbelief that the legendary Lena Horne once stayed overnight in their neighborhood, for instance, Mr. Fisher tells her: "'Hold on there, Miss Lady. Don't press ugly on that pretty face. Tell me now, how come you think Lena Horne couldn't have stayed at Mrs. Jackson's?'" (p. 12). This question becomes the launch for a story about Duke Ellington set during a time when, as Mr. Fisher tells the children, "'most all the famous black folks who came to town stayed at somebody's house'" (p. 12). Similarly, in the children's book *Jewels* (Rochelle, 1998), briefly described in chapter 2, it is the porch where Lea Mae and people from the neighborhood gather every night during the summer to hear 'Ma Dear's stories about the past and to talk about their meaning. At the end of the summer, as Lea Mae prepares to go back North with her parents, she tells 'Ma Dear: "'One day I'm going to write down all of the stories. I'm going to be able to tell a story just like you. . .'" (unnumbered pages).

As described by the previous writers (as well as others), the porch is one traditional space where many Black children have historically been audience to adult models of how to tell a good story and to engage with others in extended verbal interaction. But the porch as an actual physical space is only symbolic. The porch might as easily be a picnic table, a card table, or a dinner table at a family reunion, church homecoming, or other celebratory event where adult storytelling abilities and other valued rhetorical skills are also likely to be on prominent display. It is not surprising that the trip South to attend a family reunion, a church revival, or to spend time with extended kin is an event that occurs with frequency in African American children's literature. In this body of literature, the journey South to renew one's kinship ties takes on symbolic proportions. It is a literary journey that can be usefully contrasted with the symbolic "journey into the forest" that characterizes much traditional children's literature, especially folk and fairy tales. The journey into the forest, whether literal or metaphoric, is almost always a solitary one, in which the child protagonist must confront unforeseen challenges and obstacles with only him- or herself to count on. Although the child protagonist typically returns home at the end of the book—in what Shelby Wolf (2004) describes as the basic "home-away-home " pattern in children's literature—the journey into the forest is a developmental journey toward independence, toward coming to define oneself as an individual separate from family and community. In contrast, the journey South in African American children's literature is a developmental journey toward connection, toward a definition of self in relationship to one's extended family and to the cultural traditions of the larger Black community.

In *Tanya's Reunion* (1995) by Valerie Flournoy, for example, Tanya looks forward to spending some "alone time" with Grandma when they leave early to help the folks down South prepare for the big family reunion. Once they arrive at the family farm, however, Tanya is overwhelmed by the unfamiliar customs of her extended family and disappointed at having to share her grandmother's attention with so many other people. Over the course of the next several days, she gets to know her cousins, explores the farm that is such an important part of her family's history, and listens with fascination to stories about her family's past. Similarly, in *Freedom's Gifts: A Juneteenth Story* (1997) by Valerie Wesley, Lillie is far from excited about visiting her extended family in Texas and participating in the Juneteenth festivities there, a commemoration of the day in June, 1865 when enslaved Africans in Texas first learned about the Emancipation Proclamation. But when Aunt Marshall tells her stories that link Juneteenth Day to her own family history and to an ancestor with whom Lillie shares remarkable similarities, Lillie change her feelings and wants to learn more about her own family and cultural heritage. She promises to ask her daddy to bring her back every summer.

As is the case with Tanya, and with many other protagonists who appear in African American children's literature, Lillie's trip South to participate in an extended family celebration represents movement toward a sense of identity more firmly grounded in her connection to family and to the larger African American community. The fact that so many children's writers have chosen to represent the journey South to attend reunions and other extended family celebrations in their fiction is testament to the importance of these events as ritual spaces in which children both witness and participate in valued linguistic and cultural practices. The frequency with which these events are depicted in children's literature also hints at their possible significance in the writers' own lives as they were growing up.

The novelist Paule Marshall (1983) traces the earliest and most significant influence on her writing not back to the stories she heard told at family reunions, but to conversation in the basement kitchen of the brownstone house in Brooklyn where she grew up. There, Marshall's mother and her friends, exhausted from cleaning White people's houses all day, would gather around the kitchen table for tea, cocoa, and conversation in the late afternoons. Reflecting back on the importance of those conversations for her later development as a writer, Marshall writes:

> For me, sitting over in the corner, being seen but not heard, which was the rule for children in those days, it wasn't only what the women talked about—the content—but the way they put things—their style. The insight, irony,

wit and humor they brought to their stories and discussions and their poet's inventiveness and daring with language . . . (pp. 7–8)

Like Hurston, who picked up "glints and gleams" out of what she heard on the Eatonville porch to store away for future use, Marshall drew upon the "metaphors, parables, Biblical quotations and sayings" (p. 8) that characterized the women's conversation in the kitchen, their "poet's inventiveness and daring with language," in shaping her own rhetorical voice and in developing the "standard of excellence" that would guide her future writing (p. 12).

Reminiscent of Paule Marshall "sitting in a corner being seen but not heard" as her mother and friends talked animatedly around the kitchen table, Marcyliena Morgan (2002) recalls her own listening perch under a table: "There were always people 'passing through' our home . . . From my perspective, whoever visited the family visited me, and I always tried to find a comfortable spot under a table or out of the way so that I could hear the fantastic stories told by our many guests" (p. 1). In her children's book *ellington was not a street* (2004), poet Ntozake Shange describes her childhood memories of hours spent listening to her father and his famous friends talking about literature, philosophy, and politics in the Harlem home where she grew up.

In his autobiography, Malcolm X (1995) provides a testament to the potentially powerful and long-lasting effects of the spoken word upon a young listener in being able to recall, verbatim, phrases from the speeches his father made at political meetings that Malcolm attended with him as a very young child in Lansing, Michigan. Recalling his father, Malcolm says:

> . . . the image of him that made me proudest was his crusading and militant campaigning with the words of Marcus Garvey. As young as I was then, I knew from what I overheard that my father was saying something that made him a "tough" man . . .
>
> I can remember hearing of "Adam driven out of the garden, into the caves of Europe," "Africa for the Africans," "Ethiopians, Awake!" And my father would talk about how it would not be much longer before Africa would be completely run by Negroes—"by black men," was the phrase he always used. "No one knows when the hour of Africa's redemption cometh. It is in the wind. It is coming. One day, like a storm, it will be here" . . .
>
> I remember seeing the big, shiny photographs of Marcus Garvey that were passed from hand to hand. My father had a big envelope of them that he always took to those meetings . . . and I remember how the meetings would always close with my father saying, several times, and the people chanting after him, "Up, you mighty race, you can accomplish what you will!" (p. 9)

One can imagine the young Malcolm repeating these phrases over and over to himself, perhaps as he fell asleep at night, "holding them on his tongue, experimenting with them, playing with them," as Toni Morrison has said, savoring their sound as much as their sense.

In an interview with John Rickford, playwright August Wilson noted that Black language "was just in the air" in the Pittsburgh neighborhood where he grew up. He recalled in particular the cigar store where the elderly men from the neighborhood would congregate and "talk all kinds of stuff" and he, the future playwright, would stand around and listen (Rickford and Rickford, 2000, p. 29). Other ritual public spaces in which Black language and rhetorical traditions are both enacted and passed down to the next generation are barbershops and beauty salons. Of these, Harris-Lacewell (2004) writes:

> Barbershops and beauty salons have both a mythic and an actual relevance among African American people. . . Barbershops are the archetype of the black public space, consisting of a relatively permanent physical space, but with constantly changing memberships. . . The one constant is that black people in these spaces believe themselves to be free to talk to one another beyond the gaze of racial others (p. 9).

In both literature and popular film, Black barbershops and beauty shops are portrayed as discursive spaces in which talk is at least as important as getting one's hair cut or styled. The same holds true of its portrayal in children's literature. In *The Barber's Cutting Edge* (1994) by Gwendolyn Battle-Lavert, for example, the barbershop owner, Mr. Bigalow, offers both haircuts and lessons on words. Fittingly, his "cutting edge" turns out to be not a razor or a pair of clippers, but the dictionary he keeps in the back room. *Bippity Bop Barbershop* (2002) by Natasha Anastasia Tarpley tells the story of a little boy's first haircut: "Jazz music, loud voices, and laughter blend with the buzzzzzzz of clippers and the soft *sweesh-sweesh* of scissors skimming loose hairs from a freshly cut head" (Tarpley, 2002, unnumbered pages).

In *No Bad News* (2001) by Kenneth Cole, young Marcus is feeling pretty blue about life when he arrives at Jackson's Barbershop for his haircut, a state of mind picked up on by all the customers gathered in the shop ("'What's up with that sad look on your face?'" [unnumbered pages]). Barber and customers quickly proceed to cheer him up. In the end, "what was to be a ten-minute haircut turned out to be an hour of history, laughter and hope" (unnumbered pages). As Marcus gets ready to leave, one of the customers stands up from his chair and reminds him, with elderly wisdom and stylistic flair: "'Son, you can't see anything with your head held low. And you need to not only *see* the good news. You need to *be* the good news'" (unnumbered pages).

In *Janna and the Kings* (2003) by Patricia Smith, Saturdays are special because that's the day Janna goes with Granddaddy to "her favorite place in the whole world"—Terrell's barbership—where the customers feel like kings and Janna feels like a princess. "There was always lots of talking, and no matter what the kings talked about—baseball, the old days, a TV show—they always, *always* asked Janna what she thought" (unnumbered pages). When Granddaddy dies suddenly, Janna is inconsolable and Saturday is the saddest day of the week. One day, she tentatively opens the door of the barbershop and is instantly greeted with love:

> . . . all the kings' voices reached Janna at once—Mister Odell's, Terrell's, Amos's. The words "pretty" and "there's our baby" and "sweetheart" washed over her, just as they used to. Janna kicked her feet and grinned up at the familiar faces gathered around her. Slowly she began to feel like a princess again. Granddaddy wasn't gone. Janna could feel him here among the other kings, in this place they both loved. (unnumbered pages)

As a final example, in another delightful picture book, *Saturday at the New You* (Barber, 1994), Shauna spends Saturday mornings helping out at her mother's busy neighborhood beauty salon, where the regular customers include Ms. Escobar, one of the teachers at Shauna's school, and a "bratty little thumb-sucking" girl named Tiffany who drives Shauna crazy with her demanding ways. In their portrayals of an African American barbershop and, in Barber's case, a beauty salon, these writers succeed in capturing some of the flavor of a cultural and linguistic space where at least some African American children may be exposed on a regular basis to adult models of rhetorical excellence.

Arguably, the most powerful ritual space in which Black children are exposed to the range and beauty of African American linguistic traditions is the Black church. The Black church not only meets the spiritual needs of its members, but, to quote Zora Neale Hurston, nurtures their love of "magnificence, beauty, poetry and color" as well (quoted in Pitts, 1993, p. 5). According to C. Eric Lincoln and Lawrence Mamiya in their classic study, *The Black Church in the African American Experience* (1990): "Much black culture is heavily indebted to the black religious tradition, including most forms of black music, drama, literature, storytelling and even humor" (p. 8). Anthropologist Patricia Jones-Jackson (1987) observes that "from the time when young children begin going to church services, they learn that rhetorical skills are to be praised, practiced and deeply venerated as essential characteristics of learned people" (p. 30). Describing the young Martin Luther King, Jr.'s language socialization in Ebenezer Baptist Church in Atlanta, for example, Richard Lischer (1995) writes:

> In the canon of King family legends is the story of little Martin who one Sunday in church looked up to his "Mother Dear" and said, "When I grow up I'm going to get me some big words." . . . Like his father before him, Martin memorized passages from the King James Version of the Bible and practiced them until he had incorporated its Elizabethan cadences into his own pattern of speech. With his young church friends he studied other preachers in the neighborhood, not out of piety as much as fascination with their technique and the power they wielded over their congregations. (p. 40)

The rhetorical skills valued in the church and in the Black community more generally are particularly in evidence during the sermon. In her study of the African American sermon as literary text, Beverly Moss (2003) quotes Mitchell's (1970) six stylistic features of the traditional Black sermon:

1. The use of rhythm.
2. The use of intonation.
3. The repetition of words, phrases, sentence patterns, aphorisms, and so on.
4. The use of role-playing and other storytelling techniques.
5. The personal involvement of the minister in what she/he is preaching about.
6. The minister's ability to play with language, to give the congregation the "well-turned" phrase. (p. 26)

In examining the sermons of three Black ministers in Chicago, Beverly Moss (2003) found that the ministers used all of these stylistic features in their sermons (as well as other rhetorical devices including the use of call and response, code-switching, collective pronouns and shared knowledge). The use of rhythm, intonation, repetition, and the ability to play with language (numbers one, two, three and six in the previous list) are well illustrated in the following example from one of the sermons in Moss's data:

> God gives proof that if you kill a King you cannot kill what King stood for
> That if you silence a Tutu,
> Ban a Boesak,
> Defeat the candidacy of a Chisolm,
> Derail the movement of a Jackson, or denounce the teachings of a Malcolm X,
> The truths that undergird these men and women of integrity will keep on
> coming and keep on coming and keep on coming. (pp. 92–93)

In addition to the highly skillful use of rhythmic phrasing, alliteration and repetition (on many levels) evident in the previous passage, the minister plays masterfully on the word *king* in the first line. Although it is not possible to fully capture intonational features in a written transcript, it is likely that the minister's use of rhythmic intonation as he spoke added significantly to the power of the words. Indeed, according to Walter Pitts (1993), a noted authority on the Afro-Baptist worship service, one of the most distinctive features of the Black sermon, as well as the prayers that occur during the Devotion, is their melodic quality. "In fact," Pitts asserts, "sermon and prayer may become so melodious as they develop that church musicians can easily accompany the preacher's and deacon's patterns of intonation on their instruments" (p. 59). Moss contends that "the rhythm of the typical African American sermon is as meaningful as the actual words" (2003, p. 148), a phenomenon characteristic of poetry.

One of Moss's findings in her study of the three Chicago ministers is the extent to which two of the ministers in particular relied upon storytelling (number four in Mitchell's list) to get points across in their sermons (on the importance of storytelling in African American sermons, see also Jones, 1976; Mitchell, 1970; Smitherman, 1977). In a number of cases, the minister's storytelling included the use of dialogue or "direct speech," as illustrated in the following short excerpt from Moss's sermon data. Here the minister is illustrating his mother's life-long habit of "talking back," in call-response fashion, to preachers:

> She be sittin' there sayin' "Well, well," "Don't you see?"
> "Help yourself!" (laughter from congregation)
> "Yes sir"
> "Glory"
> Preacher say "He's a Burden Bearer"
> My mama say "Yes he is"
> Preacher say "He can make a way"
> My mama say "Yes he can"
> Preacher say "The Lord will provide"
> My mama say "Yes he will" (p. 105)

Another stylistic/rhetorical feature not included in Mitchell's list, but that was highly characteristic of the interaction recorded by Moss, as well as by other researchers, is the use of call and response (illustrated in the previous example), an interactional pattern in which members of the congregation provide continuous verbal and nonverbal feedback to the minister's words. When the minister and congregation are in sync with one another, the call-response interaction produces a sermon that is to a significant extent co-constructed by the minister and congregation, creating what Moss calls a "community text." As Moss notes, the call-response pattern is "a phenomenon that has reached beyond sermons to most aspects of public performance in African American communities (political rallies, concerts, movies and has influenced many African American orators" (p. 89). As an example of the latter, Moss cites "the sermonic 'talks' of academic Cornel West" (p. 89).

In order to explore Moss's point more fully, consider the following excerpt from a speech given by Cornel West at Harvard University in the wake of Hurricane Katrina:

> Katrina coincides with "povertina." . . . Not just New Orleans. It could have hit the South Side of Chicago, it could have hit South Central Los Angeles, could've hit Harlem, could have hit Roxbury, all of these fellow human beings struggling with a disgraceful education system, wrestling with dilapidated housing, wrestling with no healthcare, no child care, access to a job with a living wage hardly available, just under the radar screen, invisible, no serious focus on their plight. (*Boston Globe*, 9/18/05, p. A32)

While this written excerpt provides no evidence of the call-response inter-action that may have occurred when West actually delivered his speech, the excerpt does evidence the same stylistic features identified in Mitchell's list and in other research on the Black sermon, most notably the use of rhyth-mic repetition that builds to a larger point or conclusion and creative plays on words (*Katrina/povertina*). One of Moss's major points is that the Black sermon, as community text, powerfully shapes the way in which large num-bers of African Americans use language. Interestingly, in the introduction to her book, Moss describes how during the process of writing it, she came to the realization that she uses techniques of rhythm, repetition, and emphasis in her own writing very much like those employed by the ministers in her study, stylistic techniques that she had evidently acquired, at least in part, through her life-long participation in the Black church. The beautiful children's book, *Rock of Ages* (2001) by Tonya Bolden, is essentially a poem in praise of the Black church and its role in sustaining and inspiring African American people over the centuries. In the following stanza, Bolden names just a few of the many women and men of words and song whose voices have been nurtured in the Black church:

> Cradle, too, was she for
>   creative fire:
> where Aretha, Leontyne, Sam, Dinah, Della
>   first found voice,
> where Brother Baldwin laid hands on rhythms
>   he worked with words,
> where Martin learned to speak.   (unnumbered pages)

While not all African Americans use the stylistic features described here on a public stage or with the same degree of mastery as people like Cornel West, Louis Farrakhan, or Maya Angelou, many Black people do use them to some degree or other. They are essentially the same stylistic features employed by the women who gathered around the kitchen table in Paule Marshall's kitchen after cleaning other people's houses, the same features to be found in the stories that have been told by ordinary people on porches and dinner tables, in barbershops and beauty shops, and on bar stools and street corners in Black communities for generations. They are the same features that characterize the "art of conversation" among Black people in diverse social settings—from pool rooms to college dorm rooms, where personal experience and points-to-be-made are often turned into a story, a process Smitherman (2000a) describes as "narrativizing." As Smitherman explains:

> *Narrativizing* is a characteristic feature of general Black discursive practices. Everyday conversational talk may be rendered as a "story." Narrativizing is a Black rhetorical strategy to explain a point, to persuade holders of opposing

views to one's own point of view, and to create word-pictures about general,
abstract observations about life, love, and survival. (p. 275)

The "ordinariness" of rhetorical skill among members of the Black community is vividly illustrated in a story that appears in Shirley Brice Heath's classic ethnographic work, *Ways With Words* (1983). The storyteller, Ms. Dovie Lou Farrell, is a resident of a small, working-class African American community in the Piedmont Carolinas. Her story, created totally "in the moment" and told to a group of female friends one afternoon, was occasioned by a neighbor woman's comment that Ms. Farrell's husband had been seen with another woman. Clearly, as can be seen in the following story, Ms. Farrell aims to put the nosy neighbor in her place and to entertain her listeners in the process with a highly imaginative "news flash" about her husband and a local stripper dressed in white mink:

> Now you know me—I'm Dovie Lou, and you may think I'ma put up wid that stuff off Hennin's ol' lady, right? Who, who, after all, gives a hoot about her—or him, for dat matter? I been here quite a while—gonna be here a time yet too. She holler off her porch "Yo man, he over in Darby Sat'day night". I say "Shit, what you know 'bout my man? My man." It was a rainy night, you know ain't no use gettin' fussied up to go out on a night like dat. Tessie 'n' I go play bingo. But dat ol' woman, she ak like she some Channel Two reporter or sump'n:
>
> "P.B. Evans was seen today on the corner of Center and Main Street. He hadda bottle in each hip pocket, and one under his London Fog hat. Sadie Lou [a well-known stripper in a local topless bar] was helpin' him across the street, holin' her white mink in front of him to keep his shiny shoes from gettin' wet. The weather tomorrow promises to be cloudy for some."
>
> What she think she doin', tellin' *me/looks around to audience/* 'bout my ol' man? Sayin' "He lookin' mighty fine, yes sireeeeee." (long pause) She betta keep/*casting a sharp look in the direction of the Hennings' house/* her big mouf 'n' stay shut up in dat house. (pp. 168–169)

As in the traditional Black sermon in which the minister often employs narrative and storytelling techniques to get his or her point across, Ms. Farrell "narrativizes" her "point" as well. Within the narrative, she uses dialogue and alliterative, rhythmic description to animate four distinct characters: her "big mouf" nosy neighbor, her hapless husband, an imaginary Channel Two reporter, and her own bad, not-to-be-trifled-with self. Like the skilled Black minister, she is able to code-switch effectively between BC and SE. Her instantaneous shift into SE when she assumes the voice and intonational patterns of the Channel Two reporter illustrates both her bilingual abilities and her verbal artistry, as part of the humorous effect of her story is achieved through the stylistic contrasts between the two varieties. She uses highly visual images and plays on words (e.g., predicting "cloudy weather" for "some"), pausing, intonation, and nonverbal behavior to wonderful effect. Although not captured in the written transcription of the story, Heath describes the call-response interaction that occurs between Ms. Farrell and her audience as the story is told: "Throughout the story, the audience laughed, nodded, and provided 'yeah,' 'you right,' 'you know it'" (p. 169), just like a church congregation in a more sacred context.

Dovie Lou Farrell's story is a masterpiece, all the more impressive for being impromptu. What is remarkable is that she has no official status as a storyteller in her small Piedmont community, nor are the excellent rhetorical abilities she possesses atypical of others who live there. Rather, like most African Americans, Ms. Farrell has been socialized in a cultural community that nurtures and rewards sophisticated verbal skills, and not surprisingly, her linguistic behavior reflects it. To quote a description used by hip-hop scholar Imani Perry (2004) in another context, Dovie Lou Farrell is "average and amazing at once" (p. 137).

Was the development of Dovie Lou's Farrell's rhetorical abilities influenced by her participation in the Black church? It is impossible to say as Heath does not describe her church-going habits. But, in a sense her church-going habits hardly matter, for the influence of the Black church stretches far beyond the confines of its actual physical spaces. Its spiritual and rhetorical traditions are deeply woven into the fabric of African American culture. The language of the Black church is "in the air" everywhere. Moss writes: "Millions of African Americans, be they devoted church goers or not, are influenced by the model of literacy, and therefore of literate text, that emerges from the African American church. Therefore many African American students come to school with that model of a community text as part of their linguistic competence" (2003, p. 152).

Only a small number of African American children's books center exclusively on the Black church. In addition to Bolden's *Rock of Ages* briefly described earlier, another one is *Come Sunday* (1996) by Nikki Grimes, a collection of poems about one little girl's experiences in the Black church. The following excerpt from "Lady Preacher" allows the reader to imagine the powerful impact the Black sermon has likely had on generations of children growing up in the church:

> *The Holy One has a word for us today, children,* she'll say, and right away I feel a shiver go up my spine, 'cause I'm pretty sure it's God who's doing the talking, and not just Sister Beverly. The whole church knows it too, 'cause when she preaches, even our pastor has to say *Amen, sister! Praise the Lord!* (unnumbered pages)

Most often, the Black church appears in children's books as a backdrop, a taken-for-granted part of everyday Black life, or, in books with a historical perspective, as an integral part of the struggle for social justice.

It is no accident that the people whose reflections I have drawn upon in this chapter are all people whose life's work has centered around language in some way, whether as novelist, storyteller, playwright, preacher, political leader, literary scholar, linguist, or anthropologist. Such people are probably more likely than most of us to have thought consciously about their early linguistic influences. Certainly they are more likely than most to have had those reflections appear in print. But this does not mean that the linguistic influences they describe are peculiar to their experience. As Gates asserts, his father's mastery of Black language rituals and his love of "talk about talk" are not atypical in African American communities. As African American children participate in the key activity settings of home, church, neighborhood, and community, they are exposed to adult models of language use that become incorporated into their own developing linguistic repertoires.

It is hard to exaggerate the importance of these models in young people's language development, for as the theories of Lev Vygotsky (1978) and Mikhail Bakhtin (1981) have helped us to understand, children acquire their own speaking voices largely by internalizing the voices of those around them. The "glints and gleams," the images and metaphors, of other people's conversation, the careful building-to-a-point of stories, sermons and arguments, the quick and witty comebacks to constant verbal challenge that Black children hear around them every day are the organizational and stylistic building blocks of their own facility with language.

Chapter 5
Children Using Language

Children are not only listeners but also participants in the communicative interactions that occur in their communities. We know children's early socialization experiences—their on-going participation in the everyday linguistic and cultural routines that occur in their homes and communities—are the foundation for later learning and development. The linguistic and communicative proficiencies they acquire in early life influence their ongoing capacity to learn and develop as speakers, thinkers, and communicators. We also know that every cultural community teaches children to develop the skills and abilities they value (Erikson, 1968; Rogoff, 2003; Tomasello, 1999; Vygotsky, 1978). Thus, if verbal adeptness is a behavior that is valued in African American communities (and there is significant research to suggest that it is), then it is reasonable to posit the notion that African American children are likely to make rapid developmental progress in this area, and, indeed, the small body of research we currently possess on Black children's language socialization and behavior suggests that this is the case (Goodwin, 1990; Heath, 1983; Vernon-Feagans, 1996).

One question that is difficult to answer then is why so little of the rich cultural and linguistic socialization experiences of African American children gets taken into account (or even recognized) in literacy teaching and learning. Arguably, these experiences ought to be a rich foundation for further school learning. Why is it that teachers have not been able to build more successfully on this foundation?

An idea with a long legacy in educational thinking concerns the contrast in the socialization and enculturation experiences of African Americans in comparison to those of their White peers, and how this contrast works to the disadvantage of African American children. This contrastive relationship has been variously theorized in the literature as cultural incongruity (Vogt, Jordan, & Tharp, 1987; Zeuli & Floden, 1987), cultural asynchrony (e.g., Irvine,

1991) and a mismatch of cultural capital (e.g., Lareau, 1987). In literature on teaching African American children that is written from this cultural difference perspective, teachers are typically admonished to recognize and build upon children's cultural and linguistic strengths. What has not yet been made explicit in this literature so far, however, is a careful delineation of exactly what those linguistic and cultural strengths are.

In this chapter, I take an initial step toward specifying some of those linguistic and cultural strengths as they are contextualized in African American children's early socialization experiences. I characterize this effort as an "initial step" because, as mentioned earlier, at this point we possess only a small body of research about language socialization in African American communities. In attempting to delineate the specific linguistic abilities that African American children bring to school, I am very much cognizant of the dangers inherent in attempting to draw meaningful generalizations about the verbal abilities of a population of children based upon a relatively modest body of research. In addition, almost all of the research on African American children's socialization has been conducted in poor and working-class communities, sounding an important cautionary note about generalizing findings from this research to other socioeconomic groups within the larger African American speech community. We need far more research on Black children's language socialization in a variety of situational contexts before we can make definitive statements about shared linguistic-cultural abilities. Nonetheless, I believe it is long past time for us to take an initial stab at identifying them.

Many scholars have argued that our failure to do a better job of educating African American children is related in part to the negative assumptions that many teachers make about the cognitive and verbal abilities of Black children (Richardson, 2003; Perry, 2003; Steele, 1992). Too often, African American children entering school are viewed in terms of specific skills they may lack as compared to White mainstream children (e.g., recognizing the letters of the alphabet, knowing appropriate book reading behaviors). Meanwhile, the impressive, and far more important, linguistic abilities they do possess go unrecognized and therefore uncapitalized upon in the classroom. Teachers unfamiliar with African American linguistic practices and with language socialization in Black communities may not even be able to recognize the abilities children are bringing because those abilities may manifest themselves differently from what they have come to expect from experience in their own communities. To repeatedly admonish teachers that they need to build on children's strengths without specifying what those strengths are is not likely to yield improved teaching and learning.

For teachers to be effective with African American children, they must not only have the right cultural optic for recognizing the strengths to build on, but understand those strengths well enough to be able to create appropriate instructional practices and sociocultural learning contexts. It is hard to overstate the importance of making accurate appraisals of children's linguistic-cognitive abilities not only when they first arrive in school but in all subsequent decisions about instructional practice. Judgments made about children's intellectual and scholastic capacity have a continuous and lasting effect on their academic efficacy and school performance (Jencks & Phillips, 1998). The practices and behaviors that teachers recognize as "signs" of verbal ability and precociousness will determine much of children's experience of school. If we could recognize the performative, cognitive, and linguistic abilities African American children bring to school from their language socialization in home and community contexts, we could then proactively create the social and intellectual foundations for powerful literacy learning in school contexts. We might also become more aware that linguistic socialization is a developmental trajectory animated by ongoing interactive instructional experiences in school, and that this development can be either enhanced or degraded based upon how the adults value and fortify the abilities children bring.

In the remainder of this chapter, I draw from the existing research on Black children's language socialization in order to enumerate and describe the linguistic abilities that many African American children are likely to bring with them to school.

Rising to a Verbal Challenge: *"Now what you gonna do?"*

Perhaps the most detailed description of Black children's language socialization is contained in Shirley Brice Heath's (1983) description of language use in Trackton, a small, working-class Black community located in the Piedmont Carolinas. In Trackton children are socialized within the context of a community where "successful verbal performance under challenge is thought to be a sign of quickness and intelligence" (p. 80). From the time they are about a year old, Trackton babies are reinforced by the adults and older children around them for any display of aggressive play or counter-challenge, particularly one that combines verbal and non-verbal behavior (pp. 79–80). One such successful display occurred one day when Darett, a teenager, came upon 16-month-old Teegie playing on the porch:

> Darett went up to the side of the porch, reached through the rails, and began to tug at Teegie's bottle. Teegie pulled back, but Darett soon pulled the bottle away anyway. Teegie stood up, stuck his lips out, made a sucking noise, and "strutted" across the porch, interpreted by the audience as an imitation of Darett's walk. The audience picked up on the ludicrousness of "smart-cat Darett" strutting while sucking on a bottle; in the midst of howls of laughter, Teegie turned to Darett and said, "Go on, man." Darett found the performance highly acceptable and gave the bottle back, tickled Teegie, and said, "You gonna be all right, boy, you be just like me.'" (p. 80)

As in this example, Trackton preschoolers are routinely presented with some kind of verbal or physical challenge and then asked, "*'Now* what you gonna do?'" As Heath notes, the preschoolers "are powerless to counter physically" and so "must outwit, outtalk, or outact their aggressors" (p. 84). Children who are not able to stand up for themselves verbally in this way are likely to be considered "slow" or "dull," like Nellie, a preschooler whose "dullness" was exemplified for the community by the fact that "'she don't stan' up for herself; she don't say nut'n'" (p. 99). Thus, from the time they are babies, Trackton children begin to develop a sense of self-efficacy strongly tied to their ability to respond well to verbal challenge.

Findings from a number of other studies (Corsaro, 1996; Goodwin, 1990; Mahiri, 1998; Vernon-Feagans, 1996) suggest that the ability to respond quickly and appropriately to verbal challenge is also highly valued in peer and sibling interactions among Black children. In his study of peer culture in an urban Head Start center in which the students, teachers, and other staff were primarily Black, William Corsaro (1996) found that children engaged in a large amount of oppositional talk (a finding consistent with other studies):

> . . . children constructed social identities, cultivated friendships, and both maintained and transformed the social order of the peer culture through opposition. Peer interaction and play routines were peppered with opposi- tional talk like "Why you following me like that for?" and "Get that block out the way!" (pp. 441–442)

Corsaro found that children seldom responded negatively or ran to tell the teacher when challenged by their classmates. "Rather," Corsaro writes:

> The children normally responded in kind, and serious verbal or physical disputes were rare. In fact, oppositional talk and teasing were valued . . . as part of the verbal enrichment of everyday play routines. Particularly clever oppositions or retorts were often marked as such with appreciative laughter and comments like "good one," or "you sure told her," by the audience and, at times, even the target child. (p. 442)

In this Head Start Center, as in Trackton, the ability to answer a verbal challenge, that is, to stand up for oneself with style and wit, was rewarded with appreciative audience response. In the case of many preadolescent youth in inner city settings, this capacity to adroitly handle confrontation is a requirement for being ready to "come off the stoop" and come out on the street among other youth indepen- dently of the protection of an older sibling (Canada, 1995). Corsaro's observation that oppositional talk and teasing were valued by the children as "part of the verbal enrichment of everyday play routines" suggests that this kind of opposi- tional talk is engaged in largely for the opportunities it provides to show off and practice one's verbal prowess, rather than being an activity aimed primarily at winning or resolving a "real" conflict (e.g., settling who has access to a particular play space or toy). What Corsaro observed in younger children, and Canada noted among preadolescent males, are instances of an acquired capacity to handle the challenge "*'Now'* what you gonna do?'" Also worthy of note is the way in which the children enrolled in the Head Start Center used oppositional talk to construct both their social identities and their relationships with other children. In this way, oppositional talk, with its repeating challenge/response structure, provided the context for children's social, linguistic, and cognitive development as they struggled to come up with responses that would best their "opponent" and establish their own position within the peer community.

Focusing on peer interactions among a multiage group of children (ages 4 through 14) who played together after school on "Maple Street" in a working-class Black neighborhood in Philadelphia, Marjorie Goodwin (1990) found that the principal activity the children engaged in was talk, much of it oppositional talk. As with the preschoolers described by Corsaro, the Maple Street children used oppositional talk as a vehicle for displaying their linguistic facility. Drawing on the theoretical framework of sociologist Erving Goffman, Goodwin describes the Maple Street children's disputes as "miniature versions of what Goffman calls 'character contests'—'moments of action [during which] the individual has the risk and the opportunity of displaying to himself and sometimes to others his style of conduct'" (p. 142). By demonstrating their verbal virtuosity, Maple Street children jockey for position within the neighborhood social order. Just as oppositional talk in the Head Start Center provides a context for children's development, oppositional talk on Maple Street serves similar functions, providing children "with a rich arena for the development of proficiency in language, syntax, and social organization" (p. 141). Goodwin observes that Maple Street disputes seldom end in compromise or settlement (p. 156); instead "the end of an argument generally occurs without any sharp indication that either position has 'won' or 'lost'" (p. 157), often as a result of one of the participants shifting the contentious frame to a humorous one with a clever play on words or metaphorical usage (p. 170). The ultimately nonserious, playful nature of Maple Street disputes is suggested in a comment made by one of the children, Vincent, in reaction to an adult's attempt to intervene in a dispute:

> That stupid Mr. Dan gonna come up there
>   and say
> "Y'all better come on and shake hands."
> Don't mean nothin' cuz we be playin' together
> next day anyway. (p. 156)

Goodwin writes: "Despite the absence of a clear outcome, disputing allows participants the opportunity to construct and display character, a process important to their social organization as well as social development" (p. 188). As in Trackton and the Head Start Center, here again we see the use of oppositional talk (e.g., issuing a verbal challenge, engaging in an extended argument sequence) whose principal purpose is to display verbal skill (i.e., "character") rather than to definitively "settle" an issue.

Corsaro suggests that the primarily Black teachers and staff at the Head Start Center did not view children's oppositional talk in a negative light, but as a normal, taken-for-granted, aspect of peer interaction and play routines at the Center. Similarly, in her study of adult-child interactions in Sunday school at a Black Baptist church in Salt Lake City, Wendy Haight (2002) found that children sometimes issued verbal challenges or made argumentative statements directed at their teachers and that these were responded to by teachers in a positive, even encouraging, way. Haight writes:

> Even the youngest children initiated verbal conflicts with their teachers, and teachers did not correct children for engaging in topic-relevant verbal opposition . . . Teachers seemed to use playful teasing to reframe potentially negative exchanges, to enliven the classes, and to engage children in mutually enjoyable, affectively positive social exchanges. (p. 141)

Interestingly, scholar and teacher Jabari Mahiri (1998) found that in the community sports setting where he examined communicative interactions between and among African American youth players and their coaches, players were allowed to criticize not only one another's performances, but the coaches' as well; ". . . it was accepted that everyone had a right to express opinions about team strategies, midgame decisions, and player performances" (p. 35). This was the case even when a player's opinion was expressed in highly oppositional and emotional ways.

In both the community sports center and the Sunday school setting that Haight describes, the Black adults who were in charge not only allowed, but, by their responses, actively encouraged the expression of oppositional views, suggesting that, far from viewing argumentation as something negative, the adults in these settings viewed argumentation as both intellectually stimulating and as an important context for learning. In her analysis of one particularly argumentative exchange between a student, Javon, and one of the teachers, Sister Justine, Haight notes the skillful way in which Sister Justine continually reframes the argument as playful and intellectually engaging rather than as hostile. At one point, for example, when Javon refuses to concede Sister Justine's point, Sister Justine says playfully, " 'Oh, well, you need your little butt whipped' " (p. 138), leading to laughter from the class as well as a continuation of the lively exchange between her and Javon. At other points during the interaction, Sister Justine issues playful challenges/accusations of her own (e.g., " 'You lying' "), role plays (e.g., " 'I was like, "Excuse me!" ' "), and talks in different voices (e.g., a "fake annoyed voice," a "shaky, old voice"; pp. 138–139). Sister Justine uses her own facility with language to engage in an argumentative exchange with a student that ends up stimulating both Javon's, and likely the entire class's, thinking about the real-life implications of important biblical concepts. In this exchange, as in the others of which it is illustrative, adults and children participate together in argumentative interactions that hone children's verbal skills, foster their ability to think quickly on their feet, fuel their engagement with ideas, and reinforce their identities as able speakers.

Both Heath's examination of adult/child interactions in Trackton and Haight's analysis of teacher/student interactions in Sunday school suggest that verbal challenges addressed to children by adults often end up engaging children in what Haight (2002) describes as "hypothetical talk" (p. 97), and by extension, of course, hypothetical reasoning. In the Sunday school setting, Haight found that hypothetical talk typically cast the children in a major role, asking them to imagine what they would do if a particular set of circumstances were to occur. She notes that "remarkably, even the youngest children participated in narratives referring to hypothetical events" (p. 100). An example from Haight's data illustrating children's familiarity with hypothetical talk is this eight-year-old's response to a question about how one could recognize the pastor as a Christian if he weren't carrying around a Bible: " 'He'd always be quoting scriptures and asking, 'What if, and what if, and what if' " (p. 97).

Heath recounts the way in which an older Trackton adult, nicknamed "the mayor," issues weekly challenges to preschooler Lem about " 'keepin' " the bag of candy Lem typically receives on Friday afternoons. The mayor's challenges (" 'What you gonna do, I try to take dis? Let me keep it for you . . .' ") lead Lem to try out a number of strategies to keep his candy safe (p. 84). Eventually, when he is about two years old, Lem comes up with a consistently effective strategy: he sticks his candy bag in a hole between the boards in the porch that is too small for the mayor's hands to fit in. Analyzing the "thinking ahead" or hypothetical reasoning involved in Lem coming up with his successful solution to the threat posed by the mayor, Heath writes: "To win the game, Lem had had to size up the possible responses of other adults, to figure out a tactic which made the most of his strengths and caught the mayor in his weaknesses" (p. 85). The constant verbal challenges issued to children in Trackton (e.g., "*Now* what you gonna do?") provide multiple opportunities for them to mentally play out different hypothetical possibilities before enacting the response they judge to be most effective in the particular situation at hand.

Based on findings from the research discussed previously, it seems to me that teachers seeking to identify a foundation on which to build effective literacy instruction for African American children can reasonably expect that many (though certainly not all) children who have been socialized in African American communities will share with one another the following:

1. A sense of identity and self-efficacy strongly linked to one's ability to use language well;
2. A view of argumentation/conflict talk as a stimulating and intellectually engaging activity;

3. Skill in, and a liking for, oral performance; and
4. The ability to think quickly on one's feet and to engage effectively in verbal debate.

In order to add to this list of socialized dispositions and linguistic abilities likely fostered through socialization in the African American speech community, I turn now to further analysis of Black children's verbal behaviors as these have been described in the research literature.

Understand[ing] and Appreciat[ing] Implications

Findings from research on language socialization in White mainstream communities reveal that adults frequently engage children in question/answer exchanges in which the child's anticipated response is predictable and invariant: "What does the doggie say?" "How many toes do you have?" "What's your sister's name?" Through their participation in linguistic routines that call for set responses to questions about people and objects in their environment, many mainstream children not only build a base of factual, predictable knowledge about the world (e.g., numbers, colors, letters, labels for everyday objects), but also learn to expect adult approval for displaying that knowledge. As a result, it is likely that many mainstream children come to believe that to be "smart" is to be an information giver, to produce the "right answer" to factual questions posed to them by adults.

In sharp contrast, Heath found that this type of *known-answer* question is almost never asked in Trackton. Trackton adults simply do not ask children questions to which the answer is obvious or which are designed to "test" children's factual knowledge about the world. In verbal exchanges between children and adults and older children in Trackton, responses to someone else's words are seldom predictable. "If a child says 'bye-bye,'" Heath writes, "an adult may respond by a wave and 'bye-bye,' or he may grab the child roughly and say 'You tryin to make me go home, boy?'" (p. 85). Similarly, "questions which seem to have set answers are often used to challenge young children: 'What's my name?' 'What's your name?' 'Who gave you dat?'" (p. 111). As Heath explains, children are not expected to give "literal accurate answers" to these questions, but instead, to provide answers that fit the relationship they have with the questioner. For example, when teenage Darett asks Lem "What's your name?", he does so to elicit "Peanuts," the special nickname he uses for Lem. The same question posed by different speakers might require a variety of other responses. Thus Heath's data suggest that children raised in African American communities may be more likely than those raised in White mainstream communities to participate in verbal exchanges that require them to take multiple contextual factors into consideration in order to respond appropriately to another person's question or challenge.

Heath's data also suggest that adults in Trackton are quite conscious of the fact that their ways of talking with children differ from those common in White mainstream communities. Not surprisingly, adults' comments about those differences reveal that their ways of interacting with children around language are intentional and are viewed by them as constituting an effective means of preparing children for adult participation in the African American speech community. Following, for example, are comments made by Trackton resident Annie Mae Jones about her grandson Teegie:

> He gotta learn to *know* 'bout dis world, can't nobody tell 'im. Now just how crazy is dat? White folks uh hear dey kids say sump'n, dey say it back to 'em, dey aks 'em 'gain 'n 'gain 'bout things, like they 'posed to be born knowin'. You think I can tell Teegie all he gotta know to get along? He just gotta be keen, keep his eyes open, don't he be sorry. Gotta watch hisself by watchin' other folks. Ain't no use me tellin' 'im: "Learn dis, learn dat. What's dis? What's dat?" He just gotta learn, gotta know; he see one thing one place one time, he know how it go, see sump'n like it again, maybe it be de same, maybe it won't . . . (p. 84)

In her statements Teegie's grandmother makes clear that in her view asking children questions like "What's dis?" "What's dat?" is a useless, even "crazy" activity because what something is or means at any particular point depends upon context (i.e., ". . . he see one thing one place one time, he know how it go, see sump'n like it again, maybe it be de same, maybe it won't' "). Drawing on the work of several African American scholars (Gates, 1988; Mitchell-Kernan, 1972 ; Morgan, 2002), I earlier characterized the African American speech community as one that places a strong value on indirection in discourse, on conveying and deciphering meanings that are not directly stated or made explicit (see also Gundaker, 1998; Smitherman, 1977, 2000a; Spears, 1998; Troutman, 2001). Recall, for example, Morgan's (2002) description of the African American community where she grew up as one in which people "expressed great love and respect for conversations that were deeply ambiguous" (p. 1). Here Morgan is describing a preference for ambiguity as opposed to explicitness in discourse that some scholars (Gundaker, 1998; Levine, 1977; Morgan, 1993; Nielsen, 1997) have traced back to traditional West African oral and written rhetorical traditions. The flip side of this preference for ambiguity, of course, is that explicitness, or, what from an African American discourse perspective might be phrased as "stating the obvious," is *not* valued, a point of view clearly evident in Annie Mae Jones' comments quoted previously as well as in the following comments made by James Bullock, an African American father and teacher quoted in Gundaker (1998):

> Black people get the point quickly. It's essential to their survival. Once they see something or once it's been said they assume everybody gets it. They don't like to repeat it. They don't see any reason to spell things out. . . . But

in school they want you to spell it out. That's what they grade you for. That's how you show you are smart. Black kids show they're smart by showing how far they can go playing all around the point but they consider it stupid to spell out what everybody gets. (p. 164)

Like Annie Mae Jones who characterizes it as useless (i.e., "'ain't no use . . .'") and "crazy" to ask children questions to which the answer is obvious, James Bullock does not mince words: Black kids "consider it *stupid* to spell out what everybody gets." Thus when Black children do not hasten to raise their hands to respond to known-answer questions in the classroom, it is possible that their reluctance has more to do with their puzzlement—even incredulity—over the fact that they are being asked to state what is obvious than it does with whether or not they actually know the answer to the question being asked. As developmental theorist Barbara Rogoff (2003) hypothesizes, children in this position may fail to respond as the teacher expects in an effort to "avoid being made a fool of by giving an obvious answer to what must be a trick question—otherwise why would a knowledgeable person ask it?" (p. 247).

Yet, as Bullock points out, spelling things out, stating obvious answers, is a large part of what children are graded for and evaluated upon in school. Indeed, research shows that known-answer questions are the most frequently asked type of question in many school settings, including of course on standardized tests of achievement (Cazden, 1988; Stubbs, 1983). Clearly, as every study that has been done of language use in African American communities suggests, use of this type of question to assess children's learning is a practice highly unlikely to reveal the true depth of Black children's knowledge and understanding about a given topic.

While many children raised in African American communities may receive little practice answering questions like "What's this?" "What's that?," some research suggests that they are likely to receive extensive practice answering another question, albeit one more likely to be implied than directly articulated: "What does this (e.g., this word, this statement, this gesture) *mean*, in this particular situation?" It is in figuring out the answer to this question that many children who are members of the African American speech community demonstrate their intelligence and the depth of their understanding about the world. When seven- or eight-year-old Claudia Mitchell-Kernan, for example, figures out the meaning of Mr. Waters's signifying monkey tale *as it applies to* her own behavior, Mr. Waters applauds her developing ability to "hold a conversation," i.e., to understand and appreciate implications. When preschooler Lem figures out the meaning of Darett's question, "What's your name?" *as it applies to* the special relationship between them, he is rewarded by Darett's approval of his keenness in being able to figure out the contextually appropriate meaning of his question. And when Lem gets a little older and responds to the mayor's renewed offer to "keep" his candy (see earlier example) with the scornful retort, " 'You ain't *keep* nut'n, you eat it' " (Heath, 1983, p. 85), he gives evidence of his growing ability to see beneath the literal meaning of someone's words in order to uncover the "true meaning" of what is being said. As Heath (1983) writes: "Trackton children are expected to recognize that the same form of language—or anything else—is not expected to carry the same meaning at all times. Instead children are expected to learn how to know when meanings are not literal, but conveyed meanings" (p. 105).

Because of its attention to, even preoccupation with, the multilayered meanings of discourse, the African American speech community has some-times been described as "double-voiced." In my view, the concept of "double voicing"—and its interpretative parallel, "double vision"—are useful ones for describing important cognitive/linguistic abilities that many children develop as a result of their cultural socialization in African American communities, but that frequently go unrecognized by their teachers in mainstream settings. Fol-lowing the example of literacy scholar Grey Gundaker (1998), I use the terms *double voicing* and *double vision* to refer to "two or more ways to see/hear, inscribe/interpret, or see/represent" (p. 11). Gundaker provides an example of the concepts double voicing and double vision and their centrality in African American culture in her analysis of the multiple meanings symbolized by a church sign she observed in Chattanooga, Tennessee in which the word *JES—US* appears across the horizontal face of a cross. This sign, Gundaker writes:

> Combines double-voiced associations (including "that talk," in the dialect spelling j-e-s for "just" and the emphatic preaching intonation Jeeeez-us) with double-visual readings to enfold an in-group within the outstretched arms of Jesus and the cross. Variations on the theme of the in-group, "just us," also play against a word of special import for African Americans, "jus-tice." For example, the name of one black-owned publishing house special-izing in Afrocentric literature is Just Us. The rap performer Just-Ice doubles the concepts of justice and cool in his name.
>
> Double vision, therefore, not only implies a capacity to see multiple planes of existence and how they relate or conflict with one another; it also lays claim to deep knowledge, initiates' knowledge, whether of religious matters or secular concerns of a self-aware, self-defined community. (p. 25)

Perhaps the most familiar example of double-voiceness associated with the African American community is that of the spirituals, whose lyrics sometimes communicated hidden messages about escaping to freedom on the Under-ground Railroad (Douglass, 1845/1968; DuBois, 1982; Jones, 1993; Levine, 1977; Smitherman, 1977). Thus, for example, when enslaved African Ameri-cans sang "steal away to Jesus" or "I am bound for the land of Canaan," they could just as well have been singing about, in Smitherman's terms, "dis heah" as "after here" (1977, p. 48), about freedom in Canada as freedom in Canaan. However, although it is true that African American spirituals sometimes func-tioned as a secret system of communication during the period of enslavement, these spirituals were not double-voiced in any simplistic or invariant sense. What a particular spiritual, or a particular phrase, meant in any specific instance depended upon the context. As scholar Arthur Jones (1993) writes: ". . . none of these songs had any fixed meanings but were available 'in the air' to any African person needing them for any specific purposes . . . they [the spirituals] could be improvised or utilized in various ways" (p. 58). Thus as Bernice Reagon explains, one "can't say that every song that has 'Canaan' means Canada. . . . It means Canada if it *meant* Canada" (quoted in Jones, 1993, p. 58). In this sense, the terms double voicing and double vision are misnomers for the contextual nature of meaning being discussed here because these terms suggest merely two ways of meaning, whereas, as the example of the spirituals suggests, in the African American communicative tradition there are always multiple interpretative possibilities. And as many scholars of African American language, literature and culture have asserted, to be a member of the African American speech community involves being open to, alert to, these multiple possibilities of meaning.

Raised in communities in which, to quote Mitchell-Kernan, "holding a conversation" means being able to "understand and appreciate implications," many African American children receive extensive practice in figuring out what something "really means" long before they ever set foot in a classroom. More specifically, to the list of those socialized abilities and dispositions likely possessed by many children raised in African American communities, we can add those that appear in boldface in the following list:

1. A sense of identity and self-efficacy strongly linked to one's ability to use language well;
2. A disposition toward argumentation/conflict talk as a stimulating and intellectually engaging activity;
3. Skill in, and a liking for, oral performance;
4. The ability to think quickly on one's feet and to engage effectively in verbal debate;
5. **A strong tendency to take context into account in figuring out the meaning of a word, statement or extended piece of discourse;**
6. **A highly developed sensitivity to audience in communicative interactions; and**
7. **The ability to discern multiple possibilities of meaning in discourse and to "read between the lines" of what is literally being said.**

Repetition with a Difference

The literary scholar Henry Louis Gates (1988) has described *repetition with a difference* as a recurring process within African American oral, literary, and musical traditions. Very briefly summarized, what Gates means by this is that many Black oral performers, as well as literary and musical artists, comment upon and pay homage to prior texts within the Black tradition by repeating central patterns or tropes of those texts with what Gates refers to as "a signal (signifying) difference" (p. 51). Gates provides numerous examples of this process from Black music and from the African American literary tradition— from jazz, for instance, the way in which Jelly Roll Morton's 1938 recording "Maple Leaf Rag (Transformation)" repeats and transforms elements of Scott Joplin's 1916 recording of "Maple Leaf Rag" (p. 63); from literature, the way Alice Walker draws upon and extends Zora Neale Hurston's use of the vernacular voice in *Their Eyes Were Watching God* (1937) to create the narrative voice of her 1982 novel *The Color Purple* (pp. 239–258).

From the Black oral tradition, one of the examples Gates cites to illustrate the process of *repetition with a difference* is the Signifying Monkey tales, alluded to earlier in the example of Mitchell-Kernan learning how to "hold a conversation." Gates notes that the Signifying Monkey tales apparently originated during the period of enslavement and that literally hundreds of these tales have been recorded since the early years of the twentieth century. As Gates explains, all of the individual tales contained within the larger corpus of Monkey tales "speak to one another" in the sense that they involve the same three characters (the monkey, the lion, and the elephant) in a recurring plot sequence (i.e., the lion is duped by the rhetorically masterful monkey, and as a consequence of acting upon a literal [and therefore mistaken] interpretation of the monkey's words, is beaten by the physically more powerful elephant). In addition to these thematic similarities, the tales also share structural similarities, including their rhyming structure and the use of certain formulaic phrases. Differences among the individual tales, then, typically consist of relatively minor changes in the way these familiar elements are used. Gates writes: "It is as if a received structure of crucial elements provides a base for poeisis, and the narrator's technique, his or her craft, is to be gauged by the creative (re) placement of these expected or anticipated formulaic phrases and formulaic events, rendered anew in unexpected ways" (p. 61).

The challenge, then, is for the narrator to be linguistically creative despite having to work within the very tight constraints dictated by the fact that so many thematic and structural aspects of the Monkey tales are already specified. Gates has persuasively argued that because so many aspects of the tales are "givens" and likely familiar to the narrator's audience, what gets highlighted in an "innovative" version of a Monkey tale is not so much meaning as the language itself (what Gates calls the "signifier"). What stands out, in other words, is the *way* in which something is said, the narrator's skill in using language to render what is (seemingly) familiar "anew" in "unexpected ways"—that is, repetition with a difference.

As a number of scholars, including Gates, have noted, repetition with a difference is a pattern that also characterizes everyday discourse in African

American communities, especially in interactional routines like signifying, toasting, rapping, and playing the Dozens. The Dozens, which Gates once described as "that age-old black ritual of graceful insult," is a particularly well-known African American linguistic routine (in Afterword to Hurston, 1937/1990, p. 192). For those unfamiliar with it, the Dozens can be briefly described as a verbal battle of wits in which two opponents trade insults, typically about each other's mothers. Linguist Lisa Green (2002) and others have pointed out that the Dozens has set rules that are punctiliously followed by players whether or not they are consciously aware of what those rules are. These rules include, for example, the specification that the players be known to one another, that the insults traded be exaggerated and untrue, and that the audience be judge of the winner (p. 138). These ritualized insults must also conform to a specified grammatical structure, which Morgan (2002), drawing on the work of Hutcherson, calls the "anatomy" of a mother joke (p. 58). As Morgan explains, for example, "your mother" statements typically begin with *Your mother (is) so* followed by an adjective, as illustrated in the following examples:

1. Your mother is so fat that when she sits on a quarter she gets two dimes and a nickel. (Quoted in Morgan, 2002, p. 59)
2. Your mother is so old that when she reads the Bible she reminisces. (Quoted in Morgan, 2002, p. 59)
3. Your mother is so stupid (that) she thought a lawsuit was something you wear to court. (Quoted in Green, 2002, p. 138)

Just as with the teller of a Monkey tale, the Dozens player must be creative within the constraints provided by the required grammatical structure as well as by the other rules to which "your mother" statements must conform (e.g., that the insult be exaggerated and untrue). Here, again, because the Dozens player is working within a frame in which so many thematic and structural aspects are already givens (i.e., the "repetition" part), emphasis is focused upon the language itself, the *way* in which something is said (i.e., the signal/ signifiying "difference").

The Dozens have been described in the literature as a language socialization device, a form of rhetorical training for eventual participation in the adult discourse community. Capturing this educative function of the Dozens in the Black speech community, Gates (1988) quotes H. Rap Brown who remarked in his autobiography that he and his friends " 'played the Dozens like white folks play Scrabble' " (p. 72). Also emphasizing their teaching role, Morgan (2002) asserts: "Your mother statements are a device to practice and perform verbal skill and this practice often occurs in the presence of family members, including mothers who help judge their effectiveness and comment on the wit and irony in the statements, often offering other examples which they deem more impressive" (p. 58).

The literature on Black children's language socialization suggests that in many working-class communities, children of all ages regularly engage in playful linguistic routines that include Dozens-like insult exchanges, play songs and jump rope rhymes, storytelling, joking, and other forms of signifying (Goodwin, 1990; Heath, 1983; Mahiri, 1998; Vernon-Feagans, 1996; Wyatt, 1995). According to Heath (1983), for example, "school-age boys and girls [in Trackton] model a wide range of methods of verbal play, imaginative exaggeration, and ways to vary treatment of themes in their exchanges of insults and play songs" (p. 175). These "play song-like insults" typically contain either internal or end rhyme, as illustrated in the example below taken from Heath's data:

> Yo' ma, yo' ma
> Yo' greasy greasy gran' ma
> Got skinny legs 'n fat behind
> Enuf to scare ol' Frankenstein (p. 175)

Heath notes that spontaneous, in-the-moment creations that include clever language play are particularly admired and likely to be picked up and repeated by other children. Similarly, Goodwin (1990) observed that on Maple Street, both boys and girls frequently engage in what she calls "playful ritual insult battles" (p. 186). Just as the Signifying Monkey tale teller or the Dozens player must demonstrate his or her verbal creativity within the constraints provided by a linguistic structure in which many elements are already set, children involved in ritual insult battles on Maple Street must tie what they have to say in some clever and ingenious way to statements made by the previous speaker. As Goodwin explains, "the point is not to negate or contradict prior talk but to show that second speaker can take a feature of first speaker's talk . . . and transform it" (p. 186).

This process of constructing one's verbal comeback by transforming an aspect of previous speaker's statement is essentially the process of repetition with a difference that I have been describing throughout this section, as is illustrated in the following example from an interchange between two Maple Street children:

> MARTHA: I don't know what you laughin' at.
> BILLY: I know what I'm laughin' at.
>   Your head.   (p. 177)

Here Billy constructs his insult by essentially repeating the structure of Martha's statement with three (signifying) differences: the change from a negative to a positive construction in the first part of the sentence (*I don't know* what/*I know* what), a switch in pronouns in the second part of the sentence (*you* laughin' at/*I'm* laughin' at), and the addition of new lexical information at the end (*Your head*). As Goodwin points out, in exchanges such as these, the second speaker's repetition of structural and lexical elements from the first speaker's statement "[makes] the relevant difference in the second utterance . . . stand out with particular salience" (p. 182). This process of repetition with a difference is illustrated as well in the following additional examples from Goodwin's data:

TONY: You sound terrible.
MARTHA: We sound just like you look.   (p. 183)

MALCOLM: She a dropout.
RUBY: I *know* you a dropout.
MALCOLM: She says she know she a dropout.   (p. 186)

As Goodwin illustrates with multiple examples throughout her text, in regularly occurring playful insult disputes, Maple Street children receive extensive practice in rendering another person's language "anew" in clever and unexpected ways.

An indication of how early many Black children begin to engage in the kind of creative language play described here comes from data collected by linguist Toya Wyatt. In a study of language use among three- to five-year-old African American children, Wyatt (1995) found numerous examples of preschoolers engaged in collaborative rapping sequences and in verbal disputes that she characterizes as an elementary form of the Dozens (Wyatt's findings in this regard are consistent with those of Heath, 1983). Analyzing a rap spontaneously produced by two boys, DD and DN, Wyatt writes:

> . . . during the rap sequence, the children appear to recognize the importance of rhythm, rhyme, and group collaboration. They also know the importance of trying to "play off" each other's lines and making verbal contributions that relate in some fashion to the previous contribution. Perhaps even more important, however, they recognize that their performances must be spontaneous as evidenced from DD's response to Wyatt's question about the origin of his rap: "Cuz, cuz, I just got it from my body, man." (p. 15)

Unquestionably, one of the most impressive examples contained in the linguistic literature of a preschooler's ability to "play off" someone else's lines comes from Heath's Trackton data. In this example, preschooler Lem is not engaged in verbal play with other children, but instead is responding to a teasing challenge issued by his mother, who is exasperated with him for taking off his shoes when he wasn't supposed to. She asks Lem: " 'You want me ta tie you up, put you on de railroad track?' " Heath reports that, after hesitating only a moment, Lem offers the following lyrical response:

Railroad track
Train all big 'n black
On dat track, on dat track, on dat track

Ain't no way I can't get back
Back from dat track
Back from dat train
Big 'n black, I be back   (p. 110)

Of note here is preschooler Lem's already skillful use of rhyme (e.g., track, black, back), alliteration (e.g., **B**ig 'n **b**lack, I **b**e **b**ack), and repetition [with a difference] (e.g., Back from dat track/Back from dat train), all the more impressive, of course, for having been created on the spot, or, as preschooler DD might have phrased it, "from his body, man."

The linguistic creativity demonstrated by African American children as they skillfully transform another person's words into the point *they* want to make is the "stuff" out of which great speakers and writers are made, rich ground, to be sure, in which to help anchor a successful literacy curriculum. More specifically, the research discussed in this section suggests the following additions (in boldface) to the list of linguistic abilities and dispositions likely fostered through socialization in many African American communities:

1. A sense of identity and self-efficacy strongly linked to one's ability to use language well;
2. A disposition toward argumentation/conflict talk as a stimulating and intellectually engaging activity;
3. Skill in, and a liking for, oral performance;
4. The ability to think quickly on one's feet and to engage effectively in verbal debate;
5. A strong tendency to take context into account in figuring out the meaning of a word, statement or extended piece of discourse;
6. A highly developed sensitivity to audience in communicative interactions;
7. The ability to discern multiple possibilities of meaning in discourse and to "read between the lines" of what is literally being said;
8. **Sensitivity to verbal nuance and experience in interpreting metaphorical/figurative language;**
9. **Experience in rhyming as well as in the use of other kinds of poetic language, including, for example, the use of rhythm, alliteration, repetition, well-turned phrases and plays on words; and**
10. **Skill with in-the-moment verbal improvisation.**

Narrative and Storytelling Abilities

In a study that compared a group of low-income African American children and a group of middle class White children the summer before they entered kindergarten, Vernon-Feagans (1996) examined children's use of language in peer and sibling interactions. She found negligible differences between the two groups on quantitative measures of linguistic complexity or in the abstract level of their talk. In other words, neither group possessed an advantage in terms of the grammatical and semantic complexity of their language, a finding consistent with other studies comparing the language development of African American and White children (e.g., Blake, 1984; Bridgeforth, 1989; Stock-man & Vaughn-Cooke, 1982). Vernon-Feagans did, however, find significant differences between the two groups in the kinds of verbal interactions that accompanied their play. The African American children engaged in four times as many interactions that involved extended storytelling as the White chil-dren did. Indeed, pretend play and storytelling constituted a major portion of Black children's play in the study. According to Vernon-Feagans, the stories told by the Black children were characterized by a level of imagination and theme development unequaled in any of the narratives produced by the White children. Focusing on even younger children than the mostly five-year-olds discussed by Vernon-Feagans, Heath (1983) found that the spontaneous pro-duction of what she describes as "story-poems," in which events are described in a "series of verse-like utterances," was characteristic of children as young as two and three in Trackton (p. 171). Lem's railroad track poem quoted earlier is an example of the linguistic sophistication and lyrical quality evidenced in some of the "story-poems" produced by preschoolers in Trackton.

A number of studies suggest that stories told by children and adults in working class African American communities are often highly imaginative and tend to be fictional as opposed to literal, factual accounts of events (Heath, 1983; Labov, 1972; Mahiri, 1998; Nichols, 1989; Sperry & Sperry, 1996; Vernon-Feagans, 1996). Typically, such narratives include a great deal of dramatic dialogue (Goodwin, 1990; Heath, 1983; Nichols, 1989). In her study of interac-tion among children and teachers during Sunday school in an African Ameri-can church, Haight (2002) also reports a high incidence of stories involving hypothetical events and notes that even the youngest children in her study participated in the creation of such narratives. A particularly vivid example from a young child comes from Vernon-Feagans's data (1996). The following narrative, spontaneously "composed" by five-year-old James, sitting alone on a bench looking up at the sky, creates an imaginative scenario about what might occur were James to "'get [me] an airplane and fly up to the sky.'"

> I like to know how it feels being up to the sky. I gotta get me an airplane and
> fly up to the sky, see how it looks. And then I'd look but I wouldn't look down
> from the sky. I wouldn't look down or maybe I'd fall down. But I wouldn't
> jump out of a plane. Not without a parachute. Cause I know if I jump out of a
> plane without a parachute I'd be in big trouble. If I jump, if I had a parachute,
> I would. I'd jump right out. With the parachute I'd land safely. I won't fall on
> the ground. I land just like this, then I walk and go back to the plane again
> cause when I jump it's gonna be scary. But I hope mine don't crash. Cause if
> it would it's gonna be in big trouble. (pp. 109–110)

James's ability to reason hypothetically about the possible consequences of various actions he envisions undertaking in his imaginative story (e.g., "'. . . if I jump out of a plane without a parachute . . .'") is impressive. It is worth underscoring here, as well, that except for other Black boys, no children in the study produced monologues of anywhere near the length, semantic complexity, or linguistic sophistication represented in James's monologue.

As in James's monologue, a distinguishing feature of the hypothetical narratives told in the Sunday school context studied by Haight is that they typically cast the children themselves in a major role. Similarly, Heath describes how children in Trackton "hear themselves made into characters in stories told again and again" (p. 167) and often tell imaginative stories about themselves. Likewise, Goodwin (1990) reports that in their verbal disputes with one another, children on Maple Street create fictional scenarios in which their opponents are cast as characters engaged in unflattering behaviors. Both Heath and Goodwin emphasize the way in which the African American children in their studies use imaginative stories to negotiate their relationships with other people (on this point, see also Bloome, Champion, Katz, Morton & Muldrow, 2001). Goodwin notes, for example, that "when stories are used in dispute processes, they permit the playing out of an event in full dramatic regalia" (p. 239). As alluded to above, such "full dramatic regalia" typically includes the use of dialogue and sometimes body language and other nonverbal behavior as well. Telling a story whose purpose is to illustrate Tony's cowardice, for instance, Maple Street's Chopper animates Tony's alleged response to three boys asking for money by raising his hands up in the air and saying in a shaky, high-pitched voice: "'I Ain't Got n(h)(hh)o m(h)oney'" (p. 245). Thus, as Goodwin points out, "instead of simply reporting what Tony said, Chopper *enacts* his behavior at the moment of climax" (p. 244).

Significantly, Tony eventually retaliates against Chopper for his negative characterization of him not by getting overtly angry or by resorting to physical aggression, but by making up a counter story that casts Chopper in a negative light. The contest is a rhetorical one, and in this case (as research suggests is typical in the Black community), the "measure of a man" is not his physical might, but his mouth, his store of verbal wit and eloquence (Goodwin, 1990; Kochman, 1981; Labov, 1972; Smitherman, 1977). And, as Goodwin's and others' research amply demonstrates, such battles of wit are as much the "testing ground" of girls and women as of boys and men (see especially Etter-Lewis, 1991; Foster, 1995a; Goodwin, 1990; Mitchell-Kernan, 1972; Morgan, 2002; Troutman, 2001).

Here again we see the importance attached to verbal ability in African American communities and, consequently, the likelihood that children raised in those communities will not only be verbally adept, but, as suggested earlier, have developed a sense of identity and efficacy in the world closely linked to their ability to use language well. Research on the uses of story in African

American communities suggests that storytelling abilities are an important part of a larger repertoire of verbal abilities that children develop as a result of their on-going participation in the everyday life of their communities and that they regularly draw on to make sense of—and in—the social interactions that occur there.

Studies of storytelling in African American communities also consistently highlight the interactive, participatory nature of this event. Even the youngest storytellers learn to adjust their narrative performance based upon subtle and not-so-subtle reactions and cues from their audience, and even the most proficient storytellers, of all ages, are constantly in danger of losing the floor, momentarily at least, to a more skillful performer. In the following story recorded by Heath (1983), for example, preteens Terry and Tony work at some points collaboratively, and at some points competitively, to create their imaginative scenario:

TERRY:	Didja hear 'bout Aunt Bess' cat las' night?
TONY:	No, what 'bout dat ol' cat?
TERRY:	Dat cat get in a fight.
TONY:	A fight?
TERRY:	Yea, it kilt a dog.
TONY:	Ain't no cat can kill no dog.
TERRY:	Dis cat, he kilt a big dog, dat ol' German shepherd stay down by ol' man Oak's place.
TONY:	What'd you do?
TERRY:	Me? I kilt a horse.
TONY:	You ain't kilt no horse, (pause) more'n likely a mouse. Where?
TERRY:	On Main Street. Yesterday.
TONY:	And you kilt one, for sure?
TERRY:	Yea, me 'n dat ol' cat, we built a big fire, stirred it aroun', Threw oil in it, got it goin' good, and I rode dat horse right in.
TONY:	Ya did?
TERRY:	Yup =
TONY:	= I know, it took a while to git de cat outta de fire, 'bout (pause) maybe a week or so, 'n Mr. Rowe [who owns a bicycle shop on Main Street] give us a bicycle, 'n we ride de horse, 'n my friend, Steve, he ride de horse, too 'n we come back and foun' dat ol' cat done kilt dat big dog.
TERRY:	Why?
TONY:	'Cause dat cat say "Wow, I'm de greates', ain't no dog kin git me," (pause) like ain't no fire gonna git *me* (pause) 'n my horse (pause) 'n my bicycle. (pp. 183–184)

At the beginning of this jointly constructed narrative, Terry clearly has the spotlight. Tony, however, participates actively in the telling by asking questions (e.g., "No, what 'bout dat ol' cat?") and posing challenges (e.g., "Ain't no cat can kill no dog.") that work to facilitate Terry's performance. But in the latter portion of the interaction, Tony takes over control of the story (i.e., "I know . . .) by stepping into the opening created by Terry's brief hesitation after the word *Yup* and continuing on with his own version of what happens next. Interestingly, Terry then obligingly takes up the role of facilitator to and participant in Tony's telling with his question "Why?" near the very end of the story. Apropos of important linguistic abilities highlighted earlier—that is, the ability to think quickly on one's feet and facility in the use of such stylistic/rhetorical features as rhyme, rhythm, repetition, and alliteration—it is also worth noting Tony's skilled, in-the-moment use of repetition, parallelism, and dramatic pausing in his closing lines: " ' . . . like ain't no fire gonna git *me* (pause) 'n my horse (pause) 'n my bicycle.' "

Terry and Tony are preteens; in the verbal performance reproduced here from Wyatt (1995), the performers are preschoolers, DD and DN, demonstrating the same process of collaborative production, as well as the same (albeit fledging) use of characteristic BC stylistic and narrative features such as rhythm, repetition, and dramatic dialogue:

DD: (Rap tempo) Everytime I see her, I'm gonna give her a kiss . . . /Ah, Ah/Ah, Ah/An' I lover her! . . . An' tell her I love her . . . I lover her!/

DN: I love her . . . I'ma lover her everytime . . ./

DD: An' she can tell me everytime . . . An' I answer the phone, I say get off the phone mom! . . ./

DN: She's my girl . . . and I'ma see her . . . Everytime, she call me, I say ma, get off the dag-gone phone . . . I wanna talk to the girl/??: (Laughing)

DN: Everytime, I see her . . . I'm gonna kiss her . . . I'm gonna love her and I'm gonna kiss her . . ./

DD: Everytime, she call me . . . I'ma . . . kiss the phone . . . I'm say hello . . . Who is it? . . . It's my girlfriend, man!/Don't joke around with me man/ (pp. 14–15)

From a developmental perspective, what is particularly significant about collaborative storytelling is the opportunities it provides for participants to learn from one another in the process of constructing a story together. In both of the previous examples, it is apparent how statements made by one participant work to facilitate or scaffold the narrative performance of the other participant. In the process of co-construction, participants are thus facilitating one another's narrative development, in essence, teaching each other how to tell an effective story. In a report based on their on-going study of young African American children's spoken and written narrative development, researchers David Bloome, Tempii Champion, Laurie Katz, Mary Beth Morton and Ramona Muldrow (2001) emphasize not only the social uses of narrative among the children they studied, but also the ways in which the children (preschoolers and kindergartners) built upon one another's images, ideas, and language in creating both their oral and written stories. The collaborative nature of story-telling in working class African American communities (and in the research alluded to earlier) is, of course, in sharp contrast to narrative performance in many school settings, where both oral and written narratives are almost invari-ably expected to be the production of a single student working alone.

In describing the theoretical framework for their study, Bloome, et al., make a useful distinction between the processes of *adoption* and *adaptation* in narrative production:

> Adoption would include children's mimicking and reproduction of narra-tives in the ways that they experience them (e.g., they may attempt to tell "The Three Little Pigs" in the same manner in which they were told the story). Adaptation would include various hybridizations and transformations of extant narratives (cf Bakhtin 1953/1986), sometimes overt and sometimes subtle . . . (2001, p. 49)

Clearly, it is adoption that is valued over adaptation in many school literacy tasks, particularly those that serve some sort of assessment function. Early literacy assessments, for example, commonly include story-recall tasks that require children to essentially repeat the narrative they have just heard read aloud to them. Yet, as discussed in the section on "repetition with a differ-ence," many African American children are likely to assume that meeting a verbal challenge—for example, coming up with a story "worth telling"—calls for creativity and linguistic innovation. To simply parrot back what someone else has said is hardly considered skilled verbal performance or constitutive of an effective story.

Indeed, Vernon-Feagans speculates that the African American children in her study may have performed less well on a kindergarten paraphrasing task than their White counterparts precisely *because* of their more creative use of language and their superior storytelling abilities (documented in the earlier part of her study). Rather than simply retelling the story when asked to paraphrase, the African American children added to and embellished the story, in the process frequently creating a "different, but often more interest-ing, vignette" (1996, p. 198). But although their stories were frequently more interesting than the original, the process of embellishment led the African American children to exclude elements of the original story, for which they were heavily penalized when their performance on the task was evaluated.

As I have attempted to illustrate throughout this section, whether or not those abilities receive recognition by teachers or on tests, many children social-ized in African American communities are likely to possess considerable skill in producing lengthy, highly creative, and stylistically sophisticated stories, often featuring themselves or other familiar people as imaginary protagonists.

To the list of linguistic abilities likely fostered through socialization in African American communities, then, we can add the following bold-faced items:

1. A sense of identity and self-efficacy strongly linked to one's ability to use language well;
2. A disposition toward argumentation/conflict talk as a stimulating and intellectually engaging activity;
3. Skill in, and a liking for, oral performance;
4. The ability to think quickly on one's feet and to engage effectively in verbal debate;
5. A strong tendency to take context into account in figuring out the meaning of a word, statement or extended piece of discourse;
6. A highly developed sensitivity to audience in communicative interactions;
7. The ability to discern multiple possibilities of meaning in discourse and to "read between the lines" of what is literally being said;
8. Sensitivity to verbal nuance and experience in interpreting metaphorical/figurative language;
9. Experience in rhyming as well as in the use of other kinds of poetic language, including, for example, the use of rhythm, alliteration, repetition, well-turned phrases and plays on words;
10. Skill with in-the-moment verbal improvisation.
11. **Extensive experience in the collaborative construction of narratives and stories; and**
12. **Skill in the construction of imaginative stories that frequently fictionalize the self (and/or other familiar people) and that often include dramatic dialogue.**

A Final Note

The list presented in this chapter of linguistic abilities likely fostered through socialization in African American communities is not meant to be exhaustive. Rather, it represents an attempt to specify those socialized abilities whose existence can reasonably be inferred from the relatively small body of research that currently exists about African American children's language socialization. I have little doubt that future research in this area will not only allow us to add to this list of socialized abilities, but also to acquire a deeper and more nuanced understanding of those abilities discussed here.

As the reader may have noted, most of the preceding discussion centered on language socialization experiences in human interaction. I have not ventured in this chapter into discussion of any language abilities likely fostered through African American children's interactions with books. Contrary to popular misconceptions, we know that many African American children of all social classes have considerable experience with books before they enter school and that many continue to read extensively at home after school entry (Compton-Lilly, 2003; Gadsen, 1993; Taylor & Dorsey-Gaines, 1988). We know as well that African American culture in general places a very high value on the power and importance of literacy (Anderson, 1988, 1995; Cornelius, 1991; McHenry, 2002; Perry, 2003; Peterson, 1995; Royster, 2000).

It is also the case, however, that despite being heirs to a cultural tradition that greatly prizes literacy, a large number of African American children enter school with little prior exposure to books, either because their families cannot afford them or because the difficult circumstances of their lives have led their families to lose touch with this important cultural value. Because this is the case, I have chosen to focus here on linguistic abilities likely to be possessed by children socialized in African American communities *whether or not they have any experience with books or other literacy artifacts before entering school and/or whether or not they read extensively afterward.* What have been highlighted in this chapter, then, are oral abilities and performance features that, as I have tried to illustrate throughout, provide a strong, rich, and entirely sufficient foundation in which to anchor successful literacy instruction for African American children at any grade level.

Part 3
Using African American Children's Literature to Teach Essential Comprehension Strategies

Chapter 6
Drawing on Children's Strengths

To date, much of the literature about BC and reading instruction has focused almost exclusively on phonological and grammatical components of the language rather than on the kinds of pragmatic abilities discussed in chapter 5. In some respects, this focus is not surprising. A good deal of the research about Black children and reading has been aimed at trying to make sense of the low literacy achievement of many poor and working-class Black children, a pattern of low achievement that has persisted over decades and that stands in marked contradistinction to Black children's sophisticated verbal abilities. Black Communications features in this research as one potential source of difficulty for BC speakers learning to read. And, indeed, there is some compelling evidence to suggest that systematic differences between the phonological and grammatical patterns of BC and SE may cause difficulties in learning to read for some children, especially when teachers do not take those systematic differences into account in designing and implementing instruction. (This topic will be explored at great length in part 4.) However, our exclusive focus on these structural aspects of language—and on explaining failure—have led us to largely ignore other aspects of BC and of socialization in the BC discourse community that may in fact provide BC users with potential advantages in the process of learning to read (Foster, 2001). In order to more fully explore, and build upon, those advantages, we must look not only beyond a narrow definition of BC, but also beyond the narrow definition of reading that underlies, and circumscribes, most discussions about the relationship between BC and the reading process.

Complicating Our Notion of the Reading Process

Educators often talk about the process of reading as broadly divided into two major components: decoding (i.e., the ability to translate written symbols into their spoken equivalents) and comprehension (i.e., the ability to make meaning of text). We might think of the first as being in service of the latter, the means to an end, if you will—that is, one decodes text for the purpose of understanding it. Although both decoding and comprehension are critical to the definition of what it means to be literate in our society, it is important to remember that the latter is not necessarily dependent upon the former. Clearly, it is possible to comprehend a text read aloud by someone else.

Lessons from the Past

In her seminal study of African American literary societies in northern, urban Black communities from the late 1820s to the 1920s, Elizabeth McHenry (2002) describes the way in which these societies embodied a conception of literacy as a communal rather than an individual activity. Because of the limited educational opportunities available to African Americans throughout this period, many Black Americans (even those never literally enslaved) were not able to read (i.e., decode) text for themselves. This lack of decoding ability did not, however, preclude their active participation in the workings of the literary societies McHenry describes. Because texts were read aloud, all could take part in analyzing and debating the writer's ideas in the discussions that followed the oral readings. Thus, the practices of these literary societies were based upon the assumption that the verbal sophistication and reasoning ability necessary to comprehend complex text were not in any way dependent upon the ability to decode that text for oneself.

This assumption that one could understand text without literally reading it oneself did not mean, of course, that African Americans of the time did not value individual literacy. Jupiter Hammond's 1787 exhortation to his fellow Blacks to "let all the time you can get be spent in trying to learn to read" is one that has echoed throughout African American history (quotation in McHenry, 2002, p. 35). Given the intense racism and lack of educational opportunity that surrounded them, however, learning to read just wasn't possible for many Black people of the time, despite how fervently they may have wished to learn. But because the African American literacy societies McHenry describes did not make access to text dependent upon first being able to decode it, members who could not read by themselves were still able to become, in the deepest sense, literate, to develop what one Black writer in 1840 called "'a literary character'" (quoted in McHenry, p. 85).

Current Thinking in the Field

This essential distinction between one's ability to decode text and one's ability to comprehend it is not one that teachers necessarily have at the forefront of their consciousness during early literacy instruction. While few teachers would likely quarrel with the notion that even the youngest readers struggling to decode the simplest text need to be making sense of what they read, it is often assumed that children's development of so-called "higher order" comprehension abilities—for example, drawing inferences, interpreting metaphorical language, determining important ideas in text—must, for the most part at least, wait upon their achievement of fluency in decoding. At its most extreme, this view is well captured in literacy researcher Jean Chall's famous statement that one "learns to read" in the primary grades and "reads to learn" in the later grades.

Significantly, this is emphatically *not* the view held by most educators and researchers who are currently writing and thinking about the development of children's comprehension abilities. Many have specifically identified reading aloud by the teacher—of text that is typically well beyond children's current decoding levels—as an important instructional context for developing both children's vocabularies and their comprehension abilities (e.g., Baker, Scher, & Mackler, 1997; Calkins, 2001; Cunningham, 2005; Dickinson & Smith, 1994; Ewers & Brownson, 1999; Harvey & Goudvis, 2000; Keene & Zimmermann, 1997; Leung, 1992; Robbins & Ehri, 1994; Wolf, 2004). Thus, current thinking in the field of reading—that the development of children's comprehension abilities does not have to wait upon their acquisition of decoding skills—is clearly in alignment with the read-aloud practices and sense of communal literacy that characterized the African American literary societies discussed earlier.

Tracked for Failure

Unfortunately, however, African American children, particularly low-income children attending under-resourced schools, are seldom the beneficiaries of either the latest thinking about best practices represented in the research literature or of the potentially innovative teaching ideas to be gleaned from a careful study of African American historical experience. Indeed, a substantial body of research collected over the last two decades reveals that a disproportionately large number of African American children are placed in the lowest educational tracks or in remedial reading programs where they are far more likely to be hunched over their desks filling out worksheets than gathered together with their classmates for an intellectually stimulating discussion of a book read aloud by their teacher (e.g., Allington, 1983; Barr & Dreeben, 1988; Braddock, 1995; Cooper & Sherk, 1989; Darling-Hammond, 1995; Dreeban & Gamoran, 1986; Epstein, 1985; Oakes, 1985; Slavin, 1987, 1989). Needless to say, in the vast majority of cases, these placements have nothing to do with children's intellectual or verbal aptitudes.

This last point is powerfully illustrated in the research by Vernon-Feagans (1996) described in chapter 5. Examining children's language use in peer and sibling interactions during the summer before they entered kindergarten, Vernon-Feagans found that the working class Black children in the study were at least

as verbally sophisticated as the middle-class White children in the study, producing narratives that were longer and more imaginative than any produced
by their White counterparts. Nonetheless, when they arrived in kindergarten,
most of the African American children were placed in low-ability groups,
where they remained throughout the second grade when Vernon-Feagans and
her colleagues ended their study. Tracked into these low-ability groups, the
Black children spent large amounts of time filling out prepackaged worksheets
and received instruction that was frequently disorganized and sometimes actually incoherent.

The instruction the African American children received was in sharp contrast to what occurred in the overwhelmingly White high-ability groups where
instruction was more logically sequenced and considerably more intellectually
engaging. Ironically, Vernon-Feagans found that some of the rhyming activities teachers engaged in with the high-ability groups (while the low-ability
groups filled out worksheets) were strikingly similar to the rhyming games
that researchers had observed the African American children routinely playing
in their neighborhoods. Although Vernon-Feagans's study is unusual in terms
of the length of time she and her colleagues spent documenting children's verbal abilities before school entry, her description of the poor quality literacy
instruction they received once they arrived in school is highly consistent with
findings from the studies cited here.

Drawing on a number of those studies, Linda Darling-Hammond (1995)
describes the kinds of learning activities that constitute "reading instruction"
for children in these low-track placements:

> . . . students . . . too often sit at their desks for long periods of the day, match-
> ing the picture in column (a) to the word in column (b), filling in the blanks,
> and copying off the board. They work at a low cognitive level on fairly bor-
> ing literacy tasks that are profoundly disconnected from the skills they need
> to learn. Rarely are they given the opportunity to talk about what they know,
> to read real books or to construct and solve problems . . . (p. 183)

Clearly we are dealing here with the narrowest possible definition of reading.
Unfortunately, this same body of research also reveals that African American
children attending schools in high poverty areas do not have to be placed in a
low or remedial track to be likely recipients of low-quality literacy instruction
in which "teaching reading" becomes essentially synonymous with teaching
children to decode simple text.

Moving Toward Change

One of the most important suggestions that can be made to improve reading
outcomes for African American children in the early grades is for teachers
to clearly separate comprehension instruction from instruction in decoding.

As literacy educator Dorothy Strickland (2005) points out, while decoding or phonics instruction is undeniably an important component of early literacy instruction, it is by no means a *precursor* to it. She advises teachers to "allow neither students nor their parents to think they are receiving instruction in reading, when they are merely receiving instruction in phonics" (p. 153).

The distinction between comprehension and decoding is one that even young children are capable of making. As one illustration of how this distinction might be made for children, literacy educator Lucy Calkins (2001) offers the following example of a teacher talking with her first-grade class:

> "I'm going to tell a story, and I want you to really picture it in your minds. Here goes. Imagine that you can look inside your brain, and inside your brain you see lots of little people who look just like you do, and they all have jobs. When it's math time, you have some little people, the math people, that go to work."
>   . . . "Now look toward the front of your brain, right behind your forehead. There are a few of these little people. Their job is reading. They are the readers . . . First graders grow really strong at figuring out the words in books, and one of the workers does just that. He or she works really hard to figure out the words. We've all been getting good at that . . . There is another part of reading that we need to work on in this class and that is *thinking about the story*. The worker that does this has big ideas and helps us be sure we understand what we're reading. This is the thinking-about-books reader . . ." (p. 306)

As Calkins points out, there is "nothing magical" about the specific metaphor this teacher uses to make the distinction between comprehension and decoding understandable to her students. Other metaphors might have been chosen. What is essential is that children (and, Strickland would add, their families) understand that thinking, talking, and writing about stories read aloud by someone else constitutes "reading" every bit as much as sounding out words does.

The Critical Importance of Read-Alouds

It is important for teachers to begin capitalizing on Black children's sophisticated linguistic abilities from the moment they enter school. Thus while they are still working on their decoding skills, children need to be *simultaneously* and *extensively* engaged with texts that contain high level vocabulary, interesting and challenging content, and language that is as rich and complex as that routinely used in their own communities. Read-alouds are the principal vehicle for providing this engagement. Unfortunately, there is reason to believe that reading aloud is an activity particularly likely to get squeezed out of the instructional day in many classrooms, probably because it is not perceived as contributing in any direct way to children's knowledge about letter-sound relationships. In their study of 42 Head Start classrooms, for example, Dickinson and Sprague (2001) found that over a two-day period, only 65% of the teachers they observed spent any time at all reading aloud to children. What's more, the average length of time spent reading to children in these "read-aloud classrooms" was two minutes, and researchers observed little conversational interaction around the books.

This view of storybook reading by the teacher as essentially separate from the real nuts and bolts of learning to read is clearly borne out by my observations in primary classrooms serving large numbers of low-income Black children. In my experience, many teachers in such settings view reading aloud to children as an "extra" or "bonus," a pleasurable activity that provides a kind of balance to the serious literacy work that gets accomplished when children are doing phonics activities or sounding out words in their basal texts. As such, reading aloud is an activity that can easily be (and in my observation, often is) hurried through, or even dispensed with, when the schedule is tight.

It is not the actual experience of being read aloud to that matters so much, but rather the access to complex text that read-alouds afford. Without this access, the early literacy curriculum is essentially devoid of any literary or intellectual substance. It is true that children need extensive practice with the predictable text that characterizes basal readers and leveled books in order to learn how to decode. But if such necessarily simplified reading fare constitutes the majority of children's exposure to text in a classroom, then one can virtually guarantee poor outcomes for many Black children, especially those who enter school with little prior book experience and thus are more dependent on school for their introduction to the meaning and purposes of text. For Black children who have been socialized into a deep love for language in their communities, who create complex imaginative stories, rap songs, and play lyrics, who engage one another in verbal battles of wit and best their opponents in rhyme—for children whose *play* is conversation—being subjected to a literacy curriculum comprised almost entirely of basal reader selections and the literal, known-answer questions that typically follow can only be experienced as mindless, boring, and profoundly disconnected from most of what they have already learned and presumably come to love about language.

On the other hand, when teachers read books aloud to children and then create interesting and intellectually challenging learning activities around them, they open myriad possibilities of connection for children between what James Baldwin has called "[the] passion, [the] skill . . . the incredible music" of Black language and the metaphorical, magical world of literature. As well, they create opportunities for children to work on high-level vocabulary development and reading comprehension skills far in advance of their ability to actually decode text on their own.

Multiple Readings

It is important for books to be read aloud to children more than once. High-quality children's literature, almost by definition, begs rereading in order for children to fully explore its complexity. It is as if the initial reading of the book sets the stage for deeper engagement with the text on subsequent readings. Having established the broad outlines of character and plot the first time around, children's minds are freer to linger on the nuances, to puzzle out an initial confusion, to suddenly hear a word or turn-of-phrase unnoticed the first time the book was read. Consider, for example, the effect of multiple readings of the same book on children's acquisition of new vocabulary from text. While a large body of research suggests that books read aloud to children can be an important source of vocabulary development (Dickinson & Smith, 1994; Ewers & Brownson, 1999; Leung, 1992; Nagy, 2005; Robbins & Ehri, 1994), a number of studies further found that repeated readings of a text, as opposed to a single reading, resulted in significantly greater vocabulary learning (Cunningham, 2005; Elley, 1989; Senechal, 1997; Senechal & Cornell, 1993).

Written text not only contains more varied and unusual vocabulary than spoken language, but more complex syntax as well. Consider, for example, the following excerpt from *Leola and the Honeybears* (1999) by Melodye Benson Rosales, a picture book suitable for reading aloud to kindergartners:

> Now way down deep in the Pine Hollow Woods stood a charming little inn. It was owned by a family known as the Honeybears . . .
>   Woodland folks from far and near came to visit the Honeybears' inn. They dined on delicious daily delights like dandelion stew, double-dipped daffodil custard, and sweet daisy-dough cakes. Cheerful chatter and hearty laughter always filled the inn. (unnumbered pages)

It is through repeated readings that children come to eventually process and make sense of the unusual vocabulary and complex sentence structure of literary text. They are often aided in this process by the author's skillful use of repetition. In *Leola and the Honeybears*, for instance, Papa Honeybear sits on a "GREAT, BIG oak chair," Mama Honeybear on a "MIDDLE-SIZED easy chair" and Lil' honey on a "LITTLE wooden chair," adjectives repeated numerous times in the text (unnumbered pages). And Leola keeps remembering, and then dismissing, her Grandmama's rules about polite behavior using the same rhythmic phrasing each time, as illustrated in the following two examples:

> "I know my Grandmama said, 'Never go inside folks' houses until first being politely asked,' but I don't think she'd mind *this time*." (unnumbered pages)
>   "I know my Grandmama said, 'Never make yourself *too* comfortable in folks' houses until first being politely asked,' but I don't think she'd mind *this time*." (unnumbered pages)

These repetitive language chunks—often memorized through repeated readings by even very young children—become entry points or "bootstraps" into the discourse, anchoring children's developing understanding of the story as a whole.

Multiple readings of the same book serve the ends of comprehension in other ways as well. Many of the strategies that highly skilled readers employ to understand complex text—for example, making connections to prior knowledge, asking questions as they read, mentally summarizing a dense chunk of text—entail rereading (perhaps several times) significant portions of text. If teachers are going to use read-alouds effectively as a context for helping children develop sophisticated comprehension strategies, then they will need to model those strategies by doing what highly proficient readers actually do when processing rich text, such as pausing to reread and visualize the images in a passage filled with figurative language, or stopping to think through, and read again, a particularly difficult section of text. When teachers read a book straight through and never revisit it, children get the message that books are like so many other things in this society—to be rapidly consumed, perhaps only half-digested, and then quickly discarded for a new one. This is not a good message to be giving if we want children to be academically successful.

In an intellectual world where texts "speak" to other texts, where the meaning of an individual text is at least partially derived from, and consequently dependent upon, its relationship to other texts, no good book is ever "done." Consider an example from the academic literary tradition. William Faulkner takes the title for his novel *The Sound and the Fury* from the fifth act of Shakespeare's play *Macbeth,* and in doing so, establishes conditions whereby the reader must be familiar with a sixteenth-century play in order to fully understand the meaning embedded within his twentieth-century novel. Within the novel itself, one of the main characters, Quentin, has an obvious psychological forebear in the character Hamlet. Much of Quentin's musings on the day he commits suicide, for instance, are reminiscent of Hamlet's famous "to be or not to be" soliloquy. Although Hamlet is never directly mentioned within the novel, his words are echoed there. The reader who cannot "hear" Hamlet when Quentin speaks does not really hear all of what Quentin—and ultimately, of course, Faulkner—has to say.

At first glance, it may seem somewhat far-fetched to be drawing an analogy between academic literary traditions and read-alouds in the kindergarten and primary classroom. Not so, however. Consider, for example, how obviously *Leola and the Honeybears* speaks to *Goldilocks and the Three Bears.* The kindergarten and first-grade children who hear echoes of Goldilocks's story in Leola's have a richer appreciation for the story than those who do not. Similarly, when second- and third-graders view *Leola and the Honeybears* within the context of the African American folktale tradition, as reflected, for example, in the works of Virginia Hamilton, Julius Lester, and Patricia C. McKissack, not only is their understanding of these particular books deepened, but they also develop frames of analysis that can help them make meaning of other texts and of different folktale traditions. Not surprisingly, current reading research reveals that proficient readers are constantly making text-to-text connections as they read. Such connections do not leap off the page on first reading, however, especially when children are first learning to comprehend text. Rather, they emerge on second and third readings and as teachers model for children, and allow them to practice, the strategies skilled readers use to understand rich text.

Making Read-Alouds Magical

A number of years ago, I observed a first-grade "morning meeting," a time when children gather on the rug for calendar activities, sharing time, and, often, read-alouds. The teacher had asked me to come in and observe four African American children (there were 6 Black children in this class of 18) who, according to the teacher, routinely engaged in disruptive behaviors during meeting, such as calling out, talking with other children, hitting or poking classmates, and leaving the meeting area to play or stand in other parts of the room. On this particular morning, the student teacher was leading the meeting. As I watched events unfold, I did indeed record numerous instances of inattentive or disruptive behavior by these four children. I also noted the length of time during which children were expected to sit quietly while another child carried out a highly routinized, time-consuming task, such as searching for and attaching the correct felt numbers to the calendar or counting classmates to determine whether anyone was absent.

After the calendar activities, the student teacher read aloud a book about a little girl who feels sad because she doesn't receive an invitation to a birthday party. Although the reading was animated, the student teacher read in a very soft voice, making it difficult to hear her when there were noises or distractions in the room. She interrupted her reading several times because of the noise in the room. Twice she told the class that she would not continue reading until everyone was silent. Both times, however, she resumed reading while some children were still talking. When she finished the book, the student teacher invited children to share experiences of a time when they hadn't gotten invited to a party or when they felt left out in some way. Children called on for sharing remained in their places, and most spoke so quietly that it was difficult to hear what they were saying. They all looked at the student teacher when they spoke. Again, the student teacher interrupted the activity several times to ask for silence. She did not solicit children's responses, but called only on children whose hands were raised. None of the six African American children in the class raised their hands to speak. Along with a few others, the four African American children I had been asked to observe appeared totally disengaged from what was going on.

I recount this incident in detail here because I believe it is representative of what happens in some classrooms during "read aloud" time. Despite the teacher's laudable intention to engage children with text, the books that are chosen and the way they are read and discussed end up boring children rather than exciting their interest. I was not surprised that it was the African American children in particular who were so disengaged from the story and discussion in the circle time event described here. As discussed in part 2, many African American children have been raised in communities in which the standards of skilled oral performance are set very high. They are used to seeing adults who "hold the floor," not necessarily because of their particular social position (e.g., teacher, preacher, committee chair), but by virtue of their ability to use language well. As a consequence, many Black children expect adults, especially "adults in charge," to be able to handle themselves well verbally—to command authority with their voice and quick wit, and to speak and read with passion and energy. Thus, it is particularly important for teachers of African American children to practice reading aloud with enthusiasm and dramatic flair.

Some educators of young children believe that one of the most important function that read-alouds serve is to entice young children to fall in love with words. Many African American children are likely to enter school already in love with words. Talking about the love of words in the African American community, Toni Morrison compares their function to that of a preacher's: "to make you stand up out of your seat, make you lose yourself and hear yourself" (in LeClair, 1981, p. 27). In a sense, the teacher reading aloud must be like the preacher, making the language of text so magical and mesmerizing that children will literally "stand up out of their seats."

Based on an observational study of practices employed by 25 "expert" teachers (nominated for the study on the basis of their reputation and their students' high reading performance), Fisher, Flood, Lapp and Frey (2004) identified seven essential components of an effective interactive read-aloud:

1. Books chosen were appropriate to students' interests and matched to their developmental, emotional and social levels.
2. Selections had been previewed and practiced by the teacher.
3. A clear purpose for the read-aloud was established.
4. Teachers modeled fluent oral reading when they read the text.
5. Teachers were animated and used expression.
6. Teachers stopped periodically and thoughtfully questioned the students to focus them on specifics of the text.
7. Connections were made to independent reading and writing. (pp. 10–11)

In a follow-up study of 120 additional teachers who did not meet the same selection criteria, the researchers found that teachers did not typically employ all of these practices; in particular, "the data suggest that these teachers did not consistently preview and practice the books, provide models of fluent reading, or connect their read-aloud to other literacy activities" (p. 14). The researchers speculate that because the teachers did not consistently preview and practice books they had selected to read, they were unable to read them aloud in a fluent way. They write:

> The ability to fluently read text silently does not equate with the ability to fluently read text aloud. In other words, being a good reader is not sufficient. Teachers must also become good orators so that they can "tell the story" as they read it. This takes practice and coaching. We encourage teachers to practice reading selections aloud so that when they present them to their students they will be able to read with clarity and expression. They should also be able to use natural voice modulation to illustrate key points and changes in emotions without interrupting the listeners' "transfer of imagery" (Lipman, 1999) as they personally visualize the story. Teachers need to be well practiced because their voices are the vehicles that so fluidly convey the story and enable student listeners to develop their personal images and responses. (p. 15)

The 25 expert teachers the researchers observed not only read with animation and expression, typically changing their voice to represent different characters, but also used movement, hand gestures, facial expressions, and props of various kinds to perform the story they were reading. Because of their oral performative abilities, they made books come alive for children.

Creating Opportunities for Authentic Discussion

In the sharing time observation described previously, it was not only the student teacher's oral reading that may have been less than engaging for children, but also the slow pace and the rigid question/answer format of the ensuing "discussion," a format that provided no openings for children to voice their own reactions to or questions about the text. In my experience, Black children's comments and insights about text are most likely to surface when the interactional norms in the classroom allow children some degree of spontaneous entry into the instructional conversation. Teachers who insist that children can only speak when called upon and in response to specific questions posed by the teacher may never see the true extent of their African American students' critical engagement with text or the full range of their verbal abilities.

As the research discussed in chapter 5 suggests, the impressive verbal abilities that Black children are likely to bring with them to school are developed and displayed within the context of peer interactions and in community settings where the conditions and norms of interaction differ markedly from those found in school. The call-and-response style of interaction that characterizes communication in many African American social settings, for example, contrasts greatly with the teacher's strict control over speaker turns in most classrooms. Thus the kind of quick verbal comebacks and in-the-moment improvisation that identified children in Trackton (Heath, 1983) and in the Maple Street neighborhood (Goodwin, 1990) as being particularly verbally adept are unlikely to surface in the traditional classroom setting, where children are not expected—indeed, are not permitted—to make spontaneous responses to other people's speech. Interestingly, the teacher-controlled discussion format that prevails in many classrooms contrasts sharply with the interactional practices Haight observed in her study of the African American Sunday school described in chapter 5. In this Sunday school context, clearly a Black cultural space, children's spontaneous contributions to discussion occurred with regularity in all classes. Similarly, several studies of African American adult/child book interactions found that in reading books to young children, Black mothers asked fewer questions and allowed them to engage in more spontaneous commentary about the text than did their White counterparts (Anderson-Yockel & Haynes, 1994; Hammer, 2001).

Adherence to strict, teacher-designated turn-taking rules not only runs the risk of silencing children, but can also stifle critical thinking and limit children's full engagement with text. When children are allowed to build spontaneously upon one another's statements and ideas in discussion (i.e., Gates's notion of "repetition with a [signal] difference"), they often come up with insights and subtle nuances of meaning that seem clearly inspired by the collaborative nature of the interaction. As I have observed time and again, when children are actively encouraged to voice what they are thinking or wondering about during a book discussion, their questions and comments frequently push everyone's thinking in new directions.

One example that comes to mind (this one told to me by a teacher) involves a class discussion of *The Hard-Times Jar* (2003) by Ethel Footman Smothers. The main character in this story, eight-year-old Emma, loves books and writing stories more than anything else. She longs to own a book of her own, but she and her family are migrant workers with little money to spend "on extras" (unnumbered pages). When her parents enroll her in a local school, Emma is dazzled by her teacher's large collection of books and thrilled to find out that children can read as much as they want to during activity period. Even though the books aren't supposed to leave the classroom, one Friday Emma secretly borrows two of them to read at home. When her mother discovers the books under Emma's bed, she makes her return them and apologize to the teacher. She also gives Emma six quarters from the hard-times jar to buy a book of her own.

A teacher in one of my children's literature courses read this book aloud to her largely African American second-graders. Because this teacher actively encourages students to raise questions and make relevant observations during book reading and discussion, her children usually have a lot to say about books. They had many questions and "wonderings" about *The Hard-Times Jar. How come Emma loved writing stories so much? How did she make her books from grocery bags and safety pins? Could they try it? Could they write their own "Lizzy Lizard" stories?* Many children in the class didn't know that some migrant workers are African American, and they wanted to talk more about the lives of migrant workers. They had other questions as well. *Was it very wrong for Emma to take the books home? Did she intend to keep them?*

At one point, a child raised a question that seemed to be inspired by the illustration depicting Emma's apology to her teacher: "Does the teacher think Emma is lying?" This question eventually led children back to a discussion about the racial composition of Emma's classroom (she is the only Black person there) and then, not surprisingly, to some sensitive issues about race in their own school environment. This turned out to be an important discussion for the students and one that this teacher was convinced would not have occurred were it not for the open-ended discussion format in her classroom. Despite this open-ended format, the teacher says that she seldom has trouble with discipline or with children making silly or irrelevant remarks during book discussions because the majority of children are so intellectually and emotionally engaged in the conversation.

As discussed in part 2, many African American children are used to participating in social situations such as Sunday school, church services, family gatherings, and community events in which language is highly interactive. African American preachers, politicians, storytellers, teachers, and plain old conversationalists expect their listeners to interject comments into the discourse. In the communicative tradition in which many Black children are raised, sitting quietly while someone else speaks is neither a sign of engagement nor of respect, as it is in the mainstream, Eurocentric communicative tradition. Many African American children enter school expecting to be active in discourse and to be praised for skillful use of language. Thus when teachers create openings that invite their participation in authentic discussion, many Black children are likely to respond with insightful comments and with verbal facility.

Strategy Instruction

As emphasized earlier in this chapter, it is essential that systematic instruction in the comprehension of engaging, high-quality text begin as soon as children enter school rather than waiting upon children's ability to read independently. This does not mean, of course, that teachers shouldn't work simultaneously on helping children learn to decode text. On the contrary, the sooner children are reading books on their own, the better. The comprehension strategies that will be discussed in the next three chapters are ones that children can practice both with books read aloud by the teacher and with books they read on their own. However, long after children have acquired the ability to read text independently, read-alouds still serve an important function in literacy instruction by providing a shared context for teachers to talk about and model strategies for making meaning of complex text.

Increasingly over the past two decades, reading researchers have turned their attention to examining the reading process from the perspective of what skilled readers actually *do* when comprehending text. Collectively, this body of research has identified a number of important strategies that good readers consistently employ to facilitate their understanding of text (e.g., Dole, Duffy, & Rohler, 1992; Fielding & Pearson, 1994; Hansen, 1981; Harvey & Goudvis, 2000; Keene & Zimmerman, 1997; Palinscar & Brown, 1984; Pearson & Gallagher, 1983). The strategies of *connecting, visualizing, questioning, inferring* and *summarizing/retelling* are especially relevant to young readers. Many reading experts agree that these strategies should be taught explicitly to children beginning as early as the preschool level.

Although there is no generally agreed upon, set-in-stone order in which these strategies should be taught, many experts agree that connecting should come first as children's ability to make a meaningful connection to text is likely necessary for them to successfully employ other comprehension strategies. For example, children are not likely to focus on sensory images or infer deeper meanings in a text that bears no connection to their prior knowledge and experience. In this sense, connecting is probably the most fundamental comprehension strategy and the one with which most teachers will probably want to begin strategy instruction. Teachers need to spend a good chunk of time—six weeks or so, and perhaps even longer—helping children acquire reasonable facility with a particular strategy before they introduce another one. The goal is for children to develop a repertoire of strategies that they can draw on in conscious and deliberative ways as they encounter different kinds of text. Studies indicate that highly skilled readers are flexible in their use of strategies, often employing multiple strategies with a single text depending upon the specific characteristics of the text and their purposes for reading it. Thus it is clear that these strategies often support one another in aiding children's comprehension of complex text. Because children's ability to use multiple strategies is so important, in my discussion of strategies in subsequent chapters, I frequently draw on more than one strategy in discussing ideas for using particular books.

It is also clear that children do not master comprehension strategies once and for all. Children will likely, and should, revisit strategies they learn about in earlier grades. For example, children who practice making predictions and inferences about the books they read and listen to in first grade have much to gain from a focus on inferring in later grades, where they will doubtless explore the process of making inferences, as well as other strategies, in greater depth and detail. It is also important to note that researchers have identified a number of other comprehension strategies (e.g., determining importance, synthesizing) in addition to the five mentioned earlier. In my view, these are strategies more appropriate to slightly older students than the ones I focus on in this book.

In the next three chapters, I draw upon books from the corpus of African American children's literature to discuss the five strategies of connecting, visualizing, questioning, inferring, and summarizing/retelling. At the end of each chapter, I include additional recommended titles, along with suggested speaking and writing activities to extend and enhance the strategy instruction discussed in the chapter.

Chapter 7
Making Connections

Connecting to text by consciously activating prior knowledge is one of the most powerful strategies good readers use to aid comprehension. Before reading a book aloud, teachers often elicit such connections from children by asking questions designed to tap into their prior knowledge about important themes and experiences presented in the book. For example, prior to reading aloud Natasha Anastasia Tarpley's *I Love My Hair!* (1998), a story about a little girl getting her hair styled by her mother, a teacher might ask questions like the following: *How many people have had their hair combed or styled by someone else? Did you like it? How did it feel? What is one of your favorite hair styles?* Having children think about and share their answers to questions like these encourages them to make authentic connections with the story—for example, to empathize with the feelings of Keyana, the little girl in the book, and to visualize more vividly the scenes and situations Tarpley describes.

Asking children questions that help them connect with a book prior to hearing or reading it is an excellent method of enhancing their comprehension of the text. However, as with all the comprehension strategies that will be discussed, the primary goal of teaching students about connecting is for children to begin consciously using this strategy on their own, to purposefully call up experiences from their own lives that relate to the text at hand. To that end, children will need considerable practice with this strategy as well as many opportunities to hear their teacher model the strategy for them.

Drawing again on *I Love My Hair!* imagine that on her second reading of the book, a teacher pauses after the following passage:

> When Mama gets to especially tangled places, I try my hardest not to cry, sucking in my breath and pressing my hands together until they're red. But a few tears always manage to squeeze out. "Mama, stop!" I cry when I can't stand the comb tugging at my hair any longer. (unnumbered pages)

Let's assume that the teacher stops at this point because this passage conjures particularly vivid (and painful) memories of her own experiences when her big sister combed out her hair. The teacher begins modeling her connection by saying the following:

> This description of Keyana trying so hard not to cry and the way she has her face all scrunched up in this picture reminds me of when I was little and my big sister Yvonne used comb my hair out every Sunday night . . .

After describing her memory in a little more detail, the teacher underscores for children how making this personal connection to the text helps her to understand the story better. She says, *Remembering how it used to hurt so much when Yvonne pulled my hair makes it easier for me to sympathize with Keyana in this part of the story.* Teachers need to repeatedly model and emphasize the point that the purpose of making connections is to better understand the text. Otherwise, the process of "making connections" can become an end in itself, with children enthusiastically offering examples of connections only tangentially related to meaning in the text.

The Power of African American Connections

I Love My Hair! is a book with which many African American children easily connect because it describes a set of experiences with which most—girls *and* boys—are familiar. Unfortunately, however, this is not the case for many of the books used in early elementary classrooms, even in classes where the majority of children are African American. Many Black people have written with great eloquence about the difference it made in their own intellectual and emotional lives to encounter books written by and about other Black people (e.g., Gates, 1990; Harris, 1993; Malcolm X, 1965; Marshall, 1983). A sizeable number of African American children's writers have cited their desire to see more such books available to future generations of Black children as a major catalyst for their decision to write children's literature (e.g., Eloise Greenfield, Patricia McKissack, Walter Dean Myers, Andrea Davis Pinkney). Children need to see themselves represented in the pages of the books they read. Nothing is more critical to helping children make connections to text.

In my role as literacy educator, teachers often ask me what percentage of the literature they use in the classroom should represent African Americans and other people of color. My response is two-fold. First, I believe that regardless of the context in which they teach, all teachers have an obligation to insure that the literature they use and make available in the classroom is broadly representative of the racial and cultural diversity of the nation as a whole. Essentially this means that teachers should strive to include some literature in the curriculum that reflects the experiences and perspectives of at least the following large (and in themselves heterogeneous) groups: African Americans, Arab Americans, Asian Pacific Americans, Caribbean Americans, European Americans, Latinos, and Native Americans. Second, and just as importantly, teachers need to insure that a significant portion of the literature they use reflects the particular racial and cultural backgrounds of the students in their classrooms. This means, for example, that in a classroom made up primarily of African American children (as many classrooms in the United States are) the largest percentage of the literature used should be by and about Black people.

Finding this literature is not a difficult task. At this point in time, African American children's writers have produced a substantial body of literature of extraordinary quality on just about every topic of interest and relevance to early childhood and elementary school students—from alphabet and counting books to chapter books and novels dealing with preadolescent issues like identity, friendship, social values, and family conflict. While much of this literature contains visual images, language patterns and cultural references that reflect the lives of African American children, this cultural specificity does nothing to detract from the ability of this literature to simultaneously represent themes, values, and experiences of importance to a much broader range of children.

Eloise Greenfield's classic picture book *She Come Bringing Me That Little Baby Girl* (1974/1993), for example, contains illustrations of African American characters as well as some grammatical and intonational patterns that are characteristic of Black Communications, yet the story—about a little boy who wonders if his parents will love him as much after the birth of his sister—speaks to the fears of almost every child anticipating the birth of a sibling. Similarly, Natasha Anastasia Tarpley's *Bibbity Bop Barbershop* (2002), with its lively images of an African American barbershop on Saturday morning, is at once wonderfully evocative of Black cultural experience and potentially resonant with the experiences of any child spending special time with a father or other important adult. *Leola and the Honeybears* (1999) by Melodye Benson Rosales ostensibly retells the classic story of *Goldilocks and the Three Bears*, but in words and pictures that conjure up a Black cultural world and its values instead of a European one. Its success in representing themes of universal importance to children in ways that capture the particulars of Black experience is what makes the work of so many African American writers appropriate for use with all children, but particularly effective and compelling for use with Black children.

In *Because You're Lucky* (1997) by Irene Smalls, a boy named Jonathan has to make some hard adjustments when his younger cousin, Kevin, comes to live with the family. *Because You're Lucky* is a great book for illustrating and practicing the strategy of *connecting* because it contains many potential openings for children to make connections to their own experiences. For example, one common childhood experience dealt with in the book is the frustration of having to share someone you love and the feelings of loss, jealousy, and anger that can result. When Jonathan and Kevin get into a fight and Jonathan's mother refuses to take sides, Jonathan lashes out at his mother: " 'You always believe Kevin. You don't believe me. You're my mother. Not his. I hate Kevin' " (unnumbered pages). Also, like Jonathan, many children have had ambivalent feelings about a person or situation in their lives. In the story, Jonathan hates sharing his room with Kevin, but when Kevin moves into the guest room, Jonathan misses his company and can't get to sleep. And like Kevin in the story, many children have probably felt out of place and uncomfortable in a new situation at some point in their lives. As these examples illustrate, *Because You're Lucky* is filled with possible "connecting points" for children from a diversity of backgrounds. But what makes the book particularly powerful and easy to connect with for Black children is Smalls's success in evoking a Black cultural world. It is worth examining in some detail how she does that.

To begin, the book embodies a number of traditional African American core values and practices that have been described in the literature. One is the tradition of extended and fictive kinship discussed in chapter 2. Taking in and raising children not literally one's own is a traditional and highly valued practice within African American communities. Smalls illustrates the cultural value attached to this practice in the book's opening lines:

> The question traveled through the family like wild-fire. Cousin Cheryl called Great-Aunt Myrtle, who called Nana Louise, who called her goddaughter Yvonne, who called her brother Jimmy, who called Aunt Laura. Who was going to take Hazel's boy, Kevin? Softhearted Aunt Laura was the first to say yes. (unnumbered pages)

Another African American cultural value illustrated in the book is captured in the historic Black phrase "lifting as we climb," the notion that Black people who are more advantaged than others have an obligation to share with those less fortunate and to help them also achieve a more advantageous position in life, especially in terms of education. When Jonathan asks his mother why he has to share his clothes and other possessions with Kevin, she responds:

> "Because you're lucky. You have a home, a family, so many things, and so much love. You're lucky that you have so much. You can easily share some of it." (unnumbered pages)

The importance attached to family in African American culture is also clearly reflected in the book by the things Jonathan's mother says. She tells her children, for example, that " 'family has to stick together,' " and when Kevin feels bad because his cousins aren't very welcoming, she reassures him by saying, " 'They'll come around. You're family' " (unnumbered pages). Finally, the high value African American people place on literacy is subtly highlighted both in the written text and in the illustrations that accompany it. As Jonathan and

Kevin start to become closer, Jonathan shows him around the public library and teaches him how to use the computer, sharing with his cousin the things that he has learned to value. In illustrations depicting the family's home, books are prominently displayed, neatly arranged in bookcases and stacked in piles on tables and desks.

In addition to reflecting these important cultural values, the book also celebrates the physical beauty of African American people, both in the expressive faces depicted by the illustrator, Michael Hays, and in descriptions of people contained in the written text—e.g., "carmel-colored Kevin with the long curly lashes" and Jonathan with his "sturdy nut-brown body" (unnumbered pages). In terms of the language itself, *Because You're Lucky* contains many examples of the kind of rhythmic repetition and alliteration characteristic of many texts in the Black oral and written traditions. Here are two examples:

> He came without a toothbrush or a toy. He came without a change of clothes, and he came without a mommy or a daddy. (unnumbered pages)
>
> Jonathan had so many clothes and so many toys. They spilled out of drawers, were scattered on the floor of the closet, stuck out from under the bed, and sprawled on top of the dresser. (unnumbered pages)

It is important for teachers to model and to elicit from children connections to text that have to do with the kinds of specifically (though not necessarily exclusively) African American values and practices represented in *Because You're Lucky*. For instance, after reading the book aloud a couple times, the teacher might initiate a discussion about different kinds of blended families, perhaps focusing on the mother's statement: " 'Kevin wasn't mine before, but he's mine now' " (unnumbered pages). The teacher can ask questions that spark personal connections for children. Do their parents or other family members talk to them about the importance of sharing with and helping others? When Jonathan's mother says, " 'family has to stick together,' " do those words remind them of anything they've heard people in their family say? After reading this book aloud in a second-grade classroom a few years ago, I talked about all the books that appear in the illustrations. "This family must love to read," I observed, and then made a connection to Malcolm X's autobiography where he describes loving to read so much that the combined strength of 10 people could not have torn him away from his books.

In their portrayals of characters in a variety of historical and present day circumstances, many African American children's books reflect traditional African American beliefs about the power and importance of literacy and education. Highlighting these beliefs in talking about the books (as in the previous Malcolm X example) helps forge a strong connection between high academic achievement and African American cultural identity. A teacher I know in South Carolina, for example, read her third-grade class *More Than Anything Else* (1995) by Marie Bradby, a book narrated in the fictional voice of Booker

T. Washington. In the story the young boy Booker, newly freed from enslavement, has a burning desire to learn to read. Watching a Black man reading a newspaper aloud one day, he imagines his future:

> . . . I have found hope and it is as brown as me. I see myself the man. And as I watch his eyes move across the paper, it is as if *I* know what the black marks mean, as if *I* am reading. As if everyone is listening to *me*. I hold that thought in my hands. I will work until I am the best reader in the country. Children will crowd around me, and I will teach *them* to read. (unnumbered pages)

Although his family has little in the way of material things, Booker's mother somehow manages to get her son a book that starts him on his journey to literacy. After listening to this story, a student in the class raised his hand excitedly with an important connection: "It reminds me of what my grandmother always says—read, read, read." The teacher then pointed out to him that the boy in the story and the student's grandmother shared the same belief in the importance of reading, just like so many African Americans throughout history. In effect, the teacher told this child: *literacy is your cultural and historical legacy.*

As will be discussed in the section on visualizing in the next chapter, it is critical for teachers to also talk explicitly about the literary elements of text. Teachers' comments about stylistic features—even remarks as simple as *I love all those /k/ sounds in "Caramel-colored Kevin with the long curly lashes"* or *I really like how Smalls uses repetition here*—are a strong incentive for children to begin consciously noticing similar features in the language they hear at home, on the radio, in their church, and in other community and family settings. Discovering connections between the stylistic features used by people around them and the literary language of the books they read and listen to in school helps children relate to text in a deeper and more meaningful way. Thinking about those connections also fosters children's meta-linguistic awareness (i.e., the ability to think consciously not only about *what* is being said or written, but also about the *way* it is being said or written). Not surprisingly, this is an ability especially critical to good speakers and writers.

Text-to-Text Connections

The literature on comprehension instruction talks about three kinds of prior knowledge/experience connections that children need to learn to make: text-to-self, text-to-text, and text-to-world. Most of the examples I've talked about in this section so far have involved text-to-self connections in which readers consciously call up experiences from their own lives to better understand what they are reading or listening to. But when I talked about how I drew a connection between the family's apparent love of reading in *Because You're Lucky* and Malcolm X's statements about reading in his autobiography, I was making a text-to-text connection. The distinctions among these different kinds of connections are somewhat artificial. Nonetheless, they are useful to make in teaching because they encourage children to think in a very conscious way about the specific sources of knowledge they have available in making connections to text. Helping children learn to make text-to-text connections is particularly important. Being able to draw in a very deliberate way on books one has previously read in order to make sense of a new book is an essential academic skill. Throughout their years in school, in every subject they study, students will be continuously called upon to weigh and compare information and ideas from various sources. Understanding how texts "speak" to other texts is thus critical to school success.

Thematic Connections Among Texts

One way that teachers can encourage children to see and make text-to-text connections is by selecting a number of books for instruction that focus on the same theme. There are many possibilities here. Some themes that are especially appropriate to African American children's literature include the following: *family; friendship; standing up and speaking out; music, art and dance; literacy for freedom; pursuing your dreams; conflict resolution; folktale wisdom; dealing with racism and injustice; celebrating community*; and *storytelling*. Books about Black history constitute a kind of "supra-theme" in African American children's literature. These include both fictional and nonfictional accounts of major historical events and time periods (e.g., enslavement, the Great Migration North, the Harlem Renaissance, the Great Depression, the Civil Rights Movement) and biographies of famous Black Americans. When teachers read and discuss multiple books about the same time period or the same historical figure, children have a chance to experience how their understanding of a new book is deepened when they think consciously about things they've already learned about the subject matter through previous reading.

For example, *Langston Hughes: American Poet* (2002) by Alice Walker and *Coming Home: From the Life of Langston Hughes* (1994) by Floyd Cooper are two picture book biographies (appropriate for use with third-, fourth-, and fifth-graders) that paint quite different, but essentially complementary, portraits of the life of Langston Hughes. By first reading the shorter book by Cooper, teachers help children acquire a framework or "mental map" for making sense of Walker's more detailed portrayal of Hughes's life. Both books deal with the major figures in Hughes's early life—his mother, father, and grandmother—but each author describes these characters and their influences on Hughes in different ways. Discussing and comparing these descriptions not only helps children acquire a richer, more complex picture of Hughes's life, but also helps them see that writers bring their own individual slant or perspective to the people and events they write about.

In order to illustrate how knowledge from one source helps a reader more fully comprehend another book on the same topic, the class could compile a list of all the things they learned about the life of Langston Hughes from reading or listening to Cooper's book. Then after completing Walker's book, children could expand this list, adding both new knowledge they've gained about Hughes's life and ways in which they saw these two books "speaking" to each other. Here is just one example. As its title suggests, *Coming Home* represents Hughes's life as a continuous search for home, first, as a child, in a physical place, and later, as an adult, in his connection to Black people and to his poetry. Although Walker does not talk explicitly about home as a theme in Hughes's life, the teacher might ask children to think about how Cooper's notion of home helps them better understand some of the events from Hughes's life that Walker describes (e.g., Hughes's decision to attend Columbia University because of its proximity to Harlem).

The teacher might also read aloud more of Hughes's poetry (there are two examples in the Walker text). The teacher could read as well *Visiting Langston* (2002) by Willie Perdomo, about a little girl poet who goes with her father to visit the house where Hughes once lived in Harlem, and *Love to Langston* (2002), Tony Medina's biography in poems. Afterward, if one of the students hasn't already done so, the teacher might point out to children how much more understandable and meaningful these books were for them as a result of their already knowing so much about Langston Hughes.

Books with Recurring Characters

In addition to using multiple books on the same theme, another way in which teachers can both teach and encourage text-to-text connections is by using books with recurring characters. Reading books with characters who reappear in a series allows children to develop a store of background knowledge about a set of characters that they can use to make predictions about how those characters are likely to behave in new situations. Each of the six books in the Jamaica series by Juanita Havill, for example, deals with a problem that a little girl named Jamaica must figure out how to solve (often with the good advice of her parents). In *Jamaica's Blue Marker* (1995), the fourth book in the series, Jamaica's problem is Russell, a little boy who's always bothering her in school—borrowing her markers, messing up her pictures, and throwing sand at her on the playground. One day the teacher tells the class that Russell and his family are moving. She suggests that the class make cards to say goodbye. Angry with Russell for all the things he's done to her, Jamaica doesn't want to make him a card. Reading this book aloud in a kindergarten classroom, I stopped after the following passage:

> Mrs. Wirth passed out paper. Then she showed everyone how to fold the paper into a card. Jamaica didn't want to make a card for Russell. She was

glad he was moving. Then he wouldn't bother her anymore. She put the paper in her desk. (unnumbered pages)

"Hmmm," I said, "I wonder if Jamaica is going to end up making Russell a card or not. This is the fourth Jamaica book we've read. All of you know a lot about Jamaica. Based on everything you know about her from the other books we've read, what do you predict? Will Jamaica make a card for Russell?" In the discussion that followed, I tried to get children to articulate as clearly as possible what it was we had read in the previous Jamaica books that influenced their predictions. One of my goals in the discussion was to help make children consciously aware of how they were using knowledge from the books we had already read to better understand the Jamaica book we were currently reading. I reminded them that making those connections is something all good readers do and that they were becoming very good readers.

Unfortunately, at this point in time, there are not a lot of books available with recurring African American characters. This makes the ones that do exist, such as the Jamaica series, the Everett Anderson series by Lucille Clifton, and the Little Bill series by Bill Cosby, especially valuable. In addition to their usefulness in teaching text-to-text connections, in my experience, these books also foster deep personal connections to text for many children. When this happens, teachers can encourage children to make up new adventures for their favorite characters during writing time.

Doing an Author Study

Having children read or listen to books by the same author is still another way for teachers to encourage text-to-text connections. One of the most successful "author studies" that teachers with whom I have worked over the years have done in their classrooms includes five books by Patricia C. McKissack, each featuring a little girl protagonist: *Flossie and the Fox* (1986), *Mirandy and Brother Wind* (1988), *Nettie Jo's Friends* (1989), *The Honest-to-Goodness Truth* (2000), and *Goin' Someplace Special* (2001). The five girls in these books are among the most delightful and engaging heroines in children's literature. Each goes on a journey of sorts and must face and overcome obstacles along the way. If she is to make it to Miz Viola's with her basket of eggs, Flossie must first outwit a clever fox. To capture the wind and win the junior cakewalk dance, Mirandy must keep trying in the face of failure and seek answers where others are afraid to go. In order to find the sewing needle she desperately needs, Nettie Jo has to come to the aid of others and to summon the courage to enter the scary woods. Libby Louise cannot reach an understanding of the "honest-to goodness truth" without first figuring out how to see beyond the literal, an enterprise that almost costs her all her friends. And to get safely to "someplace special," the city's public library, 'Tricia Ann must confront and deal with the racism that assails her on the way. Although all of these books are set in an earlier time period (the most "modern" is *The Honest-to-Goodness Truth,* set in the 1950s), the dilemmas these girls face are highly relevant to the lives of children in the twenty-first century. What does it mean to tell the truth? How does one persevere in the face of racism? How can one overcome an adversary bigger, and seemingly more powerful, than oneself?

While the girls' journeys differ in their particulars, the strengths that each one brings to the challenges she faces are remarkably similar. These strengths are rooted in traditional African American cultural values. The behavior of all five girls, for example, demonstrates their ability to think quickly and to use the power of the mind to figure a way out of difficult circumstances. Flossie ends up outwitting the fox by pretending not to believe he's really a fox. Having succeeded in capturing Brother Wind to be her partner at the cakewalk dance, once there, Mirandy realizes that she really wants to dance with Ezel instead and quickly figures out an imaginative solution to her dilemma. Similarly, when confronted with the problems of various animals she encounters on her journey, Nettie Jo comes up with ingenious remedies using the old discarded items she's collected along the way. As Libby Louise's truth-telling adventures keep going wrong, she thinks about why—looking at ideas "from the outside in, and then from the inside out"—and eventually arrives at a clear understanding of her problem (unnumbered pages). Finally, in *Goin' Someplace Special,* 'Tricia Ann mentally overcomes the humiliation of having to sit in the back of the bus by consciously setting her mind on something else.

While each of these heroines has the courage to speak her mind when necessary, they are all unfailingly polite and courteous, especially to their elders. The mannerly Flossie even curtsies for the fox on first introduction. When the conjure woman asks Mirandy why she's come, Mirandy reflects that, as a conjure woman, Mis Poinsettia should already know, but carefully refrains from saying so for fear of sounding sassy, the same reason why Libby Louise is so reluctant to tell Miz Tusselbury her real opinion of her overgrown garden. On the crowded city bus, 'Tricia Ann gives up her seat for her grandmother's friend, Mrs. Grannell, and Nettie Joe "spoke politely" to Miz Rabbit (unnumbered pages). Conjuring up a Black cultural world, adults in these books are almost always described and addressed with the traditional African American forms of politeness discussed at length in chapter 2, title plus name—for example, "Mr. John Willis, the hotel's doorman" (*Goin' Someplace Special,* unnumbered pages).

Unlike a classic pattern found in European American children's literature, in which protagonists undertake a solitary journey relying solely on their own individual resources to overcome the challenges encountered (e.g., *Hansel and Gretel; In the Night Kitchen* [Sendak, 1970]), the girls in the McKissack books draw strength and courage from the advice of their elders and from their reliance on traditional African American values. Setting off into the woods with her basket of eggs, Flossie is momentarily afraid: "'What if I come upon a fox?'" she thinks, but then remembers her grandmother's words ("'a fox be just a fox'") and decides "'that aine so scary'" (unnumbered pages). Just so, at the lowest point on her journey to the library, 'Tricia Ann calls up her grandmother's words ("'You are somebody . . .'") for strength to keep going. In her search for what it means to tell the truth, Libby discusses the question with both her mother and her elderly neighbor, Miz Tusslebury. In similar fashion, in looking for ideas about how to capture Brother Wind, Mirandy sounds the wisdom of her entire community, beginning with her grandmother and ending with the conjure woman, Mis Poinsettia. Finally, Nettie Jo succeeds in obtaining a sewing needle not because of her sharp eyesight (finding a needle in the countryside doubtless being even less likely than finding one in a haystack), but because of her courtesy and kindness toward others, traditional African American values that the other four girls also display. In addition, perseverance, determination, and coolness under pressure are other important cultural values all five enact.

Representing both general linguistic diversity within the African American speech community and distinctive linguistic patterns associated with specific time periods, the characters in these books use a variety of speech patterns and styles. They also display nonverbal behaviors often associated with the Black speech community—for example, hands on hips, shoulders squared in determination, head tossed in the air. In *Flossie and the Fox*, Big Mama "clicked her teeth and shook her head" (unnumbered pages). These books, especially *Mirandy and Brother Wind, Flossie and the Fox,* and *Nettie Jo's Friends*, are also distinguished by McKissack's use of lexical items associated with the African American speech community at an earlier time in history. (One child referred to these as "McKissack words.") "'**Why come** Mr. J.W. can't catch the fox with his dogs?'" Flossie asks her grandmother. "'**Why come** you here?'" "Mis Poinsettia asks Mirandy. Big Mama warns Flossie to "'**be particular** 'bout them eggs,'" and Mama Frances tells 'Tricia Ann: "'I trust you'll **be particular**, and remember everything I've told you.'" Mirandy "**commenced** to grinding pepper," Flossie "**commenced** to skip along," and Libby Louise's eyes **commenced** to fill with water.'" And at one point or another in their adventures, Mirandy "got **purely** upset," Libby Louise "was **purely** surprised," and Flossie declared: "'I just **purely** don't believe it.'" Finally, there are all the adverbs ending in *like* instead of *ly* as in this example from *Nettie Jo's Friends:* "'Girl,' she say real **confident-like**, 'I'm gon' go gathering and find us a needle.'" Other examples of "like adverbs" from the books include the following: **matter-of-fact-like, unsteady-like, disgusted-like, quiet-like, stern-like**, and **determined-like**. There are many other examples of distinctive vocabulary in these books that children find intriguing and quickly come to identify as "markers" of McKissack's writing.

Familiarity with an author's characteristic themes and writing style helps readers make mental predictions about what a "new" book by the same author is going to be like. Asking children to think aloud about predictions they have about a book based on their prior knowledge about the author enables them to see and name patterns in the books that might otherwise have escaped their conscious awareness (e.g., "It's going to be about a girl and she has to solve a problem"; "I think she's going to use different words from us"; "There's going to be a grandmother."). This heightened awareness of patterns across texts helps children become deeper, more insightful readers. Even predictions that turn out to be wrong in a literal sense can lead children to understand textual patterns and connections in a more complex and nuanced way (e.g., "There wasn't a grandmother, but Miz Tusslebury is kind of like a grandmother.").

As I hope my detailed description of these five McKissack books illustrates, many of their intertextual connections have to do with cultural patterns and practices that are specifically (though not exclusively) African American—for example, using the power of the mind to overcome obstacles, standing up and speaking out, drawing on the wisdom of elders, persisting in the face of racism, remaining cool under pressure, making quick verbal comebacks, displaying respect and kindness toward others, using expressive body language. One of the purposes good literature serves is to reinforce cultural values and practices essential to a people's survival. In this sense, having children practice making text-to-text connections with literature from the corpus of major African American writers like McKissack not only accomplishes the end of good strategy instruction, but also helps children make meaning of their own experiences within the broader, collective context of African American historical and cultural experience.

Text-to-World Connections

Text-to-world connections extend out to the world at large and, very importantly, to the world of nonfiction text as well. Children need experience reading and listening to a variety of written genres, including nonfiction, informational text. One way that teachers can incorporate nonfiction text into the literacy curriculum is by having the class explore topics related to the stories used for read-alouds. There are many possibilities. For instance, Lenny Hort's *How Many Stars in the Sky?* (1991), in which a boy and his dad explore the night sky together, could launch a class exploration of the solar system. There are many informational texts about stars and the solar system suitable for use with children as young as preschool age (e.g., *I Am a Star* (2001) by Jean Marzollo, *Our Stars* (2002) by Anne Rockwell, and *Zoo in the Sky: A Book of Animal Constellations* (1998) by Jacqueline Mitton).

Reading stories about Anansi the spider, as well as other folktales in which animals appear as characters, could lead to children doing research on animals featured in the tales. After doing this research and finding out as much as possible about the animals' characteristics and habitats, an interesting question for children to speculate upon is why particular animals—the spider, the fox, and the rabbit, for instance—should figure so prominently in African American folktales.

Three picture books about the life of Michael Jordan—*For the Love of the Game: Michael Jordan and Me* (1997) by Eloise Greenfield, *Salt in His Shoes: Michael Jordan in Pursuit of a Dream* (2000) by Deloris Jordan, and *Jump: From the Life of Michael Jordan* (2004) by Floyd Cooper—all focus primarily on Jordan's determination and willingness to work hard in pursuit of his dreams. For interested children, these books could lead to further nonfiction reading about basketball as well as about other sports and prominent sports figures. Reading aloud *Just Like Josh Gibson* (2004) by Angela Johnson, about a girl in the 1940s who wants to play basketball, and *Allie's Basketball Dream* (1996) by Barbara E. Barber, about a contemporary girl who loves to shoot hoops, could easily inspire a nonfiction study of women in sports.

A Net to Catch Time (1997) by Sara Harrell Banks, *Father and Son* (1992) by Denize Lauture, *Beauty, Her Basket* (2004) by Sandra Belton, *New Year Be Coming!* (2002) by Katherine Boling, *Circle Unbroken: The Story of a Basket and Its People* (2004) by Margot Theis Raven, and *Little Muddy Waters: A Gullah Folk Tale* (1997) by Ronald Daise all center on Gullah culture and life in the Sea Islands off the coast of Georgia and South Carolina. Nonfiction study based on these books could lead in several directions, including exploration of African American history, of geography, and even of marine animals (a topic especially appealing to young children). *Father and Son* is illustrated with the work of the world-famous Sea Island artist Jonathan Green, opening up the possibility of children pursuing further study of his life and work.

Finally, let me offer one more example from a list that could easily fill a chapter in itself. A recurring image or trope within African American children's literature is the train, both literal trains that often transport children to the South to visit relatives and the metaphoric freedom train that traveled on the Underground Railroad to freedom in the North. That trains should be recurring images in African American children's literature is not surprising. Because of its long association with freedom, the train is an image with deep symbolic significance in African American history. In addition, throughout much of the twentieth century, when even advanced educational credentials did not guarantee decent jobs for Black people, many Black men were able to obtain relatively well-paying jobs as Pullman porters on the railroads. In *Mac and Marie and the Train Toss Surprise* (1993) by Elizabeth Fitzgerald Howard, a brother and sister eagerly await the surprise their Uncle Clem, a porter on the Seaboard Florida Limited, has promised to toss from the train as it travels through their town on its way north to Baltimore. Books like *Mac and Marie and the Train Toss Surprise* and Vaunda Micheaux Nelson's *Almost to Freedom* (2003), set during the period of enslavement, can be used as jump-ing-off points for exploring the history of the Underground Railroad, the story of the Pullman porters, or even railroad history and information about trains in general. In many parts of the country, trains are still an important means of transportation. Taking the class to visit a train station (perhaps even taking a train ride) is a great way for a teacher to foster text-to-world connections. Children who return from an adventure at the train station to reread or listen again to a book in which a train figures centrally are likely to hear that same story with a new level of awareness.

Other Kinds of Text-to-World Connections

As this last example illustrates, text-to-world connections don't always involve books. Andrea Davis Pinkney's engaging biographies *Duke Ellington: The Piano Prince and His Orchestra* (1998) and *Ella Fitzgerald: The Tale of a Vocal Virtuosa* (2002), for instance, are made even more magical and mean-ingful to children when they can actually listen to recordings the teacher brings in of the artists' music. Consider another example. Deborah Hopkinson has written two picture books that depict the role that quilts may have played in signaling and directing travelers on the Underground Railroad: *Sweet Clara and the Freedom Quilt* (1993), mentioned in chapter 2, and *Under the Quilt of Night* (2001). Children will gain a better understanding of how secret messages may have been embedded in quilt patterns—and thus a better understanding of Hopkinson's books—when they can experiment with pattern making them-selves (an interesting map-making activity appears at the end of *Sweet Clara and the Freedom Quilt*).

As still another example of text-to-world connections, imagine that you are studying the Civil Rights era in your third-grade classroom. One of the ways that you've decided to study this period in history is by reading aloud (and having children read) fictional accounts of children's experiences dur-ing this time. You've probably read to your students *The Other Side* (2001) by Jacqueline Woodson, *Fishing Day* (2003) by Andrea Davis Pinkney, and *Freedom Summer* (2001) by Deborah Wiles, all books about children who bravely reach across the rigidly enforced racial divide to extend friendship or kindness to another child. You've also read to them Carol Weatherford's *Free-dom on the Menu* (2005), an account of the Greensboro sit-ins told from the perspective of a child, and *A Sweet Smell of Roses* (2005) by Angela Johnson about two girls who participate in a Civil Rights march, and of course *Goin' Someplace Special*. In addition, you've been able to purchase multiple copies of Patricia C. McKissack's *Abby Takes a Stand* (2005), a fictional story about a 10-year-old girl who takes an active role in her community's struggle for equal rights in Nashville, Tennessee in 1960. Because it's at an appropriate reading level for them, many of the children in your class are reading this book independently and discussing it in their literature circles (or as you and your class refer to them, "literary societies"). Discussions about all these books have been exciting ones, with children drawing many interesting and thought-provoking connections among the various books. As a result of their reading and discussions, you believe that your students are not only becoming better, more strategic comprehenders of text, but are also developing a deep, multilayered understanding of this historic time period.

Then, one day during a particularly exuberant book discussion, you suddenly realize that you've overlooked one important source of potential text-to-world connections for the children in your class: the memories of their own family members and of other people in the community who, like the book characters, were also children during the Civil Rights era. Inspired by Casey King's and Linda Barrett Osborne's *Oh, Freedom!: Kids Talk About the Civil Rights Movement With the People Who Made It Happen* (1997), you decide to address this oversight by having children interview adults in their families and communities, and you invite some of these adults to speak to the class. You are amazed at how much richer your children's insights are as a result of listening to adults from their communities talk about their experiences and their own self-to-text connections with the books the class has been reading. What is even more amazing to you is how much your students are learning about what good readers do. You think about this in the coming weeks every time you hear children in a book discussion say something like, "I talked to my auntie about her experience . . ." or "I asked my dad about that. . . ."

Speaking and Writing Connections

Recommended Books for Connecting

The following African American children's books are excellent choices for modeling and practicing *connecting*. Speaking and writing routines that encourage children to share personal stories related to the literature—both orally and in writing—deepen comprehension and help children develop a sense of narrative structure.

Saturday at the New You (1994) by Barber E. Barber

Young Shauna spends a day at her mother's hair salon.

Speaking: Ask children to share their experiences at the beauty or barber shop. Invite family members and other people from the community to talk about their beauty and barber shop experiences and about hairstyles that were popular when they were growing up.

Writing: Visit a local beauty or barber shop. Afterward, have children write a language experience story about their visit.

Grade Levels: Kindergarten and first

Thematic Connections:

Battle-Lavert, G. (1994). *The barber's cutting edge.*
Grimes, N. (1997). *Wild, wild, hair.*
Hilliard-Nunn, N. P. (1997). *Foluke: The Afro queen.*
Tarpley, N. A. (1998). *I love my hair!*
Tarpley, N. A. (2002). *Bippity Bop barbershop.*
Yarbrough, C. (1979). *Cornrows.*

<hr>

Shades of Black: A Celebration of Our Children
(2000) by Sandra L. Pinkney

Color photographs and a poetic text celebrate the physical beauty and diversity of African American children.

Writing: After reading the book aloud, help children make life-size self-portraits by tracing each other's body outlines on large pieces of butcher paper. After cutting out the outlines, children can use a variety of art materials to add their hair, facial features, skin color, and clothing. Have children write or dictate sentence strips describing their special features (e.g., *My hair is as soft as cotton balls; My skin is the color of butterscotch*) to attach to their self-portraits.

Speaking: Hang the self-portraits in the classroom and host an "art opening" for families and/or another class in the school. Children can introduce their portraits and recite their sentence strips.

Grade Levels: Kindergarten and first

Thematic Connections:

Hooks, Bell. (2002). *Homemade love.*
Hudson, C. W. and Ford, B. G. (1990). *Bright eyes, brown skin.*
Myers, W. D. (1993). *Brown angels: An album of pictures and verse.*
Smith, C., Jr. (2000). *Brown sugar babies.*

<hr>

Jamaica Tag-Along (1989) by Juanita Havill

<hr>

Jamaica's big brother, Ossie, won't let her play basketball with the boys.

Speaking: Invite children to share an experience about a time when they couldn't play or got left out. Encourage children to draw on their own experiences as they debate whether or not Ossie should have let Jamaica play.

Writing: Have children draw and write or dictate a story about a time when they had fun playing with an older or younger friend.
Grade Levels: Kindergarten and first

Thematic Connections:
Barber, B. E. (1996). *Allie's basketball dream.*
Johnson, A. (2004). *Just like Josh Gibson.*
Rodman, M. A. (2005). *My best friend.*

When I Was Little (1992) by Toyomi Igus

Noel is visiting his Grandpa Will in the country. While they are fishing at the river, Grandpa Will compares life now to what it was like when he was a little boy.

Speaking: Have children interview a grown-up in their family about differences between life now and when they were little. Encourage children to make text-to-world connections by debating whose life was more fun: Grandpa Will's "back in the day" or Noel's today.
Writing: On paper divided in half and labeled "Then" and "Now," have children illustrate and write about one difference between their own lives and the childhood memories of the grown-up they interviewed.
Grade Levels: First and second

Thematic Connections:
Johnson, D. (2000). *Quinnie blue.*

The Patchwork Quilt (1985) and *Tanya's Reunion* (1995) by Valerie Flournoy

In these stories, Tanya learns precious lessons from her grandmother about the value of family traditions and the importance of working together.

Speaking: Ask children to share their experiences with a grandparent or beloved elder. Children can also share stories about family reunions, celebrations, and traditions, such as quilt making. Invite family members to share family stories and traditions with the class.
Writing: Have children write two or more family stories featuring the same central characters.
Grade Levels: First and second

Thematic Connections:
Crews, D. (1991). *Bigmama's.*

Pinkney, G. J. (1992). *Back home.*
Pinkney, G. J. (1994). *The Sunday outing.*
Taulbert, C. L. (1999). *Little Cliff and the porch people.*
Taulbert, C. L. (2001). *Little Cliff's first day of school.*
Woodson, J. (1998). *We had a picnic this Sunday past.*

From Miss Ida's Porch (1993) by Sandra Belton

People gather on a porch to tell family stories.

Writing: Children can collect their own family stories. Have them choose a favorite to write and illustrate. Compile the stories into a class book of "porch stories."

Speaking: Children can build a "porch set" and perform their stories for other classes and/or for families.

Grade Levels: Second and third

Thematic Connections:

Hopkinson, D. (1999). *A band of angels: A story inspired by the Jubilee Singers.*
Howard, E. F. (1991). *Aunt Flossie's hats (and crab cakes later).*
Johnson, A. (1989). *Tell me a story, Mama.*
Medearis, A. S. (1994). *Our people.*
Nolen, J. (1999). *In my momma's kitchen.*
Rochelle, B. (1998). *Jewels.*
Wood, M., & Igus, T. (1996). *Going back home: An artist returns to the South.*

Louise's Gift (1996) by Irene Smalls

Nana, the eldest member of Louise's family, gives each of the children in the family a symbolic gift. When Louise receives a rumpled piece of blank paper, she is disappointed with her gift until events later in the day help her understand that she has the gift of creativity.

Speaking: Encourage children to talk with peers and family members about what makes them special.

Writing: After children have come up with several qualities that make them special, ask them to write a short essay describing the one quality of which they are most proud. Children can also describe, in words and illustrations, a symbolic gift they would like to give a special person in their lives.

Grade Levels: Second and third

Thematic Connections:
Cosby, B. (1997). *The treasure hunt.*
Curtis, G. (1998). *The bat boy and his violin.*
Medearis, A. S. (1994). *Annie's gifts.*
Miller, Tom. (1996). *Can a coal scuttle fly?*
Walter, M. P. (1999). *Suitcase.*

---

*The Palm of My Heart: Poetry by African American Children (*1996) edited by Davida Adedjouma

---

This collection of poetry written by African American children between the ages of 8 and 14 celebrates the joys of being Black.

Writing: Using these poems as inspiration, encourage children to write their own identity poems.
Speaking: Invite children to recite their poems in an assembly for families and/or other classes in the school.
Grade Levels: Third and fourth

Thematic Connections:
Adoff, A. (1973/2002). *Black is brown is tan.*
Grimes, N. (1997*). It's raining laughter.*
hooks, b. (2004). *Skin again.*
Lester, J. (2005). *Let's talk about race.*

Delivering Justice: W. W. Law and the Fight for Civil Rights (2005) by Jim Haskins

---

A biography of Westley Wallace Law, a mail carrier in Savannah, Georgia who helped organize a boycott of downtown stores during the Civil Rights Movement. The biography illustrates how ordinary people can become leaders and heroes in the struggle for social justice.

Speaking: Organize children into pairs or small groups and invite them to brainstorm ideas for making their class or school a better and more equitable place.
Writing: Have partners write an action plan for change to present to the class.
Grade Levels: Third and fourth

Thematic Connections:
Bridges, R. (1999). *Through my eyes.*
Evans, F. W. (2001). *A bus of our own.*
Giovanni, N. (2005). *Rosa.*
Myers, W. D. (2000). *Malcolm X: A fire burning brightly.*
Myers, W. D. (2004). *I've seen the promised land: The life of Dr. Martin Luther King, Jr.*
Pinkney, A. D. (2000). *Let it shine: Stories of Black women freedom fighters.*
Ringgold, F. (1995). *My dream of Martin Luther King.*

Sometimes My Mommy Gets Angry (2003) by Bebe Moore Campbell

Annie must draw upon her inner resources in order to cope with her mother's mental illness and sometimes erratic, hurtful behavior.

Speaking: Ask children to think about and share their own strategies for coping with difficulties. Invite guest speakers to talk about their special strategies for dealing with difficult circumstances.

Writing: On note cards, have children write and illustrate affirmations and "powerful strategies." Create a class book of empowering strategies. Children can also write letters of admiration and encouragement to the character Annie.

Grade Levels: Third and fourth

Thematic Connections:
McKissack, P. C. (2001). *Goin' someplace special.*
Medearis, A. S., & Medearis, M. (2000). *Daisy and the doll.*
Ringgold, F. (1991). *Tar beach.*

Chapter 8
Visualizing and Inferring

Visualizing—the process of forming mental images as you read—has been identified as an important strategy that highly proficient readers use to deepen their understanding of both fiction and nonfiction. But the special properties of children's fiction make it an especially appropriate genre for introducing students to the practice of visualizing as they read. One of the distinguishing characteristics of high-quality children's fiction is its reliance on figurative language and on "sound effects" to create meaning. The following passage is taken from Julius Lester's *John Henry* (1994), a picture book account of the life of the legendary Black hero John Henry, reputed to have had superhuman strength and monumental courage. As you read it, try to visualize the scene Lester is describing, allowing his words to form pictures in your mind. When you have finished, take a few moments to reflect on how Lester's use of figurative language and his plays on the sounds of words aided you in your effort to create mental images as you read:

> Chips and dust were flying from the boulder so fast that John Henry vanished from sight. But you could still hear his hammers—RINGGGG! RINGGGG!
>
> The air seemed to be dancing to the rhythm of his hammers. The boss of the road crew looked up. His mouth dropped open. He pointed into the sky.
>
> There, in the air above the boulder, was a rainbow. John Henry was swinging the hammers so fast, he was making a rainbow around his shoulders. It was shining and shimmering in the dust and grit like hope that never dies. . .
>
> John Henry sang and he hammered and the air danced and the rainbow shimmered and the earth shook and rolled from the blows of the hammer. Finally, it was quiet. Slowly the dust cleared.
>
> Folks could not believe their eyes. The boulder was gone. In its place was the prettiest and straightest road they had ever seen. Not only had John Henry pulverized the boulder into pebbles, he had finished building the road.

> In the distance where the new road connected to the main one, the road crew saw John Henry waving good-bye, a hammer on each shoulder, the rainbow draped around him like love. (unnumbered pages)

One of the things that may have struck you as you read this passage is the sheer number of visual and aural images it contains. Figures of motion predominate: chips and dust flying, air dancing, hammers swinging, rainbow shimmering, the earth shaking and rolling. Like many writers of folktales, throughout the book Lester uses *similes* (comparisons that typically include the word *like* or *as*) to create colorful and unusual images. This particular passage from the book contains two. In the third paragraph, the rainbow is described as "shining and shimmering in the dust and grit *like hope that never dies*," and the end of the passage contains an image of John Henry with "the rainbow draped around him *like love*."

Just as "the air seemed to be dancing to the rhythm of [John Henry's] hammers," so this passage dances to the rhythm of Lester's lyrical prose. Although it contains no actual rhymes, the passage is highly rhythmical. His use of *onomatopoeia* (words that sound like their referent) in the second line—"RINGGGG! RINGGGG!"—allows the reader to literally hear the reverberating sound of the hammers hitting against the boulder, the repeating *G*'s and the exclamation points signaling a rising tone on the ends of the words so that they echo slightly past their saying. The very repetition of the word creates a kind of rhythmic balance. Lester also uses *alliteration* to marvelous effect in this passage: the repeating /s/ sound in the first line, the soft /sh/ sound on *sh*ining and *sh*immering (contrasting powerfully with the hard consonant sounds that begin *d*ust and *g*rit) in the third paragraph, the massive boulder *p*ulverized into *p*ebbles in the fourth.

A good share of the rhythmic quality in the passage is created through Lester's use of *repetition* and *parallelism*. Note, for example, the sentence that begins the fourth paragraph: "John Henry sang and he hammered and the air danced and the rainbow shimmered and the earth shook and rolled from the blows of the hammer." This sentence—the longest in the passage—contains five clauses connected to one another with the word *and*. The first four clauses are rhythmically balanced with one another; each contains a simple subject and verb followed by *and*. This repeating, parallel structure lends the first part of the sentence a kind of musical quality, which is then balanced by the last clause, near the same number of beats as the four clauses before it. Adding to its musicality, the sentence also contains a number of repetitive sounds (the /sh/ of *sh*immered and *sh*ook, the /m/ of ha*mm*ered and shi*mm*ered and ha*mm*er, the faint echo of the /l/ in ro*l*led in the sound of b*l*ows).

This long sentence is followed by two short sentences that bring a sudden end to the action depicted in this sentence ("Finally, it was quiet. Slowly the dust cleared."). Again, these sentences are in almost perfect rhythmic balance with one another, both beginning with an *ly* adverb followed by a three-word clause and both containing roughly the same number of syllable beats. (A similar rhythmic structure is also evident in the three short sentences that together create the image of the road crew boss staring in amazement at John Henry's work in the second paragraph.) In the final image contained in the passage, John Henry waves goodbye, his retreating figure framed in the two roughly symmetrical, rhythmic phrases that end the sentence: ". . . a hammer on each shoulder, the rainbow draped around him like love."

This is an impressive piece of writing to be sure. But at this point, some readers may be wondering what discussion of literary elements like simile, onomatopoeia, alliteration, repetition, and parallelism have to do with six-, seven-, and eight-year-olds. Isn't such discussion more appropriate to a high school English class than to a primary classroom? Not so, especially if you are talking about African American children.

Connections to Black Children's Language Socialization

As described at some length in part 2, the playful linguistic routines many Black children regularly engage in include the very same linguistic and stylistic features—albeit in more neophyte form—that lend Lester's writing so much of its imagistic and lyrical power.

Consider first Lester's use of figurative language in the passage, and in particular his propensity to describe one thing or situation in terms of another, as in the similes discussed earlier—the rainbow "shimmering and shining in the dust *like hope that never dies*" and, in the final description of John Henry, "the rainbow draped around him *like love*." Making comparisons or drawing analogies between two, often seemingly unlike, entities is the essence of what it means to use language in a figurative, rather than a literal, way. Sometimes the comparison or analogy between two things is made explicit, as in these similes. Other times the comparison is only implied, as in a metaphor—for example, "autumn of life" to describe older age or "spring chicken" to describe a young person or, from Andrea Davis Pinkney's picture book *Ella Fitzgerald: The Tale of a Vocal Virtuosa* (2002): "When Chick and Ella performed together, *they were grits with gravy*—they brought out the best in each other." (unnumbered pages).

If one thinks carefully about Black children's language socialization described in chapter 2, it is apparent how much of that experience seems to prepare children to think about and use language in figurative, as opposed to literal, ways. In Heath's (1983) study of language socialization in Trackton, for example, she found that young children were seldom asked questions that called for them to produce a literal, factual response (e.g., What color is that? How many pieces do you see?). Instead, the kind of question most frequently asked of children was the "analogy question," calling for an open-ended response based on children's experiences. Heath describes:

> Analogy questions test children's abilities to see things which are similar in their environment, and the prevalence of these questions in adult-child interactions may perhaps point to the importance Trackton adults give to this ability. They ask their young "What's dat like?" "What do you think you are?" (said, for example, to a child who is hopping about, dragging himself on his stomach, or crawling under a piece of furniture). (p. 105)

Heath reports that the adult conversations she observed in Trackton were full of such comparisons, often expressed in simile and metaphor (e.g., a local politician is so low-down he can't get under a rock). She also observed that adults frequently commented on children's behaviors using comparisons (e.g., " 'You act like some monkey.' "). As a result, Heath speculates, Trackton children likely developed ways of seeing and, as her data suggest, ways of responding to the world around them in terms of comparisons or analogies between one thing and another.

Black children's jokes, rhymes, and playful insults collected by a number of researchers (Heath, 1983; Jemie, 2003; Labov, 1972; Mahiri, 1998) contain many examples of imaginative analogies as well as other kinds of figurative language and word play—for example, " 'You're so stupid you failed lunch.' " " 'Your breath is so bad it smells like elephant breath' " (examples in Jemie, 2003, p. 4). Indeed, the Dozens, the highly ritualized language game briefly described in chapter 5, depends upon just this kind of imaginative, typically hyperbolic, comparison between two seemingly disparate situations or conditions—as does much of Lester's verbal artistry in the book *John Henry*. In one popular Dozens example, for instance, "Your mother is so old that when she reads the Bible she reminisces," and in another example from *John Henry,* "Ferret-Faced Freddy was so mean, he cried if he had a nice thought" (unnumbered pages).

Consider as well the "sound effects" Lester draws on to create the highly rhythmic quality of the passage—his use of poetic devices such as alliteration, repetition, and parallelism. Then think about the Dozens-like insult exchanges, play songs, jump rope and hand-clapping rhymes, rapping sequences, storytelling, joking and other forms of signifying described in the research on Black children's language use (Goodwin, 1990; Heath, 1983; Mahiri, 1998; Vernon-Feagans, 1996; Wyatt, 1995). These involve similar kinds of sound effects. Hear in your mind, for example, the rhymes and near-rhymes of jump rope songs, the syncopated rhythm of feet hitting pavement as children jump to their beat:

All in together, Girls!
How do you like the

Weather, Girls?
When it's your Birthday,
Please jump in. (in Chambers, 2002, p. 8)

Listen to fingers snap and hands clap in time with children chanting clapping rhymes:

Oh, Mary Mack, Mack, Mack
All dressed in black, black, black,
With silver buttons, buttons, buttons
All down her back, back, back.   (in Mattox, 1989, p. 15)

Recall the playful insults exchanged by children on Maple Street, their clever plays-on-words building rhythmically on the previous speaker's utterance:

Martha: I don't know what you laughin' at.
Billy: I know what I'm laughin' at.
              Your head.   (Goodwin, 1990, p. 177)

Tony: You sound terrible.
Martha: We sound just like you look.   (Goodwin, 1990, p. 183)

Imagine children as young as three, four, and five, perfectly on beat, as they recite the rapid-fire rhymes from a popular rap song. Finally, think about Lem from chapter 5, the Trackton preschooler who spontaneously created a poem filled with the kind of alliteration, rhyme, and rhythmic repetition that he must have heard all the time in the verbal interactions of the older children and adults around him:

Railroad track
Train all big 'n black
On dat track, on dat track, on dat track
Ain't no way I can't get back
Back from dat track
Back from dat train
Big 'n black, I be back.   (Heath, 1983, p. 110)

Playful disputing and games of verbal one-upmanship, ring games, hand-clapping games, double-dutch, rapping, and collaborative storytelling are all forms of play or "performance" in which many Black children routinely engage and in which the rhythmic, near-to-music dimensions of language are foregrounded. As such, they are contexts for learning about the poetic possibilities of language.

Learning how to use the figurative and aural aspects of literature to create mental images as one reads or listens to text is a task that potentially draws upon a number of the linguistic abilities and predispositions listed at the end of part 2, in particular the following:

1. The ability to discern multiple possibilities of meaning in discourse and to "read between the lines" of what is literally being said;
2. Sensitivity to verbal nuance and experience in interpreting metaphor-ical/figurative language; and
3. Skill in rhyming as well as in the use of other kinds of poetic lan-guage, including, for example, the use of rhythm, alliteration, repeti-tion, well-turned phrases, and plays-on-words.

I am not arguing here of course that Black children enter school as masters of metaphor and simile or adept in the use of poetic devices like rhyme and alliteration. As Toya Wyatt (1995) observes in her analysis of "playing the Doz-ens" and "rapping" routines she observed being performed by the preschoolers in her study, young children's use of features like rhyme, rhythm, alliteration, and other kinds of word play in their performances is often immature, repre-senting children's fledging efforts to incorporate stylistic elements whose full mastery is still outside their developmental grasp. What is significant, however, is not the too-short grasp, but the reach itself—the awareness on the part of even the very young children observed by Wyatt that stylistic elements like rhyme and rhythm are an essential part of what constitutes skilled linguistic perfor-mance. As emphasized throughout this section, these elements are also part of what constitutes skilled literary production. Teachers who use high-quality children's literature as a primary vehicle for introducing children to essential comprehension strategies like visualizing are likely to find many Black chil-dren especially attentive to and appreciative of the stylistic elements of text.

The Importance of Explicit Modeling

We know from research that visualizing helps keep proficient readers engaged and enhances their understanding of text. However, forming mental images or "mind pictures" as one reads is not a process that happens automatically. Chil-dren must be explicitly taught to use this strategy as they read or listen to text. Thinking aloud to model this strategy is an excellent way to introduce students to visualizing. Imagine, for example, that you have just finished reading aloud the entire text of *John Henry.* Now you are reading the book again, this time stopping every couple of pages or so to talk about your own visualizing pro-cess. Suppose you have just read the passage excerpted previously. After doing so, you might stop and share something like the following with your students:

> This part about the rainbow reminds me of a time when I was walking in the park one morning and it started to rain a little bit. The rain felt so good on my face that I just kept on walking. Then all of a sudden the sun came out even

though it was still kind of raining. Then, as I walked up a little hill, there was a rainbow shining in the distance. It was beautiful! I was so surprised when I saw it because it seemed to come out of nowhere, just like the rainbow does in this story. When I read Lester's words I can see the boss's face tilting up. I can see his mouth dropping open. I can see his finger pointing into the sky. I can feel his surprise and amazement. It says here that the rainbow was "*shin-ing* and *sh*immering in the dust and grit." I love that *sh* sound in *sh*ining and *sh*immering. When I read those words, I can see the sunlight in the rainbow colors—pink and green and yellow and orange.

There are so many rich possibilities for visualizing in this one short excerpt (not to mention in the text as a whole) that a teacher could not possibly talk about them all, nor is it necessary to do so. In using this particular text for modeling visualizing, however, teachers should talk explicitly about the literary concept of similes, not only because there are so many in this particular book, but because similes, metaphors, and other kinds of comparisons abound in literature as well as in science and social studies texts. In my experience, first- and second-graders are not too young to both appreciate and understand such figurative uses of language.

A number of the similes used by Lester in *John Henry* are fairly abstract, as are the ones contained in the previous passage—the image of the rainbow *"shining and shimmering in the dust and grit like hope that never dies"* and the image of John Henry with *"the rainbow draped around him like love."* One second-grade teacher I know talked about her mental image for the first of these by telling her students that when she read the words "like hope that never dies," she saw her grandmother's face and the faces of other Black people throughout history who had endured all kinds of hardships and setbacks in their struggle for equality, but who never gave up hope that the world would someday be a better place. Another second-grade teacher told her class that this same simile made her visualize a dog she had loved as a child. One day shortly after she and her family had moved to another house, the dog ran away. Even though everyone told her that the dog was never coming back, for years afterward she held onto the hope that one day her beloved dog would come bounding through the yard. This same teacher also shared that when she read the words "the rainbow draped around him like love," she could feel her mother's arms around her on a long-ago night when she woke up scared from a nightmare. In each of these examples, the teachers modeled the use of multiple strategies—visualizing *and* making text-to-self connections—to help students understand an author's use of abstract, figurative language.

Examples of Other Texts

Children need multiple opportunities both to hear their teachers model visualizing and to practice the strategy themselves, both with books read aloud by the teacher and with books they read independently. There are many books by African American writers that are appropriate for modeling and practicing visualizing. One of the best is *I Love My Hair!* (1998) discussed in the previous chapter. The book is filled with similes and other kinds of figurative comparisons—for example, Keyana's hair is "thick as a forest, soft as cotton candy"; her ponytails "flap in the air like a pair of wings" (unnumbered pages). Because of its many figurative images, *I Love My Hair!* is perfect for practicing visualizing with children as young as preschool. After reading the book through once, for example, the teacher might ask children to close their eyes and imagine what they smell, hear and feel as s/he rereads the opening lines:

> Every night before I go to bed, Mama combs my hair. I sit between her knees, resting my elbows on her thighs, like pillows. Mama is always gentle. She rubs coconut oil along my scalp and slowly pulls the comb through my hair . . . (unnumbered pages)

Did they smell the coconuty scent of the hair oil? Could they feel Mama's fingers gently massaging their scalps? Could they hear the sound of the comb sliding through their hair? Could they feel Mama's thighs like pillows around their bodies? As children share their sensory images from this and other books, it is important to keep reminding them that visualizing—trying to see, hear, feel, taste, and smell what the author is describing—is part of what all good readers do to help them better understand what they are reading. Even as they listen, they are becoming better readers when they allow the words on a page to form pictures in their minds.

Another good book for practicing visualizing with young readers is Angela Shelf Medearis's *Poppa's New Pants* (1995). When Poppa buys a pair of pants that are too long for him, Big Mama, Aunt Viney, and Grandma Tiny all claim to be too busy to hem them. But then in the middle of the night, unbeknownst to one another, each of them sneaks into the kitchen where little George is sleeping and proceeds to cut and hem the pants as a surprise for Poppa in the morning. Startled awake by the noises each makes in the process, George can't figure out who or what is in the room, but he's definitely pretty scared. The result is several hilarious descriptions, perfect for visualizing. Here is one (replete with sensory images and similes):

> I pulled the covers down inch by inch. I pried open my eyes and slowly looked around the room. A big, white ghost was drifting through the doorway, and it was coming toward me!
>   I dove down to the foot of the pallet and curled up into a ball. I was shaking all over like a wet dog. I felt something brush past me heavily. Then the rocking chair moaned loudly as it creaked back and forth, back and forth. I heard that snip, snip, snip, rustle, rustle sound and all was quiet again. My teeth were rattling so loud, I thought some of them were going to fall out!

> I stayed balled up under those blankets like an armadillo for the rest of the
> night. (unnumbered pages)

After discussing the sights, sounds, and tactile sensations children may have
experienced as they listened, the teacher might ask them to draw their favorite
image of the passage.

Visualizing helps keep readers engaged and enhances their understanding
of text, but using this strategy effectively requires metacognitive awareness. In
other words, we want children to intentionally create mental images as they
read or listen to text and to be consciously aware of how those images are
helping them better understand the text. An excellent book for modeling how
visualizing helps readers comprehend text more deeply is Belinda Rochelle's
picture book, *When Jo Louis Won the Title* (1994). Jo Louis is a little girl who's
embarrassed by her name until her grandfather, John Henry, shares the story
behind it. Moving to the North from Mississippi in 1938, John Henry arrived
in Harlem on the very night that Joe Louis won the world heavyweight box-
ing title (" 'a special night for me . . . a special night for black people everywhere' "). On that same magical night, John Henry also met his future wife. In
a lyrical passage perfect for visualizing, John Henry describes his arrival in
Harlem on that long-ago night:

> I headed straight to Harlem. I had never seen buildings so tall. They almost
> seemed to touch the sky. Even the moon looked different in the big city.
> The moonlight was bright and shining, the stars skipped across the sky. The
> streets sparkled in the night sky's light. It was true! The streets did seem to
> be paved in gold! I walked up and down city streets that stretched wide and
> long. I walked past a fancy nightclub, where you could hear the moaning of
> a saxophone and a woman singing so sad, so soft, and so slow that the music
> made me long for home. And then, all of a sudden the sad music changed
> to happy music. That saxophone and singing started to swing. Hundreds of
> people spilled out into the sidewalks, waving flags, scarves, waving hand-
> kerchiefs and tablecloths. Hundreds of people filled the streets with noise
> and laughter, waving hats and anything and everything, filling the sky with
> bright colors of red, white, green, yellow, blue, purple, and orange. (unnum-
> bered pages)

The teacher could instruct children to close their eyes and visualize the scene
as he or she reads Rochelle's evocative words aloud. Then, after children share
their images, the teacher might want to think aloud, describing how visualizing the scene helped him/her to better understand the story. For instance, the
teacher might say something like the following:

> Picturing that night in Harlem—hearing the sound of the music, seeing all
> the people on the sidewalk, laughing and cheering and waving colorful hats
> and scarves and handkerchiefs in the air—helps me understand how impor-
> tant and magical that night was for Black people. Now I understand better

why the name Joe Louis is so special to the grandfather because he was actually there on that exciting night. He was part of it. I bet he'll never forget that night. I think Jo Louis could understand how special her name was because her grandfather made that scene come alive for her, let her picture it all in her mind too. It was almost like she was there with him in her imagination. Good storytellers and good writers do that all the time—paint pictures with their words. And if you see those pictures in your mind when you listen or read, you understand the story better, just like I did when I pictured that night in Harlem and got a better understanding of how special that night was for the grandfather.

Like many high-quality children's books, the passage from *When Jo Louis Won the Title* is filled with rhythmic sound elements and vivid images. Just as young children are capable of appreciating and understanding sound features like alliteration and figurative language like similes, so too are they capable of learning and remembering the technical terms for these concepts. Knowing the technical terms enables children to use these concepts in a conscious and purposeful way, both as readers and as writers. In practicing and discussing visualizing with the previous passage, for example, the teacher might ask students to identify the literary elements Rochelle uses that make it easier for readers to visualize the scene in Harlem—for example, the alliteration and rhythmic repetition in "a woman singing so sad, so soft, and so slow that the music made me long for home."

Similarly, in talking about Lester's choice of "RINGGGG" to capture the sound of John Henry's hammer and of "KERBOOM BLAMMITY-BLAM- MITY BOOMBOOM BANGBOOMBANG" to mimic the sound of dynamite exploding, children can learn the term onomatopoeia. That term then becomes part of the literary tool kit children have available to help them recognize and talk about examples of onomatopoeia in other books they read or listen to, such as the "Tap! Tap! Clicky-clacky!" sound of Keyana's hair beads as she walks down the street in *I Love My Hair!* or the "RUM-A-TUM-TUM, RUM-A-TUM-TUM, RUM-A-TUM-TUM-TUM-TUM" sound made by the big red drums in Angela Shelf Medearis's description of the sights and sounds of turn-of-the century New Orleans in *Rum-A-Tum-Tum* (1997), another book that works well for practicing visualizing.

Inferring

The ability to make inferences while reading is the hallmark of the highly proficient reader. Discussing this strategy in their highly acclaimed book *Mosaic of Thought* (1997), Ellin Keene and Susan Zimmerman write:

> An inference can be a conclusion drawn after considering what is read in relation to one's beliefs, knowledge, and experience. Inference can be a critical analysis of a text: a mental or expressed argument with an author, an

active skepticism about what is stated in a text, or recognition of propaganda. Inference is, in some situations, synonymous with learning and remembering. It is the process of taking that which is stated in text and extrapolating it to one's life to create a wholly original interpretation that, in turn, becomes part of one's belief or knowledge. (p. 153)

The process of *inferring* leads us beneath the surface of text to engage with its deeper, less obvious meanings and to ponder its most intriguing questions. What, for example, are we to make of Jeremy, the White child in Mildred D. Taylor's *Mississippi Bridge* (1992), who wants so much to ally himself with the Black characters in the story, but who can find neither the means nor the courage to fully do so? What motivates this boy, whose racial consciousness seems out of sync with the time and place and family in which he lives? Jeremy is an enigma, a mystery—one which the author does not explain, at least not in any straightforward, explicit way. Because Taylor doesn't directly tell the reader what to think about Jeremy or fully describe the motivations behind his behaviors, "making sense" of him requires the reader to infer, to "read between the lines" of what is literally spelled out on the page. To reach an understanding of who Jeremy is, the reader must pull together the various bits of information about him, the "glints and gleams" of his character revealed in the text, and weave these into an interpretation that is not literally *in* the text but that somehow fits with it and with the reader's own knowledge about the world.

As suggested here, inferring entails not only close reading of the text, but also bringing to bear one's own knowledge and experience on its interpretation. This is one reason why it is critical that children learning to read be able to see their own lives reflected in the books chosen for instruction. In *Jamaica Tag-Along* (1989) by Juanita Havill, for instance, young readers are able to make inferences about how Jamaica is feeling at various points in the story (something seldom described explicitly by the author) in part because the experience of being excluded from play by other children, whether siblings or peers, is a common one. In addition, for many African American children, the fact that the characters in the story are mostly Black and that they dress, talk, and behave in culturally familiar ways likely makes it even easier to speculate upon and infer Jamaica's feelings. It is the mental interplay between children's own knowledge about the world and the interpretive clues provided in the text and illustrations that enables them to make meaningful inferences as they read.

As discussed in part 2, the ability to interpret meanings not made explicit or stated directly lies at the heart of communication in the African American discourse community. Children not only hear this ability displayed in the adult interactions around them, but participate themselves in ritualized forms of language play and other verbal interactions in which meanings are conveyed through indirection, innuendo, and figurative comparisons (Heath, 1983; Goodwin, 1990; Vernon-Feagans, 1996). In their interactions with both adults and peers, children socialized in the Black discourse community are expected to know how to interpret language in nonliteral ways. Recall, for example, Claudia Mitchell-Kernan's childhood anecdote about learning to "understand and appreciate implications" recounted at the beginning of chapter 4. In that anecdote, young Claudia, age seven or eight at the time, earns the approval of her elderly neighbor, Mr. Waters, when she demonstrates that she can "read between the lines" of his story about the signifying monkey and discern its implications for her own behavior. Her ability to do so signals to Mr. Waters that she is getting to the age where she can finally " 'hold a conversation' " in the African American community.

As a result of their socialization in a discourse community that places such strong value on conveying and interpreting implicit meanings, I speculated in chapter 5 that many school-aged African American children are likely to have developed both:

1. A strong tendency to take context into major account in figuring out the meaning of a word, statement, or extended piece of discourse; and
2. The ability to discern multiple possibilities of meaning in discourse and to "read between the lines" of what is literally being said.

Children skilled in using context and in "reading between the lines" to interpret meaning in oral discourse are likely to employ those same strategies in trying to make sense of books read aloud by the teacher (provided, of course, that the books are interesting to children and written at an appropriate level). It is very unlikely, however, that children are conscious of using these strategies. Doubtless, many Black children take their ability to decipher implied meanings for granted, as simply "part and parcel" of getting along in the world. It is hard to imagine, for example, a Black child, or any child for that matter, spontaneously thinking to herself as she reads or listens to text: "Oh, here I go again, reading between the lines and making an inference!"

Yet, strange as it may sound, that is exactly the kind of statement we want children to be making, both out loud and in their own heads, as they learn to use inferring in a deliberate way, as one important strategy available to them for understanding text. The reading research literature is overwhelmingly in agreement that proficient readers use strategies like inferring in highly conscious ways, particularly when they encounter difficult text. In teaching children to purposefully employ this strategy as they read or listen to text, we are asking them to bring to conscious mind meanings likely processed at an intuitive level, outside of explicit awareness. Just as significantly, we are asking them to articulate the thinking behind those inferences (e.g., "What *specifically* in the story led you to infer that Jeremy is ashamed of his family's behaviors?").

Thus, teaching about inferring is a process of helping children become conscious of *how* they know what they know about a particular text.

A Prediction Is a Kind of Inference

When teachers ask children to make predictions during a reading lesson, they are essentially asking them to infer—that is, to put together information gleaned from the text with their own background knowledge in order to draw meanings not (yet) explicitly stated. Beginning as early as the preschool level, many teachers regularly ask children to make predictions about what a book is going to be about or what is going to happen next in a story. But teachers do not always probe the reasons behind the predictions children make. Children need to know that a prediction is not the same as a guess. A guess can be random, tossed off the top of the head, right because it's lucky. A prediction always has reasons behind it.

Imagine, for example, that a teacher is reading his kindergartners *Jamaica's Find* (1986), another book in Havill's series. In this one, Jamaica finds a stuffed dog at the park. Although she very much wants to keep it, after talking with her mother and thinking about it herself, Jamaica decides to take the dog back to the park and turn it in to the Lost and Found. In the end, she meets the girl who lost it and makes a friend. The illustration on the book's cover pictures Jamaica looking intently into the eyes of the gray-and-black dog she is holding. If the teacher were to read the title, show the cover, and ask the class what they thought the book was going to be about, many hands would likely go up. Most children would probably correctly predict that the book was going to be about Jamaica finding a dog. The teacher, however, needs to push for more than just the prediction itself. He or she needs to get children to articulate the thinking behind the prediction. After a child has stated the reasons for her prediction, the teacher might then say something like the following:

> I like the way Tameeka used both the words and the picture to predict what she thinks the book is going to be about. The words "Jamaica's Find" made Tameeka think that the book is going to be about Jamaica finding something. And the picture of Jamaica holding the dog made her think that what Jamaica is going to find is a dog. Good predicting, Tameeka! You used the words *and* the picture as clues.

If the class has previously read other Jamaica books, the teacher might encourage the children to think about how what they know about those books could help them make predictions about *Jamaica's Find*. If no ideas are forthcoming from children, the teacher can do a think-aloud:

> I have another prediction about this book. I predict that Jamaica is going to have to make a hard decision in the story. Do you know why I think that? Do you remember when we read *Jamaica Tag-Along?* In that book, Jamaica had to make a hard decision about whether or not to let Berto play. Remember? And in *Jamaica's Blue Marker,* she had to decide if she should make Russell a goodbye card even though she was mad at him. So now I'm thinking that in

this book, she might have a decision to make too. I'm using text-to-text connections to make a prediction. I'm using what I *already know* about the other Jamaica books we read to make a prediction about this one.

In talking about the thinking processes behind their predictions and inferences, it is important for children to differentiate between when they are drawing on background knowledge and when they are drawing on the text itself. Teachers should emphasize the importance of both. For example, the teacher might stop at the page that illustrates Jamaica showing the dog to her mother and ask children to predict how the mother is going to respond. After listening to two children's predictions and the reasons behind them, the teacher might say something like the following:

> We heard two interesting predictions. Jamal predicted that Jamaica's mother isn't going to let Jamaica keep the dog. He said that whenever he finds something at the playground, his mother says that he can't keep it because it's old and dirty. And Jamal remembered that earlier in the book, it says there are food and grass stains on the dog. So Jamal put those two things together to make his prediction. He is using *both* the words in the book and what he knows about *his* mother to make a prediction about what Jamaica's mother is going to say. Kendra had a different prediction. She predicted that Jamaica's mother is going to like the dog because she's smiling at Jamaica and the dog in this picture. Kendra is using the illustrations to make her predictions. Both Jamal and Kendra did a very good job of predicting. Good readers use what they already know and what's actually *in* the book—the words and the illustrations—to make predictions about what might happen next in a story.

In thinking about the notion that a prediction is a kind of inference, readers may be wondering at this point exactly how a prediction and an inference differ and whether or not the distinction between them is important to make for children. In *Strategies That Work: Teaching Comprehension to Enhance Understanding* (2000), Stephanie Harvey and Anne Goudvis suggest that the main difference is that a prediction gets confirmed or contradicted at some point in the story whereas the accuracy or truth of an inference may remain unresolved at story's end (p. 108). Thus, in asking children whether or not they think Jamaica will decide to take the dog to the park's Lost and Found, the teacher is calling for a prediction because the answer will eventually be revealed in the text. The question of *why* Jamaica decides to return the dog, on the other hand, calls for an inference because at no point in the story does Havill explicitly convey this information to the reader.

At one level, this distinction is a major one. The most profound meanings we extract from text—the ones that resonate with our lives in powerful ways and that we remember long past the time of reading—are the meanings least likely to be stated directly by an author. This is as true of high-quality children's literature as it is of adult literature. On the other hand, the mental processes involved in predicting and inferring are essentially the same. In doing either, readers draw on both their own store of knowledge about the world and the clues provided in text to arrive at hypotheses, conclusions, and interpretations that an author has not (yet) made explicit. What is important in reading instruction is helping children to become conscious of those mental processes, whether the teacher is talking specifically about predicting or, more generally, about the process of inferring.

By the time teachers talk explicitly with children about the concept of inferences, many children may already have had lots of practice making predictions about text. In that event, teachers can highlight the similarities involved in predicting and inferring while also underscoring the point that, unlike the case with a prediction, the validity of an inference may never be directly confirmed in the text.

Talking With Children About Inferring: Becoming "Reading Detectives"

It may have struck readers of this text that some African American children might interpret a teacher's request to hear the thinking behind their inferences as a call to belabor the obvious, to spell out in excruciating detail what should, from the child's perspective, be patently self-evident. Such a possibility is easily avoided, however, if teachers frame discussions about children's inferential thinking as opportunities for children to display their superior reasoning powers and their sophisticated verbal skills. Children need to know that the ability to read between the lines and to discern meanings not directly stated in text is the essence of what it means to be a good reader. When they explain their thinking about a particular passage to their teacher and classmates, children aren't "stating the obvious"; they are "making a case" for their interpretation.

Teachers may want to use the metaphor of "reader as detective" in talking with children about inferring. An effective and engaging model for the detective is the literary character Sherlock Holmes with his trademark props (his detective cap, pipe, and magnifying glass), his famed attention to subtle detail, and his careful "recap" of his reasoning as the end of every case ("'. . . nothing clears up a case so much as stating it to another person'" [Doyle, 1996, p. 45]). Although the Sherlock Holmes stories are beyond the comprehension level of most young children, based on their own reading of them, teachers can make this colorful character and his analytic methods come alive for children. Then, during read-alouds, a magnifying glass (even one constructed of paper) might become a class signal for digging beneath the surface of a text to reflect on its deeper implications or underlying themes. Or, pausing at an appropriate place in a text, a teacher might encourage children to draw inferences by saying something like the following: "Hmmm, I wonder what Sherlock Holmes might make of this!"

Flossie and the Fox (1986) by Patricia C. McKissack is an excellent text to use for practicing inferring with second and third graders. In this clever "play" on Little Red Riding Hood, Flossie outwits the fox who is after her basket of eggs by pretending not to believe he's really a fox. It is not until the last page of the book, however, that McKissack explicitly tells the reader that Flossie has known the fox's true identity all along. Up until the book's closing, the reader or listener who cannot read between the lines of what is literally written on the page will be every bit as duped and confused as the fictional fox. While reading this book aloud, a teacher might pause somewhere in the middle of the text and say something like the following: "Hmmm. I'm trying to get this straight in my mind. Does Flossie actually know he's a fox or not?" As children voice their views, they should be asked to explain the thinking behind their inference. When I discussed this question (i.e., Does Flossie know he's a fox?) with a group of third-graders, children were able to support the inference that Flossie did know by pointing out very subtle textual cues—for example, that her grandmother's warning before she left had probably led Flossie to expect a fox; that when the fox first appeared, he displayed all of the behaviors her grandmother had described; that Flossie was too smart to be fooled, as evidenced by her skill with language. In retracing their reasoning for the group, children were becoming more aware of their own thinking processes as readers and were articulating a strategy (e.g., "okay, let me stop and think this through") that they could deliberately draw on in making sense of text in the future.

In *Off to School* (1995) by Gwendolyn Battle-Lavert (a book suitable for use with first- through third-graders), Wezielee longs to start school. But like the children of other migrant families, she must wait until after the harvest. In the meantime, she has responsibility for cooking the midday meal for her parents and siblings, who have been working hard in the fields all morning. Home by herself, Wezielee spends most of her mornings daydreaming about school and somehow always manages to ruin the meal she is cooking—for example, adding too much salt, burning the cornbread. Finally, her hungry family has had enough, and Papa tells Wezielee that she can start school early, leaving the cooking to someone else. " 'We know you're gonna be the best in the class,' " Papa tells her, as the whole family smiles. A question left unanswered in the book is whether or not Wezielee's ruined meals are an accident, that is, the result of her being absent-minded, or a deliberate strategy on Wezielee's part to get to go to school early. To answer the question, children must go beyond the literal words in the text and make an inference. Children can defend their position on this question (i.e., their inference) with both evidence from the text and arguments drawn from their own experiences in the world.

Another book that teachers can use to practice inferring with first- through third-graders is *Visiting Day* (2002) by Jacqueline Woodson. Based on Woodson's childhood memories of visiting a beloved uncle in prison, *Visiting Day* describes the monthly trips a little girl and her grandmother make to visit her father in prison and the happiness and hope for the future they share in being together. Nowhere, however, does the book explicitly state that the father is in prison. Readers must infer this information on the basis of the illustrations and textual clues (e.g., ". . . the bus pulls up in front of the big old building where, as Grandma puts it, Daddy is doing a little time" [unnumbered pages]). Before starting to read this book aloud, teachers could tell students that the author doesn't directly say where the visits in the story take place. Students could be directed to listen for clues in the text that help them figure this out and to hold these clues in their heads until the discussion.

I Dream of Trains (2003) by Angela Johnson is another book especially useful for practicing inferring (probably most appropriately with second- or third-graders). The boy narrator of this story and his family are sharecroppers in Mississippi. For the narrator, the sound of the train whistle blowing past him in the fields conjures dreams, both about Papa's stories of the legendary Casey Jones and about his own future far away from the fields in Mississippi. A question to explore with children, one that leads them beyond the literal to sound the deeper meanings of the text, is why the train is so important to the narrator.

There are many other excellent books from the corpus of African American children's literature that could be used to help children gain a clear understanding of what readers actually do when they make inferences about text. Whatever books teachers choose to work with, the most essential ideas to get across when talking with children about inferring are: (a) that this strategy always involves figuring out something that they think is true about the story (or informational text) that isn't said directly, and (b) that inferences are based on a combination of readers' own knowledge and clues from the text itself.

Lucy Calkins' Question: "What's *really* going on?"

To nudge students to dig deeper into a book in order to infer meanings not stated directly, literacy educator Lucy Calkins (2001) sometimes pauses at a particularly rich point in the text and asks children: *"What's really going on here?* or *"What does the author want me to realize here?"* (p. 481). A good book to use these questions with is Jacqueline Woodson's *Our Gracie Aunt* (2002) about a little boy, Johnson, and his sister, Beebee, who are left alone by their mother. After several days, a social worker arrives and takes them to stay with their Aunt Gracie, a woman whom they've never met. Warm and loving, their Gracie Aunt promises to take special care of them until their mother can be with them again. There are many places in the book where asking second- or third-graders to think about "what's *really* going on" would likely enhance their understanding of the story. Here is one example, which occurs when the social worker first arrives to find the children alone in their apartment:

> "Where's your mama" Miss Roy wanted to know.
> Beebee got real quiet. After a while she said, "She went someplace."

"How long has she been gone"
I counted the days on my fingers.
"Since a few minutes ago," Beebee said. (unnumbered pages)

Asking children to reflect on Beebee's response and to grapple with its deeper significance enriches children's understanding of the story and allows them to empathize with Beebee's feelings of protectiveness toward her mother. *"What's* really *going on here?"* is one of those wonderfully generative questions that teachers can ask children and children can ask themselves over and over as they read. It is a question that never gets old because it works with every rich text at every grade level and almost always leads readers to connect with deeper meanings in the text.

Using Inferring to Make Sense of Difficult Text

By thinking aloud with children, teachers can model how the strategy of inferring can help readers think through things that may be puzzling or confusing in a text. Faith Ringgold's *Aunt Harriet's Underground Railroad in the Sky* (1992) is a case in point. As with many of Ringgold's books, much of the action in this complex story occurs as part of a young child's dream. As a result, it is easy for young readers to become confused about what part of the story is real and what is fantasy unless they pay careful attention to textual clues and use them to make inferences about what is happening. By sharing their own inferences in a think-aloud, teachers not only help children better understand this particular book, but also model a strategy for reasoning through complexities in other texts. A second- or third-grade teacher might begin the think-aloud with the book's title and cover illustration:

> *Aunt Harriet's Underground Railroad in the Sky.* Hmmm. I'm trying to figure out what this book is going to be about. I know that "Underground Railroad" is a term used to describe escape routes from the South to the North during the days of slavery. I also know that Harriet Tubman was a person who helped enslaved people escape on the Underground Railroad. I'm remembering that poem we read by Eloise Greenfield—"Harriet Tubman didn't take no stuff/Wasn't scared of nothing neither." Remember that poem? I'm wondering if *Aunt* Harriet in the title is the same as Harriet Tubman. Maybe this woman pictured on the cover is supposed to be Harriet Tubman. But then the girl on the cover looks like Cassie from *Tar Beach*, and the little boy looks sort of like her brother BeBe, except, who's that baby on his back? Maybe they just *look* like the characters from *Tar Beach*. Anyway, everyone looks like they're flying. Even the train does. So definitely I think the book is going to be about flying and probably about escaping from slavery. I think I'll start reading:
>
> > *One day, my brother Be Be and I were flying among the stars, way, way up, so far up the mountains looked like pieces of rock candy and the oceans like tiny cups of tea. We came across an old ramshackled train in the sky.* (unnumbered pages)

> Okay, now I know this *is* another book about Cassie and BeBe. I'm making an inference that Cassie is taking this trip with BeBe in her imagination. I know kids can't really fly. I know trains don't really travel in the sky. And I know that in *Tar Beach,* Cassie also imagines that she's flying. So I think this book is about another trip that Cassie takes in her imagination, only this time she's taking BeBe with her. It doesn't say that here, but I'm inferring that it's true.

After reading a few more pages of the text, the teacher might pause and continue the think-aloud:

> I have another inference. It doesn't say this directly in the book, but I think Cassie is imagining herself in another time period. I think she is taking a trip back to the time of slavery because of the words "GO FREE NORTH OR DIE" printed on the side of the train. And here Cassie meets Harriet Tubman. So Aunt Harriet in the title *is* Harriet Tubman, and she lived a long time ago. So putting all those clues together, I'm inferring that in this book, Cassie is imagining herself going back into history and meeting people who lived a long time ago.

There are many other places in this book where teachers might want to pause and think aloud with children about inferences. One example is the following short passage, in which Ringgold is describing the lives of enslaved Africans:

> A legal marriage was not allowed. So instead a man and woman would jump the broom. (unnumbered pages)

After reading these sentences aloud, a teacher might share the following:

> I'm not sure exactly what "jump the broom" means because it doesn't really say in the book. But I'm inferring that it must be a way that enslaved people got married because Ringgold says "a legal or church marriage was not allowed so *instead* a man and woman would jump the broom." The word *instead* tells me that jumping the broom was something they did *in place of* or as a *substitute* for a legal or church marriage.

In modeling the process of making inferences, teachers should utilize illustrations as well as the written text. At one point in *Aunt Harriet's Underground Railroad in the Sky*, for instance, Ringgold writes: "It was against the law for a slave to learn to read or write" (unnumbered pages). However, the illustration accompanying this sentence depicts a White woman evidently teaching a group of enslaved African Americans to read. Similarly, the illustration on the next page depicts what looks like a prayer meeting with a Black preacher and Black worshippers while the accompanying text, building on the previous sentence, reads: "Or have a meeting, even to preach the word of God" (unnumbered pages). After reading these pages aloud, a teacher might stop and say something like the following:

> I have another inference. It says here that it was against the law for enslaved people to learn to read or write. It also says that it was against the law for them to hold prayer meetings. But the illustrations show enslaved people doing both those things. So I'm inferring—even though the author doesn't directly say this—that some enslaved people did learn to read and write, and some did hold prayer meetings, even though it was against the law.

Many times when children confront text that is difficult or confusing in some way, their first impulse is to simply tune the text out, to give up on trying to understand it. Teachers need to help build children's confidence in their ability to think through complexity as they read or listen to text. As with any other academic task, children's belief that they can do so grows out of their clear understanding of exactly what is involved in the process (hence the importance of modeling) and their repeated success in accomplishing it themselves (hence the importance of lots of guided practice).

Using Inferring to Explore Different Points of View

One of the most important abilities children develop during the early years of school is the ability to think about and imagine the perspectives of others. Certainly this ability is critical to children's understanding of literature. Good readers must be able to infer the feelings and motivations of central characters and to envision what the world might look like through their eyes. An excellent book for illustrating the importance of point of view in literature is *Fishing Day* (2003) by Andrea Davis Pinkney. The book is set in the Jim Crow South and the plot revolves around a young Black girl's decision to offer a helping hand to a troubled White boy. In the Author's Note at the end of the book, Pinkney offers some insight into her motivation for writing it. She says in part:

> Though I didn't grow up in the Jim Crow South, where segregation was the law of the land, *Fishing Day* is a story I've lived a thousand times. Throughout my childhood I saw quieter examples of racism's sting. There were no visible "Whites Only" signs in my youth, but segregation still existed, even though its labels weren't posted in public.
>   . . . for me, the separate-sides-of-the-river scenario would play itself out again and again—on the school bus, on the kickball team, in the school cafeteria; where white children stuck together, black children stuck together, and few of us made attempts to mix.
>   I hated feeling that I was on one side of an invisible fence, and that white children were on the other. Worst of all, I grew to hate my desire to befriend white children whose games and laughter seemed just like mine. And, all the while, I couldn't help but wonder if *they* wanted to be friends with *me*.

> I wrote *Fishing Day* in an effort to recast some of the painful times of
> my childhood. To show that children, if given the chance to formulate their
> own ideas about differences and tolerance, will often do what is right. . .
> (unnumbered pages)

Pinkney's memories of sometimes wanting to befriend White children
and of wondering whether or not they also wanted to befriend *her* suggests
the importance of being able to imaginatively place ourselves, if only momentarily, in the mind, and circumstances, of another human being. The belief that
it is possible to do so lies at the heart of all good literature, and certainly at the
heart of Pinkney's book. There are four characters in *Fishing Day:* Reenie and
her mother, who are Black, and Peter (Pigeon) and his father, who are White.
Although they fish on the same river, they never speak ("In all the time we've
been fishing alongside Pigeon and his daddy, we've never said a word to them,
and they've never said a word to us. Not a word" [unnumbered pages]). Peter
and his father are very poor and need the fish they catch in order to eat. But
unlike Reenie and Mama, they don't have much luck with the fish. Reenie and
Mama know it's because they make too much noise and don't use the right
bait. After Reenie reels in a really big fish, Peter starts flinging stones. One of
them hits Reenie in the knee. Hugging her close, Mama tells Reenie that Peter
is a hurting child. "'And he can't help but spread his hurt around,'" she gently explains (unnumbered pages). When Peter's daddy disappears for a while,
Reenie decides to offer Peter some of the corn she and Mama have been using
for bait. He soon catches a fish. The next day, Reenie and Peter wave to one
another as the truck he's riding in passes Reenie and Mama on their way home
from church.

Teachers can help children infer the motives, thoughts, and feelings of
these four characters by asking questions that focus on the significance of
various events in the story. As always, children's explication of the reasons for
their judgments is critical. Possible questions might include the following:

- How does Reenie feel about Peter at the beginning of the story? How
  do you know?
- How does Mama feel about the Jim Crow laws? How can you tell?
- What is Mr. Troop thinking as he watches Reenie and Mama catch so
  many fish? How does he feel? How can you tell?
- After Reenie and Mama move to a place further down the river, the
  book says: "Mama's quiet." What is she thinking about? How can
  you tell?
- Why does Reenie decide to help Peter? Explain your thinking.
- Why is Peter "scared and glad, all at the same time" when he sees
  Reenie walking toward him? What is he thinking? How do you know?
- How does Reenie feel about herself and her decision to help Peter at
  the end of the book? How do you know?

Useful for focusing on perspective taking with kindergarten and first-graders are the eight books in the Everett Anderson series by Lucille Clifton. In these books, Everett, who turns from age six to seven over the course of the series, experiences a number of life-changing events, including the death of his father, his mother's remarriage, and the birth of a baby sister. In the most recent book in the series, *One of the Problems of Everett Anderson* (2001), Everett has to figure out what to do when his friend keeps showing up at school with bruises and won't explain why. Writing in poetry, Clifton succeeds in beautifully capturing Everett's complex and often ambivalent reactions to the changes in his life. In *Everett Anderson's 1 2 3* (1977/2002), Everett worries a lot about all the time his mother is spending with Mr. Perry, who's just moved into the apartment next door. He's not sure how he feels about Mr. Perry coming into his life (he doesn't want a *new* father), but at the same time, Everett tries to understand the way his mother feels: "It's not much fun talking to yourself all day, and so he tries to understand the way that Mr. Perry likes to be talking to Mama a lot lately" (unnumbered pages). Clifton doesn't try to neatly resolve Everett's ambivalence. Faced with the prospect of a new stepfather, at the end of the book Everett is cautiously optimistic: "It's still hard to get used to Three Everett thinks, but he thinks he will" (unnumbered pages). Because Clifton's portrayal of Everett's feelings throughout the series is so perceptive and true to life, many children are able to bring their own life experiences to bear in drawing inferences about Everett's feelings and motivations.

Speaking and Writing Connections

Recommended Books for Visualizing

The following speaking and writing activities encourage children to use sensory images and details to create poems, songs, stories, and dramatizations about themselves and the world around them. These routines enhance children's speaking vocabulary and give them tools to make their writing come alive with similes, metaphors, and other forms of descriptive and figurative language.

Bigmama's (1991) by Donald Crews

The author uses sensory images to describe a family's trip to the South for a family reunion.

Speaking: Ask children to close their eyes and visualize a time when they were at a large family gathering for a special event. Invite children to share their sensory images. What was the setting? Who was there? What did they do, see, taste, hear, and smell?

Writing: Have children draw a picture of themselves at their special family event and write or dictate sentences about what they saw, heard, smelled, tasted, and/or felt.

Grade Levels: Kindergarten and first

Thematic Connections:

Hudson, W. (1993). *I love my family.*

Patrick, D. L. (2004). *Ma Dear's old green house.*

Woodson, J. (1998). *We had a picnic this Sunday past.*

Woodtor, D. P. (1996). *The big meeting.*

Max Found Two Sticks (1994) by Brian Pinkney

A boy uses a pair of sticks to imitate the rhythm of the things he hears around him—for example, pigeons startled into flight, rain hitting against the windows, train wheels thundering down the tracks.

Speaking: Ask children to close their eyes and listen to a series of different sounds (e.g., tapping on the table, ringing a bell, playing notes on a xylophone). After each sound, challenge children to guess its source.

Writing: Ask children to focus on the sounds they hear around them while they fall asleep at night. The next day, compose a class "Night Sounds" poem as a shared writing activity.

Grade Levels: Kindergarten and first

Thematic Connections:

DeGross, M. (1999). *Granddaddy's street songs.*

Greenfield, E. (1996). *Night on Neighborhood Street.*

Medearis, A. S. (1997). *Rum-a-tum-tum.*

Rashka, C. (1992). *Charlie Parker played be bop.*

Walter, M. P. (1980). *Ty's one-man band.*

When I Am Old With You (1990) by Angela Johnson

A little girl lovingly imagines all the things she and her grandfather will do when they are old together. They will go fishing, eat bacon on the porch, and play cards "till the lightning bugs shine in the trees" (unnumbered pages).

Speaking: Share with children a memory of a time when you felt warm, safe and loved. Use lots of sensory detail to describe where you were, who you were with, and what you saw, heard, smelled, and felt. Then encourage children to share similar experiences with their partners.

Writing: Invite children to draw a picture of a time when they felt warm, safe, and loved. Have them write or dictate a caption for their picture that describes where they were and who they were with. Children can add words to their pictures that describe what they were seeing, hearing, smelling, and/or feeling.

Grade Levels: Kindergarten and first

Thematic Connections:

Barrett, J. D. (1989). *Willie's not the hugging kind.*
Greenfield, E. (1976/1991). *First pink light.*
Lauture, D. (1992). *Father and son.*
Smalls, I. (1992). *Jonathan and his mommy.*
Smalls, I. (2005). *My Nana and me.*
Smalls, I. (2006). *My Pop Pop and me.*
Smith, E. B. (1994). *A lullaby for Daddy.*
Tarpley, N.A. (1998). *I love my hair!*

Honey, I Love, and Other Love Poems (1978) by Eloise Greenfield

---

This lyrical poetry collection contains many sensory images for children to practice visualizing as they listen to the poems read aloud.

Speaking: Have children recite their favorite poems in pairs or small groups. A number of the poems, including "Way Down in the Music," "Rope Rhyme," and "Harriet Tubman," can be dramatized as well as recited.

Writing: Encourage children to write poems about the things they love, modeled after the title poem in the collection, "Honey, I Love." Remind children to use sensory images to describe the things they love.

Grade Levels: First through third

Thematic Connections:

Giovanni, N. (1971/1985). *Spin a soft Black song: Poems for children.*
Greenfield, E. (1988). *Nathaniel talking.*
Mattox. C. W. (Ed.). (1989). *Shake it to the one that you love the best: Play songs and lullabies from Black musical traditions.*

JoJo's Flying Side Kick (1995) by Brian Pinkney

JoJo is nervous about taking the test for her yellow belt promotion at the Tae Kwon Do Center. Her mother suggests that she visualize herself doing the perfect kick. She does, and earns the yellow belt!

Speaking: Ask children to create a mental picture of themselves performing a difficult task (e.g., hitting a home run, playing a song on the violin). Have children draw their visualizations and share them with a partner. Model the activity by using lots of sensory detail as you visualize aloud and create a picture of yourself performing a difficult task.

Writing: Have children write a story about their pictures, using lots of sensory details.

Grade Levels: First through third

Thematic Connections:

Barber, B. E. (1996). *Allie's basketball dream.*

Johnson, A. (2004). *Just like Josh Gibson.*

McKissack, P. C. (1989). *Nettie Jo's friends.*

Mitchell, M. K. (1993). *Uncle Jed's barbershop.*

Bruh Rabbit and the Tar Baby Girl (2003) by Virginia Hamilton

In this retelling of a classic African American tale that originated during the period of enslavement, Bruh Rabbit uses his quick thinking abilities and his skill with language to outwit his physically stronger adversary. Read the book aloud without sharing the illustrations so children can visualize Bruh Rabbit's delightfully described encounter with Tar Baby Girl. Ask children to draw their visualization. Revisit the book and have children compare their drawings with James Ransome's illustrations.

Writing: Either individually or in small groups, have children write and illustrate their own Bruh Rabbit adventure. Encourage children to use concrete images as they describe the characters and their actions.

Speaking: Invite children to dramatize their original Bruh Rabbit adventures.

Grade Levels: Second and third

Thematic Connections:

Arkhurst, J. C. (1964). *The adventures of Spider: West African folk tales.*

Berry, J. (1997). *First palm trees. An Anancy spiderman story.*

Diakite, B. W. (2003). *The magic gourd.*

McKissack, P. C. (1986). *Flossie and the fox.*

McKissack, P. C., & Onawumi, J. M. (2005). *Precious and the Boo Hag.*

Uptown (2000) by Bryan Collier

A boy describes his Harlem neighborhood with a series of striking images. Uptown is: "A caterpillar." "Chicken and waffles." "A row of brownstones." "The orange sunset over the Hudson River" (unnumbered pages).

Speaking: Share and describe in sensory detail a favorite neighborhood place. Invite children to share their own favorite neighborhood places with their partners.

Writing: Have children create a neighborhood brochure describing their favorite neighborhood places with sensory images that capture the sights, sounds, smells, and tastes around them.

Grade Levels: Second and third

Thematic Connections:

Greenfield, E. (1996). *Night on Neighborhood Street.*

Myers, W. D. (1997). *Harlem: A poem.*

Smalls, I. (1991). *Irene and the big, fine nickel.*

Wyeth, S. D. (1998). *Something beautiful.*

Going North (2004) by Janice Harrington

The author uses aural imagery to wonderful effect in describing a family's journey from rural Alabama to start a new life in Lincoln, Nebraska. As the family travels north in their yellow station wagon, the tires "make a road-drum, a road-beat . . .". In the car, Jessie bounces Baby Sister on her "lap, lap, lap" as they speed by "brown girls jumping rope, rope, rope" (unnumbered pages).

Writing: Take a field trip to any place that is likely to be filled with interesting sounds—for example, a train station, a park or nature preserve, a playground, a busy shopping area. Have children record the sounds they hear around them. Encourage them to capture the rhythms of the sounds as accurately as possible in their descriptions. Turn the children's collective aural images into a class poem.

Speaking: Invite children to experiment with pace and tone as they recite the class poem individually and in small groups.

Grade Levels: Second and third

Thematic Connections:

Lester, J. (1994). *John Henry.*

Medearis, A. S. (1995). *Poppa's new pants.*

Pinkney, A. D. (1998). *Duke Ellington: The piano prince and his orchestra.*

Pinkney, A. D. (2002). *Ella Fitzgerald: The tale of a vocal virtuosa.*

Nathaniel Talking (1988) by Eloise Greenfield

A collection of poems told in the voice of nine-year-old Nathaniel: "It's Nathaniel talking/and Nathaniel's me/I'm talking about/My philosophy" (unnumbered pages). The author explains that the lyrics of two of the poems in the book are similar to the lyrics of a type of music called "twelve-bar blues." She includes directions for children to write their own twelve-bar blues poem.

Speaking: Invite children to read aloud their favorite poem and explain why they like it.

Writing: Have children use Greenfield's directions at the end of the book to compose their own twelve-bar blues poem.

Grade Levels: Third and fourth

Thematic Connections:
Grimes, N. (1994). *Meet Danitra Brown.*
Grimes, N. (2002). *Danitra Brown leaves town.*
Grimes, N. (2005). *Danitra Brown, class clown.*
Norman, L. (2006). *My feet are laughing.*

Lies and Other Tall Tales (2005; collected by Zora Neale Hurston) adapted and illustrated by Christopher Myers

The book contains humorous comparisons such as those typically found in versions of "playing the Dozens," for example, ". . . I knowed a man so smart, he had the seven-year itch and scratched it out in three months" (unnumbered pages). In Myers's delightful Artist's Note, he explains that "Playing the dozens is an African American cultural practice, which if you haven't heard about it, you better ask your mama! It includes mama jokes and humorous dissing, which if you don't know what dissing is, you don't have the sense God gave a flea" (unnumbered pages).

Speaking: In pairs, ask children to compose their own "mama joke" comparisons, following the structure: "_____ is/are so _____ that _____." Invite children to share their figurative comparisons with the class.

Writing: Working in pairs or small groups, have children write their own tall tales about legendary or made-up characters. Encourage them to use the kind of exaggerated comparisons contained in the book.

Grade Levels: Third and fourth

Thematic Connections:
Lester, J. (1994). *John Henry.*
McKissack, P. C. (1992). *A million fish . . . more or less.*
Pinkney, A. D. (1996). *Bill Pickett: Rodeo-ridin' cowboy.*

Recommended Books for Inferring

The following speaking and writing routines feature role-plays, character monologues, character interviews, and character letters. These engaging activities promote oral and written language development while motivating children to step inside the shoes of the characters and infer their thoughts, feelings, and motivations.

Jamaica's Blue Marker (1995) by Juanita Havill

Jamaica agrees to share her markers with Russell, even though she doesn't want to. She becomes so angry after Russell scribbles on her drawing that she doesn't want to write him a good-bye card when the teacher announces that he is moving away.

Speaking: Ask children to imagine that Jamaica and Russell have a chance to talk after she gives him her blue marker as a going-away present. Encourage them to infer what each of the characters might say. Then have partners role-play a conversation between Jamaica and Russell. Invite partners to perform their role plays for the class.
Writing: Ask children to write a good-bye card to Russell.
Grade Levels: First and second

Thematic Connections:
Havill, J. (1989). *Jamaica tag-along.*
Havill, J. (1993). *Jamaica and Brianna.*
Jones, R. C. (1991). *Matthew and Tilly.*

Everett Anderson's Nine Month Long (1978) by Lucille Clifton

Everett must deal with the challenges of having both a new stepfather and a new baby sister.

Speaking: Ask half of the class to assume the role of Everett Anderson. The other half can be the audience. Have children in the audience ask Everett questions about how he is feeling at various points in the story. To answer the questions, children must infer Everett's feelings.
Writing: Ask children to write letters to Everett Anderson, offering him advice about having a new sibling or stepparent.
Grade Levels: First and second

Thematic Connections:
Clifton, L. (1970). *Some of the days of Everett Anderson.*
Clifton, L. (1971/1991). *Everett Anderson's Christmas coming.*

Clifton, L. (1974/1992). *Everett Anderson's year.*
Clifton, L. (1976/1992). *Everett Anderson's friend.*
Clifton, L. (1977/2002). *Everett Anderson's 1 2 3.*
Clifton, L. (1983/1988). *Everett Anderson's goodbye.*
Clifton, L. (2001). *One of the problems of Everett Anderson.*
Greenfield, E. (1974/1993). *She come bringing me that little baby girl.*

Visiting Day (2002) by Jacqueline Woodson

A girl and her grandmother visit Daddy in prison.

Speaking: Children can take turns role-playing an imaginary scene in which the girl in the story talks with her best friends about how she feels about her daddy being in prison. Children can enact a similar scene between the grandmother and her best friends and between Daddy and two of his friends.

Writing: Ask half the class to imagine that they are the girl in the story. Have them write a letter to Daddy in the girl's voice and from her point of view. Have the other half of the class write response letters in Daddy's voice.

Grade Levels: Second and third

Thematic Connections:
Woodson, J. (2002). *Our Gracie Aunt.*
Wyeth, S. D. (1995). *Always my Dad.*

Grandpa's Face (1988) by Eloise Greenfield

Tamika's grandfather's expressive face changes from "glad to worried to funny to sad" (unnumbered pages). Grandfather's face tells Tamika how he is feeling and how much he loves her. While watching her grandfather rehearse for a play one day, Tamika sees him make a mean and angry face that frightens her until Grandpa reassures her that it is just a pretend face.

Speaking: Before reading the book, play a charades activity recommended by Harvey and Goudvis (2000) to introduce the inferring strategy to young children. Give a volunteer an index card with a feeling word (sad, happy, angry, frustrated, worried, excited, etc.) written on one side. Include an illustration to clarify meaning. Ask the child to whisper the word to you to make sure he or she has "read" it correctly. Then coach the child to act out the feeling with facial expressions and gestures. Invite the rest of the class to guess the feeling.

Writing: Give each child a feeling word to illustrate. Have children complete the following sentence frame below their picture: "I feel _____ when _____." Bind the pages together to make a class book of feelings.

Grade Levels: First and second

Thematic Connections:
Crews, D. (1991). *Bigmama's.*
Greenfield, E. (1983). *Grandmama's joy.*
Igus, T. (1992). *When I was little.*
Johnson, A. (1990). *When I am old with you.*

The Jones Family Express (2003) by Javaka Steptoe

Steven wants to find a special gift for his favorite aunt. He ends up making her a present that wonderfully captures the spirit and energy of his aunt and of their large extended family.

Speaking: Write each child's name on a piece of paper and put the names in a basket. Have each child pick a name from the basket. Ask children to draw a picture of a perfect gift for the child whose name they picked. Display each picture and challenge the class to guess who each gift is for. Encourage children to explain the reasoning behind their choices.

Writing: Have children write a description of a special gift they would like to give to someone they love. Encourage children to identify the character traits that make their gift a good choice.

Grade Levels: Second and third

Thematic Connections:
Flournoy, V. (1995). *Tanya's reunion.*
Grimes, N. (2001). *Stepping out with Grandma Mac.*
Medearis, A. S. (1995). *Poppa's new pants.*

Aunt Harriet's Underground Railroad in the Sky (1992) by Faith Ringgold

Cassie and BeBe travel back into history to meet Harriet Tubman.

Speaking: Hold a "press conference" with Cassie and Bebe. Invite classroom reporters to ask Cassie and Bebe questions about their journey back into history.

Writing: Ask children to choose a person from history they would most like to meet. Have them explain the reasons for their choice and describe what they would like to ask the person. What message do they think the person would like to give to children today?

Grade Levels: Second through fourth

Thematic Connections:

Farris, C. K. (2003). *My brother Martin: A sister remembers growing up with the Rev. Dr. Martin Luther King, Jr.*

Lawrence, J. (1993). *Harriet and the promised land.*

Ringgold, F. (1995). *My dream of Martin Luther King.*

Ringgold, F. (1999). *If a bus could talk: The story of Rosa Parks.*

Flossie and the Fox (1986) by Patricia C. McKissack

Flossie outwits a sly fox.

Writing: Have children work with partners or in small groups to write a narrative describing the encounter with Flossie from Fox's point of view.

Speaking: Ask children to think about how the fox might tell his side of the story. What tone of voice would he use? What gestures and facial expressions would he make? Then invite children to read or perform their narratives aloud.

Grade Levels: Second and third

Thematic Connections:

Berry, J. (1997). *First palm trees: An Anancy spiderman story.*

McKissack, P. C., & Onawumi, J. M. (2005). *Precious and the Boo Hag.*

Uncle Jed's Barbershop (1993) by Margaree King Mitchell

Uncle Jed has a life-long dream to open a barbershop, a dream he must keep deferring both because of the Great Depression and because he is always using his savings to help others. To fully make sense of the story, children need to make a number of inferences as they read or listen.

Speaking: Before reading, tell children about a dream you had when you were growing up. Then have children share their own dreams with a partner. After reading, pose discussion questions that require children to make inferences about the story. Here are some examples: *Why was Uncle Jed the narrator's favorite relative? Before Uncle Jed started cutting hair, why did Black people have to travel 30 miles to get a haircut? Why didn't people believe him when Uncle Jed talked about his dream of opening his own barbershop? What did Uncle Jed feel when his dream finally came true?*

Writing: Have children write a personal essay about their dream, detailing the steps they think will be necessary to make it come true and predicting how they will feel when they accomplish their goal.
Grade Levels: Second through fourth

Thematic Connections:
Bradby, M. (1995). *More than anything else.*
Howard, E. F. (2000). *Virgie goes to school with us boys.*
Johnson, A. (2003). *I dream of trains.*
Johnson, A. (2004). *Just like Josh Gibson.*
Joseph, L. (1998). *Fly, Bessie, fly.*
Mitchell, M. K. (1997). *Granddaddy's gift.*
Ringgold, F. (1991). *Tar beach.*
Ringgold, F. (1995). *My dream of Martin Luther King.*
Tarpley, N. A. (2003). *Joe-Joe's first flight.*
Tarpley, N. A. (2004). *Destiny's gift.*

Rosa (2005) by Nikki Giovanni

In her lyrical account of Rosa Parks's historic refusal to give up her seat to a White passenger on a bus in Montgomery, Alabama on December 1, 1955, Giovanni writes: *"When the policeman bent down to ask 'Auntie, are you going to move?' all the strength of all the people through all those many years joined in her. Rosa Parks said no"* (unnumbered pages).

Writing: Ask children to write about what they think Rosa Parks may have been thinking at this historic moment.
Speaking: One by one, invite children to stand and voice their thoughts in the voice of Rosa Parks.
Grade Levels: Second through fourth

Thematic Connections:
Greenfield, E. (1995). *Rosa Parks.*
Ringgold, F. (1999). *If a bus could talk: The story of Rosa Parks.*

The Other Side (2001) by Jacqueline Woodson

Two young girls, one Black and one White, decide to step over the fence that racially divides their town and become friends.

Writing: Open to the page where the two girls run into each other while walking with their mothers downtown. In the illustration, the girls look back at each other as their mothers lead them in opposite directions. Ask children to imagine what each of the girls is thinking in the picture. Then ask children to draw the scene with "thought bubbles" above the characters' heads. Have them write the girls' thoughts in the bubbles.

Speaking: Ask partners to enact an imaginary scene in which the girls actually stop and talk to one another. Invite partners to perform their role plays for the class. Have the audience interview the characters about why they chose to say what they did.

Grade Levels: Second through fourth

Thematic Connections:

Pinkney, A. D. (2003). *Fishing day.*

Wiles, D. (2001). *Freedom summer.*

Chapter 9
Questioning and Summarizing/Retelling

I can never think about the strategy of questioning without visions of Bloom's taxonomy rising to mind. Bloom's Taxonomy of Educational Objectives, developed in the 1950s, laid out a classification system for ordering the difficulty level of questions. It began with literal recall questions at the bottom of the hierarchy and extended upwards to increasingly more abstract, analytical questions. The questions at the top were naturally presumed to be more cognitively complex and demanding than those at the bottom. Like many other reading teachers in the 1970s, I spent countless hours making up questions for various texts based on this taxonomy and then, to my mind, at least, "teaching comprehension" by asking students to provide the answers. Looking back now, I can see that in doing so I was making two false assumptions about reading comprehension that, unfortunately, are still not uncommon today.

One was the assumption that simply by asking students questions about a text after they had read it, I was necessarily teaching them how to comprehend text. From research on the thinking processes of skilled readers, we now know that the questions that matter the most in terms of comprehension are the questions that readers learn to ask themselves as they engage with text. This doesn't mean that teacher-generated questions about text are useless, however—far from it. For one thing, teachers need to ask questions that model for children the kinds of questions good readers ask as they read. They also need to ask questions that guide children in the use of other important comprehension strategies as happens, for example, when teachers ask children what they visualize in listening to a particular passage or how something in a text might connect to their own lives. Finally, teachers need to ask questions that inspire great classroom discussion, that push children's thinking, and that send them back to a text with new and deeper questions of their own. But this carefully thought out, strategic use of questions is very different from the predictable set of hierarchically sequenced comprehension questions that typically passed for reading instruction when I began teaching.

The second assumption I made back then that turned out to be erroneous—and one that is particularly dangerous for teachers of Black children to make—is that comprehension ability develops in the same linear, sequential order laid out in Bloom's taxonomy of questions. This would imply, for example, that a child's ability to answer a higher order question (e.g., one requiring her to draw inferences from text or make a critical judgment) is somehow dependent upon her ability to respond appropriately to lower order questions (e.g., ones requiring literal recall of information from the text). A teacher influenced by this view is unlikely to even consider the possibility that children who consistently fail to answer literal recall questions correctly might nonetheless do very well with questions requiring sophisticated inferential reasoning. Yet three decades of research in cognitive science suggest that this is perfectly possible (Rogoff, 2003). Based on this research, we now know that much of what children are able to think about and do is not dependent upon a preordained developmental sequence, but rather upon the specific cultural practices they have routinely participated in as fledging members of a particular social community.

Based on what we know about language socialization in African American communities, we might predict that some Black children would experience difficulty with literal recall or what are often termed known-answer questions because, as discussed in chapter 5, the Black discourse community tends to place little value on the recitation of obvious knowledge. Therefore some Black children are likely to have had little practice answering this type of question. On the other hand, the community tends to place very high value on being able to come up with a novel, creative response to questions that are more open-ended and that do not call for a single, predictable answer. Thus we might predict that many Black children would excel in responding to the kinds of questions that appear at the upper end of Bloom's taxonomy, those requiring critical and creative interpretive abilities.

These are precisely the results that literacy educator Angela Rickford (1999) obtained in her study of reading comprehension in an urban middle school classroom in which the majority of students were African American. To assess their comprehension of six African American narratives read aloud to students at two-week intervals, Rickford asked a series of questions for each narrative that students had to respond to in writing. For all six narratives, story-specific questions included the following four types: general questions, literal meaning questions, interpretive reading and critical evaluation questions, and creative reading questions (pp. 96–97). Rickford found that students did significantly better on questions requiring interpretive thinking, critical evaluation, and creative reading than they did on questions requiring only literal recall.

The questions students did best with not only focused on so-called higher order interpretive abilities, but, as Rickford points out, also tapped into students' experience with and skill in argumentation and problem solving (p. 103). For example, included in the interpretative reading, critical evaluation set of questions for each story was a question that required students to make a moral judgment about the behavior of a major character within the story and to show the reasoning behind this judgment. Similarly, another question for every selection asked students to circle three qualities that best described a particular character's feelings with respect to a key story event and then to provide reasons for their choices. The creative reading questions invited students, working together in small groups, to respond to the stories in more collaborative and creative ways. For one story entitled "Brer Rabbit in Love," for instance, students were asked to compose a short song or rhyme modeled after a rhyming song in the story. Another question for each selection invited students, again working in small groups, to write a new ending for the story. Like the examples just discussed, all of Rickford's nonliteral, more intellectually challenging questions drew upon linguistic and cognitive abilities fostered through socialization in the African American speech community. Rickford speculates that it was precisely this "goodness of fit" between the types of questions asked and students' prior language experiences that accounted in part for their superior performance on the higher order, more cognitively demanding questions.

This "goodness of fit" can clearly be seen by reflecting on Rickford's questions in light of the 12 attitudes and abilities listed at the end of chapter 3. The second item on that list, for example, suggests that as a result of their language socialization experiences, Black children are likely to have developed a view of argumentation/conflict talk as a stimulating and intellectually engaging activity. As described here, the majority of Rickford's nonliteral questions required students to make a judgment or take a stand about an issue or a character's actions. For none of these questions was there a single correct or even best answer. All were open to interpretation, to argument and dispute. All required justifying one's point of view. In his study of language use among Black adolescent boys in Harlem, Labov (1972) found that, like the students in Rickford's study, this kind of linguistic task—that is, taking a stand on an issue and defending it—was one in which his subjects particularly excelled, leading them to construct highly complex and forceful arguments in support of their positions. As was described in chapter 5, many Black children have had extensive experience both observing and participating in speech events that require defending one's point with wit and logic. Thus Rickford's questions provided a context for students to demonstrate verbal reasoning abilities honed through years of practice in their peer groups and communities. It is little wonder then that they performed so well in response to these questions.

Unfortunately, as discussed earlier, the most frequently asked type of question in most elementary classrooms continues to be the known-answer question, calling forth only children's most basic, literal-level recall of information from a text (Cazden, 1988; Stubbs, 1983). Reflecting on the ubiquity of this question type in classroom discourse, literacy educator Lucy Calkins (2001) writes:

> I do not know why it is ingrained in us as teachers to pepper children with oral, workbooklike, fill-in-the-blank questions. We want to say, "Let's talk about the reasons children made fun of Crow Boy," but because we are accustomed to the conversational pattern that dominates classrooms, we say, "Did the children in this book like Crow Boy? Did they make fun of him?" (p. 61)

Calkins maintains that breaking this known-answer question habit is essential to helping children "think, talk and eventually write well about texts" (p. 61). As Calkins makes clear in her discussion, grilling children with known-answer questions about a text does not facilitate literacy development for anyone. But I would argue that this practice is especially harmful to many Black children, for two reasons. One is that, in contrast to many White mainstream children, not only do some Black children have little out-of-school experience with questions that call for the display of obvious knowledge, but stating the obvious is a discourse practice that may be explicitly devalued in their speech community. Thus some Black children may find teachers' over-reliance on this question type particularly unengaging and perplexing. As a result, some African American children may not respond when teachers ask known-answer questions, a situation that leads directly to my second point about why teachers' prevalent use of this question type differentially impacts Black children.

We know that some teachers—unfortunately, way too many—bring very low academic expectations to their work with African American children. Needless to say, these teachers know little about language use in African American communities or about the sophisticated linguistic abilities children are likely to develop there. Thus when Black children in their classrooms repeatedly respond to known-answer questions by saying, "I 'on' know," shaking their heads, or simply remaining silent, such teachers are likely to misinterpret these behaviors, viewing them as signs of ineptitude and lack of understanding rather than as possible signals of children's boredom and lack of engagement with the kinds of questions being asked. The educational consequences of such misinterpretation are, of course, enormous. Instead of seeing that they need to significantly raise the level of classroom discourse to accommodate more sophisticated and challenging discussion, such teachers are likely to move in the opposite direction—even further simplifying an instructional approach that is already way too slow-paced and intellectually vacuous to be effective for African American children.

Asking Good Questions

Questions that stimulate children's critical thinking about text aim straight at the heart of what is most meaningful in a particular text. In many instances what is most meaningful is what is most puzzling and hard to interpret in any simple, definitive way. For example, in Mildred D. Taylor's *Mississippi Bridge* (1992), Black passengers about to embark on a bus trip in a heavy rainstorm must surrender their seats to a group of White passengers who show up at the last minute. Disaster strikes soon after when a nearby bridge collapses, plunging the bus and its all-White passengers into the churning waters of the Mississippi River. Over the years, I have seen classes of graduate students and fourth- and fifth-graders alike debate endlessly, and with insight and eloquence, in an effort to answer the most basic and profound of all story questions: "Why?" In discussing this book with students, I often begin by sharing that as many times as I've read *Mississippi Bridge*, I still have unanswered questions about it. Why, for instance, is Jeremy (a White character) so fascinated with the Logans (a Black family)? Why can't Jeremy find the courage to stand up for his beliefs? Why does Josiah risk his life trying to save White passengers when he has been kicked off the bus and treated in such a cruel and racist way? My questions typically generate lots more from students, many of them equally "unanswerable" in any definitive way, but elicitative of much critical thought and animated discussion. Remarkably, I have found (both in my own experience and in talking with teachers with whom I work) that when encouraged to voice their authentic questions about this text, fourth- and fifth-graders raise questions that are frequently as complex and thought-provoking as those raised by adults.

Even kindergartners are capable of asking (and answering) complex questions about the stories their teachers read aloud. Consider, for example, Juanita Havill's *Jamaica Tag-Along* (1989), part of the series of Jamaica books mentioned earlier. In this well-loved story, Jamaica's big brother, Ossie, refuses to let her play basketball with him and his friends. Later, building a sand structure on the playground by herself, Jamaica is approached by a much younger child who clearly wants to help her. Rejecting him initially, she suddenly recalls how she felt when Ossie wouldn't let her play and so decides to let the little boy help her after all. A deceptively simple story, *Jamaica Tag-Along* taps into important themes in young children's lives—the question of "who gets to play" and the fear, and pain, of being rejected by other children. Previewing and predicting what this story might be about with a group of kindergartners, I said: "I'm wondering if this story is going to remind me of when I was little and my mother always told me that I had to let my little sister play, even when I didn't want to." Modeling the questioning process for children, I paused several times in my reading to pose other questions, for example, "I have a question. I'm wondering what Ossie means by 'serious ball'?" "I wonder why Ossie doesn't want Jamaica to play." "I'm wondering how Jamaica is feeling right now." Soon children were sharing their own "wonderings." We ended our discussion of the book with heated consideration of one little boy's question: "Do you have to let kids play even if you don't want them to?"

An Important Caveat: Learning How to Deal with Known-answer Questions

As discussed earlier, asking children factual, known-answer questions about a book they have just read or listened to is not likely to help them become better comprehenders of text. Nonetheless, known-answer questions are ubiquitous throughout the educational system, from preschool to graduate school. For better or worse, students are rewarded and viewed as intelligent for knowing the right answer, for being "information givers" in response to factual questions posed by teachers and, frequently, on standardized tests as well. Even though the content of questions obviously becomes more sophisticated as children progress up the educational ladder, their underlying form and function remain the same: to test the respondent's ability to produce a single, specific, predetermined answer. Because being able and willing to respond appropriately to these questions is essential to success in many school settings, teachers need to make sure that students receive practice with this question type (a point also underscored by Angela Rickford, 1999).

A number of educational researchers have stressed the importance of teachers being explicit and direct when helping children acquire mastery of new discourse forms (e.g., Delpit, 1996; Heath, 1983). As some African American children are likely to be unfamiliar with known-answer questions, especially during the early years of school, I advocate talking explicitly with children about their use. Reading aloud with young children, for example, you might say something like the following:

> In school, we sometimes play a question game when we talk about books. I ask a question, and, if you know the answer, you raise your hand. I may not be able to call on you to say the answer out loud because I can only call on one person at a time in the game, but I'll notice that your hand is up. Sometimes the questions will be silly. Look at this page [show illustration]. When we play the question game, I might ask you, "How many owls are sitting on the branch?" It's a silly question, isn't it? It's a silly question because we can all see that there are three owls in the picture. But even if the question is silly, when you know the answer, raise your hand, because that's how we play the game.

I have often found it helpful to use a puppet when talking with young children about known-answer questions. I sometimes have the puppet voice reactions I suspect the children may be having. For example, when the puppet covers its eyes in frustration and says (in a very scornful voice), "That's a really silly question!," in my response to the puppet I am able to validate what some children may be thinking and communicate my own awareness that, yes, the questions we ask in the "question game" *are* often kind of silly. This is critical because it is important for children to feel that their teacher's comments and responses "make sense"—that is, that they either fit with, or differ in understandable ways from, the assumptions about language children bring with them from home. In this way, children who have been socialized in a discourse community where stating the obvious is not valued learn that during *some* learning activities in school stating the obvious is valued. This understanding enables children to participate successfully in this particular discourse practice without having to simultaneously reject their own community's standards of skilled verbal performance.

With older children, teachers can talk even more directly and analytically about the practice of asking known-answer questions. Why, for example, are these the type of questions typically asked on standardized tests? Why do so many teachers use them? What kinds of knowledge do these questions tap into? How do these kinds of questions (what I often refer to with children as "right answer" questions) compare to the more open-ended kinds of questions that guide authentic discussion about a topic? What kinds of questions are easier to respond to, and why? Children can collect data about the kinds of questions they hear addressed to preschoolers in their homes and communities. To gain greater awareness of the specific aspects of text that known-answer questions tend to highlight, children can practice making up known-answer questions for various reading selections. They can experiment with and discuss how reading a text for the purpose of answering factual, recall questions is different from reading the same text with a different purpose in mind. The more children are able to think consciously, and talk explicitly, about different kinds of questions and the assumptions behind them, the more versatile and skilled they become in performing a range of academic tasks, from the more prosaic (e.g., circling the correct answer on a multiple-choice test) to the more profound (e.g., discussing or writing about the meaning of a character's actions).

Summarizing/Retelling

The ability to summarize—to capture in a succinct way the essence or gist of a text—is one that children will need to call on repeatedly throughout their school years. In the National Research Council's 1998 report, *Preventing Reading Difficulties in Young Children,* the ability to summarize major points from both fiction and nonfiction texts is listed as a benchmark third-grade accomplishment (Snow et al., 1998, p. 83). In kindergarten and first grade, summarizing most often takes the form of retelling—recounting the major events of a story (or portion of a story) in the sequence in which they occurred in the text.

In the book *So Much* (1994) by Trish Cooke, for example, the members of a large extended family gather to celebrate a birthday. As family members arrive for the party, they greet the baby who lives in the house in a special way, all emphasizing that they love the baby *so much*. Auntie Bibba loves him so much that she wants to squeeze him. Uncle Didi wants to kiss him. Nannie and Gran-Gran want to eat him, and Cousin Kay-Kay and Big Cousin Ross want to fight him. A kindergartner's retelling of this story would entail, in part, telling which relatives arrived in what order and what each said and did to the baby.

In *Shortcut* (1992) by Donald Crews, another book that works well for practicing retelling, a group of children decide to take a shortcut home by walking along the railroad tracks, even though they know they shouldn't. They have lots of fun playing on the tracks until they suddenly hear the sounds of an approaching train. Frightened, they scramble to safety and arrive home unharmed. Kindergartners or first-graders retelling this story would need to include the major events that occur—the decision to take the shortcut, the playing on the tracks, the children's sudden awareness of an oncoming train, the scramble to safety, the arrival home—and to recount these in narrative order.

When first practicing retellings, young children sometimes leave out critical story events—the arrival of Uncle Didi in *So Much,* for example, or the children playing on the tracks before they hear the train in *Shortcut.* Nonetheless, these less-than-perfect efforts are still recognizable as retellings. What is critical to a retelling is the inclusion of most or all of the key story events and their presentation in sequential order. What is *not* permissible in a retelling is adding events that do not occur in the text, such as adding a relative to the list of visitors in *So Much* or having an airplane land on the railroad tracks in *Shortcut.* Interestingly, this is precisely what the African American children who were part of Vernon-Feagans's (1996) study of language socialization at home and in school did on a retelling task administered during the fall they entered kindergarten. Rather than simply retelling the story as most of the White children did, many of the African American children added to and embellished it. Vernon-Feagans writes:

> By doing so they frequently ended up creating a different, but often more interesting, vignette. For instance, one little boy, in paraphrasing the story about John buying a cake for his mother's birthday, proceeded to elaborate on other items he would buy for the birthday party, including hot dogs and potato chips. Even after a reminder that he was to only retell the vignette we had told to him, he created an elaborate story about how he would surprise his mother by inviting many of their relatives and friends. (p. 198)

In changing the story they heard, the Black children were demonstrating a skill highly valued in the African American discourse community, the ability to revise, to build upon, a previous speaker's utterance or story in a process the literary scholar Henry Louis Gates (1988) has called "repetition with a difference" (see chapter 5). But although the Black children's stories were often more interesting and imaginative than the original, they did not constitute retellings and thus the children were heavily penalized when their performance on the task was assessed. Ironically, then, as Vernon-Feagans intimates, the Black children may have performed poorly on the retelling task precisely *because* of their creative use of language and their sophisticated storytelling abilities.

Obviously it would be an error to predict the behavior of all Black children on the basis of how this particular group of kindergartners responded to a retelling task. Nonetheless, we know from numerous studies that the African American speech community in general places strong value on the speaker's introduction of a new semantic or rhetorical "twist" on the topic currently under discussion. A good oral performance, then, is one in which the speaker adds something unexpected, witty, and verbally inventive to the perspective that has already been voiced or to the story that has already been told. Thus the revisions that the Black children made to the story in Vernon-Feagans's study make sense within the frame of what we know about the Black discourse community. In this sense, their response to the retelling task was a predictable one, one that teachers of Black students should be prepared to deal with in teaching children how to retell or summarize text.

One effective way of doing that is for teachers to explicitly contrast retellings and summaries with more imaginative responses to text. In discussing *So Much*, for example, children could be asked to focus on two separate kind of responses to the book, one a retelling of what actually happened in the story and the other an activity in which children create an imaginary relative to add to those who came to the party in the story, perhaps a character modeled after someone in children's own families. The first kind of response could be labeled *retelling* and the other could be labeled something like *new telling*. Teachers might want to highlight the differences between these two kinds of tellings by posting the following sets of directions on large chart paper somewhere in the classroom:

Retelling
1. *Tell only things that happened in the story.*
2. *Tell about what is most important in the story.*
3. *Don't tell all the details.*

New Telling
1. *Use your imagination to tell a new story.*
2. *Tell about what the characters did and what they said.*
3. *Use lots of interesting details.*

Books in a series are especially good for contrasting retellings and new tellings. For example, children can do retellings of the stories in the Jamaica series by Juanita Havill or the Little Bill series by Bill Cosby and then do new tellings by making up new adventures for these same characters. In creating new stories about characters they've encountered in multiple books, children are drawing not just on their imagination and skills with language, but on their prior knowledge of text and their growing knowledge about literary character as well. Of course children's new tellings do not have to be limited to extending the adventures of book characters or adding to an already existing story. Children can also use stories read aloud to them (or that they read independently) as jumping-off points for creating their own characters and adventures. In response to *Shortcut*, for instance, children might do new tellings about a time when they did something that they were warned not to do.

The possibilities are clearly endless. What is critical is that these two very different kinds of responses to text—one that sticks closely to the text's story line and the other that uses the text as an imaginative launching pad—be carefully distinguished for children and that they have multiple opportunities to practice both. By explicitly contrasting these forms (i.e., retelling and new telling) for children, teachers are helping them to develop a comparative perspective on different forms and ways of using language. Contextualizing new knowledge in terms of what children already know is perhaps the most basic principle of learning. If teachers have reason to believe that "repetition with a difference" may be a more familiar and valued form of verbal performance in children's communities than is retelling, then talking about what constitutes a retelling in contradistinction to what constitutes a new telling makes sound pedagogical sense. All children, regardless of their prior language socialization, benefit from becoming familiar with, and practiced in, multiple ways of processing and responding to text.

Acting Out Stories Is a Kind of Retelling

Especially for kindergartners and first-graders, dramatizing a book is an effective and engaging way of retelling the major narrative events. Using the book *So Much* with kindergartners, for instance, the teacher could ask children to volunteer to play the nine different characters who appear in the book. The rest of the children could play the role of audience the first time the story is enacted and then be encouraged to take on character roles the next time. The fact that the text of *So Much* is so rhythmic and repetitive makes it easy for children to remember key lines from the book. The teacher can prompt children who might forget what their character is supposed to be doing and saying by holding up an illustration of the character and saying something like the following:

> Remember Auntie Bibba? What does she say to the baby? What does she do with the baby? Think back to when you were listening to the story.

Teachers can bring in props to make the dramatization more fun and realistic. For *So Much* these might include the doorbell that announces each family member's arrival in the book and music to accompany the scene in which everyone dances at the party.

After children have put on numerous performances (perhaps several days later), the teacher might have them exercise their skills in "repetition with a difference" by revising the play, creating new characters who greet the baby in unique and special ways. The class could brainstorm who the characters would be and what they would say and do to the baby. The teacher should be sure to emphasize that the first play is "just like the book," while the second play is different from it, a new creation.

Another book that works particularly well for dramatized retelling with kindergartners is Irene Smalls's *Jonathan and His Mommy* (1992), in which a little boy and his mommy walk down the street together in all kinds of fun and special ways. When they take "big giant steps," for example, they talk in "big giant voices," and when they take "itsy-bitsy baby steps," they talk "in tiny baby voices about baby things" (unnumbered pages). The book follows their progress from home and back again. The entire class can dramatize this book together as they parade around the room re-creating (i.e., retelling) the actions and conversation in the book. Afterward, children can do a "new telling" by creating new steps for the whole class to learn and follow.

Folktales and fairy tales are particularly appropriate for retelling because their repetitive language and predictable story structure aid children's recall. *Leola and the Honeybears* (1999) by Melodye Benson Rosales, for example, makes a great retelling-through-dramatization book for kindergartners as does *Head, Body, Legs: A Story from Liberia* (2002) by Won-Ldy Paye and Margaret Lippert. Teachers may want to make puppets available for children to use during choice time to dramatize stories the class has been reading.

Examples of books that work well for dramatic retellings with first- or second-graders include the Jamaica books by Juanita Havill, Patricia McKissack's *Nettie Jo's Friends* (1989), and Angela Shelf Medearis's *Poppa's New Pants* (1995). Again, children can first dramatize (i.e., retell) the events as they occur in the book and then create "revisionist" dramas of their own. As an example, recall my earlier reference to *Jamaica's Find* (1986), in which Jamaica returns a stuffed dog to the Lost and Found and ends up meeting the dog's owner, Kristen. After dramatizing various scenes from the book, children could improvise a scene that doesn't actually occur in the story, such as what happens when Jamaica and Kristen see each other at the park the next day or when Jamaica goes home and tells her family about returning the dog and meeting Kristen. Again, there are myriad imaginative possibilities.

Summarizing Is Like Retelling, Only . . .

When summarizing something they've read or listened to, readers pay relatively less attention to telling all the major events that occurred in the text in strict chronological order and relatively more attention to specifying what is most important in the text. In this sense, summarizing is a more sophisticated skill than retelling. An important aid to both comprehending and summarizing fictional text is learning about story structure. Stories include the basic elements of character, setting, plot, and theme. Teaching children to look for these elements as they read or listen to stories not only scaffolds their understanding of the story, but also provides a reliable structure for producing an effective summary. Before reading aloud *Jamaica and Brianna* (1993) by Juanita Havill, for example, a first- or second-grade teacher might say something like the following:

> As I read the book aloud, I want you to listen for the story elements. Remember how we talked about the fact that every story has these four elements? Every story has characters, the people who act in the story. Every story has a setting, which is where the story takes place. Every story has a plot, which is what happens in the story. And every story has a theme, which is the big idea or the lesson in the story. Characters, setting, plot, and theme—these are the four elements that go together to make a story.
>
> Remember when we read *Jamaica's Find* last week? We talked about the characters and made a list of them. We had Jamaica on our list, her mother and father and her brother, Ossie. There was also the man at the Lost and Found and Kristen, the little girl who lost the dog. Those were the characters. We also talked about the setting. The setting is where the story takes place. In *Jamaica's Find,* the story took place at the park and in Jamaica's house. We talked about the plot, too. Remember, the plot is what happens in the story. In *Jamaica's Find,* Jamaica found the dog at the park. She couldn't decide if she would keep it or not. Finally she decided to take it to the Lost and Found, and she met Kristen, the little girl who lost it. That was the plot, what happened in the story. When we talked about the theme of the story, people had different ideas, didn't they? Keisha said that the big idea in the story was that when you find something that isn't yours, you have to give it back, even if you want it. Kevin said that the big idea or lesson was that it's important to do the right thing. We heard lots of good ideas about the theme.
>
> Now we're reading this new Jamaica book, *Jamaica and Brianna*. As I read, listen for the characters (who are the people in the story?), the setting (where does the story happen?), the plot (what happens in the story?) and the theme (what's the big idea or the lesson in the story?).

After reading the story, the teacher might ask children to share their ideas about character, setting, plot, and theme with partners before the whole class discussion. Later, children can write short summaries of the book and draw a picture of their favorite part of the story. Children will need lots of practice working with story elements before these become a routine way for them to think about the stories they listen to and read on their own. This practice is well worth the effort, however, as these elements are powerful tools for helping children identify what is most essential in a fictional text.

One of the ways children can practice summarizing is by writing short summaries of individual chapters in books read aloud by the teacher. A second- or third-grade teacher, for example, might read aloud *Abby Takes a Stand* (2005) by Patricia C. McKissack, the story of a little girl's involvement in the Civil Rights Movement in Nashville, Tennessee. The book is divided into 12 short chapters. At the end of each chapter, the teacher could pause and ask children to write a very brief summary of the chapter, focusing on the elements of character, setting, and plot. When the book is finished, the teacher might want to ask children to write a summary of the entire book, including a discussion of theme.

Junebug (1995) by Alice Mead and its sequel, *Junebug and the Reverend* (1998), work well for doing chapter summaries with third- and fourth-graders. Because its chapters are untitled, another way to practice summarizing with *Junebug* is to have children make up titles that capture the main idea or gist of each chapter. Children can also write book reviews of books they've read on their own. These reviews can be written for classmates who haven't yet read the book. The summaries included in the review should capture the essence of the story without giving away any details or story outcomes that would spoil the book for a new reader.

Because the ability to summarize effectively is so critical to academic success, it warrants extensive practice with many different kinds of text, including factual, expository text, for which the ability to distinguish central ideas from illustrative details is so crucial to full comprehension. To give children needed practice in summarizing, teachers should both read aloud and have children read expository texts from multiple content areas—books as well as newspapers and children's magazine articles about topics such as animals, the ocean, music, dance, plants, space, medieval knights and castles, current events, sports, everything under the sun, and beyond, that children could possibly be interested in. In teaching children how to summarize ideas from text, teachers need to model the process by "thinking aloud" during oral reading. Pausing at strategic points in the text, teachers should summarize the major ideas presented up to that point, making sure to emphasize that they are using "their own words," not the exact wording of the text, to restate the big ideas in the passage.

One subject area ripe for exploration, and too often overlooked or given too short shrift in the early elementary grades, is African American history. Books about this history provide a great context for practicing skills in summarizing. A case in point is Toni Morrison's children's book *Remember: The Journey to School Integration* (2004), a book especially suitable for reading with children in grades two through four. Morrison uses powerful photographs and words to chronicle what she terms the "journey" to school integration. In the book, she divides this journey into three distinct phases: "The Narrow Path," "The Open Gate," and "The Wide Road" (unnumbered pages). After reading this book straight through once, on the second reading, the teacher might pause after each of these phases and ask students to summarize this particular phase of the journey in their own words. (Children can do this orally and/or in writing.) Morrison's wonderfully evocative metaphors for these three phases of the journey to school integration could then be used to organize further exploration of this period in American history.

In *Let It Shine: Stories of Black Women Freedom Fighters* (2000), Andrea Davis Pinkney presents brief biographies of 10 African American women who effected change in the world by standing up for social justice. Reading the individual biographies aloud to third- or fourth-graders over a period of days, the teacher could ask children, in preparation for summary writing, to think about what they consider to be the most essential information contained in the biography. For the first two or three biographies, the teacher might want to work collectively with students to create a class summary. Then children could work individually, in pairs, or in small groups to write brief summaries for the rest of the biographies. Before leaving discussion of the book, teachers should ask children to reflect upon what these 10 women, some born in the eighteenth and nineteenth centuries and some in the twentieth, held in common. In addition to Pinkney's collection, *Let It Shine,* there are numerous individual biographies of both well- and lesser-known African Americans that could be used effectively for simultaneously practicing summarizing and learning more about African American history.

Speaking and Writing Connections

Recommended Books for Questioning

The following speaking and writing routines use questions to set a purpose for listening, reading, researching, and gathering and organizing information. Posing key questions provides a framework to support and enhance comprehension, as well as to help children elaborate on their writing.

My Nana and Me (2005) by Irene Smalls

A little girl does special things with her grandmother.

Speaking: As you preview the book, ask children what questions they have about the girl and her Nana. Record their questions. Then ask: *What do you think the girl and her Nana like to do together?* Set a listening purpose by asking children to think about this question as they listen to you read. After reading, record and discuss children's answers to this question, as well as the other questions children posed before reading.

Writing: Have children draw a picture of themselves doing something special with a grandparent or other important adult. Conduct a shared writing activity by describing children's descriptions of their pictures (*Duane likes to play the drums with Aunt Mary; Aisha likes to go to the park with Grandpa*).

Grade Levels: Kindergarten and first

Thematic Connections:

DeGross, M. (1999). *Granddaddy's street songs.*

Flournoy, V. (1985). *The patchwork quilt.*

Greenfield, E. (1988). *Grandpa's face.*

Howard, E. F. (1991). *Aunt Flossie's hats (and crab cakes later).*

Smalls, I. (1992). *Jonathan and his mommy.*

Smalls, I. (1999). *Kevin and his dad.*

Smalls, I. (2006). *My Pop Pop and me.*

Sleeping Cutie (2004) by Andrea Davis Pinkney

Little Cutie LaRue has an exciting bedtime adventure.

Speaking: Build interest in the story by asking children whether they like to go to bed at night. Then preview the book and ask children what questions they have about the girl and the owl pictured on the cover. Children may ask: *Who is the owl on the cover? Is the little girl dreaming? Is her name Little Cutie? Does she like going to bed?* Ask children to listen for the answers to their questions as you read the story aloud. After reading, discuss children's findings. Then ask children which parts of the book are real and which parts are imaginary. As you reread the book, have children focus on figuring out what is real and imaginary in the story. After reading, invite children to share their own special bedtime rituals with partners.

Writing: Children can draw a picture and write or dictate a bedtime story about themselves.

Grade Levels: Kindergarten and first

Thematic Connections:

Cosby, B. (1999). *One dark and scary night.*

Jonas, A. (1984). *The quilt.*

Medearis, A. S. (1995). *Poppa's new pants.*

Two Mrs. Gibsons (1996) by Toyomi Igus

The author describes her African American grandmother and her Japanese mother. They are different in many ways, but similar in their love for the author.

Speaking: Preview the book and ask children what questions they have about the two Mrs. Gibsons. Set a listening purpose by asking children to focus on the questions: *How are the two Mrs. Gibsons different? How are they the same?* After reading, use a Venn diagram or other graphic organizer to help children compare and contrast the two characters. Ask children if they have further questions about the two Mrs. Gibsons that they wish the author had answered. Afterward, have children work in pairs and use a Venn diagram to answer the same questions—*How are we different? How are we the same?*—about themselves.

Writing: Working in the same pairs, have children write one way they are different and one way they are the same.

Grade Levels: Kindergarten and first

Thematic Connections:

Falwell, C. (2001). *David's drawings.*

Hru, D. (1993). *Joshua's Masai mask.*

Johnson, D. (1992). *The best bug to be.*

Medearis, A. S. (1994). *Annie's gifts.*

Donavan's Word Jar (1998) by Monalisa DeGross

In this short chapter book, Donavan is confronted with a perplexing question: what to do with his rapidly growing collection of interesting words. Donovan seeks advice from his mother, his father, his teacher, and his grandmother before happening upon an ingenious solution to his dilemma.

Speaking: While reading the book aloud, stop at the end of each chapter and have children generate questions they hope will be answered in the next chapter. Ask children if they know anyone who has an interesting collection. What do they want to know about the collection? Work with children to develop a set of questions to interview someone at school, home, or in their communities about his or her collection.

Writing: Have children draw a portrait of the person they interviewed and write a short report about his or her collection. Invite children to share their reports with the class. Encourage children to ask one another questions.

Grade Levels: First through third

Thematic Connections:

Angelou, M. "I Love the Look of Words," in Feelings, T. (Ed.). (1993). *Soul looks back in wonder.*

Cosby, B. (1997). *The treasure hunt.*

Smothers, E. F. (2003). *The hard-times jar.*

Something Beautiful (1998) by Sandra Dennis Wyeth

"Where is my something beautiful?" is the question at the heart of this beautiful picture book. Walking around her neighborhood, the young narrator is discouraged by the things she sees—for example, trash in the courtyard, graffiti scrawled on buildings, a homeless woman sleeping on the sidewalk. When *beautiful* becomes one of her vocabulary words at school, the narrator sets out in search of what is beautiful in her surroundings.

Writing: Write the following question on the board or on chart paper: *Where is your something beautiful?* Then, in pairs, have children identify at least five beautiful things in their surroundings and choose their favorite to illustrate and write about. Tell children that their writing is a first draft.

Speaking: Ask a volunteer to read aloud his or her draft. Model how to ask questions to help the writer describe his or her "something beautiful" in more detail. You might ask, *What does it look like? Can you compare it to something else? What does it sound like? What does it feel like or smell like? What makes it special for you? How does it make you feel?* Then have children read their drafts to their partners. Encourage partners to ask one another questions to help elaborate on their descriptions.

Writing Again: Have children revise their drafts, incorporating details that respond to their partner's questions.

Grade Levels: First and second

Thematic Connections:
Cole, K. (2001). *No bad news.*
Greenfield, E. (1996). *Night on Neighborhood Street.*
Grimes, N. (1997). *It's raining laughter.*

Beauty, Her Basket (2004) by Sandra Belton

A young girl from the Sea Islands and her cousin Victor learn about the tradition of making sea grass baskets and about the strength and courage of their enslaved ancestors.

Speaking: After previewing the book, ask children what questions they have about the story. Children who do not live in the Sea Islands area of the United States are likely to have more questions after the first reading of the story. Discuss and record these questions before reading the book a second time. After the second reading, ask children what questions they still have about topics or issues raised in the story. Pose two or three sample questions, such as the following: *Where are the Sea Islands? Why do the characters talk the way they do? Do many people* *still make sea grass baskets? What other traditions did enslaved Africans bring with them from their homelands?* Ask children how they think they can find answers to their questions and together make a list of possible sources of information.

Writing: In small groups, have children research the answers to their questions and prepare brief research reports.
Grade Levels: Second and third

Thematic Connections:
Banks, S. H. (1997). *A net to catch time.*
Daise, R. (1997). *Little Muddy Waters: A Gullah folk tale.*
Raven, M. T. (2004). *Circle unbroken: The story of a basket and its people.*

My Brother Martin: A Sister Remembers Growing Up With the Rev. Dr. Martin Luther King, Jr. (2003) by Christine King Farris

Dr. King's older sister paints an intimate portrait of the civil rights leader's boyhood and the events and relationships that shaped him.

Speaking: Before reading, ask children what they know about Dr. Martin Luther King, Jr. Record their responses in the first column (What We *K*now) of a K-W-L chart. Then ask children what they would like to know about the civil rights leader, particularly about his childhood. Record their questions in the second column (What We *W*ant to Know) of the chart. Ask children to listen for answers to their questions as you read the book aloud. After reading, review the questions in the second column of the chart. Discuss and record children's answers in the third column (What We *L*earned). Identify any unanswered questions and talk about how children might find the answers to them.
Writing: Have small groups choose a question to research. Invite groups to write a research report and share their findings with the class.
Grade Levels: Third and fourth

Thematic Connections:
Myers, W. D. (2004). *I've seen the promised land: The life of Dr. Martin Luther King, Jr.*
Rappaport, D. (2001). *Martin's big words: The life of Dr. Martin Luther King, Jr.*

Meet Danitra Brown (1994) by Nikki Grimes

In a series of spirited poems, a young girl introduces readers to her best friend Danitra Brown, "the most splendiferous girl in town."

Speaking: As you read the poems aloud, ask children to listen for words and information that describe Danitra—her physical appearance, her personality, her likes and dislikes, her dreams and goals. After reading, organize the class into teams. Instruct each team to come up with a set of questions about Danitra to pose to a competing team. Encourage them to include both literal, known-answer questions (e.g., *What is Danitra's favorite color?*), as well as open-ended, interpretive questions (e.g., *Why is Danitra a good friend?*). Using a quiz-show format, challenge teams to ask and answer each other's questions as you moderate.

Writing: Have children choose their favorite open-ended question to write about.

Grade Levels: Third and fourth

Thematic Connections:
Grimes, N. (2002). *Danitra Brown leaves town.*
Grimes, N. (2005). *Danitra Brown, class clown.*

Champion: The Story of Muhammad Ali (2002) by Jim Haskins

A biographical tribute to Muhammad Ali.

Speaking: Invite children to come up with questions they would like to ask Ali about the events described in the book. Several children can take turns playing the role of Ali while the other children play the role of interviewers. Prompt the interviewers to ask children playing Ali questions about key events in his life, such as how he felt as a boy when he saw Black people being treated unfairly or why he thought it was important not to fight in Vietnam even though he was stripped of his championship title as a result.

Writing: Have children generate a set of research questions about Ali's life that they would like to explore. After doing research, individually or in pairs, have children write their own brief biographies of Ali's life, highlighting the events and details they feel are most important.

Grade Levels: Third and fourth

Thematic Connections:
Bolden, T. (2004). *The champ: The story of Muhammad Ali.*
Shange, N. (2002). *Float like a butterfly.*

Creativity (1997) by John Steptoe

Charles, who is African American, wonders why Hector, his new classmate from Puerto Rico, looks so much like him: "How could that guy be from Puerto Rico? He was the same color as me, and I'm not from

Puerto Rico. His hair was black like mine, but it was straight" (unnumbered pages).

Speaking: Stop after reading the previous passage (it appears on the first page of the book) and ask children what questions they have about the story at this point. Record children's questions before continuing to read. Discuss which questions were answered by the reading. Then encourage children to come up with a new set of questions. These might include the following: (a) *What are the histories of Indians, Africans, and Spaniards in Puerto Rico?* (b) *What is the history of Afro-Cubans?* (Charles finds out that his father is part Cuban.) (c) *What does Charles's father mean when he talks about different ways of speaking English?* (d) *What about different ways of speaking Spanish?*

Writing: Have children research and write about their questions in small groups.

Speaking Again: Invite groups to give oral presentations about their research.

Grade Levels: Third and fourth

Thematic Connections:

Chambers, V. (2005). *Celia Cruz: Queen of salsa.*
Picó, F. (1994). *The red comb.*
Velasquez, E. (2001). *Grandma's records.*

Recommended Books for Summarizing/Retelling

The following speaking and writing routines include dramatic retellings, creative new tellings, book reviews, and book reports. While scaffolding comprehension, these activities help children develop sequencing skills and an understanding of story elements and structure.

Kevin and His Dad (1999) by Irene Smalls

Rhythmic text describes all the things Kevin and his dad do together one Saturday, from cleaning the house to taking in a movie.

Speaking: Invite children to retell the story by acting out the activities Kevin and his Dad do.

Writing: Ask children to do a new telling by drawing a picture and writing or dictating a story about what Kevin and his dad do on another day of the week. Alternatively, children can draw a picture and write or dictate a story about special things they do with a favorite adult. Encourage children to use rhymes when they write or dictate their stories.

Grade Levels: Kindergarten and first

Thematic Connections:
Greenfield, E. (1976/1991). *First pink light.*
Johnson, A. (1997). *Daddy calls me man.*
Johnson, D. (1998). *What will Mommy do when I'm at school?*
Smalls, I. (1992). *Jonathan and his mommy.*

Full, Full, Full of Love (2003) by Trish Cooke

At Sunday dinner at Grandma's house, Little Jay Jay keeps asking: "Is dinner ready, Gran?" Each time, he gets momentarily distracted by some interesting activity.

Speaking: Prompt children to retell the major events in the story through drawing, interactive writing, drama or conversation.

Writing: Invite children to draw, write or dictate a new telling by adding an episode to the story in which Jay Jay gets distracted by some other fun activity. Alternatively, children can draw a picture and write or dictate a story about dinnertime at their house.

Grade Levels: Kindergarten and first

Thematic Connections:
Cooke, T. (1994). *So much.*
Falwell, C. (1993). *Feast for ten.*

Do Like Kyla (1990) by Angela Johnson

A little girl does everything her big sister Kyla does, from tapping at the birds outside their bedroom window in the morning to saying, "The End," when they finish their bedtime story at the end of the day.

Speaking: Invite children to retell the story by acting out the major events.

Writing: Have children write or dictate a new telling in which Kyla, the older sister, does everything her little sister does. Alternatively, children can draw a picture and write or dictate a story about things they do that are just like someone special in their lives.

Grade Levels: Kindergarten and first

Thematic Connections:
Caines, J. (1988). *I need a lunch box.*
Crews, N. (1998). *You are here.*
Howard, E. F. (1988). *The train to LuLu's.*
Howard, E. F. (1999). *When will Sarah come?*
Johnson, A. (1997). *The rolling store.*
Medearis, A. S. (1995). *The adventures of Sugar and Junior.*

Jamaica's Find (1986), *Jamaica Tag-Along* (1989), and
Jamaica and Brianna (1993) by Juanita Havill

In each of these stories, Jamaica faces a common childhood dilemma.

Speaking: Have children retell the stories by acting them out.

Writing: Have children do a new telling by writing or dictating an original Jamaica story. Prompt the story-writing process by asking questions such as the following: *Where will your story take place? What kind of problem will Jamaica have to solve? What happens first? What happens next? What will Jamaica say? What will she do? How does the story end?*

Grade Levels: Kindergarten through second

Thematic Connections:
Clifton, L. (1970). *Some of the days of Everett Anderson.*
Clifton, L. (1971/1991). *Everett Anderson's Christmas coming.*
Clifton, L. (1974/1992). *Everett Anderson's year.*
Clifton, L. (1976/1992). *Everett Anderson's friend.*
Clifton, L. (1977/2002). *Everett Anderson's 1 2 3.*
Clifton, L. (1978). *Everett Anderson's nine month long.*
Clifton, L. (1983/1988). *Everett Anderson's goodbye.*
Clifton, L. (2001). *One of the problems of Everett Anderson.*
Havill, Juanita. (1995). *Jamaica's blue marker.*
Havill, Juanita (1999). *Jamaica and the substitute teacher.*
Havill, Juanita (2002). *Brianna, Jamaica, and the dance of spring.*

Ma Dear's Aprons (1997) by Patricia C. McKissack

The story describes the assorted colors of aprons Ma Dear wears on different days of the week and the activities that she and little David Earl engage in on each of those days.

Speaking: On different color paper cut in the shape of aprons, have children draw or write something to help them remember the major story events. Prompt children to place the paper aprons in appropriate sequence and use them as props to retell the story to a partner or to the class.

Writing: Have children work in pairs or small groups to do a "new telling" by choosing one of the days of the week and making up an adventure that happens to David Earl and Ma Dear on that day (e.g., one of the sheets they hang on the clothesline every Monday suddenly blows away and . . .). Alternatively, children can write about their favorite day of the week, explaining what makes the day so special for them.

Grade Levels: First and second

Thematic Connections:

Barber, B. E. (1994). *Saturday at the New You.*

Johnson, A. (1990). *When I am old with you.*

Johnson, D. (1990). *What will Mommy do when I'm at school?*

The Stories Julian Tells (1981) by Ann Cameron

This short chapter book tells the adventures of Julian and his younger brother, Huey.

Writing: Children can write book reviews focusing on the story elements of character, setting, plot, and theme.

Speaking: Invite children to act out their favorite adventure from the book. Children can also create original Julian and Huey adventures and act out their new tellings.

Grade Levels: Second and third

Thematic Connections:

Cameron, Ann. (1986). *More stories Julian tells.*

Cameron, Ann. (1987). *Julian's glorious summer.*

Cameron, Ann. (1988). *Julian, secret agent.*

Cameron, Ann. (1990). *Julian, dream doctor.*

Cameron, Ann. (1995). *The stories Huey tells.*

Cameron, Ann. (1999). *More stories Huey tells.*

Cameron, Ann. (2001). *Gloria's way.*

Cameron, Ann. (2004). *Gloria rising.*

Show Way (2005) by Jacqueline Woodson

Woodson traces her maternal lineage back to her great, great, great, great grandmother by talking about how the African American quilting tradition was woven into the fabric of her foremothers' lives. Pause frequently when reading this story aloud, so children can follow the connections among the various characters.

Speaking: Have children retell the family history Woodson recounts, perhaps illustrating Woodson's maternal family tree by drawing the various characters or writing their names on paper quilt squares and then arranging them in sequential order. Encourage children to talk with their families to trace their own maternal or paternal lineage. Children can create paper quilt squares depicting each of their forebears and make presentations to the class.

Writing: Children can write about an object, story, or tradition passed down in their own families.

Grade Levels: Second through fourth

Thematic Connections:
Hopkinson, D. (1993). *Sweet Clara and the freedom quilt.*
Hopkinson, D. (2001). *Under the quilt of night.*
Nelson, V. M. (2003). *Almost to freedom.*
Ransom, C. (2003). *Liberty Street.*
Smalls, I. (1996). *Irene Jennie and the Christmas masquerade.*

Money Troubles (1998) and *One Dark and*
Scary Night (1999) by Bill Cosby

The beginning chapter books in the Little Bill series are divided into three or four short chapters. Chapter 1 presents the problem or situation to be solved. Chapter 2 (or 2 and 3) complicates the action. In the final chapter, the problem or situation is resolved.

Speaking: Discuss with children how the stories are structured. Encourage children to use this structural format to summarize the stories in the Little Bill series.

Writing: Conduct a minilesson on opening sentences, using the Little Bill books as a model. Point out that the books all have a formulaic opening in which Little Bill greets the reader, introduces himself, and sets the stage for the story to follow. For example, *Money Troubles* (1988) begins: "Hello, friend. My name is Little Bill and I am going to be famous. I'll tell you why" (unnumbered pages). Encourage children to do a new telling by writing their own Little Bill story, using the same formulaic opening and the same story structure. Alternatively, children can write books about their own real or imagined adventures, again using the same format.

Grade Levels: Two through four

Thematic Connections:
Cosby, B. (1997). *The best way to play.*
Cosby, B. (1997). *The meanest thing to say.*
Cosby, B. (1997). *The treasure hunt.*
Cosby, B. (1998). *Shipwreck Saturday.*
Cosby, B. (1998). *Super-fine valentine.*
Cosby, B. (1999). *The day I was rich.*
Cosby, B. (1999). *Hooray for the Dandelion Warriors!*
Cosby, B. (1999). *My big lie.*
Cosby, B. (1999). *The worst day of my life.*
Cosby, B. (2000). *The day I saw my father cry.*

The Story of Ruby Bridges (1995) by Robert Coles
and *Through My Eyes* (1999) by Ruby Bridges

Both books chronicle the experience of Ruby Bridges, who, in 1960, was the first Black child to attend a New Orleans public elementary school. Bridges uses subheadings to organize her account, making the book perfect for practicing summarizing.

Writing: After reading each major section in *Through My Eyes*, pause to allow students to write very brief summaries.

Speaking: Encourage children to compare and contrast Coles's picture book and Bridges's first-person account. Ask children to identify and discuss which details of Bridges's experience Coles chose to include in his book. Which details might children include if they were writing a book about Ruby Bridges? Why?

Writing Again: Children can write and illustrate their own "stories of Ruby Bridges."

Grade Levels: Third and fourth

Thematic Connections:

Evans, F. W. (2001). *A bus of our own.*

McKissack, P. C. (2001). *Goin' someplace special.*

Morrison, T. (2004). *Remember: The journey to school integration.*

Walvoord, L. (2004). *Rosetta, Rosetta, sit by me!*

Mufaro's Beautiful Daughters: An African Tale (1987) by John Steptoe

This classic African folktale highlights the value of generosity and kind-heartedness and explores the relationship between appearance and reality.

Speaking: Children can retell the tale by dramatizing it.
Demonstrate how to create "story boards" to help children remember the sequence of events. The book can also be used to explore traditional folktale themes and conventions, for example, the appearance of talking animals, the magical forest or far-from-home setting, the ritual test of character, the use of hyperbole and simile, the triumph of good over evil.

Writing: Drawing upon these traditional themes and conventions, and working in small groups, children can write and perform their own folktales. Alternatively, children can do a new telling by telling the story from another character's point of view or by changing one or more of the story elements in some essential way.

Grade Levels: Third and fourth

Thematic Connections:

San Souci, R. D. (1989). *The talking eggs: A folktale from the American South.*

San Souci, R. D. (1992). *Sukey and the mermaid.*

San Souci, R. D. (1996). *The house in the sky.*

San Souci, R. D. (1998). *Cendrillon: A Caribbean Cinderella.*

Part 4
Learning to Decode

Chapter 10
Emergent Literacy

Most children entering kindergarten and many entering first grade are at the emergent stage of literacy development. They are not yet what Snow, Burns, and Griffin (1998) colloquially term "real readers," able to take up an unfamiliar text and derive meaning from the print (p. 42). Although some may already know the letters of the alphabet and even recognize some words by sight, children at the emergent stage have little systematic understanding of how alphabet letters are related to speech. A solid understanding of the systematic and predictable relationships between print and speech—that is, phonics—is critical to children becoming fluent, independent readers. Not surprisingly, many reading researchers and other experts in the field have identified direct, explicit instruction in phonics as an essential component of an effective early literacy curriculum (e.g., Adams, 1990; Chall, 1967; Foorman, Francis, Fletcher, Schatschneider, & Mehta, 1988; Juel, 1988; Snow et al., 1998).

The Centrality of Phonemic Awareness

But before children can fully benefit from instruction in how specific letters and letter sequences map onto specific speech sounds (i.e., phonics instruction), they must first be aware that speech itself can be broken down into smaller units—into words, syllables, onsets and rhymes, and, most importantly, phonemes, the units of sound that most closely align with individual letters (e.g., /k/ /a/ /t/). As Snow, et al. (1998) explain: "Unless and until children have a basic awareness of the phonemic structure of language, asking them for the first sound in the word *boy*, or expecting them to understand that *cap* has three sounds while *camp* has four, is to little avail" (p. 54). This "basic awareness of the phonemic structure of language" is essentially what is meant by the term *phonemic awareness*. Phonemic awareness has two components: the understanding that words can be broken down into separate sounds (phonemes) and the ability to manipulate those sounds in various ways (e.g., the ability to orally blend the separate phonemes /k/ /a/ /t/ into the word *cat* or to orally produce *at* when asked to "say *cat* without the /k/").

Phonemic awareness can be difficult for children to achieve because in speech, phonemes have no actual acoustic reality. Neither, for that matter, do words. In the stream of speech, there are no identifiable breaks for individual words. The only breaks or pauses that do occur when people talk occur between syllables. As word boundaries do not actually exist in speech, it is not surprising that children occasionally have trouble figuring out exactly where they are. As illustration, the linguist Steven Pinker (1994) provides the following examples of "near-misses" from the speech of young children:

> I don't want to go to your ami [from *Miami*]
> I am heyv! [from *Behave!*)
> Daddy, when you go tinkle you're an eight, and when I go tinkle I'm an eight, right? [from *urinate*] (p. 267)

Similarly, individual phonemes have no clear, easily separable identity in speech. In speech, individual phonemes are interconnected or *co-articulated* with one another. In the word *bet*, for example, it is difficult to "hear" and pronounce the vowel sound /e/ in isolation from its surrounding consonant sounds /b/ and /t/. Yet children must be able to "hear" the /e/ as a separate sound in order to learn to read and spell. Even adults sometimes have trouble "hearing" all the distinct sounds in a word—identifying, for instance, that the word *straight* contains five phonemes or that the word *sing* has three.

In most situations, most of us perceive a word not as a series of separate sounds, but as a chunk of meaning. In other words, we pay attention to meaning, not sound. As Pinker (1994) puts it, "the actual sounds go in one ear and out the other; what we perceive is *language*" (p. 159). This is true both in listening and in reading. Skilled readers are only occasionally dependent upon their ability to "sound out" words because they recognize most words on sight or rely on spelling patterns to figure them out. As a consequence, they are likely to have stopped paying attention to individual sounds in words. Thus, not surprisingly, many people preparing to become elementary teachers find that they have to make a conscious effort to "hear" individual phonemes, that is, to recapture, or in some cases, acquire, the degree of phonemic awareness that is necessary for them to aid children in learning to read.

Phonemic awareness, then, is a *metalinguistic* awareness, one that requires conscious attention to aspects of language that typically pass under our radar as we go about using language to negotiate meaning in our everyday lives. It is only through deliberate, conscious effort on our part that individual phonemes end up making it onto our radar screen. Little wonder, then, the child who, when asked to identify the first sound in the word *cow*, tentatively responded

" 'Moo?' " (recorded in Bear, Invernizzi, Templeton & Johnston, 2000, p. 103). Because phonemes are so abstract and outside of conscious awareness, phonemic awareness must be taught explicitly in the early literacy curriculum. Relatively few children spontaneously acquire phonemic awareness (Adams, Treiman, & Pressley, 1998).

Just how important is phonemic awareness to the process of learning to read? The answer is "very." It is difficult for children to learn to decode text and to spell if they do not understand how the alphabet is related to individual speech sounds. In *Preventing Reading Difficulties in Young Children,* a landmark review-of-the-research report put out by the National Research Council, Snow et al. (1998) note that there are literally dozens of studies that confirm a close relationship between children's level of phonemic awareness and reading ability, both in the early grades and beyond. What's more, these findings about the importance of phonemic awareness have been corroborated by research with children in other countries, including Sweden, Norway, Spain, France, Italy, Portugal, and Russia (Adams, Foorman, Lundberg, & Beeler, 1998). A number of researchers have identified phonemic awareness and alphabet knowledge as two of the strongest predictors of success in early reading (Adams, 1990; Beck & Juel, 1995; Chall, 1996; Snow et al., 1998; Stanovich, 1986).

Phonemic Awareness and Alphabet Knowledge

Just as children must recognize that words are made up of separable sounds before they can begin matching letters to sounds in systematic and predictable ways, so too they must also recognize—and, ideally, be able to write—at least some of the letters of the alphabet. Underscoring their importance in the process of learning to read, Blevins (1998) describes phonemic awareness and alphabet knowledge as the two skills that "open the gate" for early reading (p. 16). They are the foundational abilities upon which successful phonics instruction depends. Learning to recognize and write most of the alphabet and acquiring some basic phonemic awareness are thus two of the most essential learning goals in the kindergarten year (Snow et al., 1998). Because of their importance in the learning-to-read process, I will discuss both phonemic awareness and alphabet knowledge at considerable length in this chapter and the next. Before doing so, however, I want to place these abilities within the larger context of the emergent literacy curriculum. In doing so, I am envisioning phonemic awareness and alphabet knowledge as two pieces of a picture puzzle entitled, "Effective Emergent Literacy Instruction." Before I metaphorically pick up these two pieces to examine them in closer detail, I want to make sure that readers understand how these pieces fit within the broader instructional picture. What are the other pieces of the puzzle to which they connect?

Letter-Sound Knowledge

First, and most closely connected, is letter-sound knowledge—children's aware- ness, for example, that the letter *m* "stands for" or represents the /m/ sound. It is important to point out that instruction in the alphabet and in phonemic aware- ness need not be complete before children begin making some letter-sound connections. Although children eventually have to become secure in their knowledge of all the letters, children who know only a subset of letters well can already begin making connections between sound segments and letters. Similarly, children can learn some letter-sound correspondences at the same time they are developing phonemic awareness. As the teacher draws children's attention to the /b/ sound while reading aloud the title of *Bippity Bop Barber- shop* (Tarpley, 2002), for example, it is a short step for children who have been learning the alphabet to make the connection between the /b/ sound they hear at the beginning of these words and the written symbol *b*. Bear et al. (2000) point out that children's awareness of sounds is actually heightened by print (p. 104). A number of literacy researchers have suggested that there is, in fact, a reciprocal relationship between children's level of phonemic awareness and their knowledge of sound-print correspondences. As pointed out earlier, a basic level of phonemic awareness—specifically, the insight that spoken words are composed of individual sounds—is necessary before children can be expected to connect letters with sounds. But, then, once children begin making those connections, the focused attention on sounds this process necessarily entails ends up further increasing their phonemic awareness. This increased level of phonemic awareness, in turn, supports children's growing knowledge of let- ter-sound connections. Research has consistently shown that phonemic aware- ness, alphabet knowledge, and letter-sound knowledge work in concert to help establish the foundation for successful reading instruction (Ball & Blachman, 1991; Cunningham & Cunningham, 1992; Gillam & van Kleeck, 1996; Hohn & Ehri, 1983; Lundberg, Frost, & Peterson, 1988; Snow et al., 1998). In terms of the puzzle analogy, these three separate but interlocking pieces form a sig- nificant portion of the instructional puzzle at the emergent level.

Experiences With Text

But by far the biggest and most important piece of the picture puzzle is chil- dren's experience with meaningful text. This includes the read-alouds and dis- cussions of complex text that were the focus of the last four chapters as well as children's interactions with various other kinds of text. Children at the emer- gent stage need exposure to a variety of texts including alphabet books; big books; books that contain multiple examples of rhyme and alliteration; easy, predictable books that can be partially or wholly memorized; poems, songs, chants, and jingles written on chart paper for children to recite; and children's own talk written down. When teachers read aloud complex text and discuss it with children, children glimpse the connection between books and the world of ideas, and they learn important comprehension strategies. They learn new vocabulary. As children chorally recite a familiar big book or a poem written on chart paper while the teacher points in synchrony to the words, they are experiencing the musicality of text and learning about directionality in print and about printed word boundaries. When teachers write down what children say about their drawings or record what children have to say about a field trip or a classroom visitor, children experience the connection between oral and written language and come to understand that whatever can be said can be written. As children "pretend" read or read from memory a familiar, predictable book, they practice the rhythm and cadence of written language and take on the identity of reader. Most importantly, children's multiple experiences with text give meaning and purpose to their work with sounds and letters. In the picture puzzle of emergent literacy instruction, "experience with text" is the puzzle piece that, once in place, puts all the other pieces in perspective.

Opportunities to Write

Experiences with writing form another crucial piece of the picture puzzle. As discussed in part 3 on comprehension strategies, it is important that children be provided many opportunities to draw and write in response to texts read aloud by their teacher. Children also need chances to draw and write stories and reports about other experiences in the classroom and in their lives (e.g., an experiment at the water table; the birth of a sibling). Especially in the beginning of the kindergarten year, these "writings" will typically be in the form of a drawing with no accompanying text. A common, and highly laudable, kindergarten practice is for teachers to ask children to tell about their drawings and then record each child's dictation below his or her picture. As teachers subsequently read their own words back to children, these become a "text" that reinforces children's developing understandings about print (e.g., left-to-right sequencing, the use of white space to separate words, the connection between print and speech). Eventually children should be encouraged to use invented spellings to write their own text to accompany their pictures.

At first, children will likely only approximate "real writing" with scribbles and letter-like forms that in their minds may represent actual words, but that in actuality bear no relationship to sound. Over time, as they learn more alphabet letters, children are likely to begin using these letters in their writing. At this point, children are using letters to represent words, but typically without any real match between specific letters and sounds. Gradually, as children learn some letter-sound correspondences (e.g., that the letter t stands for the /t/ sound), they will likely start using these to represent the most prominent sounds they hear in words (e.g., *P* for *map* or *KT* for *cat*). Because the act of writing requires children to figure out how to turn spoken language into written language, having multiple opportunities to write reinforces and extends children's level of phonemic awareness, their alphabet knowledge, and their emerging knowledge of specific letter-sound correspondences (Bear et al., 2000; Clay, 1993; Cunningham, 1990; Griffith, 1991; Snow et al., 1998; Wilde, 1997). Thus writing is a critical piece in the instructional puzzle, both in laying the foundation for formal phonics instruction and in providing children a vehicle for expressing their ideas and feelings about text and sharing them with others.

Putting First Things First

In the "big picture" of emergent literacy instruction, then, phonemic awareness and alphabet knowledge only make sense within the context of a balanced literacy curriculum that includes attention to letter-sound correspondences as well as plenty of opportunities for children to listen to, recite, and pretend-read text and to experiment with writing using invented spelling. However, placing them in context does not diminish the critical importance of phonemic awareness and alphabet knowledge to the process of learning to read. I isolate these abilities for special attention both because they are essential to early reading success and because they are often given insufficient attention in the early literacy curriculum. In their understandable desire to have children move as quickly as possible into "real reading," teachers sometimes introduce formal phonics instruction before children have the necessary foundation to fully benefit from it. If children are still confusing many alphabet letters or if they have not yet come to the critical insight that words are comprised of individual sounds, then focusing a lot of time on letter-sound connections is likely to be a fruitless enterprise for many children, potentially leading them to feel like failures and tempting teachers to conclude that the children who don't catch on quickly aren't very bright and/or are likely candidates for some kind of special intervention.

In *Becoming a Nation of Readers* (1985), Anderson, Hiebert, Scott, and Wilkinson recommend that instruction in phonics be compete by the end of second grade, suggesting that by this point, children should be well on their way to becoming fluent readers, a process that may not be fully complete until the end of third grade. In sharp contrast to this suggested instructional time frame, Snow et al. (1998) estimate that urban schools with large numbers of children of color may send about half of their students to second grade "not yet able to read conventionally" (p. 68). Clearly, these students are very far from where they would need to be to even approach fluency by the end of third grade. The seriousness of this state of affairs is underscored by at least some research that suggests that children who are behind in literacy in third grade have little chance of ever catching up (Snow et al., 1998, p. 212). When one considers the amount of literacy knowledge that children must acquire between kindergarten and second grade in order to be "on track" in third grade, it is clear how important it is for teachers to know what abilities and skills children bring with them so that instruction can build sequentially on what children already know and simultaneously fill in the gaps where children may lack specific knowledge critical to their success in learning to decode.

The Diversity of Black Children's Experiences

African American children obviously bring a wide range of literacy knowledge with them to school depending upon their prior experiences with text and other literacy artifacts at home and in daycare or preschool settings. It is likely, however, that a large number of African American children living in poverty in both urban and rural areas enter kindergarten having had few experiences with books and knowing relatively little about the alphabet. Lack of prior experiences with books may well impact the level of phonemic awareness children possess on entering kindergarten. As pointed out earlier, phonemic awareness is a metalinguistic awareness. Acquiring it requires that one pay deliberate attention to aspects of language that are typically outside of conscious awareness. Research suggests that children's phonemic awareness is fostered in large measure through book interactions (whether at home or in school) in which adults draw children's explicit attention to sound features of the language used in text (e.g., rhyme, rhythm, alliteration) and engage with them in various kinds of self-conscious play with sounds (e.g., *"Can you think of another word that rhymes with hat?"*) (Ayres, 1993; Griffith, 1991; Griffith & Olson, 1992; Hoffman, 1997; Murray, Stahl, & Ivey, 1996; Neuman, 1999; Snow et al., 1998). Children who are read to at home and/or in preschool on a frequent basis and who engage with adults in this kind of focused attention to sounds may have already acquired considerable phonemic awareness by the time they enter kindergarten. Children without these experiences will likely not.

As discussed in part 2 on language socialization, many children raised in African American communities, whatever their experience with books, are likely to be adept in their use of language and to incorporate sound elements like rhythm, repetition, and even rhyme to aesthetic and strategic effect in their speech. Research suggests that Black children routinely engage in verbal play with peers and older children that requires them to manipulate the sound elements of language in clever and creative ways and to be alert to subtle nuances of sound and meaning in the language used by others. Thus many African American kindergartners are likely to *use* sound elements of language in highly sophisticated and creative ways. In fact, they may far surpass most children raised in other communities in this regard. But *using* those elements effectively and *focusing conscious attention* on them are not the same thing.

For many Black children, the knowledge of sound elements required to invent a new rhyme in a jump rope game or to make a quick verbal comeback in the midst of a heated interaction is tacit, taken-for-granted knowledge, not an object of conscious reflection, as it needs to be when teachers ask children things like, *"How many sounds do you hear in fast?"* or *"If you take away the /s/ in sad and add /b/, what's your new word?"*

Clearly, the facility in using language and in manipulating sound elements to rhetorical effect that many Black children possess by the time they enter kindergarten constitutes a strong foundation upon which to build their phonemic awareness. But for children who enter without prior read-aloud experiences in which adults drew their conscious attention to sound elements in text, the process of building on that strong foundation won't happen automatically. To occur successfully, that process requires carefully planned and explicit instruction by the teacher.

Similarly, children who enter kindergarten (or beyond) without sufficient alphabet knowledge need systematic teaching and lots of structured opportunities to practice recognizing and writing the letters. In some studies, alphabet knowledge—specifically, letter-naming—emerges as the strongest single predictor of later success in reading (Snow et al., 1998). Knowing the names of the letters gives children a jump start in figuring out the alphabetic principle (i.e., the idea that letters represent sounds). Because the majority of letter names contain the sound the letter represents (or at least *one* of its sounds—the names of the vowels, for example, contain their "long" sounds), children can reliably depend upon their knowledge of letter names to begin making working associations between letters and sounds. In fact, during the early stages of invented spelling, children typically use letter names to sound out the words they are trying to spell (Chomsky, 1970, 1971; Bear et al., 2000; Read, 1975). (For example, *GP* may be used to represent the word *jeep* because the name of the letter *g* contains both the initial consonant and vowel sound in *jeep* [example in Bear et al., 2000, p. 143].) Thus, knowing the alphabet plays a huge role in powering the learning-to-read process. On the other hand, as Blevins (1998) points out, children who don't know the letters well may be in danger of becoming nonalphabetic readers, relying mainly on memorized "sight words" to decipher text.

The popularity of educational programs for preschoolers like *Sesame Street* with their focus on letters and sounds and the ubiquity of the alphabet song, "Now I Know My ABCs," which many kindergarten-aged children are able to sing with a great deal of pride, can make it seem like the alphabet is "shared knowledge" among preschoolers in the United States. But even among confident singers of the alphabet song, there is likely to be a tremendous range in what individual children actually know about the alphabet. It is easy to underestimate both the complexity of what is entailed in "knowing" the alphabet and the large knowledge advantage possessed by children who enter kindergarten having had lots of prior experiences with alphabet letters. At a minimum, for example, knowing the alphabet entails recognizing letters in both upper and lower case, in various print styles, in and out of "alphabet sequence," and alone and in text, as well as being able to write the letters oneself. In terms of prior alphabet experience, some children grow up in families in which adults are constantly drawing children's attention to letters—for example, in words spelled with magnetic letters on the refrigerator door, in games and puzzles, in the design and shape of objects in the environment (e.g., the *y* shape of a backyard tree). Recently, for instance, a friend shared a bath-time alphabet game that her daughter plays with her two-year-old son, Diallo. After he excitedly calls out the name of the magnetic letter his mother is holding up, Diallo squeals in delight as his mother tosses the just-named letter into the tub. This is just one of many alphabet activities that this two-year-old regularly engages in with his parents. Children like Diallo enter kindergarten with five years of accumulated knowledge about letters—their names, sounds, shapes, and their integral relationship to reading. Children without this accumulated store of alphabet knowledge need to acquire it in school, and in very short order, if they are to make good progress in learning to read.

Before moving on to specific suggestions for teaching the alphabet and phonemic awareness, I want to underscore again the essential point that African American children living in low-income communities vary tremendously in the amount and depth of literacy knowledge they bring to school (Gadsen, 1993; Heath, 1983; Morgan, 2002; Taylor & Dorsey-Gaines, 1988, Vernon-Feagans, 1996). It is not possible to predict an individual child's prior experiences with text and letters based solely on demographic factors like family income or parents' educational level. That said, it is also important for kindergarten and first-grade teachers who work with African American children from low-income communities to develop the following:

1. An "anticipatory set" for highly intelligent, verbally sophisticated children who enter school with little alphabet knowledge or phonemic awareness; and
2. A repertoire of strategies for teaching alphabet knowledge and phonemic awareness in creative, effective and time-efficient ways.

In discussing such strategies in the rest of this chapter and in the next chapter, I begin with the alphabet, which, in terms of teaching, is considerably more "straightforward" than phonemic awareness.

What the Teaching Literature Has to Say About Alphabet Learning

The literature on early literacy learning is replete with endearing anecdotes about children's alphabet "discoveries"—that the *M* at the beginning of one's own name matches the *M* in the MacDonald's sign, that one's own double *e*'s also appear on the boxes of *Cheer* detergent and *Cheerios* cereal in the grocery store, or that, amazingly enough, *lots* of people's names share letters with one another. Not surprisingly, many of these alphabet discoveries involve a personal connection with letters. In *Teaching Other People's Children,* Ballenger (1999), for example, describes a preschooler named Tatie who is so enthralled with "her" *T* that she collects all the magnetic *T*'s in the classroom and places them in her cubby (p. 45). In the same classroom, Giles repeatedly writes the letter *G*, cuts carefully around it, and then parades around the classroom with it, proudly announcing to his teacher, " 'Cindy, I no cut my *G*' " (p. 46). These anecdotes testify to the power of children's personal connections to literacy and to the intellectual excitement that can be generated when children discover or construct new knowledge on their own.

Accordingly, much of the literature on early literacy instruction places a premium on providing children opportunities to explore books and other literacy artifacts on their own or in small groups, often in learning centers located around the classroom (e.g., alphabet center, writing center, dramatic play area). The alphabet center in a kindergarten classroom, for instance, might be stocked with items such as plastic and felt letters, alphabet stamps and pads, clay or gel sealed in plastic bags for forming letters, alphabet puzzles and stencils that invite children to manipulate and experiment with letters and their shapes. Meanwhile, the writing center, with its supply of paper, crayons, markers and pencils, offers still more opportunities for exploration and practice with letters. In addition to setting up centers where children can engage in various hands-on activities involving letters, teachers are encouraged to create a print-rich classroom environment conducive to children's discovery of knowledge about letters and print—for example, various areas of the room labeled with alphabet letters, posters and signs hanging on the walls and from ceilings, children's names and pictures on bulletin boards, poetry and song charts on prominent display, books of various sorts in view around the room.

Rather than explicit teaching of alphabet letters in isolation from text, teachers are often advised to embed alphabet instruction in a meaningful context. Based on the work of Cunningham (2000), one widely advocated practice, for example, is to begin kindergarten letter instruction with children's names. In terms of "meaningfulness," this practice makes a great deal of sense. Children's own names are clearly words that have both deep personal and social significance in the classroom community. In this process, each day for the first month or so of school, a different child's name is highlighted. After the name is identified and displayed for all to see, the teacher engages the whole class in a number of activities with the name, such as clapping its syllables, counting and chanting its letters, and reciting the letters as the teacher writes the name on a slip of paper, which is then cut up into individual letters for children to reassemble (Cunningham, 2000). One of the most important activities involved in the process is the teacher's elicitation of children's observations about the name. For example, a child might observe that the name begins with the same letter as the name chosen yesterday, or that it has an *a* in the middle, or contains two *e*'s. Depending upon children's current level of knowledge and the particular names of children in the class, the teacher might also focus children's attention on specific letter or sound patterns, such as noting the different sounds that *C* represents in *Catherine* and *Cindy* or generating other words that rhyme with the name of the day (Cunningham, 2000, p. 27).

The emphasis in this work with names is on children making their own discoveries about the alphabet, even as the teacher sometimes skillfully directs their attention to features and patterns he or she may especially want to highlight. This emphasis on the importance of children generating or constructing their own knowledge about letters is well illustrated in Calkins's (2001) description of an alphabet study conducted by a kindergarten class working together in small groups:

> One group wrote name books, another sorted letters into categories such as letters with tails and letters with bumps, others made alphabet books, or used magnetic or spongy letters and paint to make names and other words. Renee's alphabet study offered opportunities for her class to be inventive within the system of the alphabet. They created things to do and made discoveries along the way. Amber and Paul noticed that the letters *a* and *g* can look differently sometimes. When Jasmine and Lisa were making kids' names out of scrabble letters, they realized that nobody had *q* in their name but lots of kids names began with *j*. They decided to check to see if this was true in other kindergarten classes. (p. 202)

An alphabet study such as the one just described is a wonderfully creative and potentially exciting classroom project. Indeed, Calkins notes that one of the teacher's goals was to teach children "that they could pore over words and letters with the same curiosity and awe they brought to their [earlier] investigation of ants and worms" (p. 203). Like children's observations and discussions about the letters and sounds in one another's names described earlier, an alphabet study offers the possibility of engaging children's intellectual energy in learning letters in a way that rote activities like tracing letters or practicing with flash cards could never do. Similarly, hands-on exploratory activities like molding letters with clay or gel in the alphabet center or practicing writing letters by making classroom signs in the writing center are infinitely more fun and interesting for children than drill and practice routines designed for memorizing letters.

But, engaging as they may be, are these constructivist-oriented, centered-based activities widely advocated in the teaching literature really the kinds of activities that, by themselves, can help children with little alphabet experience learn their ABCs?

Does It Work for All Children?

The question is whether activities like those just described provide enough basic practice in letter recognition to enable children with little letter experience to actually learn the alphabet. It has been estimated that children who come from so-called high literacy homes enter school with an average of 1,000 hours of one-on-one adult/child interactions around literacy, including not only reading experiences with alphabet and story books, but also activities like putting together alphabet puzzles, playing commercially made alphabet games and toys, and shared writing of things like lists, notes, and cards (Adams, 1990; Teale & Sulzby, 1991). Many preschool-aged children are taught how to form letters at home, including the letters in their own names and in other frequently used, special words. For children who enter kindergarten with these experiences behind them, activities like comparing and contrasting letters and letter patterns in one another's names and conducting an alphabet study build directly on prior knowledge. For children without those experiences, not so. Children just learning to recognize alphabet shapes will need many, many more experiences with individual letters than can be provided in lessons like the names activity, in which the specific information about letters that gets focused on is to a large extent serendipitous and perhaps even inappropriate (or at least irrelevant) for children just getting acquainted with letters. For example, the letters *e, a,* and *s* (along with *c* and *o*) have been identified as a group of letters particularly confusing for children, and some experts have suggested that for this reason they should not be taught at the same time (Blevins, 1998; Manzo & Manzo, 1993). Yet in the "names activity," if one of the children in the classroom is named *Sean* (or *Sarah, Leah, Andrea* . . .), these letters will, of necessity, be "taught" at the same time. Similarly, if *Cindy* and *Catherine* are two names in the classroom, children just learning to recognize the shape and sound of *C* may not get very much out of the discussion of the two sounds of *C* that will almost inevitably occur.

I am not arguing here that being exposed to information they are not yet ready to fully understand or internalize is necessarily harmful for children. What I am arguing is that teachers cannot reliably count on activities like the ones described in the last section to actually teach the alphabet to children who don't already know it, or at least much of it. Children who investigate letters with tails and bumps during an alphabet study are definitely learning something about the alphabet, but children who don't already know a lot about letters aren't learning *enough* through this activity to have such a study constitute the majority, or even a significant portion, of their alphabet instruction. Such activities, albeit intellectually stimulating and engaging, cannot *substitute* for systematic, explicit teaching of individual letters. For children who come to school without much knowledge of the alphabet, there is way too much to be learned for children to "discover" or "construct" this knowledge on their own.

Bear et al. (2000) note that learning the alphabet requires multiple exposures to individual letters "in many contexts and across many different fonts, sizes, shapes and textures" as well as multiple opportunities to practice writing the letters and to compare and contrast their distinctive features with those of other letters (p. 105). As discussed earlier, in many kindergarten classrooms, center-based activities are designed to provide children with much of this needed exposure to and practice with letters. As children make letters with pipe cleaners, stencils, clay, or paint in the alphabet center, for example, they familiarize themselves with the characteristic features of individual letters. As they manipulate the pieces of an alphabet puzzle, they literally feel the difference between the upward extending *b* and the downward extending *p*. As they scrutinize their supply of alphabet cereal to do a letter sort, they pay attention to the smallest of letter distinctions. When children work on activities like this in the alphabet center, teachers are likely to assume that children are busy learning letters. But is that necessarily the case?

In many kindergarten classrooms, children work in learning centers without direct adult guidance or supervision. If children look actively engaged with the materials in a given center, busy teachers often turn their attention to working with children on activities that seem to more clearly require direct teacher guidance. Further, teachers typically don't have time to check each child's alphabet work or to assess his or her learning before the next activity begins. Thus in the absence of teacher participation in the activities going on in the alphabet center, it is not necessarily clear exactly what children are doing with or learning from the materials there. Again, I am not suggesting that there is anything *wrong* with using center-based activities to provide children hands-on experiences with letters or to reinforce particular alphabet skills. To the contrary, such activities play a valuable role in allowing children chances to manipulate and play with letters in ways likely to add significantly to their alphabet knowledge. Such experiences are part of the multiple exposures to letters "in different contexts and across many different fonts, sizes, shapes and textures" that Bear et al. identify as so central to alphabet learning. However, at least in most classrooms, center-based alphabet activities are neither systematic enough nor sufficiently teacher directed or monitored to carry the full responsibility of teaching the alphabet to children who enter the classroom knowing little about letters.

It may seem to some readers that in talking about alphabet teaching in such detail here, I am making too much of a relatively minor aspect of the early literacy curriculum. Not so. Knowing or not knowing alphabet letters at school entry has nothing whatever to do with intelligence, linguistic ability, or one's potential to become a highly skilled, insightful reader. Yet their degree of alphabet knowledge greatly impacts children's ability to "access" the curriculum in many kindergarten and first-grade classrooms. Accurate and automatic letter recognition is a major part of the knowledge base on which successful literacy instruction depends. It is possible for teachers to begin phonics instruction (i.e., instruction in letter-sound correspondences) without children knowing all the alphabet letters. For example, if children know only the following nine letters—*a, m, t, i, s, r, f, u,* and *b*—they can generate a fairly large number of simple consonant-vowel-consonant (CVC) words (Ball & Blachman, 1991; Ericson & Juliebo, 1998). Thus children who have a fairly good grasp on some key letters may be able to do okay with just those letters in the initial stages of phonics instruction. But if their grasp on many of the other letters is only a tenuous one, they are almost inevitably headed for decoding trouble down the line unless the teacher takes care to insure that systematic alphabet instruction continues even as children are starting to use some letter-sound correspondences to form words. Once the process of instruction in letter-sound correspondences begins, it is easy for teachers to lose track of the fact that some children may still be struggling with automatic recognition of some or many letters. This is a costly oversight. It simply isn't possible for children to become skilled, fluent readers if they are not secure in their knowledge of the entire alphabet.

"Now I (<u>Really</u>) Know My ABCs"

As discussed earlier, children who enter school with little alphabet experience need lots and lots of exposure to and practice with letters. Despite many people's critique of them as boring and unchallenging, "rote-learning" activities like copying and tracing letters and working with alphabet flash cards have their place alongside more intellectually engaging activities in helping children master the alphabet. Copying and tracing letters, for example, shouldn't take the place of children experimenting with writing letters on their own at the writing center or during journal or writing workshop time. Nevertheless, copying and tracing can provide children who need it with valuable practice in forming letter shapes, a process that also helps children with letter recognition (Blevins, 1998; Clay, 1993). Similarly, working with alphabet flashcards can help many children acquire needed automaticity in letter recognition.

In his helpful book, *Phonics From A to Z: A Practical Guide,* Blevins (1998) describes 35 activities for helping children develop alphabet recognition (pp. 24–27). Some of these are time-honored activities described by other writers as well and employed by many skilled teachers. Rather than listing Blevins's activities here, I want to underscore the underlying principles that, in my view, make his suggestions such good ones and that teachers could also use to design their own alphabet activities:

1. Almost all of the activities can be done as "whole class" activities if the teacher chooses, thus providing the teacher with the opportunity to quickly assess children's learning and to identify those needing additional practice.

2. Many of the activities do not require a lot of instructional time and thus can be fit into the "nooks and crannies" of the instructional day—for example, distributing letter cards and having children "pop up" as their letter is called, doing an alphabet activity as children are lining up for lunch or recess.

3. Many of the activities are easily incorporated as a daily part of the classroom routine, thus insuring that all children will receive regular, ongoing practice with letters—for example, singing the alphabet song while pointing to each of the letters; having children walk a laminated construction paper alphabet path while saying aloud each letter name; having children "sign up" for things like attendance, checking out books, and obtaining a bathroom pass.

5. Many of the activities provide opportunities for children to compare and contrast distinctive features of different letters (Bear et al., 2000)—for example, playing alphabet concentration and other games, matching upper case and lower case letters, doing various kinds of alphabet sorts.

6. The activities make use of different learning modalities (visual, auditory, kinesthetic and tactile)—for example, children forming letters with their bodies, tracing letters in a variety of mediums, performing letter "actions" (e.g., bounce, catch, dance).

In addition to Blevins's work, educators can find ideas for teaching the alphabet in a number of sources (e.g., Bear et al., 2000; Chaney, 1993; Cunningham, 2000). A frequently made, and excellent, suggestion is that teachers read and discuss many alphabet books with children, using them to teach not only letter recognition, but to expand children's vocabulary and concepts about the world. After listening to and discussing a variety of these, children can create their own alphabet books, perhaps modeled after one they particularly enjoyed hearing. Bear et al. (2000) suggest that children look up entries for various letters in a number of different alphabet books, thereby getting an early introduction to the use of resource books (p. 124). Alphabet books should definitely be part of the classroom library collection available for children to peruse during independent reading time. There are a large number of interesting and engaging alphabet books available from which to choose (an extensive list is contained in Chaney, 1993).

Chapter 11
Fostering Phonological and Phonemic Awareness

Phonemic awareness, the ability to discriminate and manipulate individual phonemes in words, is part of a more general set of abilities often referred to as *phonological awareness*. Phonological awareness includes children's ability to do the following:

- Identify and play with rhyming elements within words;
- Identify alliteration (e.g., *the dainty dog danced in the dewdrops)* and produce alliterative words (i.e., words that begin with the same sound);
- Blend smaller elements of sound (i.e., syllables, onsets and rimes, and, finally, phonemes) into whole words;
- Segment words into smaller sound elements (i.e., syllables, onsets and rimes, and, finally, phonemes); and
- Add and remove sound elements to create new words (e.g., *Take /b/ from bat. Add /s/. What's the word?).*

In the early stages of blending and segmenting sounds, children should work first with syllables and onsets and rimes, rather than phonemes, because these larger sound elements are easier for children to discern when they are first learning to pay conscious attention to sounds within words. A *syllable* is comprised either of a vowel by itself (e.g., *a, I*) or a vowel with one or more consonants preceding and/or following it. It is always pronounced as a unit (e.g., *bak-er, fro-zen, mi-cro-phone).* Although they have probably never thought about syllables in a conscious way, most children find it relatively easy to clap or count the number of syllables in a word as, unlike phonemes, syllables have acoustic reality. As Adams et al. (1998) explain, syllables "correspond to the sound pulses of the voice as well as to the opening and closing cycles of the jaw," and thus, "the successive syllables of spoken language can be both heard

217

and felt" (p. 49). The *onset* of a syllable refers to the consonant or group of consonants that precede the first vowel, whereas the rime is comprised of the vowel and what follows (e.g., *j –ump, t –ap, st –op*). It is much easier for children to "hear" onsets and rimes than individual phonemes. According to Pinker (1994), onsets and rimes are "the pieces of word structure that are most salient to people," which is why they are the sound units that get manipulated in poetry and other forms of word play (p. 174). Given their greater "reality" or "tangibility" for children, it makes good sense to focus first on syllables and then on onsets and rimes before presenting children the more difficult task of blending or segmenting words into phonemes.

As the words *phoneme* and *phonological* suggest, most of the activities just described are done orally, although once children have learned enough letters, many benefit from also seeing the letters as they blend and segment sounds (Bear et al., 2000; Blevins, 1998; Ericson & Juliebo, 1998, Snow et al., 1998). Whether or not children are also looking at print, however, the main focus in phonological awareness activities is always on sounds. When children reach the point where they are able to discern and manipulate individual phonemes (as opposed to just syllables and onsets and rimes), they are working on the level of phonemic awareness. It is this finer-tuned awareness that is so essential to the learning-to-read process and that leads children to the discovery of the alphabetic principle, the critical realization that letters represent sounds. Activities that focus on more general phonological awareness skills—working with rhyme and alliteration and blending and segmenting larger sound chunks—establish the ground for phonemic awareness to develop. For most children, the roots of phonemic awareness lie also in their early, out-of-school experiences with the musicality of language. Some children discover this music in the cadence and rhythms of nursery rhymes and bedtime books. Others, including many Black children, experience it in oral stories, verbal debates, and jump rope games. Part of the responsibility of the early literacy teacher is to build in systematic and creative ways on both kinds of out-of-school experiences so that all children can develop the level of phonemic awareness necessary for successful decoding.

Building on Black Communications

The more successful teachers are in helping children see the connections between what they already know about using language and the literacy tasks they are expected to perform in school, the more successful early literacy instruction is likely to be. In reality, there is not all that great a distance between playing with sounds in a jump rope song or a game of ritual insult and playing with rhyme and alliteration in a poem or storybook read aloud by the teacher. But the distance can *seem* enormous to children inexperienced with books and new to an environment where much else may also be unfamiliar, including not just classroom routines, but teachers' ways of using language as well. One important way that teachers can make a connection between African American children's out-of-school experiences with language and instruction in phonological and phonemic awareness is by working with poems, chants, and books that capture the rhythms, cadence, and lexicon of Black Communications.

The literature on early literacy is in agreement that reading aloud books that contain lots of rhyming and alliteration and having children chorally recite, and even memorize, poems, songs, and chants written on chart paper are excellent ways of focusing children's conscious attention on sounds and thus fostering their phonological awareness. Many writers on the topic include extensive lists of books that contain rhyme, alliteration and other forms of sound play. Unfortunately, few of the books listed in this literature are written by African American authors or contain African American characters or themes. Some of the books most frequently mentioned are classics, books that generations of teachers have found useful in fostering children's awareness of sounds, such as *"I Can't," Said the Ant* (1961) by Polly Cameron and the many rhyming books written by Dr. Seuss. Similarly, the songs and poems suggested in the literature typically include time-honored teacher favorites like traditional nursery rhyme verses, songs by the artist Raffi (e.g., "Willaby Wallaby Woo"), and the poetry of Shel Silverstein.

While all of these—as well as many of the other more recent books and poems often referenced—are clearly "good literature" and appealing to many children, they are not the primary materials I would choose in working with African American children with little prior experience of books. There are many African American children's books and poems available to teachers that are as full of interesting and inventive word play as those typically recommended in the teaching literature and that have the added advantage of containing language, characters, and themes that are culturally familiar to many Black children. "Jack and Jill Went up the Hill" and "Humpty Dumpty Sat on a Wall," for example, are not necessarily *bad* choices for children's choral recitation, but it is likely that many African American children will respond with considerably more enthusiasm and engagement to Eloise Greenfield's (1978) poem, "Honey, I Love," which begins like this:

I love
I love a lot of things, a whole lot of things
Like
My cousin comes to visit and you know he's from the South
'Cause every word he says just kind of slides out of his mouth
I like the way he whistles and I like the way he walks
But honey, let me tell you that I LOVE the way he talks
  I love the way my cousin talks

and

The day is hot and icky and the sun sticks to my skin
Mr. Davis turns the hose on, everybody jumps right in

The water stings my stomach and I feel so nice and cool
Honey, let me tell you that I LOVE a flying pool (unnumbered pages)

Embedding the "New" in the Familiar

I am not arguing that "Honey, I Love" is *better* poetry than Mother Goose's or Shel Silverstein's (that is a different discussion), but I am arguing that it is more culturally resonant for many Black children in terms of both subject matter and language. Relatives coming up North to visit and "talking that talk" is something many Black children can relate to, as is the focus on special relationships with extended kin and the pleasure of running through the hose on a hot summer day. In addition to the skillful use of rhyme, repetition, and alliteration found in many well written poems, Greenfield also uses features that are characteristically associated with Black Communications, like the culturally toned diminutive *honey* and the stress on the word *love* that help to create the intonational patterns of BC speech.

The sense of familiarity many Black children are likely to experience in listening to Greenfield's poem can be reassuring evidence that "home language" and "book language" connect to one another in meaningful, figure-out-able ways and that the linguistic knowledge they already possess has value and currency in school. African American children in the midst of reciting "But honey, let me tell you that I LOVE the way he talks" are likely to be feeling very much "at home" in school. In using Greenfield's poem as the context for asking children to do something new with language—to focus explicitly on sounds as opposed to meaning—the only new part teachers are asking children to deal with is the task itself, as opposed to adding unfamiliar lexicon, syntax, and/or subject matter into the mix as well, as is sometimes the case with books and other materials used in the early literacy curriculum. It goes without saying that all children need to leave their comfort zone at some point and try out new ways of using language and explore new ideas and unfamiliar experiences. After all, that is what education is all about. But the importance of connecting instruction to what children already know is paramount in the early stages of literacy instruction.

Jump-Rope Rhymes and Other Familiar Play Songs

Using poetry, chants and songs that may already be familiar to some African American children is another excellent way of making those connections. As discussed in chapter 5, research suggests that a significant number of African American children participate in jump-rope and hand-clapping games in their home communities, traditional play activities that extend far back into African American history. Jump-rope chants and clapping rhymes are a rich source of material for rhyming verses that can be written on chart paper, chorally recited by the class, and used to talk about and generate rhymes. Imagine, for example, children's likely excitement as they chant and clap the following three stanzas from the centuries-old African American clapping rhyme, "Mary Mack":

> Oh Mary Mack, Mack, Mack, all dressed in black, black, black with silver
> buttons, buttons, buttons all down her back, back, back.

> She asked her mother, mother, mother
> For fifteen cents, cents, cents, cents,
> To see the elephant, elephant, elephant,
> Jump over the fence, fence, fence.

> He jumped so high, high, high.
> That he reached the sky, sky, sky,
> And he didn't come back, back, back,
> 'til the Fourth of July, 'ly, 'ly.   (in Mattox, 1989, p. 15)

Like Greenfield's poem, African American play songs and jump-rope rhymes connect in powerful ways to many children's outside-of-school experiences with language and thus help anchor early literacy instruction in what is already known and meaningful to children.

Learning to Listen in a Whole New Way

As discussed earlier, phonemic awareness (the ability to identify and manipulate phonemes within words) is a metalinguistic ability, requiring children's conscious attention to individual sound elements that usually go unnoticed in the back-and-forth of conversation. Thus, in learning to read and write, children must come to perceive language in a new way. In this regard Snow et al. (1998) write:

> For the child, Downing (1979:27) suggests, language is not an object of
> awareness in itself but is "seemingly like a glass, through which the child
> looks at the surrounding world, . . . not [initially] suspecting that it has its
> own existence, its own aspects of construction." To become a mature reader
> and writer, charged with construing and corroborating the message of an
> author, this perception must change. Moreover, each such change must be
> guided by the metalinguistic insight that language invites inspection and
> reflection. Indeed, literacy growth, at every level, depends on learning to
> treat language as an object of thought, in and of itself . . . (p. 45)

For children at the emergent stage of literacy development, "learning to treat language as an object of thought" involves learning to listen to sounds in a new, more conscious way. Children's attention to sounds in words can be facilitated by activities that begin, not with analyzing words, but with paying closer attention to the everyday sounds around them.

Activities commonly suggested for developing children's listening awareness include having children close their eyes and identify environmental sounds or sounds deliberately made by the teacher (e.g., Adams et al., 1998; Bear et al.,

2000). By closing their eyes and listening attentively to the sounds around them, for example, children might identify the sounds of breathing, swallowing, scratching, throats clearing, coughing, sneezing, the hum of an air conditioner, the subtle movements made by classmates, etc. The teacher might also ask children to close their eyes and identify the various sounds he or she makes, such as ringing a bell, rustling papers, tapping or pounding on a table, or whistling. After children have correctly identified these separate sounds, the teacher might make a series of sounds, asking children to recall their sequence. Teachers can also take children to different locations to listen for environmental sounds (e.g., the lunch room, the library, a nearby park or playground).

Connections to Text

To insure that children see the connection between listening to sounds and reading, I strongly advocate introducing these various listening activities with a relevant book. The sounds Tarpley conjures in *Bippity Bop Barbershop* (2002), for instance, are perfect for increasing children's conscious awareness of sounds in their environment. Some sounds from the book include the following:

- The secret knock that Daddy uses to wake Miles up: "Bippity-be-bop-bop! Bippity-be-bop-bop!"
- The sound of checkers slamming on the game board
- The sounds of "jazz music, loud voices and laughter"
- The "buzzzzzzz of clippers"
- The "sweesh-sweesh whisper of scissors" (unnumbered pages)

In talking about these and other sounds from the book, teachers might actually want to demonstrate some of them for (and with) children, like the rhythm of Daddy's knock on the door, the checkers hitting the game board, the buzzing clippers and sweeshing scissors. Children can close their eyes while the teacher makes these sounds in a particular order and then asks children to recall their sequence. The barbershop sounds in Tarpley's book also open possibilities for home-school connections. Teachers could write a letter to children's families, asking them to assist their child in listening to and recording sounds they hear in various neighborhood locations such as a restaurant, store, church, barbershop, or beauty shop.

Focusing on sounds in *Full, Full, Full of Love* (2003) by Trish Cooke offers similar curricular possibilities. To begin, teachers and students can simply revel in the many fun sounds used in the book—for example, *"splash, splish; wiggle, wiggle; struggle, juggle; snuggle, cuddle; yum, yum."* In reading the book aloud, for example, the teacher might stop and say something this: *"Clink, clank; clatter, clatter. I just love making those sounds! Can you make them with me?"* Teachers can encourage home-school connections with this book as well by having children listen for the sounds they hear in their own kitchen when dinner is being prepared, asking an adult to help them record those sounds. Children can share their findings with the class.

As a way to move from a focus on listening attentively to environmental sounds to listening more carefully to sounds in words and text, Adams et al. (1998) suggest that teachers randomly replace familiar wording with nonsense in a book they've read aloud to children several times before (p. 23). For example, in reading aloud the line "As Momma stacks the clean towels near the sink, I hold a brush in my hand like a microphone and pretend I'm a famous singer," teachers might replace the word *brush* with *elephant* (sentence from *Saturday at The New You* (1994) by Barbara Barber). By asking children to detect "nonsense changes" in familiar texts, teachers provide children with practice in attending to the sounds they actually hear, as opposed to those they expect to hear.

These listening activities are really warm-ups for subsequent work with rhymes and alliteration and with blending and segmenting sounds in words. They alert children to the importance of listening carefully to the actual sounds they hear both in their environment and in speech. With a little creativity on the teacher's part, listening activities can be fun and engaging. Children enjoy being sound detectors, discovering a world of interesting sounds they've never really "heard" before.

Playing With Rhymes

Working with rhymes can be equally fun and engaging for children. Developing children's sensitivity to rhyme is an important way of helping them shift attention from meaning to sounds in words. Asking children to recite and memorize rhyming poems, chants and songs is an excellent activity for fostering awareness of rhymes and one that is likely to appeal to many African American children's love of oral performance. As suggested earlier, traditional African American jump-rope rhymes and play songs work well for this purpose (for a collection of these, see Mattox, 1989). These can be performed as well as chanted, with children clapping out, or even jumping, the rhythm of the words. Linking rhyme to physical movement is a strategy highlighted in the teaching literature (e.g., Adams et al., 1998; Ericson & Juliebo, 1998). An excellent "chart paper" poem for doing just that is "Jeannie Had a Giggle" contained in *Brown Angels* (1993) by Walter Dean Myers (teachers should be sure to display the photograph of the little girl that appears with the poem in Myers's book):

> Jeannie had a giggle just beneath her toes
> She gave a little wiggle and up her leg it rose
> She tried to grab the giggle as it shimmied past her knees
> But it slid right past her fingers with a " 'scuse me if you please"
> It slipped around her middle, it made her jump and shout
> Jeannie wanted that giggle in, that giggle wanted out!

Jeannie closed her mouth, but then she heard a funny sound
As out that silly giggle flew and jumped down to the ground
Jeannie caught it with her foot just beneath her toes
She gave a little wiggle and up her leg it rose   (unnumbered pages)

As children practice reciting this poem, synchronizing their physical movements
to its rhythms, they should be encouraged to accentuate the rhyming words in
various ways, saying them one time very softly, then loudly, then elongating their
sounds, etc. Memorizing the poem helps children "own" the rhymes, establishing a secure base from which to generate new words that rhyme with those in the
poem. (Because the emphasis in these activities is on sounds, not print, it is not
necessary—in fact, it is counter-productive—to highlight differences in spelling
at this point [as in *toes, rose,* and *clothes,* for example].) Children are likely to
enjoy performing this poem for visitors or another class in the school.

Another poem that can be set to movement and that is highly appealing
to children is "Damon & Blue" from the collection *My Man Blue* (1999) by
Nikki Grimes:

Damon & Blue
Just us two
Cruising up the avenue

You strut, you glide
But mark our stride
Can't beat us when we're
        side by side.   (unnumbered pages)

Again, after children have performed this poem many times, they can suggest
additional rhyming words for those in the poem. Some of these may also represent actions children can perform, such as *slide, step wide, ride,* and *hide.*
Playing with *oo* sounds from the poem, one class and their teacher came up
with the following:

The cow says moo
The ghost says boo
The baby says goo
The owl says whoo
And now we're through!

Adding Verses

When children are feeling confident coming up with rhyming words on their
own, they can even try their hand at generating additional verses for favorite
songs or poems. Consider, for example, the rich possibilities suggested by Eloise Greenfield's poem "By Myself" (in the collection, *Honey, I Love,* 1978):

When I'm by myself
And I close my eyes

I'm a twin
I'm a dimple in a chin
I'm a room full of toys
I'm a squeaky noise
I'm a gospel song
I'm a gong
I'm a leaf turning red
I'm a loaf of brown bread
I'm a whatever I want to be
An anything I care to be
And when I open my eyes
What I care to be
is me.   (unnumbered pages)

Children can perform the poem in a call-response fashion, with the first line of each rhyming couplet issued as a *call* by one child and the second line offered as the *response* by another (the rest of the poem recited chorally). After reciting the poem together many times, children and teachers can have great fun making up new rhyming couplets. Here are some possibilities suggested by children:

I'm a fish / I'm a birthday wish
I'm a red and yellow hat / I'm a baseball bat
I'm a candy bar / I'm a twinkling star
I'm a girl / I'm someone who can whirl
I'm a shiny ring / I'm a royal king
I'm a red umbrella / I'm a real cool fella
I'm an ambulance siren / I'm a piston firin'
I'm a bird / I'm a very long word

Reading Books With Rhymes

One of the activities widely advocated for developing children's rhyme awareness is for the teacher to read aloud many books containing rhyming words. Teachers should point out the rhymes in text, accentuating them while reading and pausing to make comments such as the following:

Did you notice all the words that rhyme in this story? Remember that rhyming words are words that sound alike at the end. There are so many words that sound alike at the end in this story. Listen: *toast, most; doom, room; face, space*. Listen again to *toast* and *most*. Who can think of some other words that rhyme with *toast* and *most*? (The text referred to here is *Clean Your Room, Harvey Moon* [1994] by Pat Cummings.)

After reading a book aloud several times so that children are familiar with the text, teachers can also pause in their reading for children to supply the second word in a rhyming pair. Good suggestions for other rhyming activities, not necessarily book related, can be found in a number of sources (e.g., Adams et al., 1998; Bear et al., 2000; Blevins, 1998; Ericson & Juliebo, 1998; Fitzpatrick, 1997).

Rhyming and BC Phonology

A number of years ago, I observed a lesson that I later ended up describing in an article:

> I am watching a student teacher working with a small group of first graders. They have finished their lesson and are playing with rhyming words. The mood is light-hearted, especially when one child offers the word *kiss* as a rhyme for *miss*. The mood changes abruptly, however, when another child calls out *twis(t)*. . . "Twis? Twis?" asks the student teacher, clearly at a loss. She wrinkles her face in confusion. "What do you mean *twis*?" she asks, the heavy emphasis on "twis" making it sound like something repugnant. The child who called out his word with such enthusiasm and confidence says nothing. (Meier, 1999, p. 102)

Readers may recall from chapter 3 (or know from experience) that final consonant cluster reduction (e.g., *twis* as opposed to *twist*) is a feature of the BC phonological system. Had the student teacher been knowledgeable about BC phonology, she might have handled this situation in a better way. She might, for example, have said something like the following:

> *Twis.* What an interesting word! You know why it's so interesting? Because *twis* is a word that can be pronounced in more than one way. Sometimes people pronounce the word *twis* just like Kenny did. But sometimes people pronounce the word like this: *twist-t-t. Twis, twist.* Can you hear the difference? Can you hear the extra little sound at the end of *twist*? Listen carefully: *twis, twist; twis, twist.* Say the words with me. . . .
>
> Now, if you say the word like this—*twis*—then it does rhyme with miss and kiss, doesn't it? Just like Kenny said. Listen: *miss, kiss, twis.* Good rhyming, Kenny. They sound the same at the end. But if you pronounce the word like this—*twist*—then they don't rhyme do they? Listen: *miss, kiss, twist.* They don't sound the same at the end.
>
> There are a lot of words in our language that can be pronounced in more than one way. Usually, the difference is at the very end of the word, the very last sound you hear. So let's listen carefully to the very last sounds in words from now on to see if we can discover other words that can be pronounced in more than one way. Thank you for that interesting word, Kenny. You really got us listening. Hearing the difference between *twis* and *twist* is part of being a great sound detective. Let's say them together one more time . . .

Why Such a Big Deal About Such a Little Difference?

After reading the previous example teacher response, readers may have been left wondering, "Why all the fuss?" Wouldn't it have been better for the teacher to simply accept the child's BC pronunciation of *twist* (which, after all, does rhyme with *miss* and *kiss*) and just move on? Why discuss the difference between these two pronunciations, and why at such length? The answer lies in both the prominence of consonant cluster reduction as a feature within the

BC phonological system and its possible impact on the process of learning to read.

Studies indicate that consonant cluster reduction is a prominent feature in the speech of BC speaking children (Craig, Thompson, Washington, & Potter, 2003; Craig & Washington, 2006). Some researchers, most notably the linguist William Labov, have suggested that BC consonant cluster reduction may be a factor in the reading difficulties experienced by some Black children. In research conducted in the Philadelphia Public Schools, Labov and his colleagues have found that the reading errors of low income African American children who are poor readers tend to cluster at the ends of words, where there is the greatest divergence between SE and BC, most notably in final consonant clusters. They've also found that reading errors involving final consonant clusters seem to be particularly difficult to reduce among the students they work with in Philadelphia, even after extensive instruction (Labov, 2001; Labov, Baker, Bullock, Ross, & Brown, 1998). As a result of these findings, as well as his decades of research on BC, Labov has long advocated that teachers pay more attention to the ends of words in early literacy instruction (Labov, 1969, 1995, 2001).

Thus a very good reason for talking with children about pronunciation differences in a rhyming activity is that, in doing so, teachers are encouraging children to develop the strategy of paying more careful attention to the ends of words, a strategy likely to be very useful for BC speakers during phonics instruction. Just as importantly, by talking explicitly with children about pronunciation differences, teachers are helping children develop a frame for making sense of possible future inconsistencies between what teachers might say about the relationship between sound and print in a particular word and what BC speakers may hear when they say the same word "aloud" in their heads. Instead of the child thinking, "This doesn't make sense" or possibly even "What's wrong with me because I don't get it?," the child who has been part of many interesting discussions about alternate pronunciations has another possibility available for interpreting the apparent inconsistency—that is, "Maybe my teacher and I don't pronounce this word the same way." Finally, paying attention to subtle sound differences—such as that between the BC pronunciation *twis* and the SE pronunciation *twist*—can help increase children's level of metalinguistic awareness (i.e., the ability to reflect on language as an entity in itself). Reading research has shown that skilled readers are likely to have superior levels of metalinguistic awareness (Bohannon, Warren-Leubecker, & Hepler, 1984; Paris and Myers, 1981; Snow et al., 1998; Tunmer & Hoover, 1992).

The Systematicity of BC Pronunciations

At this point, readers may have another question. If consonant cluster reduction has such a potentially important impact on learning to read, they why all the discussion about alternate pronunciations? Why not simply encourage children to enunciate the ends of words more clearly? Many readers may have noticed that final cluster reduction also occurs in the speech of non-BC speakers. For example, my sister, an SE speaker, recently shared with me her excitement about finally getting "a *bran* new stove," deleting the *d* from the final *nd* cluster. If most English speakers sometimes reduce final consonant clusters (and they do!), then why is this feature described as specifically characteristic of BC? I suspect that this question may be in the back of the minds of the many teachers I have heard over the years making statements like the following to BC speakers: *You're forgetting to say your endings; Be sure to pronounce the last sound in the word; Look at the word again and say it correctly.*

It is essential for teachers to realize that there *is* a difference between consonant cluster reduction used by BC speakers and that used by SE speakers. For one thing, this feature is used much more frequently by BC speakers than by SE speakers. Secondly, BC speakers reduce final clusters in a wider variety of linguistic contexts. Whereas SE speakers typically delete the final consonant in a cluster only when that consonant precedes another consonant (e.g., *fas forward*, but *fast action*), BC speakers sometimes also delete the final consonant in a cluster preceding a vowel (e.g., *las dance* and *las option*) as well as when words ending in consonant clusters appear in isolation, as on a spelling test (e.g., *tol* not *told*; Green, 2002; Labov, 1969; Rickford & Rickford, 2000). But by far the most important difference between consonant cluster reduction in BC and in SE is that in BC, consonant cluster reduction in an integral part of the linguistic system, whereas in SE it is not (Green, 2002).

To illustrate the rule-governed nature of consonant cluster reduction, Green discusses plural formation and uses the words *post, wasp,* and *mask* as examples. For many BC speakers, these words are pronounced as *pos, was,* and *mas,* respectively. The systematic nature of these pronunciations, Green explains, is revealed in the way their plurals are formed. In both BC and SE, words that end in *s* form their plurals by adding *–es* (sounds like [IZ]), whereas for words ending in *t, p,* or *k,* the plural ending is *–s.* The fact that the plural forms of *post, wasp,* and *mask* in BC are *poses, wases,* and *mases* rather than *posts, wasps,* and *masks* is good evidence that their BC pronunciations (i.e., *pos, was,* and *mas*) are systematic and rule-governed (Green, 2002, pp. 113–114). Some linguists have argued that consonant clusters do not even exist in the underlying structure of BC (e.g., Smith, 1998). Those holding the view that the underlying structure of BC contains no consonant clusters highlight the historical relationship between BC and various West African languages, in which consonant clusters rarely occur.

"Two Ways to Say It"

In any case, linguists who study BC are in agreement that the absence of final consonant clusters in the speech of many BC speakers is a rule-governed feature of the linguistic system. Thus BC-speaking children who pronounce *desk* as *des* are not forgetting to say their endings or pronouncing words incorrectly. They are following the systematic, largely unconscious, rules of their language. Although it is important in this society for BC speakers to become fully bilingual (i.e., able to use both BC and SE with fluency and skill), teachers must think very carefully about how best to help children achieve that goal.

"Correcting" children who aren't really making mistakes, but, instead, following systematic, unconscious rules is not likely to be effective. As Carrie Secret (1998), a long-time, highly successful teacher in Oakland, California, points out, BC speakers often don't hear the difference between the BC and SE pronunciations of a word like *best*. They zoom right past this subtle pronunciation difference and head straight for meaning. Thus when a teacher "corrects" a BC speaker who says *bes* by modeling the SE pronunciation *best*, the child may well be confused rather than "enlightened" (i.e., *Isn't that what I just said?*). As a consequence, Secret advocates explicitly teaching children to hear the differences between the two pronunciations. In Secret's view, "children must first hear and develop an ear for both languages in order to effectively distinguish between the two" (p. 83; see also Harris-Wright, 1999, 2005 on this topic).

Over the course of 10 years studying the linguistic patterns used by BC speaking children in two urban communities in Michigan, Craig and Washington (2006) found that as they progressed in school, many of the children in their study increasingly shifted toward SE, a finding consistent with other studies (Adler, 1992; Bountress, 1983; Craig and Washington, 2004). Interestingly, Craig and Washington were able to identify two distinct points of dialect shifting: one at first grade and the other at third grade. These shifts seemed to occur in the absence of direct instruction in SE, although Craig and Washington speculate that these shifts were likely influenced by the instructional context: "The first shift appears to be triggered by immersion in the language of the classroom whereas the second appears to be influenced by formal reading instruction" (pp. 47–48). In Craig and Washington's data, dialect shifting was associated with positive academic achievements (p. 46).

Thus in focusing children's conscious attention on systematic phonological differences between BC and SE, teachers would seem to be aiming instruction in the developmental direction that many young, well-achieving BC speakers are already headed. For these children, such a focus can only contribute to, or possibly even accelerate, that process by enhancing their level of metalinguistic awareness. For children experiencing more difficulty learning to code-switch, explicit attention to pronunciation differences may help them more clearly differentiate the two varieties and therefore spur their movement toward acquisition of SE skills. And clearly, the research of Labov and his colleagues in Philadelphia suggests that explicit attention to the ends of words in particular is likely to have a beneficial effect on children's decoding skills. In any discussion of pronunciation differences between BC and SE, however, it should be clear that the goal is not to change the way children pronounce words. Rather the goal should be two-fold: (a) increasing children's ability to "hear" those differences, and (b) establishing the fact that there are different ways of speaking in our society and that linguistic differences are an interesting topic for discussion and exploration (e.g., *Wow! Let's listen for other words that can be pronounced in two different ways!*).

Rhyming activities provide an ideal context for drawing young children's attention to these differences in a natural and lighthearted way. Imagine, for example, that kindergarten or first-grade children are chorally reciting the jump-rope song "Little Sally Walker" (the song is written on large chart paper so that children can track the print as their teacher points to each word). As the children recite, the teacher notices that when they come to the lines *Shake it to the east/ Shake it to the west/ Shake it to the one that you love the best,* many of the children pronounce the rhyming words *eas, wes,* and *bes.* Afterward, to take advantage of this teachable moment, the teacher might say something like the following:

> Do you remember the other day when we were talking about words that can be pronounced in more than one way? *Twist* was one of those words. We noticed that some people say *twis* and other people say *twist.* Same word, different ways to say it. When we were reciting "Little Sally Walker," I noticed some other words that can be pronounced in more than one way. I noticed that when we said *turn to the one that you love the best,* some people said *love the bes* and some people said *love the best. Bes, best.* Can you hear the difference? *Bes, best; bes, best. Best* has a /t/ sound at the end, doesn't it? *Bes, best.* They're different at the very end, aren't they? *Bes, best.* Two ways to say the same word. Let's say them together.

If the teacher were working with children who already knew some letter-sound correspondences, the teacher would likely want to point to the print in talking about the /t/ sound at the of *best.* Eventually, as children become more advanced in decoding, the idea of two ways to pronounce a word can be expanded to the concept of "two ways to say it, one way to spell it."

As teachers engage children in coming up with additional rhyming words to match those in a poem or book, children may well offer rhymes that reflect BC phonological patterns. It is important for teachers to recognize these BC pronunciations (as the student teacher in the example earlier did not) and to use them as an opportunity for developing children's ear for subtle differences between BC and SE pronunciations. All of this emphasis on the ends of words in the early stages of literacy instruction is likely to serve children well throughout the process of learning to decode.

Alliteration: Focusing on Beginning Sounds

Drawing children's attention to the use of alliteration in books, poems, songs, and chants and encouraging them to experiment with alliteration in various ways can be considered the first steps in developing children's ability to segment words into individual phonemes. As children isolate the initial phoneme from the rest of the word, they strengthen their awareness that words are comprised of separate, and separable, sounds. There are many excellent children's books that contain examples of alliteration. Again, I recommend that teachers draw in significant numbers from the many books with alliteration that feature African American characters, themes, and settings.

One of the best of these is Irene Smalls's *Kevin and His Dad* (1999) discussed in an earlier chapter. With Mom gone for the day, Kevin and his Dad spend Saturday morning doing household chores. For example, they "hang, hang, hang the hats," "catch, catch, catch the cobwebs," and "dust, dust, dust the dog" (unnumbered pages). Children enjoy performing the various actions Smalls describes, pretending that they're "fix, fix, fix[ing] the faucets" and "squeeze, squeeze, squeez[ing] the soap" as they recite the rhythmical lines from the text. Afterward, children can make up their own alliterative actions to perform. Here are some examples made up by children: *we hose, hose, hose the hamsters; we cook, cook, cook the corn; we dump, dump, dump the dustpan; we feed, feed, feed the fish; we sort, sort, sort the socks; we shine, shine, shine the shoes; we scrub, scrub, scrub the skillet; we sponge, sponge, sponge the spoons.*

Leola and the Honeybears (1999) by Melodye Benson Rosales, mentioned in earlier chapters, also contains many delightful examples of alliteration. One example is Rosales's description of the honeybears' culinary preferences: "They dined on delicious daily delights like dandelion stew, double-dipped daffodil custard, and sweet daisy-dough cakes" (unnumbered pages). Teachers can extend the alliteration, and the vocabulary, beyond the pages of the book by asking children to think of other "delicious daily delights" that begin with the /d/ sound, such as *donuts, dumplings, dates, ding-dongs, Dots, devil's food cake, dill pickles,* and *Dove bars.* Afterward, children could brainstorm "delicious daily delights" that begin with another sound they have previously learned, such as /k/—*cakes, cookies, candy, carrots.*

Finding Other Book Connections

In addition to reading lots of books with alliteration, activities frequently mentioned for focusing children's attention on initial phonemes include versions of the popular games "I Spy" and "I'm Thinking of Something," in which the teacher asks children to guess the word he or she is thinking of, the first clue being its initial sound. Although this is not in itself a book-based activity, I advocate that teachers find some kind of book connection in doing this activity with children. For example, teachers could introduce the "I'm Thinking of Something" activity by reading aloud *What's in Aunt Mary's Room?* (1996) by Elizabeth Fitzgerald Howard. This book revolves around Susan's and Sarah's curiosity about what might be in a locked room at their Great-great-aunt Flossie's house. As the girls and their parents make their regular trip to Aunt Flossie's, they play a game they call "What's in Aunt Mary's Room?":

> "Alligators," said Sarah.
> "Alligators and baby buggies," Daddy said.
> "Alligators, baby buggies, and car seats," said Mommy.
> "Alligators, baby buggies, car seats, and Dairy Queens," I said, because we
>   were passing a Dairy Queen.   (unnumbered pages)

After reading the book through in its entirety, the teacher could go back to the part about the guessing game, noting how much fun the girls and their parents had playing with the beginning sounds in words and then telling children that they're also about to play a fun game with beginning sounds.

Another possibility for incorporating a book connection into this activity is for the teacher to tell children that all of the words they will be guessing in the game come from a particular book. *Feast for Ten* (1993) by Cathryn Falwell, for instance, is a counting book about family members who go grocery shopping and prepare a meal together. The teacher might begin the game by reminding children that all of the words to be guessed will come from *Feast for Ten* and then offering a clue such as the following: *The thing I'm thinking of starts with the /k-k-k/ sound.* At this point, children should be encouraged to come up with as many possibilities as they can, as the object of the game is not so much the accurate identification of the target word as practice with initial phonemes. The teacher can then continue with additional meaning clues as needed, always being careful to include the initial sound clue along with the new clue—for example, *When the family goes shopping, they get one to put their groceries in. /K-k-k/; The baby in the family rides inside of it. /K-k-k/.* Or, as another example, if the teacher has read children the Jamaica books by Juanita Havill, he or she could focus on words from that series—for example, *I'm thinking of how Jamaica felt when she had to return the stuffed dog to the park. The word begins with the /s-s-s/ sound.*

I emphasize these book connections so strongly because they are extremely important for children who don't have a lot of prior book experience. Children in this situation need to connect with books in as many ways as possible. Jamaica, Kevin and his dad, and Susan and Sarah need to come off the page and into the life of the classroom, becoming real in the imaginative lives of the children there. This helps make skills work meaningful to children and connected to books in obvious and tangible ways. That said, I want to distinguish what I am advocating here about the use of literature from a strict "whole language" approach to literacy instruction, in which letter-sound relationships and other skills are taught in an "incidental" way, as these are suggested by, or come up in, the particular book being read. The approach I am suggesting here is skill driven, not literature driven. The book being read does not dictate the particular skill being taught.

Rather, the teacher identifies the skill to be focused upon and then searches for books that connect in some meaningful way to that targeted skill.

Not all activities focusing on initial phonemes need to be book related. There are many useful, non-book-based activities suggested in the literature (e.g., Adams et al., 1998; Bear et al., 2000; Blevins, 1998; Ericson & Juliebo, 1998; Fitzpatrick, 1997). Some of the most valuable of these in my view are picture sorts, in which children group pictures based upon whether or not the words that describe them begin with the same sounds. Picture sorts are described in detail in Bear et al. (2000). While the sorting activities that Bear et al. describe can be instructive and engaging for children whether or not the pictures to be sorted are related to books children are familiar with, it is possible for teachers to create picture sets that represent objects and characters from books that children have previously read and enjoyed, thereby making these excellent activities even more beneficial for children with little prior book experience. A number of educators emphasize the importance of drawing children's attention to how initial sounds feel in the mouth as they are articulated (e.g., Adams et al., 1998; Bear et al., 2000). Adams et al., for example, suggest that children be frequently asked, "What are you doing with your lips, tongue, mouth, and voice as you make the sound of /m/, /b/, /p/?" (p. 57). There are many more interesting, creative ideas for working with initial sounds to be found in the references cited earlier, and interested readers are urged to consult them.

Emphasize Beginnings *and* Ends

While a great deal of attention is given to the initial sound in words, as a whole, the literature on phonological and phonemic awareness places relatively little emphasis on developing children's awareness of ending sounds (an exception is Adams et al., 1998). As discussed in the section on rhyming, drawing children's attention to the ending sounds of words is likely to be beneficial for African American children who are BC speakers. Typically, when teachers work with children on rhymes, children's attention is focused on the rime as a whole (e.g., the final phoneme /t/ in *best* is not isolated from the rest of the rime, but considered as one whole unit: *est*). As was suggested earlier, teachers who are knowledgeable about BC phonological patterns can focus children's attention on the final sounds in words as these get highlighted when children offer rhymes that reflect BC pronunciations. Teachers can also introduce and invite discussion of words that are pronounced in more than one way. These are excellent strategies to adopt. But BC speakers are likely to need more practice distinguishing and isolating ending sounds than can be provided through rhyming activities alone. It is important for teachers to highlight initial phonemes in phonemic awareness activities, but for BC speakers in particular, it is equally important for teachers to highlight ending sounds.

Ending sounds in words are usually more difficult to isolate than beginning sounds (Adams et al., 1998). Thus it may be especially useful to draw children's attention to what they are doing with "[their] lips, tongue, mouth and voice" as they articulate various endings sounds in words. Teachers might comment, for example, on the ending /p/ sound in *bop* and *shop* in the title of *Bippity Bop Barbershop*. After talking about the feel of their lips pressing together to form the final /p/, children can be challenged to come up with other words that end with the /p/ sound, such as *hop, jump, camp, shop, dip,* and *step.* As another example, the little girl in *Violet's Music* (2004) by Angela Johnson uses a badminton racket as a pretend guitar, strumming "plink, plink, pluck, pluck" (unnumbered pages). In reading this book aloud, teachers can draw children's attention to the /k/ sound at the end of these words. Children can be asked to describe what happens to their tongue when they make this sound. What other words can children think of that end with the /k/ sound?

Teachers can play "I'm Thinking of Something" with children, focusing not on initial sounds in words, but on ending sounds. Children can also do picture sorts by matching pictures of objects whose names end with a particular sound. In fact, most of the activities designed to focus children's attention on initial sounds can, and should, also be used to focus their attention on the sounds they hear at the ends of words.

Blending and Segmenting Sounds

The ability to blend individual sounds into a word and to segment a word into its component sounds are essential to reading and spelling. Research indicates that blending and segmenting speech sounds is highly correlated with early reading achievement (Griffith & Olson, 1992; Snow et al., 1998; Yopp, 1988). Blending is generally considered to be an easier skill for children to acquire than segmenting, although there is some disagreement on this point in the literature (see, for example, Ericson & Juliebo, 1998; Lewkowitz, 1980). There is widespread agreement, however, that instruction in both should begin with syllables, move to onsets and rimes, and finally focus on individual phonemes.

Blending Sounds

Teachers might introduce the concept of blending separate parts of a word by saying children's names in syllables—for example, *Ma-lik; Tiff-a-ny*—and asking children to identify the name. This activity could also be done with the names of characters from books the class has read. Oral blending activities with onsets and rimes should focus on single-syllable words. The teacher might tell children that he or she is going to say a word in parts and they have to figure out what the word is—for example, /s/.. at. Teachers can also make a book connection for this activity by choosing single syllable words that relate to a familiar book. As children move on to working with phonemes, the process is essentially the same except that now the focus is on individual sounds—for example, /s/.. /a/.. /t/.

There are many possibilities for creating blending activities that children are likely to find engaging. One activity frequently suggested is using a puppet who talks in "parts." The puppet says /b/.. /e/.. /d/, for example, and children must figure out what the puppet is saying. Teachers and children can play a version of "I'm Thinking Of" in which the clues consist of phonemes that children must blend into the word their teacher has in mind—for example, *I'm thinking of something that Jamaica found at the park. It's a /d/.. /o/.. /g/. What's the word?* Using pictures of familiar objects (ideally pictures representing objects from a familiar book), teachers can hold up each picture, saying its name one phoneme at a time. Children must blend the sounds and come up with the right word. There are many other excellent suggestions for blending activities contained in the literature, many of which incorporate physical movement and song (e.g., Adams et al., 1998; Blevins, 1998; Ericson & Juliebo, 1998).

Segmenting Sounds

As with blending, practice in segmenting sounds should start with syllables. Children can clap the syllables in their names, the syllables in a favorite poem or song, or the syllables in a refrain from a familiar book. In *I Love My Hair!* (1998) by Natasha Anastasia Tarpley, for example, Keyana's hair beads "click to the rhythm of [her] walk," helping her to remember what she and her mother need to buy at the grocery store: "Tap! Tap! Clicky-clacky! Milk, bread, peanut butter" (unnumbered pages). Children can have fun clapping, walking, or marching out the syllables in this refrain. While the syllable is what Snow et al. (1998) refer to as an "indivisible entity" in terms of acoustics (which is why most children have little trouble segmenting words into syllables), segmenting syllables into onsets and rimes depends upon children's ability to isolate the initial phoneme from the rest of the syllable or word. Children who have had lots of practice playing with alliteration and beginning sounds will likely find it relatively easy to segment words into onsets and rimes.

Teachers should work with single syllable words when doing activities that require children to segment words into onsets and rimes or into phonemes. Many experts advocate the use of objects such as pennies, chips, or some other token that children can physically manipulate when they are learning how to segment words into individual sounds (e.g., Adams et al., 1998; Ericson & Juliebo, 1998). Again, I refer interested readers to the literature for descriptions of concrete, hands-on activities that teachers can use to provide children with needed practice in segmenting sounds (Adams et al., 1998; Blevins, 1998; Ericson & Juliebo, 1998; Fitzpatrick, 1997).

Children also get considerable practice segmenting words into their component sounds when teachers allow them to write frequently, using invented spelling. In their early writing, children rely on the sounds they hear as they say words aloud. According to Bear et al. (2000), "When literacy development has occurred in a balanced environment, phonemic awareness and the ability to invent a spelling go hand in hand" (p. 97). Activities in which teachers ask children to separate words into phonemes—for example, *Listen to this word and say it sound by sound*—help to focus children's attention on individual sounds and give them valuable practice in segmentation, but putting their developing phonemic awareness "into action" through writing helps children to own and secure that knowledge.

Back to the Big Picture

In isolating specific components of the early literacy curriculum for discussion as I have in these last two chapters, I run the risk of implying that skills should be taught in lockstep, sequential order or that memorization of the alphabet and work with phonemic awareness must be complete before any kind of phonics instruction can begin. Such is not the case. Children do not have to know the entire alphabet before they begin linking sounds to spellings, for example, or have "finished" playing with rhymes before they work on oral blending. Similarly, as children practice oral blending and work with initial consonant sounds, many benefit from also seeing the print, even though the emphasis in these activities in on sounds. As Bear et al. (2000) point out, oral language activities can, and should, cross over into learning letter-sound relationships:

> Children can learn these associations at the same time they are learning to reflect on their oral language. Phonological awareness does not have to precede or follow alphabet knowledge or other components of emergent literacy instruction. Awareness of sounds is heightened by print, and because of this, it is a reciprocal, ongoing by-product of the learning-to-read process. Although phonological awareness is a key component of early reading acquisition, phonological awareness activities need not be conducted as isolated tasks. As children develop phonological awareness, teachers should seek to make connections between sounds and letters in the context of daily reading and writing. (pp. 103–104)

I have chosen to highlight alphabet knowledge and phonemic awareness in these last two chapters not because they are the only important components of the early literacy curriculum, but because they often get too little attention as teachers attempt to move children quickly into the "meat" of phonics instruction. As I have tried to argue here, children need to have a strong foundation on which to build that instruction. Without solid knowledge of the alphabet and a thorough understanding of how speech is related to print, children may not make good progress in learning to read. African American children bring enormous linguistic strengths with them to literacy instruction, but if they have had little experience with books and other literacy artifacts, they have likely had few opportunities to develop the level of phonemic awareness or the automaticity in letter recognition necessary to fully benefit from phonics instruction. To build successfully on the verbal and rhetorical abilities African American children bring to school and to insure their success in learning to decode, teachers must make sure children develop the tools they need to fully access the curriculum.

Chapter 12
Black Communications and Phonics Instruction

Perhaps the clearest and most important recommendation that can be made about teaching phonics to BC speakers is that it be done in an explicit and systematic way. In addressing the question, "What happens in schools where inner-city children [do] read at grade level?," Mary Rhodes Hoover (2005), a former professor of reading at Howard University and a life-long activist for the educational well-being of Black children, writes the following:

> The record is clear: African American students can be taught the decoding aspects of reading at high levels using any one of several phonics-based reading programs, among other methods. These highly structured, intensive approaches are appropriate for students with second dialects or languages in their backgrounds because they are similar to foreign language teaching methods—with students first being exposed to regular patterns (phonics), then passages written in these patterns (decodable text). (p. 71)

Hoover goes on to explain:

> The structure of the English language creates the need for a structured, systematic phonics approach. . . In English there are more than 14 different ways to pronounce the letter *o* as in *Spot, mother, look, open,* and *spook.* In fact, English uses 379 letters and letter combinations for 40 sounds, compared to Italian, Turkish, Spanish, or Swahili languages with the same number of symbols as sounds. This complexity would be confusing to any student; students with more than one language in their backgrounds would be particularly in need of a structured approach to reading. (p. 71)

Hoover is careful to say that "the use of these methods does not exclude the use of comprehension, vocabulary, and study skills approaches, nor does it exclude the use of whole language or some other literature approach to reading as a supplement" (p. 71).

Thus, as Hoover points out, there is no necessary contradiction between the use of quality children's literature as a context for teaching comprehension strategies (as described in part 3) and a highly structured approach to teaching phonics. Indeed, a combination of intellectual engagement with complex text, on the one hand, and structured phonics lessons, on the other, would seem to be the perfect "instructional prescription" for facilitating high literacy achievement among African American children. Providing children with opportunities to talk in meaningful ways about books and to begin developing high-level comprehension strategies while still engaged in the process of learning to decode is instruction that takes maximum advantage of Black children's sophisticated linguistic abilities and keeps them motivated to achieve. At the same time, the structured, systematic approach to phonics instruction decreases the chance that the relatively greater distance between sound and spelling that exists for BC speakers (as opposed to SE speakers) will end up causing confusion or difficulty in learning to decode.

Hoover's insistence that phonics instruction be highly structured and systematic has considerable research support behind it (Adams, 1990; Anderson et al., 1985; Chall, 1967; Honig, 1996; Stallings, Robbins, & Presbrey, 1986; Stebbins, St. Pierre, Proper, Anderson, & Cerva, 1977). As illustration, in *Preventing Reading Difficulties in Young Children,* Snow et al. (1998) report on the findings of Project Follow Through (Stebbins et al., 1977), a study sponsored by the federal government to compare the long-term effects of various reading methodologies on the academic achievement of so-called "disadvantaged" children. Although researchers concluded that " 'most Follow Through interventions produced more negative than positive effects on basic skills test scores,'" the Direct Instruction Model was a striking exception (p. 175). This model emphasized systematic teaching of basic skills. Researchers found that "students who participated during four full years (kindergarten through third grade) in the direct instruction program performed close to or at national norms on measures of reading, math, language, and spelling" (p. 176).

Snow et al. also report on the findings of a more recent major study (Foorman et al., 1998) that compared the efficacy of three widely used approaches to first-grade phonics instruction:

1. Whole language in which the emphasis is on connected text, with alphabetic learning assumed to go on implicitly;
2. Embedded phonics in which sound-spelling patterns are systematically embedded in connected text; and
3. Direct code, in which letter-sound correspondences and practice take place with various kinds of text. (p. 199)

Fitting Hoover's description of a "highly structured, intensive approach" to phonics instruction, in the direct code method, "letter-sound correspondences and spelling conventions are explicitly taught and interactively practiced and extended" and books used for independent reading are "methodically designed to review/offer practice with the sight words and phonics lessons to date" (p. 204). The Foorman et al. study focused on 285 low-income children in Houston who were receiving services through Title I. Researchers found that children taught using the direct code method made significantly more progress in word-reading skill than the other two groups. Snow et al. write:

> Controlling for differences in age, ethnicity, and verbal IQ, the researchers found that children taught via the direct code approach improved in word reading at a faster rate and had higher word recognition skills than children receiving whole-language instruction (either the research-based or the district's standard version). Furthermore, whereas a relatively large percentage of children in the two whole-language groups and the embedded phonics groups exhibited no measurable gains in word reading over the school year, the direct instruction group showed growth in word reading that appeared more or less normally distributed. (p. 205)

To insure systematicity in phonics instruction, Hoover advocates the use of a "proven" phonics-based basal reading program. Clearly, basal reading programs are not without their shortcomings. For one, as pointed out by Snow et al., partly because of the huge expense involved in revision, they tend to lag somewhat behind the most current research and thinking in the field of reading. Second, and very important, their set sequencing reduces the teacher's ability to adjust instruction, including pacing, for individual students or even for the majority of the class, as may seem warranted for some lessons. Also, in my experience, use of a highly structured program like a basal series is often frustrating for very creative teachers who have their own good ideas about how to teach particular skills in ways that may be especially well matched to the group of students they are teaching. Some of the teachers with whom I have worked in South Carolina, for example, have had wonderfully inventive ideas for teaching phonics lessons in ways that draw upon traditional African American cultural practices and discourse patterns. However, these lessons would be difficult to incorporate into instruction if teachers were constrained to rigidly following the sequence of instruction laid out in a basal program.

In addition, Labov (1969, 1995, 2001) has long faulted basal reading programs for not designing instruction in ways that would likely accommodate the needs of BC speakers. One suggestion he has made, for instance, is that basals devote more instructional attention to the ends of words. As Labov points out, this could be accomplished in part by as simple a change as introducing final lone consonants, as well as final consonant digraphs and clusters, at the same time as these are introduced in initial position. Since 1969, Labov has consistently made the following five recommendations for improving reading instruction for BC speakers:

- Distinguishing between mistakes in reading and differences in pro-
  nunciation;
- Giving more instructional attention to the ends of words;
- Presenting words in phonological contexts that preserve underlying
  forms ("old *eggs*," for example, not "He is ol*d*, the context in which
  the final /*d*/ is least likely to be heard or pronounced);
- Avoiding contractions in early reading materials; and
- Teaching grammar explicitly. (Labov, 1995)

As Labov acknowledges, making these changes in basal reading programs
would not ameliorate all reading difficulties experienced by Black children,
but might move quite far in that direction, without doing the least bit of harm
to SE speakers using the same basal program. Unfortunately, no publishing
company has as yet seen fit to incorporate these suggestions into the design of
its basal program, even on an experimental basis. There is no question that, at
this point in time, basal reading programs are designed with the needs of SE
speakers most prominently in mind.

All of that said, however, the value of basal reading programs for teaching decoding to BC speakers still outweighs their shortcomings. BC speakers
cannot afford "hit or miss" instruction in phonics. As Snow et al. (1998) persuasively argue:

> Beyond any collection of compelling objectives and engaging activities . . .
> effective instruction requires a developmental plan that extends across days
> and weeks of the school year as well as a means for monitoring progress so
> as to adjust that plan accordingly. Most basal reading programs do provide
> such a plan, as embodied in its lesson sequence. To the extent that these
> plans are pedagogically well designed, the basal programs can be seen to
> offer instructional value that extends beyond the specifics of their activities
> and materials. To the extent that the programs also provide a rationale for
> activities, including tips and tools for monitoring student progress, they are
> of great value for improving student performance in reading . . . (p. 193)

As Snow et al. point out, these benefits of a basal program would appear to be
especially significant for new and relatively inexperienced teachers for whom
many aspects of teaching are likely to be new and challenging. It takes a great
deal of both knowledge and experience to design an effective phonics program
on one's own. But whether or not it is a basal reading program per se or some
other reliable phonics program that is used for instruction in decoding, the
important point is that such instruction be systematic and explicit.

What Else Should Teachers Be Doing?

A question that keeps recurring with respect to the reading difficulties experienced by many Black children is the extent to which systematic differences

between BC and SE may be seen as contributing to those difficulties. Because the distance between the spoken and written language is relatively greater for BC speakers than for SE speakers, many linguists and educators have postulated that learning to decode is likely to be more challenging for BC speakers than for SE speakers. Hoover's recommendation that BC speakers be taught to decode using a highly structured, explicit approach is based on just that postulation. But if learning to decode really is a more challenging task for BC speakers than for SE speakers, then is using a systematic approach to phonics instruction *enough* to insure their success, or should teachers be doing something in addition, especially given the fact that basals and other phonics programs currently on the market were not developed with differences between BC and SE in mind? To answer that question, we must first consider another: What is it that we currently know about the relationship between BC and learning to read?

In the first chapter of *Black Dialect Interference and Accommodation of Reading Instruction in First Grade*, a landmark study published in 1973, Ann Piestrup noted that while there is "considerable evidence" of both reading failure and "dialect differences" among African American children, "there is little more than speculation about whether dialect differences make learning to read more difficult for Black children and about how teachers could ease possible difficulties" (p. 1). Despite the passage of more than 30 years, Piestrup's characterization of the state of our knowledge about BC and reading remains, in many respects, still apt in 2007. Thus, at this point in time, it simply isn't possible to make definitive statements about how best to apply knowledge of BC linguistic patterns in teaching children to read.

Nonetheless, research and thinking on this topic over the last 30 years has added significantly to our knowledge base on the subject and does suggest some intriguing and promising ideas for both practice and future research. Given the very serious nature of the reading problems experienced by Black children in schools across the country, it seems to me imperative that teachers and teacher educators know as much as possible about what research has to say both about the relationship between BC and reading and about practices that appear to have been successful in helping BC speakers improve their achievement in reading. In the rest of this chapter, I present an overview of research and pedagogical discussion on this topic, using some major studies in the area as a frame for highlighting key issues that have been raised. Based on this overview, in the next chapter I discuss implications for research and practice.

Teaching Black Children to Read, 1969

Linguistic and educational interest in BC (often referred to in the early literature on this topic as *Black English* or *Black English Vernacular*) was greatly spurred by President Lyndon Johnson's "War on Poverty" in the 1960s. Working on the widely shared assumption that the surest avenue out of poverty was via a good education, a number of prominent linguists in the 1960s applied their professional expertise to examining the possible role of "dialect differences" in the reading failure experienced by many Black students in urban schools across the United States. Their thinking on this topic at the time is well represented in a collection of essays entitled *Teaching Black Children to Read* (edited by Baratz and Shuy), published in 1969. Many of the writers contributing to this volume had little experience in schools, although some had extensive experience doing linguistic fieldwork in urban Black communities. Essentially, these linguists used their knowledge about the BC system to make hypotheses about its possible effects on the process of learning to read in SE. With a teaching audience clearly in mind, they described specific phonological and grammatical patterns of BC and explained their likely impact on reading. In his article, William Labov, for example, talked about the fact that there are a large number of homonyms in the speech of BC speakers that do not occur in SE and declared: "If the teacher knows about this different set of homonyms, no serious problems in the teaching of reading need occur; but if the teacher does not know, there are bound to be difficulties" (p. 39).

All the authors in this volume theorized that the BC system was sufficiently different from the SE system that learning to read in SE was likely to be a more difficult process for BC speakers than for SE speakers. Many made suggestions for practice. These ranged from increasing teacher knowledge about the systematic features of Black English to creating beginning reading materials in Black English (often called "dialect readers"). With respect to the latter, two contributors, Ralph Fasold and Walter Wolfram, wrote: "What appears to be needed, then, is a linguistic adaptation or translation of reading materials to a language system which more closely approximates the child's oral language behavior" (p. 141). Many of the writers in the volume also pointed to the deleterious effects of teachers' negative attitudes toward BC on children's reading performance. In her article, for example, Joan Baratz asserted that most of the Black child's "middle-class" teachers "have wrongly viewed his language as pathological, disordered, 'lazy speech.' " She went on to say: "This failure to recognize the interference from the child's different linguistic system, and consequent negative teacher attitudes toward the child and his language, lead directly to reading difficulties and subsequent school failure" (p. 93).

The highly speculative nature of many of the assertions that were made about the relationship between BC and reading in this collection is well illustrated in the following excerpt from the essay written by Kenneth Goodman (confidently titled "Dialect Barriers to Reading Comprehension," as opposed to "Possible Dialect Barriers . . ."): "Since it is true that learning to read a foreign language is a more difficult task than learning to read a native language, it must follow that it is harder for a child to read a dialect which is not his own that to learn to read his own dialect" (p. 14). This assertion, like many in the volume as a whole, was not supported by any actual experience or research with BC speakers learning to read. At its most extreme, the tenuous connection between theory and practice reflected in some of the essays in this volume is captured in the lead essay, in which the author, Raven McDavid, Jr., follows an assertion about the relationship between "subdialects" and reading with the following declaration: "This supposition, like many others, needs to be tested, but pending disproof, I shall continue to assert it" (p. 1).

The Piestrup Study, 1973

Soon afterward, Ann Piestrup, then a graduate student at the University of California at Berkeley, did set out to test a number of the assertions contained in the Baratz and Shuy volume as she prepared to conduct the research for her doctoral dissertation. Published as a monograph in 1973, Piestrup's dissertation remains to date one of the few empirical investigations we have of the relationship between BC and reading in actual classroom practice. Drawing on the work of a number of linguists whose essays appeared in *Teaching Black Children to Read*—for example, Kenneth Goodman, Ralph Fasold, William Labov, Walt Wolfram—Piestrup sought to investigate what role, if any, BC or "dialect," as she termed it, actually plays during the course of reading instruction. To examine that question, she and a co-investigator observed and tape-recorded instruction in 14 predominately African American first-grade classrooms in Oakland, California.

From these observations, Piestrup extracted 104 episodes that illustrated structural and/or functional conflict between BC and SE during instruction. Using categories suggested by Labov in *Teaching Black Children to Read,* Piestrup defined a structural conflict as one involving a linguistic mismatch between BC and SE, whereas a functional conflict involved a mismatch in styles or ways of using language. The following excerpt from Piestrup's data illustrates a structural conflict (the teacher is reading from a workbook):

T   ". . . how would you harm the colt?"
C1   Tear it
T   Huh?
C1   Tear it
T   Th—th—Oh! Do you, do you know what a colt is, now?
C1   Oh, kill it, kill it!
T   No, what's a colt?
C1   Somethin' you wear.   (p. 3)

In this excerpt, the child interpreted the word *colt* as *coat*. (The phonological rule specifying deletion of *l* after a vowel in BC makes these two words possible homonyms for BC speakers.) According to Piestrup, what is critical about a structural conflict that occurs during the course of instruction is the way in which the teacher responds to it:

> The conflict is not an insurmountable barrier, but a brief misunderstanding. The teacher's handling of the situation, then, is extremely important. The teacher could ignore the initial response (you harm a colt by tearing it) and call on another child for a correct answer, which would probably not resolve the structural interference for the first child. Or she could accommodate her instruction for the dialect-speaking child. (p. 4)

In the continuation of the episode excerpted from here, the teacher does in fact accommodate her instruction to clear up the misunderstanding involving *colt* and *coat*. Through spelling, pronunciation, and clarifying meaning, the teacher distinguishes *colt* and *coat* in a brief, clear, and nonjudgmental way.

Accommodation and Interference

Episodes in which teachers moved quickly and effectively to resolve conflicts between BC and SE, Piestrup termed *accommodation episodes*. In contrast, episodes in which the conflict was not resolved quickly and effectively were termed *interference episodes*. In some interference episodes, teachers simply ignored structural conflicts that arose during instruction, as illustrated in the following excerpt (the lesson is focused on initial consonants):

T	(Holds up a card with "wow" written on it.)
Class	WOW!
T	When would you say "wow"?
C1	When you got some wil' wil' clothes.
T	Well, you might say "wow" if you had on bright clothes. What about this one? (p. 18)

Despite the fact that *wow* and *wild* were being confused in this interaction, the teacher ignored (or did not recognize) this confusion and continued on with the lesson. Other times, teachers in the study handled structural conflict in a way that ended up not only disrupting the continuity of a lesson, but also likely confusing children in the process. This is well illustrated in an episode in which the teacher interrupts a child during oral reading to "correct" his BC pronunciation of the word *they* as *dey:*

C1	Dey, —
T	Get your finger out of your mouth.
C1	'Call —
T	Start again
C1	'Dey call, "What is it? What is it?" '
T	What's this word?
C2	Dey

C1 Dat
T   What is it?
C2 Dat
C3 Dey
C4 (laughs)
C1 Dey
T   Look at my tongue. <u>They</u>
C1 'They.'
T   'They.' Look at my tongue. (Between her teeth)
C1 They
T   That's right. Say it again.
C1 They
T   'They.' Ok. Pretty good. Ok, Jimmy.   (pp. 54–55)

Episodes involving functional conflict were also handled in ways that could be categorized as either "accommodating or "interfering." In one episode illustrating interference, the children begin to engage in verbal play as the teacher attempts to record their statements as part of a shared writing session:

C1   I got me a tow truck. (Giggles)
C2,3 Tow truck, tow truck
T   (Writes on large paper) "I got me a—
C3   Tow, the one you put your toes in?
C1   No!
T   Tow. It does sound like—
C1   A car, a truck dat pull a car. That's craz', stup'!
T   'I got me a tow truck;' what else?
C1   I' pull a car.
C2   (Giggles.)
T   It pull<u>s</u> a car?
C1   Yeah.
T   'I got,' can you read it yourself?
C1   No.   (p. 8)

According to Piestrup, the children's lilting cadence as they chanted "tow truck, tow truck" and the "mischievous intonation" of "Is that the kind you put your toes in?" clearly mark these statements as verbal play. The teacher, however, ignores the children's playful language, focusing instead on making sure the inflectional ending *s* is added to the verb *pull*. As Piestrup observes, the teacher not only "loses the flavor of what the children are doing," but also "defines her separateness" from them. She notes that at the end, the "corrected" child "refuses to read even his own words" (pp. 8–9). In contrast, other teachers in the study accommodated children's verbal style through such behaviors as expressing appreciation of children's creativity, encouraging verbal play related to the lesson, and engaging in verbal play themselves.

Once the classroom observations were finished, Piestrup and her co-investigator divided the teachers into accommodation and interference groups based upon their overall impressions of the interactions they had observed. Later, based on analysis of the classroom episodes, the teachers were further divided into six teaching-style groups based on characteristic behaviors: Vocabulary Approach, Decoding Approach, Standard Pronunciation approach, White Liberal approach, Black Artful approach, and Interrupting approach (p. 83). In addition to investigating whether or not conflicts between BC and SE actually occurred during instruction and how teachers responded if they did, another major purpose of the study was to examine whether or not the ways in which teachers responded to linguistic conflict had an impact on children's reading achievement and the amount of "Black dialect" they used.

To examine dialect use, Piestrup employed a sentence repetition task in which children had to repeat back into a tape recorder a series of tape-recorded sentences modeled for them in standard English. Reading level was measured by children's performance on a standardized reading test (The Cooperative Primary Reading Tests) administered by the teacher as part of the regular instructional program. Piestrup found that neither reading nor dialect scores differed significantly for children taught by teachers in the accommodation group and children taught by teachers in the interference group. However, when scores were compared based on teaching style groups, one style stood out markedly from the others—the Black Artful style. Children taught by Black Artful teachers had the highest mean reading score and lowest mean dialect score among the six groups. Their reading scores were significantly higher than those of children taught by teachers using the interrupting and White Liberal approaches, and their dialect scores were significantly lower than those of children whose teachers used the Vocabulary and Interrupting approaches. In contrast to the mean reading scores for the schools in which Piestrup conducted the study, the mean of reading scores for children from the classes taught by Black artful teachers was considerably higher than the national norm (p. 163).

The Black Artful Approach

Black Artful teachers were characterized as having an accommodating style; that is, they encouraged children's active participation in lessons and resolved conflicts between BC and SE in an expeditious and effective manner. But so did other teachers in the study. What, then, did the Black Artful teachers do *in addition to*, or perhaps differently from, what other accommodating teachers did that could account for their apparently greater success with students?

One of the teaching behaviors that Piestrup had identified as "accommodating" before she began her study (based on suggestions made in the linguistics literature) was the teacher's use of BC features in his or her own speech during informal conversation in the classroom (p. 40). Classroom observations indicated that both teachers in the Black Artful group and teachers in the

White Liberal group sometimes used BC features in their speech. However, close analysis of the data revealed that they did so in very different ways. In her analysis, Piestrup found that teachers in the White Liberal group tended to use BC features as a way to establish rapport with children or as part of a "warm-up" to interest them in the lesson (p. 145). The following example illustrates this pattern:

C3	I'm right here.
T	Huh? What page? What page are we supposed to be reading orally?
C4	I 'on't know.
T	You 'on' know? (Dialect intonation)
C5	"Scott Street."
T	Didn't we ever read—
C6	I wanna read "Treasure Hunt," I love "Treasure Hunt."
T	You do love it, huh? What page is it on, David? It's on page 29. (Dialect intonation) (pp. 97–98)

In analyzing this excerpt, Piestrup writes:

> "You do love it, huh," was pronounced with a syncopated stress and pitch similar to that of the children. "What page is it on, David," immediately shifted to standard English. The two sentences serve different functions; the first, rapport and the second, focusing on the task. (p. 98)

In contrast to this pattern of using BC features solely for the purpose of establishing rapport or "connecting with" children, teachers in the Black Artful group incorporated BC features into instruction as well. In addition, they drew on a far broader range of BC features, including characteristic discourse patterns such as signifying and extended rhythmic language play. In describing the Black Artful teachers' interactions with children during instruction, Piestrup notes that "it is not the surface features of phonology or grammar that are important but the rapid interplay with intonation and gesture familiar to Black children as one of the art forms of Black culture" (p. 103). She describes lessons in these teachers' classrooms as "uniquely lively interactions," (p. 151) in which there was "considerable encouragement, marked by an enthusiastic tone of voice both by teachers and children" (p. 136). All of these qualities are well illustrated in the following excerpt, in which the teacher helps children understand the meaning of *tattered* through engaging with them in a game of ritual insult on "the man, all tattered and torn" from "The House that Jack Built":

T	She met a boy, and this is the man all tattered and—
All	—torn.
T	Here's another word, is "tattered."
T and Class	"Tattered"
T	If you have on clothes that are all tattered, what do they look like?

Class	Ragged. Raggelly.
T	Wait, wait. One person, whatchoo say?
C2	Raggelly.
T	Raggelly.
C3	Teacher!
C4	They torn, they torn up.
C2, 3	They got, they got—
T	They got what?
C4	—they got holes in 'em.
T	Ok. Anything you wanta say, Melinda?
C5	And dey have, dey have—all the shoes are raggy too.
T	Shoes are raggy—
C2, 3	An' clothes.
T	Wait just a minute.
C4	His (clothes) are raggelly, and his pants are raggelly, and a, his—
C6	I know.
C4	—hat is raggelly.
C6	I know.
C5	—and his shirt is raggelly.
T	Danelle?
C7	And his body is ragged.
Class	(Giggles.)
C5	His body is dirty. His body is dirty. His body is—. His body is dirty.
T	Oh, he's dirty, too.
C5	Hi—His hair is dirty.
T	Oooohh!
C4	He don't wash his hair; he don't comb his hair.
C5	An' his teeth is yellow.
T	ohhh!
Class	(Giggles.)
C5	He don't brush, he don't brush his teeth.
T	He looks terrible, doesn't he?
C3	He look like a ol' man.
C5	He don' wash his hair.
Class	(Giggles.)
C2	In a old house that Jack built.
Class	(Giggles.) (pp. 103–105)

Piestrup notes not only the rapt engagement of the children in this lesson, but also the fast-paced rhythmic quality of the interaction and the fact that the teacher allowed time for children to assimilate the meaning of *tattered.* She writes: "Unlike the White Liberal teacher's brief, imitative phrases, the Black Artful teacher's dialect seemed familiar and comfortable" (p. 105). Moreover, the teacher's use of BC linguistic and stylistic features in this interaction played an important role in helping her to convey cognitive information. Using a shared discourse style, the teacher and children jointly constructed the meaning of *tattered,* thereby increasing the likelihood of children "owning" its definition.

Another characteristic of Black Artful teachers was their continual encouragement of children's efforts, as reflected in the following very brief excerpt from the data (note, as well, the teacher's use of the word *ugly* in a way likely to be familiar to Black children):

> T I don't like for you to look a little bit ugly when you miss a word, do you hear?
> Because you're not ever gonna miss that word again, OK? All right, go on.
> You're not supposed to look ugly, because you're not supposed to know everything. This is—I thought that was very good. So we know the word, don't we? (p. 106)

Like some of the other teachers in the study, Black Artful teachers also helped children to hear the differences between words likely to be homonyms for BC speakers, often anticipating words that might be confusing for children rather than waiting for a conflict to arise in the middle of a lesson. Near the end of the study, Piestrup notes that it is indeed possible to teach Black children to read in a way that capitalizes on their stylistic skills and that minimizes linguistic conflict. But, she asserts:

> This requires the kind of attentiveness shown by the Black Artful teachers, who seemed to thoroughly understand their Black students, and to have no difficulty teaching them to read. This was not simply a matter of ethnic similarity. Not all the Black teachers in the study were in the Black Artful group. What made these teachers so effective seems worth investigating further. (p. 170)

Implications of the Study

Piestrup's study does not shed definitive light on the relationship between use of BC and learning to read. For example, did the instances of structural and functional conflict she observed actually impede the process of learning to read for children in the study? Did the fact that they were BC speakers make the process more difficult for them than it would have been had they been SE speakers (a major hypothesis put forth in *Teaching Black Children to Read*)? These questions are not answered by the data. However, as discussed next, the study contains a number of critical findings and, in addition, raises key questions about instruction that we are still struggling to answer in 2007.

1. Conflicts between BC and SE do occur in the classroom.

Piestrup's study provides clear evidence that instances of potential conflict between BC and SE do in fact occur during reading instruction. Thus, even though teachers may be using an excellent, highly systematic approach to phonics instruction, Piestrup's findings suggest that linguistic differences between

BC and SE will likely surface in the context of instruction, whether it be in the form of a temporary confusion between two words that are homonyms in BC but not in SE, or in the way children pronounce words as they read aloud or participate in classroom discussion. Her study suggests, then, that teachers need to think carefully about the ways in which they will respond to children's use of BC and how they will frame discussion of differences between BC and SE. Perhaps the most important implication for practice contained in Piestrup's study is her notion of dialect or language interference as a "brief misunderstanding" that the teacher has the power to either quickly resolve or let turn into an obstacle to learning.

It is clear from Piestrup's data that the teachers in her study responded to children's use of BC in very different ways and that their responses had an impact on children. Piestrup categorized the teachers' responses into two broad groups: those that were "accommodating" (addressing potential confusions quickly and effectively) and those that were "interfering" (exacerbating potential confusion by dealing with the conflict in an ineffective way). Although these categories turned out to be too broad to fully assess the effects of these behaviors on reading performance, it is significant that the Black Artful teachers, whose students had the highest mean reading score, were clearly in the accommodation group, whereas the Interrupting teachers, whose students' reading scores were the lowest, were clearly in the interference group. Were Piestrup's study to be replicated, it might be possible to more fully explore the relationship between specific ways of dealing with linguistic differences during instruction and children's performance in reading.

2. Is the "problem" BC features or teachers' attitudes?

An important question raised in both *Teaching Black Children to Read* and in Piestrup's study is whether or not it is linguistic differences per se that may cause difficulties in learning to read for BC speakers or, rather, teachers' negative attitudes toward BC and, by extension, toward the children who use it. Piestrup speculates that in many of the episodes that involved structural and/ or functional conflict between BC and SE, it may well have been "alienation of teachers and children" that was the most significant factor in interrupting children's learning (1973, pp. 71–72). A the end of the long interchange about a child's pronunciation of *they* as *dey* quoted earlier, for example, the teacher says "'Ok. Pretty good.'" As Piestrup points out, this lukewarm assessment carries the implicit message that something is still wrong, "that a child who pronounces words in dialect is not quite right" (p. 55). She writes: "The feelings children have when the teacher implies that something is wrong with their speech may be at least as important as their misunderstanding an instructional point" (pp. 57–58). There are many instances in Piestrup's data in which a teacher asked children to repeat words multiple times using "correct" pronunciation, made vague, judgmental statements like, "'Can you say that a little bit better?'" (p. 65), or "seemed to ask by her tone of voice and gesture, 'How could you possibly not know that!'" (p. 66). The following is illustrative of interactions in which the teacher's insistence on SE pronunciations served no educative purpose (the opposite in fact) and also proved obviously alienating to children:

> The teacher heard "story" pronounced "starry" and asked "This word?" So the child changed the word to store. After the word was repeated seven times, the child sounded annoyed when he said, "First I said story, then you ask' me that word again." It took several minutes to clarify the alternatives store, starry and story. The initial reading of the sentence, "Why do you think John not afraid in the endin,' end of the story?" was semantically clear to the children. It became unclear when the teacher focused on a variant pronunciation. (p. 61)

The question of the extent to which it is BC itself or teachers' reactions to it that may cause problems in reading instruction for some children is still very much at the forefront of discussions about the relationship between BC and reading. In support of the argument that it is teachers' negative attitudes toward BC that create reading problems, a number of linguists and educators have pointed to the example of other countries in which children who speak a nonprestige variety of the national language seem to experience little difficulty learning to read in the standard language. Many also point to the widespread, often virulent, prejudice toward BC (and its speakers) in the wider society and argue that it is highly likely that this prejudice operates in damaging ways during instruction (Baratz & Shuy, 1969; Bowie & Bond, 1994; Cross, Devaney, & Jones, 2003; Goodman & Buck, 1973; Lippi-Green, 1997; Rosenthal & Jacobson, 1968). While these two factors—actual linguistic conflict and teacher attitude—are difficult to tease apart in terms of their effects on learning, nowhere in the literature is teacher prejudice toward BC and its enactment in the classroom brought to more vivid life than in Piestrup's data.

3. A little knowledge can be a dangerous thing.

One frequently made recommendation in the literature on BC and reading is that teachers learn more about the systematic features of BC (Adger, Christian, & Taylor, 1999; Baratz & Shuy, 1969; Dandy, 1991; Labov, 1972, 1995, 2001; Perry & Delpit, 1998; J. R. Rickford, 1999; Smitherman, 1977, 2000a; Whiteman, 1980; Wolfram et al., 1999; Wolfram & Schilling-Estes, 1998). It is argued that such knowledge will likely increase teachers' respect for the language and its speakers and enable them to develop more effective strategies for teaching BC speakers. There is some evidence that professional development programs focused on BC have a positive impact on teacher attitudes and increase their use of specific strategies, such as explicitly contrasting BC and SE forms during instruction (Hollins, McIntyre, DeBose, Hollins, & Towner, 2005; Towner, Hollins, & Labov, 2000). However, such programs have not (yet) been widely implemented or discussed in the literature.

While teacher knowledge about BC is obviously critical to effective literacy instruction for BC speakers, Piestrup's study, with its close-up focus on actual teaching practice, sounds an important caution against making the too-easy assumption that increasing teacher knowledge about BC will necessarily result in improved teaching practice. She notes, for example, an episode from her data that "is of particular interest as the teacher had attended lectures on dialect differences and was following a recommendation to correct grammatical divergence and point out phonological alternates" (1973, p. 64). In this episode children are making up sentences to show they understand the definitions of words when the following interaction occurs:

Class	"Win."
T	Who can give me a sentence with "win"? Lionel?
C1	A boy win a race.
T	A boy <u>win</u> a race?
C2	I know teacher.
C3	I know teacher.
T	Hmm, that sounds—
C4	Teacher, I know one.
T	—Can you say that a little better, so it sounds—I understand what you mean, but
	Erndalyn, what, how would you say that?
C5	The win' blew the hat off my frien' head.
T	OK, that's what "win" sounds like, huh. But this is the kind of "win" when we,
	when you beat somebody else, when you win a race, OK? The other word, I'll show you how it's spelled. What word is this, Erndalyn? (Teacher writes "win" and "wind") OK? And this is the kind of "win" that we're talking about. This has a—
C	"D."
T	What's on the end?
C6	A silent "d."
T	A "d." It's hard to hear.
C6,7	It's a silent "d"!
T	Well, it's not really, really silent, but it's just really hard to hear. It's there.
	Sometimes we can say it so we can hear it. Can you hear the name of it? Did you hear the "d" then? And we usually, sometimes we usu-

ally don't say it, but it's there, so Erndalyn, what does this, make a sentence with this kind of "win."

C5   I, I, I mean, I, I can win th' race. I win the race.

C7   I know.

T   How about, "I will win the race"? OK?

C5   I <u>will</u> win the race.

T   Ok, pretty good. Ok, this one.   (pp. 63–64)

Clearly, this teacher's "knowledge" about BC did not translate into more effective pedagogical practice. As Piestrup astutely observes in discussing implications for practice near the end of the study: "It would probably be feasible to instruct teachers in potential dialect conflicts, but much harder to suggest effective strategies for dealing with them artfully" (1973, p. 166).

Both the extent and kind of knowledge about BC that teachers need to possess in order to work most effectively with BC speakers is still very much open to question. For example, how much detailed knowledge of specific BC phonological and grammatical patterns do teachers need to have? How might the teacher in the episode described here, for instance, have been assisted in translating her knowledge about BC phonology into more effective practice? Did she need more detailed knowledge about the BC system, or did she need to develop some other kinds of understandings? How important is it that teachers have knowledge about the kinds of BC discourse practices and stylistic features that were incorporated so successfully into instruction by the Black Artful teachers in Piestrup's study? To be truly effective in helping Black children achieve in reading, do teachers need to be able to use those with equal or near facility?

In my own work with teachers and preservice teachers over the last 13 years, I have come to believe that teachers need more than knowledge about the BC system. They also need to be able to reflect on that knowledge from a wider sociohistorical and political perspective. I have found that the linguistic prejudice that many people bring with them into the teaching profession runs very deep and is not easily dislodged, certainly not solely through the discovery that BC follows systematic rules. One of the teachers in Piestrup's study appointed an "ending monitor" in her classroom, whose job was "to interrupt and correct the speech of other children, as in, 'She say *fin*, she didn't say *find*'" (1973, p. 55). This teacher may well have understood BC phonological rules, but it is highly unlikely that she had reflected very deeply about how her own attitudes about the language and its speakers were affecting her treatment of children in her classroom. Teachers need knowledge that will lead them to such reflection. Thus to the list of previous questions, I would add two more: What understandings should teachers possess about the history of BC and its relationship to African American history and culture? What knowledge do teachers need to have about the historical and contemporary interactions between linguistic prejudice and racism in the US?

In part because there is little current agreement about what constitutes "sufficient" or "appropriate" teacher knowledge with respect to BC, many teachers find themselves confronting language differences in their classrooms with only limited understanding of the issues. Consequently, as illustrated in Piestrup's data, they sometimes end up responding to these differences in highly ineffective and potentially damaging ways.

4. Pragmatic features matter.

Without question, Piestrup's most compelling finding was that students taught with the style she described as Black Artful achieved a mean reading score that was not only higher than the mean reading scores for the schools they attended, but that was significantly higher than the national norm. At the end of the study, Piestrup recommends that the factors that made the Black Artful teachers so effective in teaching reading to BC speakers be investigated further. Unfortunately, that recommendation was never acted upon. The research that comes closest is that of Michèle Foster. In a study focused on a highly successful Black teacher in a community college in the Northeast, Foster (1987, 1989) found that, like the Black Artful teachers in Piestrup's study, the teacher in her study used an African American discourse style not simply to establish rapport with students (like the White Liberal teachers in Piestrup's study), but to explain and discuss course content. In a more recent ethnographic study of the pedagogical practices employed by a highly effective first and second grade teacher in the San Francisco Bay area, Foster (2001) found that this teacher also employed BC discourse practices and stylistic features to teach literacy content. For example, "call-and-response was used to facilitate pupils' semantic development by increasing their awareness of letters, syllables, spelling and the meaning of words" (p. 290). This is similar to episodes in Piestrup's data in which BC discourse forms like playful ritual insult were used to teach the meaning of vocabulary words. Foster speculates that for both the teachers she studied, their high level of success with students was in significant measure attributable to their ability to employ African American discourse practices in their teaching.

More broadly, Foster has been critical of professional development programs for teachers that focus on phonological and grammatical aspects of the language to the exclusion of pragmatic aspects. Discussing her research with Vivette Blackwell, the primary grade teacher she studied in California, she writes: "Previous research, though limited, has convinced me of the positive effect that rhythm, recitation, and repetition can have on the learning, enthusiasm, motivation, and engagement of African American students. The current data analyzed herein strengthens this finding even further" (2001, p. 296). Foster goes on to say the following:

> As long as teachers and, I might add, researchers assume a narrow view of African American English, regarding it primarily as phonology and syntax instead of as a whole language system (which includes semantics, pragmatics, prosody, rhythm, repetition, etc.) imbued with and embedded in social meaning, its potential usefulness as well as its multiple dimensions will go unrecognized. (p. 296)

Arguably, it is Black teachers who have been raised in the African American discourse community who are most likely to employ BC pragmatic features in their teaching and who are therefore likely to be the most important models of how these features can be used effectively in teaching reading. A clear implication of both Piestrup's study and Foster's more recent research is that studying the practices of Black teachers who have been highly successful in teaching BC speakers to read should be a top research priority for scholars interested in contributing to the reading achievement of African American children.

A Brief Romance With Dialect Readers, 1977

One of the suggestions made in *Teaching Black Children to Read* (Baratz & Shuy, 1969) was that BC speakers be taught to read initially in BC and then gradually introduced to materials written in SE. The Bridge Series (1977), developed by psychologists Gary and Charlesetta Simpkins and educator Grace Holt, was intended to implement that suggestion. The series contained three levels of stories: (a) stories written in BC, (b) stories written in a variety that incorporated fewer, but some, BC patterns, and (c) stories written entirely in SE. The stories written in BC not only used characteristic structural patterns and vocabulary, but stylistic features as well. The series was intended not for young children, but for older students who had experienced previous difficulties with reading.

The Bridge Series was tested over a four-month period with 540 students in grades 7 through 12 in a number of schools located in different parts of the country (Simpkins, Holt, & Simpkins, 1977; Simpkins & Simpkins, 1981). A total of 417 of these students were taught with the Bridge readers while the other 123 students were taught using conventional methods. At the end of four months of instruction, children in the control group showed only 1.6 months of reading gain, whereas students taught with the Bridge readers showed 6.2 months of reading gain. As linguist John Rickford (1999) puts it, "the experimental evidence was dramatically in support of the approach" (p. 341).

Despite this dramatic demonstration of their potential effectiveness, however, dialect readers were slated for a short life on the educational scene. Many people, including many African Americans, raised strong objections to the use of BC in instructional materials designed to teach reading. As a result of these objections, the Bridge Program was quickly shelved by its publisher and the issue of dialect readers was essentially dropped for many years. While Rickford (1999) describes the objections to dialect readers as "knee-jerk negative reactions similar to those which emerged in the Oakland Ebonics debacle of 1996" (p. 341), linguist Marcyliena Morgan (2002) argues that the negative reactions of many Black parents and community members were not surprising. She writes:

> No one had been socialized around dialect readers and with the notion that a quality education included them—especially when integrated educational institutions had worked so hard to exclude black children culturally. So even during the Black Power movement, dialect readers were a problem in the hands of children and their families who viewed public schooling as a socializing agent in preparation for an equal chance and careers for their children too. It is not difficult to imagine what parents must have thought as their children shared their materials, practiced AAE grammar and read to them dialect versions of schoolbooks and classics. (p. 141)

Rickford (1999) cites a number of other studies that reported positive results with reading materials written in BC, including a 1979 study in which African American children in a Head Start program in New York City reportedly did better on a story recall task when the story was presented in BC rather than SE (p. 309). More recently, Rickford and Rickford (1995) have also experimented with dialect readers, evidently with mixed results. Nonetheless, they argue that the positive results that have been obtained with dialect readers in a number of studies make a strong case for continuing to explore their use. Rickford (1999) asserts that many in the field have rejected the idea of dialect readers "with little or no regard to the experimental evidence that dialect readers do in fact *help* to teach AAVE-speaking children to read—and without scrutinizing the attitudinal barriers to their use, or asking how they might be overcome" (p. 309).

In addition to the negative reactions expressed by many members of the Black community, a number of other issues have been raised about dialect readers. One has to do with the source of their effectiveness. Labov (1995) points out that the Bridge series incorporates both linguistic and cultural elements, making it difficult to evaluate which component is contributing most strongly to improved reading. This is an issue that, in my view, deserves further exploration. If, for example, it were the cultural dimensions of dialect readers that had the greatest positive impact on children's reading, then it is conceivable that simply incorporating large numbers of African American children's books into the curriculum could have a level of positive effect on children's reading achievement similar to that obtained in the Simpkins et al. (1975) study.

Another issue raised with respect to dialect readers is that because they incorporate words and phrases currently popular within the Black discourse community, some of this vocabulary is likely to become dated fairly quickly, necessitating that the materials be up-dated and revised on a frequent basis (Green, 2002; Labov, 1995). As examples of words no longer in popular use from the Bridge series, Green (2002) cites the following: "*split* ('leave'), *bread* ('money'), *fox* ('good looking girl') and *pad* ('place of abode')" (p. 238).

It is also important to remember that dialect readers have not been studied in any systematic way with beginning readers. Relevant to this issue is a point made by Green (2002)—that an essential factor not yet addressed in relation to dialect readers is their relationship to children's acquisition of BC patterns. She writes: "In producing written materials for AAE speakers, it is important to know not only the reading level of the speaker, but also the types of linguistic patterns that speakers of a certain age group are likely to use" (p. 238). Although Green notes that "there is not a great deal of information on acquisition of AAE" (p. 238), the recent work of Craig and Washington (2006) has moved the field quite far in terms of being able to delineate the developmental timetable for children's acquisition of various BC features. Their research makes it more possible to envision creating reading materials that accurately reflect the linguistic structures that children of a particular age group are likely to be using.

Like the few discussed here, many of the issues that have been raised about dialect readers are at this point highly speculative due to the fact that our actual experience with them has been so limited. Given that fact, coupled with the promising results obtained with dialect readers in some studies, it is hard to quarrel with Rickford and Rickford's (1995) contention that the "case" for dialect readers deserves to be re-opened and more fully explored.

Reactions to Ann Arbor: Vernacular Black English and Education, 1980

In July, 1977 a lawsuit was filed by two attorneys from Michigan Legal Services on behalf of 15 African American children who all resided in a low-income housing project located in Ann Arbor, Michigan and who attended the Martin Luther King, Jr. Elementary School located in Ann Arbor. The court case that ensued is often referred to in educational literature as the "Ann Arbor case" or the "Black English case." At the King School, African American children made up 13% of a student population comprised mostly of White upper-class children from the surrounding University of Michigan campus community. The lawsuit alleged that the school had failed to properly educate the 15 plaintiff children, placing them in danger of becoming functionally illiterate. More specifically, "plaintiffs charged that school officials had improperly placed the children in learning disability and speech pathology classes; that they had suspended, disciplined, and repeatedly retained the children at grade level without taking into account their social economic and cultural differences; and that they had failed to overcome language barriers preventing the children from learning standard English and learning to read" (Smitherman, 2000a, p. 133).

The case was eventually narrowed by the judge to consideration of only the language issue—the question was whether the school had taken adequate measures to ensure that the children's home language was not a barrier to equal educational opportunity. Linguist Geneva Smitherman was the plaintiff children's chief consultant and expert witness. In July, 1979, two years after the suit was filed, Judge Charles W. Joiner handed down a decision in favor of the plaintiff children. He ruled that by failing to overcome language barriers, the Ann Arbor School District had violated the plaintiff children's right to equal education. As Smitherman explains, "though Black English was not found to be a barrier per se, the institutional response to it was" (p. 135). In his ruling, the judge particularly highlighted the deleterious effects of teachers' negative attitudes toward children's language, stating that "the unconscious but evident attitude of teachers toward the home language causes a psychological barrier to learning by the student" (quoted in Wolfram, 1980, p. 19). The judge mandated that the Ann Arbor School District recognize BC as a legitimate rule-governed language variety and that it help its teachers figure out how to take that language into account in teaching BC speakers to read. At the time, many people were in an uproar over the judge's ruling, erroneously asserting that the Ann Arbor Schools were planning to teach children in Black English, just as people asserted about the Oakland Schools in the aftermath of the Oakland School Board's Ebonics resolution in 1997. According to Rickford and Rickford (2000), nearly 500 news stories about the Ann Arbor case were published between July, 1977 and February, 1981 (p. 186).

A considerably more supportive and scholarly response to the case, *Reactions to Ann Arbor: Vernacular Black English and Education,* a collection of articles edited by Marcia Farr Whiteman, was published in 1980. Its purpose, as Whiteman states in the introduction, was to provide "a brief state-of-the-art statement on the role of non-standard dialects in education and on some implications of the Ann Arbor decision" (p. v). The audience envisioned for the book were the "many schools [that] may want now to adapt to the spirit of Judge Joiner's decision (in a sense to come into compliance before litigation)" (p. v). However, any school system looking to this volume for a clear, step-by-step plan of action for taking BC into account in reading instruction would doubtless have been disappointed.

One contributor, Thomas Pietras, then an administrator in the Ann Arbor Public Schools, used his article as a context for expressing the Ann Arbor School District's frustration over lack of consensus in the field about what pedagogical practices were likely to prove successful in teaching reading to BC speakers. He lamented the fact that there were "no common practices adopted by other districts" from which the Ann Arbor system could learn, no generally endorsed commercial materials available, and no programs whose efficacy had been rigorously evaluated (1980, p. 59). He likened the plight of Ann Arbor teachers and administrators to that of the ancient Mariner, adrift in a sea (of sociolinguistic ideas) without "a drop to drink" (p. 60).

But while *Reactions to Ann Arbor* contains no widely endorsed blueprint for action with respect to BC and reading, it does include a number of rich ideas for practice that the Ann Arbor teachers and administrators would have been well-advised to consider trying out in the classroom. After all, the biggest reason why there was no body of established practice for the Ann Arbor school district to draw from in complying with Judge Joiner's order in 1979 was that few, if any, school districts had seen fit to experiment with any of the pedagogical ideas that had been laid out in the research up to that point.

In one particularly provocative article from the book, "Black English: Implications of the Ann Arbor Decision for the Classroom," Elizabeth Whatley discusses strategies for taking structural differences between BC and SE into account while still using traditional basals or other programmed phonics materials not designed with BC speakers in mind. Essentially, she suggests that teachers can head off possible linguistic conflict by anticipating where it is likely to occur. She uses the case of the consonant digraph /*th*/ to illustrate. Whatley explains that the BC phonological rule specifying that initial *th* can be pronounced as /*d*/ applies only when initial *th* is voiced (i.e., articulated with the vocal cords vibrating). When initial *th* is unvoiced (no vibrating vocal cords), BC speakers pronounce this digraph the same way it is pronounced in SE. Thus many BC speakers are likely to pronounce *this, that, these,* and *those* as *dis, dat, dis,* and *dose,* respectively, but to pronounce *think, thought, thing* and *thread* the same way they are pronounced in SE. Whatley points out that in most phonics programs, the digraph *th* is initially introduced with a "concrete" word and accompanying picture such as *thimble, thermometer,* or *thumb,* words in which initial *th* is voiceless. BC speakers are likely to pronounce the *th* in these words the same way as an SE speaking teacher and to experience little difficulty learning the grapheme-phoneme relationship involved.

However, many of the most frequently occurring *th*- vocabulary words in beginning reading materials contain voiced *th*. Examples include *the, this, that, them, these, those, they, there, their, than* and *then*. Many BC speakers are likely to pronounce these words with initial /*d*/. As Whatley points out, teachers who understand the BC rules for pronouncing initial *th* realize that these pronunciations are systematic and predictable. They are not likely to mistake the BC pronunciation of *they* as *dey* for a reading error, as did one of the teachers in Piestrup's study (see p. 76). Nor are they likely to assume, as that teacher did, that a child who uses this pronunciation needs a lesson in how to physically make the *th* sound ("Look at my tongue" [see p. 76]). That fact that BC speakers "put their tongue between their teeth" to articulate voiceless *th* in *thimble* and *thumb* is an obvious indication that they already know how to do this. By anticipating the fact that BC speakers may pronounce initial voiced *th* as /d/, the teacher is not caught off guard when this occurs in the middle of a reading lesson. He or she can think *in advance* about the most appropriate time and place to talk about this pronunciation difference (e.g., certainly not in the context of a child reading aloud).

Beyond this specific example of *th*, Whatley's large point is similar to one of Piestrup's—that linguistic differences do not have to turn into obstacles to children's learning when teachers anticipate their occurrence during the course of instruction and think *beforehand* about how to respond to them in sensible and understandable ways. Not surprisingly, Piestrup (1973) found that one of the characteristics of the Black Artful teachers was that they also anticipated possible linguistic conflict and moved proactively to prevent it from interfering with learning. For example, before beginning a lesson, they carefully distinguished between two words in the lesson that they anticipated would be homonyms for BC speakers. (Needless to say, of course, teachers' "anticipatory set" for linguistic diversity needs to be supported by sound knowledge of the BC system as well as by careful attention to children's actual speech patterns.)

Like both Piestrup (1973) and Foster (1987, 1989, 1995b, 2001), Whatley also emphasizes the importance of teacher knowledge about BC pragmatic features and children's out-of-school experiences with language. For example, she discusses Black children's experiences with activities that involve rhyming concepts (e.g., "sounding," "playing the dozens," jump rope, handclapping games, etc. [1980, p. 67]) and suggests ways in which teachers can build on that rhyming experience in reading instruction (pp. 66–70). Whatley's article, published in 1980, continues to have great relevance in 2007.

In his article "Knowledge into Practice: Delivering Research to Teachers," Robert Berdan (1980) stresses a point made by many—that teachers need to distinguish between BC pronunciations and reading errors when evaluating children's oral reading (e.g., Baratz & Shuy, 1969; Craig & Washington, 2006; Dandy, 1991; Hammond, Hoover & McPhail, 2005; Labov, 1995, 2001; Perry & Delpit, 1998; Piestrup, 1973; Van Keulen, Weddington, & DeBose, 1998; Wolfram et al., 1999). He writes that "dialect intervention under the guise of reading instruction, however noble the intent, is frequently perceived by the child as aversive, sometimes even as abusive" (p. 79). But, as Berdan goes on to point out, teachers can also do instructional harm by going to the opposite extreme, becoming so concerned about not "penalizing" children for BC pronunciations that they fail to intervene when children produce actual reading errors. By not giving children needed corrective feedback when they make errors in reading, teachers may end up "plac[ing] far fewer demands on children who speak Black English . . . than they do on other children" (p. 79).

Berdan sees both these inappropriate responses (i.e., "correcting" BC pronunciations and ignoring actual reading errors) as rooted in the fact that many teachers do not possess enough knowledge about BC to reliably distinguish between systematic BC pronunciations and reading errors. Although he argues that teachers' ability to make that distinction is critical to effective reading instruction for BC speakers, figuring out how to "[bring] the necessary knowledge to teachers in a form that they can and will use" is, from Berdan's perspective, a whole other question (p. 82). He is skeptical about the feasibility of professional development efforts that require teachers to engage in extensive study of BC. To explore more time-efficient approaches to delivering essential information to teachers, Berdan and colleagues conducted a study that involved going through all the selections in the reading series used by the teachers in the study and "[annotating] each day's lesson with conventional spelling representations of the range of Black English pronunciations that would be expected for each vocabulary item" (p. 83). According to Berdan, teachers' responses were very positive:

> We had teachers gleefully report new discoveries to us: when they stopped hassling their Black children, these same children were soon eager to be allowed to read out loud—something these teachers had never experienced before. One Black teacher related her own experience of growing up in a repressive language environment, and of having recreated that repressive environment in her classroom, never thinking that there might be an alternative. Somehow, just seeing in print, day by day, the pronunciations her students used, she realized that she could accept that as reading. It's hard to convey her wonderful sense of enlightenment at this discovery. (pp. 83–84)

Although the intent of this intervention was to effect a change in teacher behavior, Berdan reports that it had a significant positive effect on teacher attitudes toward BC as well. Promising as Berdan's findings were, to my knowledge, this relatively simple intervention has never been further explored. It is very much akin to Labov's oft-repeated, fairly-easy-to-implement suggestions for modifying basals and other early reading materials to make them more appropriate for use with BC speakers. In my view, both Berdan's and Labov's suggestions deserve to be taken more seriously than they have been up to this point and actually incorporated into a major basal reading program. There would be little or no risk involved in experimenting with these suggestions and a great deal to potentially be gained in terms of improving reading instruction for BC speakers.

In "Teacher Attitude Change: Does Informing Make a Difference?," the final article I will discuss from this collection, Shirley A.R. Lewis (1980) reports on research involving "Black English-related teacher workshops" that she conducted in conjunction with colleagues at Stanford University during the 1970s. Part of this research focused on identifying positive and negative teaching behaviors in literacy instruction for "Black dialectal students" (p. 88). Positive and negative behaviors were identified through analysis of video- and audiotaped classroom observations. The researchers found that one character- istic of teachers whose students made little progress over the school year was the use of "confusing behaviors." Lewis describes:

> Confusing teacher behaviors appeared to occur for two reasons. The first kind of confusion occurred because the teacher's communication was gener- ally vague: "a verb is an action word. Well, some are and some aren't, but we usually call them action words." The second kind of confusing behavior occurred when teachers gave explanations or examples which were espe- cially untrue or inapplicable for speakers of BE: "If you use two words that mean 'no,' you mean 'yes',' or 'When you say, 'he walk home last night,' you mean last night is today." (p. 88)

These researchers' notion of "confusing behaviors" is a particularly useful lens through which to view Piestrup's (1973) rich data set of classroom inter- actions. One thinks, for example, of the teacher's response, quoted earlier, to children's notion of a "silent 'd'" at the end of the word *wind*:

> Well, it's not really, really silent, but it's just really hard to hear. It's there. Sometimes we can say it so we can hear it. Can you hear the name of it? Did you hear the "d" then? And we usually, sometimes we usually don't say it, but it's there . . . (p. 64)

As Lewis suggests, such confusing explanations are likely to be particularly problematic for children attempting to make meaningful connections between two linguistic systems. Although Lewis expresses optimism about the positive role that teacher education about BC can play both in terms of teacher attitudes and student achievement, her discussion of what such teacher education would actually look like is more heuristic and speculative than definitive. Again, the question of what constitutes "adequate" and "appropriate" teacher knowledge about BC remains unresolved.

Heath's Mrs. Pat (1983): Focusing on Metalinguistic Awareness

In her ethnographic study of language used at home and at school in three communities located in the Piedmont Carolinas, Shirley Brice Heath (1983) describes the "linguistic detective approach" employed by a second-grade teacher, Mrs. Pat, to increase her students' conscious awareness of the way language varies across different speakers and contexts. Mrs. Pat's class, which included both African American and White children, listened to the speech varieties of individuals, including the principal, the school custodian, lunch- room workers, parents, visitors from the community, and radio and television announcers. Playing the role of detectives, they listened for the answers to four questions:

> What sounds did you hear when _____ talks?
> What did _____ say about how he talked?
> What did _____ write?
> What did _____ read? (p. 328)

As their investigation continued, children noted differences between spoken and written language—for example, that some words and expressions were used in speech but not in writing, and vice versa. When listening carefully to people's speech, they noticed that the way individuals articulated certain sounds didn't always match with the ways those sounds were described in their phonics materials. For instance, Heath writes, "the diphthong /aehl/ seemed 'longer' in the speech of visitors than in the discussion of the sound for 'long *i*'" in phonics lessons" (p. 329). Heath also describes how children discovered that some sounds discussed in reading lessons—such as final *ng* and final *s*—were not always heard in casual speech. As different sounds were introduced in reading lessons, children listened for those sounds in people's speech. In terms of ending sounds, for instance, children listened to see if they could hear final *t, p, d, s, ng,* and *st* (p. 330).

Children in Mrs. Pat's class developed a whole metalinguistic vocabulary for talking about language, including the terms *dialect, casual, formal, conversational,* and *standard* (p. 329). According to Heath, by the end of the year, they were able to "recognize and label discrete features of language such as sounds, endings and styles and to apply these concepts in listening to dialect poetry, conversations, radio and TV programs, and oral story-telling" (p. 334). Not surprisingly, Mrs. Pat's class also performed well on end-of-the-year reading tests: 14 students in the class read on grade level, 8 above grade level, and 2 below (p. 333). Metalinguistic awareness has been correlated with reading achievement in a number of studies (Bohannon et al., 1984; Paris & Myers, 1981; Snow et al., 1998; Tunmer & Hoover, 1992). However, the specific role that children's heightened awareness of dialect differences per se may have played in their acquisition of phonics knowledge was not investigated. For example, did children's focus on discrete sounds and endings (e.g., *–s, –ed*) increase their awareness of SE forms and thus reduce mismatches between sound and spelling for BC speakers in the class? Did children's attention to ending sounds in people's speech help them to adopt the strategy of paying more careful attention to the ends of words while reading, as Labov might have predicted? These are likely possibilities, but we do not have enough information available to answer these questions with any certainty. Clearly, though, Mrs. Pat's "linguistic detective approach" had positive effects on her second-graders' reading performance.

A number of recent studies have suggested that familiarity with SE is strongly related to reading achievement for African American children. Charity, Scarborough, and Griffin (2004) investigated the relationship between African American children's familiarity with SE, as measured by their performance on a sentence repetition task, and their performance on three subtests of the Woodcock Reading Mastery Tests–Revised. Participants in the study were 217 African American children from kindergarten though second grade who attended historically low-performing schools in several large U.S. cities. The researchers found that reading achievement for children in the study was highly correlated with their familiarity with SE.

In discussing these findings, Charity et al. consider three possible explanations for this strong correlation. One is that because of linguistic prejudice toward BC on the part of teachers, children who demonstrated greater knowledge of SE forms may have received more attention and higher quality instruction than classmates who demonstrated less familiarity with SE, leading to a correlation between reading scores and dialect differences. Another possibility Charity et al. discuss is that greater familiarity with SE may have reduced the amount of linguistic interference between BC and SE experienced by children, thus making it easier for children who knew more SE to learn sound-spelling correspondences. The third possibility raised by the researchers is that familiarity with SE may reflect a higher level of metalinguistic awareness that positively impacts reading acquisition in a more global way. As Charity et al. point out, there is no necessary contradiction among any of these. That is, they could all be factors operating in concert to facilitate higher levels of reading achievement for BC speakers who are more familiar with SE or who, said another way, possess a higher degree of bilinguality. Reflecting on the case of Mrs. Pat through the lens of Charity et al.'s discussion, it is possible that both the increased knowledge of specific SE forms and the higher level of more general metalinguistic awareness fostered by the "linguistic detective approach" made separate, but reinforcing, contributions to children's reading achievement in Mrs. Pat's class.

In their research with BC speaking children in two urban communities in Michigan, Craig and Washington (2004, 2006) have also found a strong correlation between children's ability to dialect or code switch between BC and SE and their performance on standardized reading tests. Efforts to help BC speakers learn to code switch, that is, to become bilingual, have tended to focus on children older than primary age. Kelli Harris-Wright (1999), for example, describes a long-standing bidialectal program, instituted by the Dekalb County School System in Georgia, to teach middle-school BC speakers SE skills without devaluing their BC skills in the process. The curriculum utilizes a contrastive analysis approach to teaching children about differences between BC and SE. Students also engage in assessment activities that contrast home and school speech, utilize role-playing, and provide opportunities for students to listen to and give feedback on their own and one another's speech. Harris-Wright reports that students enrolled in the bidialectal program show consistently higher gains on the Iowa Test of Basic Skills than comparable students not enrolled in the program.

Judith Baker (2002), a high-school English teacher in Boston, also uses a metalinguistic approach to help increase her students' conscious awareness of the many different "Englishes" they and the people around them speak. "Building upon a firm respect for each student's home language," Baker has students "study" their home languages in ways akin to a linguist (as well as to Mrs. Pat's second-graders). She writes: "We find patterns of speech, rules of grammar, vocabulary, tonal features, and emotional characteristics of language which we note, label, discuss and eventually compare to the features of what we call 'formal' English" (pp. 52–53). Later, students make up role-plays of various hypothetical speech situations—for example, job interviews, college classroom, the family dinner table—and afterward discuss and debate various notions of what constitutes "appropriate speech" in different social contexts.

Both of these are highly creative, and evidently quite successful, approaches to helping students develop their conscious awareness of systematic differences between their "home language" and "academic language" and thereby presumably increasing their bilingual facility. Although in reading about them one might be inclined to assume that these approaches have applicability only to older students, Heath's description of Mrs. Pat's highly sophisticated and successful focus on metalinguistic awareness with second-graders suggests otherwise. So does the knowledge we have about language socialization in the African American speech community, which suggests that children raised there not only greatly value verbal skills, but are alert to subtle nuances of meaning and able to adjust their language to fit different contexts at an early age (see chapter 5). Thus a curricular focus on the richly contextual nature of language use, as illustrated in Mrs. Pat's curriculum as well as in Judith Baker's, may well be highly engaging for even very young African American children.

More narrowly, the contrastive analysis approach, in which BC and SE forms are explicitly contrasted and children practice making "translations" between them (e.g., children might be asked to produce the SE equivalent for "She late.") is a method that has been successfully employed by a number of educators, both as an alternative to constant "correction" of BC forms and as a way to help children acquire facility in SE (Harris-Wright, 1999; Hollins et al., 2005; LeMoine, 1999; Taylor, 1989; Towner et al., 2000). However, Rickford (1999) and Foster (2001) have both raised the caution that, by itself, contrastive analysis constitutes a limited approach to dealing with linguistic differences in the classroom, especially if students end up spending long periods of time doing repetitive "translation" exercises.

Translating BC forms into their totally predictable SE equivalents is a far cry from Mrs. Pat's second-graders "writing up" the speech of a classroom visitor and then discussing their findings. Carrie Secret (1998), who uses contrastive analysis as part of a more general focus on metalinguistic awareness in her classroom, also makes the point that often contrastive analysis approaches end up emphasizing "one way" translations, having children change BC forms to SE equivalents, but seldom asking them to do the reverse, thereby, in Secret's view, essentially negating the equality of the two languages (p. 84).

Just as securing children's alphabet knowledge might usefully entail having them do some rote activities like copying and tracing or working with flash cards, so too straightforward, somewhat mechanical contrastive analysis exercises may well help students solidify their knowledge about structural differences between the two varieties. But to be truly effective, these kinds of exercises need to be part of a larger, more intellectually engaging focus on language differences, as illustrated, for example, in Mrs. Pat's curriculum. To care about them and pay attention to them, children need to understand how linguistic differences play out and make sense in the world. As just one brief example of an activity that might be used to help children acquire those understandings, readers might imagine second-graders engaged in an animated discussion about why they think Eloise Greenfield (1978) decided to switch to BC in the last line of the following poem:

KEEPSAKE
Before Mrs. Williams died
She told Mr. Williams
When he gets home
To get a nickel out of her
Navy blue pocketbook
And give it to her
Sweet little gingerbread girl
That's me

I ain't never going to spend it.   (unnumbered pages)

In this activity, children are applying their knowledge about differences between BC and SE to a real-life situation, exploring the connection between language form and use in ways that link to their own identities as bilingual speakers, gifted with two linguistic varieties at their command for making meaning in the world. Focusing on systematic differences between BC and SE in a way that is intellectually stimulating, as opposed to rote and mechanical, is also emphasized in the *dialect awareness* approach developed by linguist Walter Wolfram (1999; see also Wolfram & Schilling-Estes, 1998). While Wolfram has used the dialect awareness approach with older children and adults, as opposed to primary-level children, some of his ideas seem to me eminently adaptable for use with children at earlier grade levels.

This section began with a discussion of Mrs. Pat, a second-grade teacher described by Heath (1983) who used the "linguistic detective approach" to help increase children's level of metalinguistic awareness, an ability that has been correlated with reading achievement in a number of studies. I then speculated on the possibility that Mrs. Pat's approach may also have increased children's knowledge about SE phonological and grammatical forms. I pointed out that knowledge of SE has been linked to reading achievement for African American students in two recent studies. I next went on to discuss the contrastive analysis approach as a way of helping children develop SE knowledge, suggesting that this approach is likely to be most effective when it is part of a larger focus on developing children's metalinguistic awareness. None of this has been meant to suggest, however, that being a monolingual BC speaker causes difficulties in reading or that BC speakers need to acquire competence in SE before learning to read. Neither of these is true. No direct, cause-and-effect relationship has ever been established between BC and reading acquisition. But that said, research linking reading achievement to metalinguistic awareness in general and to knowledge of SE in particular does suggest that facilitating children's conscious awareness of differences between BC and SE on a number of different levels, including the pragmatic, may well have a positive effect on reading achievement.

Labov's Philadelphia Findings, 1999–2001

I have already briefly discussed the pedagogical suggestions made by William Labov, a linguist who has been studying BC and pondering its educational implications for several decades. Most recently, he and his colleagues at the University of Pennsylvania have been centrally involved in an after-school tutoring-in-reading program for children attending two elementary schools located in West Philadelphia. The initial focus of their research was on examining the decoding errors made by BC speakers who were one to two years behind in reading grade level. They found that while the children in their study had relatively little difficulty decoding single elements (i.e., lone consonants and vowels), their error rates increased markedly when they attempted to decode more complex structures (e.g., consonant blends and digraphs, vowel pairs). By far, their greatest number of decoding errors occurred at the ends of words, where there is greatest divergence between BC and SE.

As mentioned earlier, these findings lend very strong empirical support to Labov's long-standing recommendation that more attention be paid to the ends of words in early reading instruction. And certainly there is little question that ends of words *do* tend to get short shrift in many instructional approaches. For example, in one widely popular method for teaching decoding, the embedded phonics approach, great emphasis is placed on what are often called *word families* or *spelling patterns* (e.g., *–ap, –at, –op*). In this approach, children practice creating new words by substituting different initial letters—for example, *c*ap, *m*ap, *tr*ap. The focus is clearly on differentiating initial sounds, while the ending sounds in the particular pattern being highlighted receive little, if any, discrete attention. More broadly, there seems to be a general assumption in the literature on reading instruction that ends of words do not warrant any special attention. The following brief excerpt from *Words Their Way: Word Study for Phonics, Vocabulary, and Spelling Instruction* (Bear et al., 2000), an otherwise excellent book, is meant to be illustrative (the authors are talking about the study of beginning sounds):

> A few final consonants might be introduced and studied, but once students have learned the frequently occurring initial consonants and phonemic segmentation, most of them can easily use their knowledge of letter-sound matches to spell final consonants. When students consistently omit final consonants in their writing, you can draw their attention to them through word study activities that are similar to the initial consonant sorts. For example, your students could hunt for words and pictures of words that end like *bat*. However, the study of final consonants is covered when the students examine word families and this is probably enough for most children. (p. 151)

As I have already noted, the assumption that final consonants are adequately "covered" when examining word families is highly questionable when applied to BC speakers. In examining the more highly structured basal series used by the schools where he was working in Philadelphia, Labov and his colleagues (1998) found that lessons covering more complex structures (as opposed to the basic CVC structure) occurred so late in the instructional sequence laid out in the basal that it is conceivable that many teachers reached the end of the school year without having taught many of those lessons (pp. 15–18).

As mentioned previously, in attempting to help children overcome difficulties in decoding, Labov and his colleagues found that errors involving ending consonant clusters seemed particularly difficult to remediate, even though their success rate with other kinds of decoding errors was very impressive. Together, the fact that a high percentage of the children's decoding errors involved ending consonant clusters and the fact that these errors proved so difficult to ameliorate can be seen as the most compelling evidence we have to date that BC may impact the process of reading acquisition. But whether or not that is the case—that is, that BC actually does impact reading acquisition—the pattern of reading errors that Labov and his colleagues found to be characteristic of the BC speakers in their study establishes a very strong rationale for acting on Labov's recommendation, first made in 1969, to pay more attention to the ends of words in initial reading instruction.

Labov stresses the importance of paying special attention to those cases in which phonological and grammatical differences between the two systems may coincide, most notably with respect to the past tense marker –*ed*. In the case of the marker –*ed*, the BC cluster reduction rule, which applies with greatest frequency to clusters ending in /t/ or /d/ and /s/ or /z/ (Labov, 1972, p. 15), may coincide with BC grammatical rules allowing for past tense meaning to be communicated by context in some environments (e.g., *Yesterday, he walk to the store.*). In early research, Labov (1969) found that adolescent BC speakers were unable to reliably use the marker –*ed* to interpret past tense meaning during reading. As a result of this finding and other research, Labov has consistently recommended that grammar be taught explicitly to BC speakers and, in particular, that teachers underscore the grammatical function of certain SE inflections, most importantly in terms of reading, the past tense –*ed*.

The reason why the grammatical role of the –*ed* inflectional ending is so critical to emphasize in reading instruction is because of its possible relationship to comprehension. If children cannot reliably use the marker –*ed* to assign a past tense interpretation during reading, then their comprehension is likely to be affected. If, on the other hand, children's rendering of *walked* as *walk* while reading aloud reflects only BC pronunciation patterns—that is, children are not articulating the marker, but they are processing its meaning—then comprehension is not affected. Because the past tense is an integral component of the BC system, the latter explanation—that children are likely processing the past tense meaning whether or not they pronounce the ending—seems to make most linguistic sense. However, Labov's research with adolescents suggests otherwise, that, in fact, some BC speakers may have trouble using –*ed* to signal past tense meaning. Clearly, we would need more research to resolve this question. In the meantime, because of the significance of the past tense –*ed* marker and the fact that some research suggests that BC speakers may omit this ending in their writing, it makes good sense for teachers to focus explicitly on its grammatical function during instruction and to take careful note of whether or not children are using –*ed* to interpret past tense meaning in their reading.

In the literature about BC, a good deal of attention has been paid to speakers' use of various –*s* inflections, including plural –*s*, third person singular verbal –*s* (e.g., *he walks*), and possessive –'*s*. While lack of plural –*s* has sometimes been cited as a feature of BC, in fact, the plural –*s* is almost always intact in the speech of BC speakers, except in the case of nouns of measure [e.g., *fifty cent* but *fifty reasons*] (Green, 2002; Rickford and Rickford, 2000; Labov, 1972). Labov et al. (1998) cite research by Jane Torrey and Arnetha Ball that suggests, predictably, that BC speakers have no difficulty with semantic interpretation of plural –*s*.

Unlike plural –*s*, verbal –*s* is likely to be absent in the speech of many BC speakers because third person singular subject-verb agreement is not part of the BC grammatical system. But because it doesn't really carry any semantic meaning (the third person singular present tense –*s* is essentially a holdover from Middle English), it is not an issue in reading, that is, it doesn't affect comprehension in any way. However, it is likely to be an issue in writing instruction. Because this feature is not part of the BC system, some BC speakers have difficulty using verbal *–s* in their writing. And because it carries no semantic meaning, it is a feature of the SE system that is often hard to teach to BC speakers. Given the fact that not using SE subject-verb agreement is highly stigmatized in the larger society, there is excellent reason to focus attention on it during grammar instruction. It is important for teachers to keep in mind, though, that the lack of a subject-verb agreement rule in BC has nothing to do with comprehension of text written in SE.

Finally, studies of BC reveal that possession in attributive position in BC is likely to be marked by juxtaposition (e.g., *the girl house*) as opposed to being redundantly marked as it is in SE by both juxtaposition and use of *'s* (e.g., *the girl's house*). Some evidence suggests that young BC speakers may have difficulty assigning semantic meaning to *'s*. Labov et al. (1998) cite the example of second-grade children in one study not being able to distinguish pairs like *"the duck nurse"* versus *"the duck's nurse"* (p. 15). How much such confusions are likely to contribute to reading difficulties is hard to say at this point in time, but, again, Labov's large point that attention be paid to talking explicitly with children about the grammatical function of SE inflectional endings seems to me very well taken. In fact, as stated earlier, all five of Labov's recommendations for improving reading instruction for BC speakers seem eminently worth putting into practice. Again, they include the following:

- Distinguishing between mistakes in reading and differences in pronunciation;
- Giving more instructional attention to the ends of words;
- Presenting words in phonological contexts that preserve underlying forms;
- Avoiding contractions in early reading materials; and
- Teaching grammar explicitly. (Labov, 1995)

Before leaving the topic of Labov and his colleagues' research in Philadelphia, I want to make some comments about the reading materials they used as part of their instructional intervention with children in the study.

Based on children's oral reading of selected text, Labov et al. (1998) constructed a diagnostic reading profile for each child that identified his or her specific pattern of decoding errors. The sequence of instruction subsequently followed in individualized tutoring sessions was based upon these diagnostic error profiles. As part of instruction, children read decodable texts, that is, texts whose vocabulary was carefully selected to reflect the specific sound-spelling correspondences that children were currently working on. For example, the central narrative children read as part of their work with the silent *–e* pattern, *Dealing with Zeke*, contains a heavy concentration of silent *–e* words (Labov, 2001, p. 307). Having children read text that is closely connected to the phonics skills they are learning is a hallmark of quality basal programs and other systematic approaches to phonics instruction.

But in addition to the texts being decodable, Labov and his colleagues also took great care to make the materials culturally appropriate and stylistically appealing to African American children living in an urban environment. Labov writes:

> In order to maximize children's motivation to read, the reading texts developed by the linguistic component have incorporated the style and rhythm of hip-hop lyrics. The basic narratives used as texts were first written by the principal investigator in a prose style characteristic of African American speech patterns. A number of these, including the diagnostic readings, were re-written in a rhymed hip-hop style . . . Narrative themes incorporated issues universally relevant to children, as well as settings and scenarios unique to African American culture. (In Towner et al., p. 84)

While the decodable texts used in the tutoring program are not the same as dialect readers (i.e., they aren't actually written in BC), they do seem to incorporate some similar features, including the use of BC stylistic patterns as well as culturally familiar characters and settings. The incorporation of these features into the reading texts children used may well have played a significant role in the success of the tutoring program, although, as far as I know, this question was not specifically examined by the researchers.

Chapter 13
Implications for Research and Practice

Although there are many questions still left unanswered about the relationship between BC and reading, the research reviewed in the last chapter contains a number of implications for teachers, teacher educators, and researchers. Perhaps the strongest impression one is left with after examining educational research and discussion about BC over the past 30 years is the way in which attention to this topic has waxed and waned. As Rickford and Rickford (2000) point out, public interest in BC has been cyclical, typically precipitated by what is perceived to be a crisis—for example, President Johnson's War on Poverty in the 1960s, the Ann Arbor Black English case in the 1970s, and the Oakland School Board's Resolution on Ebonics in the 1990s. In response to the perceived crisis, there is a sudden flurry of interest in BC and its possible educational implications. As a result, some excellent, but often highly speculative and exploratory, research is produced, accompanied by intriguing suggestions for classroom implementation and further study. But before these suggestions can be fully discussed within the educational community, much less acted upon, interest in the subject dissipates. The interesting research that has been produced gathers dust on library shelves until the next educational crisis occurs and the research is once again dragged out, dusted off, and briefly considered one more time.

Ann Piestrup's 1973 data-rich study of 14 Oakland classrooms, for example, has never been replicated and is now out of print, despite its being the only empirical study we have of how differences between BC and SE actually play out during the process of reading instruction. At the end of the study, Piestrup's strongest recommendation was that future research focus on Black Artful teachers, teachers who are routinely successful in teaching Black children to read. Outside of Michèle Foster's research with Black teachers (1987, 1989, 1997, 2001), only some of it focused specifically on teaching reading, there are no studies that have taken up Piestrup's call. My own work with teachers over the past 13 years has convinced me that there are many Black

Artful teachers working successfully in classrooms across the country, but the specific practices these teachers employ in teaching reading have never been systematically studied.

Similarly, in 1980, Shirley A.R. Lewis described the intensive efforts she and colleagues at Stanford University put into doing professional development work with teachers on the topic of BC and literacy instruction. One might have hoped that Lewis's description would have spurred similar professional development efforts around the country, along with research and scholarly discussion about them. If that had been the case, the educators and researchers designing professional development for teachers in Oakland in the wake of the Oakland School Board's Ebonics resolution in 1997 would have been able to draw upon the lessons learned from over 15 years of accumulated wisdom on this topic. As it was, they were starting essentially from scratch, except for the Oakland district's own experience in this area. Teacher knowledge about BC was an issue for the educational community in 1979 as schools scrambled to make some kind of response to Judge Joiner's court order in the Ann Arbor case. Teacher knowledge about BC was an issue of concern again in 1998 when educators struggled to make sense of the Oakland School Board resolution. In between, most educators could have cared less about the subject. Meanwhile, as Piestrup's data suggests, teacher knowledge about BC has *always* been, and continues to be, an issue significantly affecting BC speakers learning to read.

There were as well many early calls for modifying literacy materials in ways that would potentially make them more effective for use with BC speakers. For example, as discussed earlier, Robert Berdan's (1980) suggestion that reading lessons be annotated with possible BC pronunciations so that teachers could more easily distinguish these from actual reading errors was tried out in Texas in the late 1970s, with highly positive results. Despite these positive results, to my knowledge no subsequent researcher, school system or publisher has experimented further with this promising idea. The annotated collection in which it was described (Whiteman, 1980) has long been out of print. Results of the 1970s intervention with the Bridge Series dialect readers were similarly positive, but, as noted earlier, the series was dropped like a hot potato in the face of public criticism. The team that designed the series had no real chance to respond to the criticisms or to experiment with possible modifications before the whole idea of using reading materials whose linguistic patterns more closely matched those of BC speakers was simply swept off the table—end of discussion. And, as I have noted a number of times already, William Labov has put forward the same set of suggestions for improving reading instruction and literacy materials for over 30 years. As Snow et al. (1998) assert, "clearly there is a rich research agenda represented in the thoughtful application of these principles in literacy instruction" (p. 241), but to date, no one has seen fit to pursue it.

As Holly Craig and Julie Washington (2006) note, research on the relationship between BC and reading acquisition has been hampered in the past by lack of knowledge about child BC. Until very recently, researchers used the linguistic research done with adolescent and adult populations to make assumptions about the BC features likely to be used by child speakers. Research on child language acquisition in general suggests that these were not necessarily valid assumptions, but during the 1970s and 1980s, we possessed only a meager body of knowledge about child BC. However, for over a decade, Craig, Washington, and their colleagues at the University of Michigan have conducted research on the characteristics of child BC (and on the development of nondiscriminatory measures for assessing the language and literacy abilities of young BC speakers). Based on their own findings as well the findings of earlier research (e.g., Craig et al., 2003; Oetting & McDonald, 2001; Seymour & Rabalate, 1985; Stockman, 1996), they have succeeded in developing a much needed child-inventory of BC features. Craig and Washington have also developed a *dialect density measure* (DDM) to characterize the extent to which individual children employ BC features in their speech (p. 43).

The inventory of child BC features coupled with the DDM now make it feasible to explore possible relationships between BC and reading acquisition in a much more precise way. Without a reliable inventory of child BC features, accurate determination of who was and wasn't a BC speaker wasn't always possible. Nor was it possible before development of the DDM to examine whether the amount of BC used by children made a difference in the effects of BC (if any) on reading acquisition. Craig and Washington are hopeful that these developments will spur new interest in exploring possible linkages between BC and reading as well as other factors that impact reading achievement for African American children. As I hope the brief discussion of existing research provided in the last chapter illustrated, we have much that is rich to build upon in designing both promising new intervention strategies and future research. What we seem to be lacking, however, is the level of sustained interest and commitment necessary to make meaningful progress on these issues.

Although many courses on literacy teaching now include some focus on the needs of English language learners (children learning English as a second language), few teacher preparation programs pay much attention to the topic of BC or to the potential needs of BC speakers in literacy instruction. Along with others, I have argued elsewhere that in order to build effectively on Black children's existing linguistic resources in literacy instruction, teachers need to possess knowledge about the systematic features of BC (Harris-Wright, 1999; Labov, 1995, 2001; Meier, 1998, 1999; Smitherman, 1999, 2000a; Vaughn-Cooke, 1999; Wolfram et al., 1999). This is hardly a generally accepted view, however. Lisa Green (2002) has made the point that many people would likely raise objections to a call for greater attention to knowledge about BC in teacher preparation, arguing that African Americans represent only one among many linguistic minority groups in this country. She hypothesizes a number of questions being raised: "Is it realistic to require teachers to learn the rules of AAE? Where does this stop? If AAE gets special privileges, what happens when the majority of children in a classroom speak different varieties of English?" (p. 240).

The reality is that the case of BC is different from the case of many other varieties of English spoken within the United States. A historical view of the way in which BC has been perceived and characterized by the wider society, dating all the way back to the period of African American enslavement and extending up to the present day, reveals the unmistakable connection between prejudice against this language variety and racism toward its speakers. For no other group in the United States has this linguistic prejudice and its overt and veiled connections to racism been as strong or as long-lived. The linguist Walt Wolfram, who frequently conducts workshops that educate participants about several different varieties of English spoken within the United States, writes:

> I recently met with a new school administrator in a public school where we had been teaching students about dialect differences for more than a decade. Although the administrator was enthusiastic about our language curriculum, one of the first questions was, "This isn't about Ebonics, is it?" This remark was clearly not intended to be a literal question about subject content, but an indirect condemnation of any educational program that might acknowledge the legitimacy of AAE. Several decades of description, application, and education, unfortunately, have had minimal impact on the public perception of AAE. (in Craig & Washington, 2006, p. xiii)

The persistence of this prejudice toward BC, even in the face of decades of research establishing its linguistic legitimacy, speaks powerfully to its connection with racism. In the wake of the Ebonics controversy in 1997, linguist Wayne O'Neil (1998) wrote:

> ... in the United States—as in many parts of the industrialized world—language prejudice remains a "legitimate" prejudice; that is, one can generally say the most appalling things about people's speech without fear of correction or contradiction. The exercise of this prejudice in the United States is often, but not only, a shield for racism, thus allowing the holders of racist views a freedom no longer readily acceptable in civil society." (p. 42)

James Baldwin made this point even more forcefully in an essay that appeared in *The New York Times* in 1979: "It is not the Black child's language that is in question, it is not his language that is despised: It is his experience" (reprinted in Perry & Delpit, 1998, p. 70). From this vantage point, educating teachers about BC is not only about helping teachers build instruction on what children already know, but, even more importantly, about insuring that teachers who have imbibed the linguistic prejudice and racism of the larger society do not inflict educational harm upon Black children, either wittingly or unwittingly.

And in any case, increasing teacher knowledge about BC does not have to occur at the expense of, or instead of, increasing teacher knowledge about other varieties of English. As a matter of fact, much of what teachers would learn about BC would also have application to working with speakers of other varieties of English. For example, final consonant cluster reduction is a prominent feature not only of BC, but also of other varieties of English that have retained influences from other languages, such as Chicano English, Puerto Rican English, Vietnamese English, and varieties of U.S. English influenced by Creole languages (Fought, 2003; Roberts, 1988; Wolfram & Schilling-Estes, 1998; Zentella, 1997). Thus a focus on ends of words in reading instruction would not only benefit BC speakers, but speakers of other nonmainstream varieties of English as well. It has also been my experience that when teachers and preservice teachers gain a good understanding of some of the prominent features of BC and understand as well something of the history of the language and its relationship to culture, they are in a much better position to make sense of the linguistic patterns and cultural practices of other language groups that may be represented in their classrooms. They are also much less likely to view speakers of varieties such as Puerto Rican English or Appalachian English as less intellectually capable than other students simply because of the way they speak. Thus, in my experience with teachers, knowledge about BC opens the door to a broadened understanding of linguistic diversity in general and its relevance in literacy teaching. But that said, first and foremost, teacher knowledge about BC is important because of its potential to make a significant difference in reading outcomes for African American children, a group whose educational needs have been poorly served in our schools for close to two centuries. That seems to me reason enough to incorporate knowledge about BC into the teacher education curriculum, particularly in colleges and universities preparing teachers who are likely to be working with large numbers of BC speakers.

What Can Teachers Do?

Teachers do not have to wait for researchers, teacher educators, and the general public to get their act together on these issues before they can improve literacy instruction for BC speakers in their classrooms. Teachers can take the initiative to work on their own, and in collaboration with like-minded colleagues, both to increase their knowledge about BC and to develop more effective strategies for teaching phonics to BC speakers. For teachers willing to take that initiative, I offer the following recommendations:

- Begin with a systematic approach to phonics instruction.
- Increase your knowledge about BC linguistic and rhetorical patterns.
- Develop a "set" for linguistic diversity.

- Focus on increasing children's metalinguistic awareness.
- Learn from the Black Artful teachers in your midst as well as those described in the literature.

In the following, I discuss each of these recommendations in more detail.

Begin with a systematic approach to phonics instruction.

Begin with a systematic approach to phonics instruction, but, as discussed earlier, do not expect any commercially produced phonics program to have been designed with the specific needs of BC speakers in mind. Therefore, you will need to make adjustments in your instruction. The most important adjustment you can make is to pay earlier and more explicit attention to the ends of words. When doing phonemic awareness activities with children, emphasize ending sounds in words. Have them listen to the difference between the sound of *worl* and *world, jump* and *jumped.* Use ending sounds as the basis for sound substitution games (e.g., "say *west* without the /t/"; "replace the last sound in *cat* with /b/"). Highlighting ends of words, talk about differences in the way people pronounce certain words. When you teach consonants and consonant blends and digraphs, focus on them both in initial position and at the end of words. Draw children's attention to the ends of words during shared writing activities and when giving them assistance with invented spelling. Do dictation exercises that require children to listen carefully to the end of the stimulus word (e.g., did the teacher say *lef* or *left?*). (Needless to say, none of this focus on the ends of words should be about correcting or changing children's BC pronunciations.)

It is also important to learn as much about linguistics and phonics as you possibly can. Some research suggests that many teachers do not possess as much knowledge about these subjects as they need to teach reading most effectively to children from any linguistic background, let alone to BC speakers, for whom the distance between speech and spelling is greater than it is for SE speakers (Blevins, 1998; Moats, 1995). Your knowledge about sound patterns in English (i.e., phonology) and about phonics should extend beyond the parameters of the particular phonics program you are using. The more you understand about the sound patterns of English and about the relationships between sounds and spelling, the more you will be able to discern the systematicity in children's invented spellings and in their decoding and thus the more effectively you will be able to tailor instruction to their needs. You will also be able to see more clearly where modifications may need to be made to the phonics program you are currently using in order to make it more relevant to the needs of BC speakers. Information about the sound patterns of English is knowledge that you can gain either through an introductory linguistics course or through study on your own. If you are studying this topic on your own, I recommend one or more of the following books as a way to get started:

Fromkin, V., & Rodman, R. (1998). *An introduction to language.* New York: Harcourt Brace.

Jakendoff, R. S. (1994). *Patterns in the mind: Language and human nature.* New York: Basic Books

Pinker, S. (1994). *The language instinct.* New York: William Morrow.

Wolfram, W., & Schilling-Estes, N. (1998). *American English.* Malden, MA: Blackwell.

To gain more knowledge about phonics, I recommend the following:

Bear, D. R., Invernizzi, M., Templeton, S., & Johnston, F. (2000). *Words their way: Word study for phonics, vocabulary, and spelling instruction.* Columbus, OH: Prentice Hall.

Blevins, W. (1998). *Phonics from a to z: A practical guide.* New York: Scholastic.

Hull, M. A., & Fox, B.J. (1998). *Phonics for the teacher of reading.* Upper Saddle River, NJ: Merrill.

Increase your knowledge about BC linguistic and rhetorical patterns.

If you are responsible for teaching BC speakers to read and write, you will benefit greatly from knowing the major phonological and grammatical differences between BC and SE as well as from knowing something about BC stylistic and rhetorical patterns. As discussed in the last chapter, the ability to distinguish accurately between BC pronunciations and actual reading errors depends upon a solid understanding of BC phonological and grammatical patterns. So does the ability to anticipate words in a reading lesson that may be homophones for BC speakers or to figure out what linguistic patterns to target in instruction. Understanding, for example, how voicing affects consonant cluster reduction in BC (briefly, that clusters are most likely to be reduced when either both consonants are voiced or both are voiceless) allows you to develop word ending lessons that focus on the specific clusters that BC speakers are most likely to reduce. Detailed knowledge about BC is also critical to helping children analyze differences between *home language* and *school language* and to assisting them in developing the ability to code-switch effectively between them. Nor can you utilize strategies like the "linguistic detective approach" or the "Black Artful Approach" without a thorough understanding of BC linguistic and rhetorical patterns. Even being able to read some African American children's literature effectively depends upon familiarity with BC discourse patterns and pronunciation features.

When you are first learning about BC, especially if you are doing so on your own or with a group of colleagues, it is easy to become overwhelmed by the technical vocabulary and level of linguistic detail contained in many books and articles on the subject. This may be the case even for teachers who are native BC speakers. Thus it is best to begin with books that are not overly detailed and technical, but that nonetheless contain rich knowledge about both linguistic and pragmatic aspects of the language. Based on my experience working with practicing and preservice teachers, I recommend the following three books to begin your study of the language:

Dandy, E. B. (1991). *Black Communications: Breaking down the barriers*. Chicago: African American Images.

Rickford, J. R., & Rickford, R. J. (2000). *Spoken soul: The story of Black English*. New York: John Wiley.

Smitherman, G. (1977/1986). *Talkin and testifyin: The language of Black America*. Boston: Houghton Mifflin; reissued, with revisions, Detroit: Wayne State University Press.

Dandy provides a broad and easy-to-understand overview of the BC communicative system. She discusses both distinctive linguistic features and verbal strategies such as "rappin," "woofin," and "playing the dozens." Drawing on examples from classrooms, she does an excellent job of explaining why it is important for teachers to know about the systematic features of BC. She also includes specific ideas for practice. Rickford and Rickford (2000) provide more detailed information about BC phonology and grammar than Dandy, but manage to do so without using a lot of technical jargon. The linguistic terms they do use are well explained. They discuss uses of BC in literature, the Black church, the media, and popular culture, providing many vivid and contemporary examples in each of these areas. They also describe the history of the language, educational implications, and connections between Black language and identity.

Finally, Smitherman's *Talkin and Testifyin* is probably the "Ur text" on Black Communications, as interesting and relevant today as it was when it was first published in 1977. Smitherman focuses on both linguistic and pragmatic aspects of the language. She includes an extensive section on the Black lexicon, linking words and concepts in that lexicon to African American history and cultural values. She describes BC discourse forms and the Black oral narrative tradition at considerable length, drawing on examples from the Traditional Black Church, literature, politics, and popular culture. Besides the breadth of her knowledge on the subject, one of the things that makes this book so distinctive is that Smitherman wrote it using a mixture of BC and SE. The result is a book that not only testifies to, but also embodies, the rhetorical power and beauty of Black language.

Once you have read these three introductory texts, you will be ready to tackle books and articles that contain more detailed information about BC phonological and grammatical patterns, information that I believe will be very useful to you in teaching phonics to BC speakers. At this level of linguistic detail, there are many excellent books and articles to choose from, a number of which were discussed in part 1 of this book and that also appear in the bibliography. Of these, I recommend two in particular:

> Craig, H. K., & Washington, J. A. (2006). *Malik goes to school: Examining the language skills of African American students from preschool—5th grade.* Mahwah, NJ: Lawrence Erlbaum Associates.
> Green, L. J. (2002). *African American English: A linguistic introduction.* New York: Cambridge University Press.

Develop a "set" for linguistic diversity.

Recall that one of the characteristics of the Black Artful teachers in Piestrup's study is that they were able to anticipate possible linguistic conflicts between BC and SE and often acted proactively to prevent misunderstandings from occurring. In one episode from Piestrup's data, for example, the teacher anticipates that children might confuse the words *feet* and *feed* and so carefully distinguishes between them before the lesson begins. She asks children to spell the two words and to use them in sentences, providing time for the distinction between them to "sink in" for children, both on the level of meaning and of spelling (Piestrup, 1973, pp. 110–111). This behavior contrasts sharply with that of the teacher in Piestrup's study who didn't seem to notice children's confusion between *wild* and *wow*, or the student teacher I observed who was totally unprepared for a child's offer of *twis(t)* as a rhyme for *kiss*. The Black Artful teachers in Piestrup's study had a "set" for linguistic diversity. Working in classrooms where many children were far more fluent in BC than SE, they expected children to use BC pronunciations and to have a slightly different set of homonyms than SE speakers. Thus they were not surprised or caught off guard by children's linguistic behaviors, floundering awkwardly for some way to respond.

The knowledge base that undergirds a set for linguistic diversity comes from two primary sources: familiarity with the systematic features of BC and careful observation of the linguistic patterns actually used by the children in your classroom. Oakland teacher Carrie Secret (1998), for example, describes how she listens to the speech of her students, noting the specific BC features they use:

> For example, I might note that Girl X and Boy Y are dropping the final *t*'s off their words—for example saying *lef* for *left* or *bes* for *best*. I then note to myself that I will need to work on that Ebonics feature with the class. (p. 82)

Significantly, even though she is presumably a fluent speaker of BC (describing it at one point as "our language"), Secret does not make up lessons contrasting

BC and SE in the abstract, making a priori assumptions about which specific BC features the children in her class are going to use. Instead, she "studies" children's actual speech. Nor does Secret respond to or comment on children's use of BC features "in the moment," singling children out and making them feel self-conscious about their speech. Instead, she plans whole-class lessons that contrast BC and SE forms in ways that are fun and engaging and that acknowledge the systematicity and value of both language varieties. With their "set for linguistic diversity," teachers like Secret use knowledge about BC to anticipate the language patterns likely used by many of the children in their class, while at the same time, given the linguistic diversity represented in the Black community, being careful to observe which of those patterns actually characterize the speech of the children with whom they are working.

Focus on increasing children's metalinguistic awareness.

In Patricia McKissack's children's book *The Honest-to-Goodness Truth* (2000), Libby Louise tattles on her classmate, informing their teacher that "'Willie don't got his geography homework.'" "'Doesn't have his homework,'" corrects the teacher, to which Libby responds, matter-of-factly, "'No, ma'am, he don't'" (unnumbered pages). Like most children who have their grammar corrected by an adult in this way, Libby Louise doesn't even register her teacher's intended correction. Similarly, Carrie Secret (1998) observes that BC speakers do not hear themselves dropping the ends of words, saying *tes* rather than *test*, for example. As language users, we focus on meaning, on getting our message across, not on the phonological and grammatical features of our speech. But if part of our task as teachers is to help BC speakers acquire bilingual fluency so that they are equally facile with BC and SE, then we have to figure out strategies for bringing these features to children's conscious attention.

As discussed in chapter 12, in terms of phonics instruction, it is particularly important that children's attention be drawn to the ends of words. The issue, of course, is how to do that in the most effective way. Often, as vividly illustrated in Piestrup's study, teachers try to focus BC speakers' attention on word endings by correcting their BC pronunciations. They use a right/wrong, correct/incorrect strategy for encouraging children to focus on the ends of words. Their goal is a good one—if the reading errors of BC speakers tend to cluster at the ends of words, then we should be paying special attention to the ends of words in phonics instruction. However, their strategy for achieving that goal is inappropriate, for at least two reasons. For one, it falsely suggests that there is something inherently wrong with children's systematic, rule-governed pronunciation patterns. Second, simply correcting children's pronunciations offers them no framework or system for making sense of the corrections. Again and again, over the years I have spent observing and working in classrooms, I have heard (and seen) children respond to a teacher's correction of their speech with incredulity or confusion (e.g., a child who is told "no, not fifty *cent*, fifty *cents*" or "not *walk*, *walks*" responds "But that's what I said!") These incidents testify to the accuracy of Secret's observation that children are not really "hearing," that is, taking conscious note of, these subtle phonological differences between BC and SE pronunciations. Also, very commonly, teachers find themselves making the same correction over and over, repeatedly reminding children, for instance, to pronounce their endings or "say the *s* (or *ed*) at the end." The necessity for continuous reminders and correction clearly reveals the ineffectiveness of the right/wrong, correct/incorrect strategy.

As a teacher who wants to help BC speakers become skilled decoders of text as well as fully bilingual, you would do well to remove all references to "correct" language from your vocabulary, replacing the notion of "correct" language with the idea that there are different ways of speaking and using language that are appropriate to different social contexts. Secret is right in her assertion that to really "hear" the SE pronunciation test, children must also "hear" the BC pronunciation tes. In other words, BC speakers must become aware of the fact that they are dealing with two separate linguistic systems that have predictable and "figure-out-able" rules. In her classroom, Secret calls these two systems Ebonics and English. In her curricular materials, Noma LeMoine (1999) calls them African American Language (AAL) and Mainstream American English (MAE). Other teachers call them home language and school language or informal language and formal language. The terms you use are not the important thing. What is important is helping children see that they are fortunate enough to have two different languages or "ways of speaking," each appropriate in different situations.

There are all kinds of creative ways in which you can increase children's level of metalinguistic awareness, that is, their conscious awareness of being speakers of two different, equally valid and rule-governed, forms of English. One of the best of these, in my view, is some version of Mrs. Pat's "linguistic detective approach," in which subtle linguistic differences become an object of "scientific inquiry" for children, not "good" or "bad," but simply interesting. Based on Patricia McKissack's African American folktale, *Flossie and the Fox* (1986), in which a little girl uses her skill with language to outwit a very "proper speaking" fox, some teachers with whom I have worked have introduced a fox puppet into their classrooms. The puppet speaks in an exaggeratedly formal fashion, speaking very slowly, using "hyper-correct" grammatical constructions and carefully enunciating the ends of words. Children in these teachers' classrooms have fun "talking like foxes" and imitating the way the fox would likely pronounce certain words. Other teachers I know use role-plays in which children adjust their language to fit the social situation they are depicting, for example, a lively interaction with friends on the playground, an explanation to the principal about a class project, a dinner table conversation at home. One teacher used children's literature containing BC features and set in an earlier time period as a launch to talk with third-graders about the history of BC and its connections to West African languages and rhetorical traditions. Afterward, children discussed features still present in the speech of African Americans today. Carrie Secret (1998) points out to her class that some of the greatest African American writers and speakers were, and are, adept at using both BC and SE. Throughout the school year, she uses many examples to illustrate her point.

The more you learn about BC, and about African American literature, history, and culture, the more ideas you are likely to come up with for creative and intellectually engaging ways to focus children's conscious attention on language and to help them make sense of the differences between BC and SE. One word of caution is in order here, however. In talking with children about different varieties of English, it is important not to imply that SE or "formal English" somehow "belongs to" or is exclusively identified with White people. As discussed in part 1, the African American speech community has historically been, and continues to be, a bilingual community, one whose members value facility in both BC and SE. SE "belongs" to African Americans every bit as much as it does to any other group of people in the United States. This notion of bilinguality as a hallmark of the Black speech community is well conveyed in one of the role-play activities Carrie Secret does with her students. She tells them:

> "Girls, you are at Spelman and boys, you are attending Morehouse College (historically Black colleges). Today you use the language the professors use and expect you to use in your classes, and that language is [formal] English." (p. 82)

Learn from the Black Artful teachers in your midst as well as those described in the literature.

If you look around you, you are likely to find at least one Black Artful teacher in your school or within your extended teacher network. Black Artful teachers are everywhere, though not nearly in large enough numbers. The most important characteristic distinguishing Black Artful teachers is that their African American students are successful literacy learners. As pointed out earlier, not all Black teachers are necessarily Black Artful, nor—as some of the teacher portraits contained in Gloria Ladson-Billings's (1994) *The Dreamkeepers* testify to—are all Black Artful teachers necessarily Black. That said, however, it is also the case that the "wisdom of practice" represented by Black teachers in our schools is a resource too often undervalued or overlooked entirely in discussions about effective literacy instruction for African American children. Lisa Delpit (1988) has written with great eloquence about the "silenced dialogue" between White educators and educators of color that exists both in many elementary and secondary schools, as well as in teacher preparation programs and in the educational research community. There is no question that this silenced dialogue works against the educational interests of Black children. The cultural understandings that many Black teachers bring to literacy teaching, their deep knowledge of African American discourse practices, and their own skills in oral performance make them powerful pedagogical models for other teachers. Both in my own experience observing and working with outstanding Black teachers, and as they are described in the literature, Black Artful teachers are characterized not only by their teaching effectiveness, but also by their deep commitment to and passion about teaching Black children (Foster, 1997; Irvine, 2002; Ladson-Billings, 1994). Because this is the case, Black Artful teachers are likely to be willing to share their expertise and ideas with other teachers, from whatever background, who are sincere in their desire to work more effectively with African American children.

In addition to observing and talking with the Black Artful teachers around you, you will also find descriptions of exemplary Black teachers in a number of books and articles. A good place to begin reading is with Michele Foster's (1997) ground-breaking book, *Black Teachers on Teaching,* a narrative account, told in teachers' own voices, of the experiences and pedagogical perspectives of 20 Black teachers born between 1905 and 1973. Additional descriptions of highly effective African American teachers can be found in the following sources:

Foster, M. (1989). "It's cooking now": A performance analysis of the speech events of a successful Black teacher in an urban community college. *Language in Society, 18,* 1–29.

Foster, M. (2001). Pay leon, pay leon, pay leon paleontologist. In S. L. Lanehart (Ed.). *Sociocultural and historical contexts of African American English* (pp. 281–298). Philadelphia: John Benjamins.

Hollins, E. R. (1982). The Marva Collins story revisited: Implications for regular classroom instruction. *Journal of Teacher Education. 31*(1), 37–40.

Irvine, J. J. (2002). *In search of wholeness: African American teachers and their culturally specific classroom practices.* New York: Palgrave.

Ladson-Billings, G. (1994). *The dreamkeepers.* San Francisco: Jossey-Bass.

Mahiri, J. (1998). *Shooting for excellence: African American and youth culture in new century schools.* Urbana, IL: National Council of Teachers of English.

Mitchell, A. (1999). African American teachers: Unique roles and universal lessons. *Education and Urban Society, 31*(1), 104–122.

Piestrup, A. (1973). *Black dialect interference and accommodation of reading instruction in first grade.* (Language Behavior Research Laboratory Monograph No. 4). Berkeley, CA: University of California.
Rickford, A. M. (1999). *I can fly.* Lanham, MD: University Press of America.

The African American teachers described in this literature listed are likely to provide you with many inspiring ideas for improving your teaching practices.

References

Adams, M. J. (1990). *Beginning to read: Thinking and learning about print.* Cambridge, MA: MIT Press.

Adams, M. J., Foorman, B. R., Lundberg, I., & Beeler, T. (1998). *Phonemic awareness in young children: A classroom curriculum.* Baltimore: Brookes.

Adams, M. J., Treiman, R., & Pressley, M. (1998). Reading, writing and literacy. In I. E. Sigel & K. A. Renninger (Eds.). *Handbook of Child Psychology: Fifth Edition, Vol. 4: Child Psychology in Practice.* New York: Wiley.

Adger, C. T., Christian, D., & Taylor, O. (Eds.). (1999). *Making the connection: Language and academic achievement among African American students.* McHenry, IL: Delta Systems.

Adler, S. (1992). *Multicultural communication skills in the classroom.* Boston: Allyn & Bacon.

Alim, H. S. (2003). "We are the streets": African American language and the strategic construction of a street conscious identity. In S. Makoni, G. Smitherman, A. F. Ball, & A. K. Spears (Eds.). *Black linguistics: Language, society, and politics in Africa and the Americas.* New York: Routledge.

Allington, R. L. (1983). The reading instruction provided readers of different abilities. *The Elementary Journal, 83,* 454–459.

Anderson, J. (1988). *The education of Blacks in the South, 1860–1935.* Chapel Hill, NC: University of North Carolina Press.

Anderson, J. (1995). Literacy and education in the African American experience. In V. L. Gadsen & D. A. Wagner (Eds.). *Literacy among African American youth: Issues in learning, teaching, and schooling* (pp. 19–37). Cresskill, NJ: Hampton Press.

Anderson, R. C., Hiebert, E. H., Scott, J. A., & Wilkinson, I. A. G. (1985). *Becoming a nation of readers: The report of the Commission on Reading.* Champaign, IL: Center for the Study of Reading and National Academy of Education.

Anderson-Yockel, J., & Haynes, W. (1994). Joint picture-book reading strategies in working-class African American and White mother-toddler dyads. *Journal of Speech, Language, and Hearing Research, 37,* 583–593.

Angelou, M. (1969/1993). *I know why the caged bird sings.* New York: Random House.

Ayres, L. (1993). *The efficacy of three training conditions on phonological awareness of kindergarten children and the longitudinal effect of each on later reading acquisition.* Unpublished doctoral dissertation, Oakland University, Rochester, MI.

Baker, J. (2002). Trilingualism. In L. Delpit & J. K. Dowdy (Eds.). *The skin that we speak: Thoughts on language and culture in the classroom* (pp. 49–61). New York: The New Press.

Baker, L. D. (1999). Racism in professional settings: Forms of address as clues to power relations. In A. K. Spears (Ed.). *Race and ideology: Language, symbolism, and popular culture* (pp. 115–132). Detroit: Wayne State University Press.

Baker, L., Scher, D., & Mackler, K. (1997). Home and family influences on motivations for reading. *Educational Psychologist, 32*(2), 69–82.

Bakhtin, M. (1981). Discourse in the novel. In M. Holquist (Ed.) & C. Emerson & M. Holquist (Trans.), *The dialogic imagination* (pp. 259–422). Austin, TX: University of Texas Press.

Baldwin, J. (1979/1998). If Black English isn't a language, then tell me, what is? Reprinted in T. Perry & L. Delpit (Eds.). *The real Ebonics debate: Power, language and the education of African American children* (pp. 67–70). Boston: Beacon.

Ball, A. (1992). Cultural preference and the expository writing of African American adolescents. *Written Communication, 9*, 501–532.

Ball, A. (1995). Investigating language, learning, and linguistic competence of African American children: Torrey revisited. *Linguistics and Education, 7*, 23–46.

Ball, E. W., & Blachman, B. A. (1991). Does phoneme awareness training in kindergarten make a difference in early word recognition and developmental spelling? *Reading Research Quarterly, 26*(1), 49–66.

Ballenger, C. (1999). *Teaching other people's children.* New York: Teachers College Press.

Bambara, T. C. (1992). Preface. In J. Dash. *Daughters of the dust: The making of an African American woman's film* (pp. xi–xvi). New York: The New Press.

Bankston, C. L., & Caldas, S. J. (1998). Family structure, school mates, and inequalities in school achievement. *Journal of Marriage and Family, 60*(Aug.), 715–723.

Baratz, J. C., & Shuy, R. W. (Eds.). (1969). *Teaching Black children to read.* Washington, DC: Center for Applied Linguistics.

Barr, R., & Dreeben, R. (1983). *How schools work.* Chicago: University of Chicago Press.

Baugh, J. (1981). Design and implementation of writing instruction for speakers of nonstandard English: Perspectives for a national neighborhood literacy program. In B. Cronnell (Ed.). *The writing needs of linguistically different students.* Los Alamitos, CA: SWRL Educational Research and Development.

Baugh, J. (1983). *Black street speech: Its history, structure, and survival.* Austin, TX: University of Texas Press.

Baugh, J. (1984). Steady: Progressive aspect in Black English. *American Speech, 50*, 3–12.

Baugh, J. (1999). *Out of the mouths of slaves: African American language and educational malpractice.* Austin, TX: University of Texas Press.

Bear, D. R., Invernizzi, M., Templeton, S., & Johnston, F. (2000). *Words their way: Word study for phonics, vocabulary, and spelling instruction.* Columbus, OH: Prentice Hall.

Beck, I., & Juel, C. (1995). The role of decoding in learning to read. *American Educator* (Summer), 1–12.

Berdan, R. (1980). Knowledge into practice: Delivering research to teachers. In M. F. Whiteman (Ed.). *Reactions to Ann Arbor: Vernacular Black English and education* (pp. 77–84). Washington, DC: Center for Applied Linguistics.

Blake, I. (1984). *Language development in working class Black children: An examination of form, content, and use.* Unpublished doctoral dissertation, Columbia University, New York.

Blevins, W. (1998). *Phonics from a to z: A practical guide.* New York: Scholastic.

Bloome, D., Champion, T., Katz, L., Morton, M. B., & Muldrow, R. (2001). Spoken and written narrative development: African American preschoolers as storytellers and storymakers. In J. L. Harris, A. G. Kamhi, & K. E. Pollock (Eds.). *Literacy in African American communities* (pp. 45–76). Mahwah, NJ: Lawrence Erlbaum Associates.

Bohannon, J., Warren-Leubecker, A., & Hepler, N. (1984). Word awareness and early reading. *Child Development, 55,* 1541–1548.

Bombardieri, M. (2005, September 18). Hurricane exposed misery of 'povertina,' West says. *The Boston Globe,* p. A32.

Bountress, N. G. (1983). Effects of segregated and integrated educational settings upon selected dialectal features. *Perceptual and Motor Skills, 57,* 71–78.

Bowie, R. L., & Bond, C. L. (1994). Influencing teachers' attitudes toward Black English: Are we making a difference? *Journal of Teacher Education, 45,* 112–118.

Boyd, V. (2003). *Wrapped in rainbows: The life of Zora Neale Hurston.* New York: Scribner.

Braddock, J. H. (1995). Tracking and school achievement: Implications for literacy development. In V. L. Gadsden & D. A. Wagner (Eds.), *Literacy among African American youth: Issues in learning, teaching, and schooling* (pp. 153–176). Cresskill, NJ: Hampton Press.

Bridgeforth, C. D. (1989). *The identification and use of language functions in the speech of 3- and 4 1/2-year-old Black children from working class families.* Unpublished doctoral dissertation, Georgetown University, Washington, DC.

Calkins, L. M. (2001). *The art of teaching reading.* New York: Longman.

Canada, G. (1995). *Fist stick knife gun: A personal history of violence in America.* Boston: Beacon.

Cazden, C. B. (1988). *Classroom discourse: The language of teaching and learning.* Portsmouth, NH: Heineman.

Chall, J. S. (1967). *Learning to read: The great debate.* New York: McGraw-Hill.

Chambers, V. (2002). *Double dutch: A celebration of jumprope, rhyme, and sisterhood.* New York: Hyperion.

Chaney, J. H. (1993). Alphabet books: Resources for learning. *The Reading Teacher, 47*(2), 96–104.

Charity, A. H., Scarborough, H. S., & Griffin, D. M. (2004). Familiarity with "School English" in African American children and its relation to early reading achievement. *Child Development, 75,* 1340–1356.

Chomsky, C. (1970). Reading, writing and phonology. *Harvard Educational Review, 47,* 287–309.

Chomsky, C. (1971). Write first, read later. *Childhood Education, 47,* 296–299.

Clay, M. M. (1993). *An observation survey of early literacy achievement.* Portsmouth, NH: Heinemann.

Compton-Lilly, C. (2003). *Reading Families.* New York: Teachers College Press.

Cooper, E., & Sherk, J. (1989). Addressing urban school reform: Issues and alliances. *Journal of Negro Education, 58,* 315–331.

Cornelius, J. D. (1991). *When I can read my title clear: Literacy, slavery, and religion in the antebellum South.* Columbia, SC: University of South Carolina Press.

Corsaro, W. (1996). Transitions in early childhood: The promise of comparative, longitudinal ethnography. In R. Jessor, A. Colby, & R. Shweder (Eds.). *Ethnography and human development: Context and meaning in social inquiry.* Chicago: University of Chicago Press.

Craig, H. K., & Washington, J. A. (2004). Grade-related changes in the production of African American English. *Journal of Speech, Language, and Hearing Research, 47,* 450–463.

Craig, H. K., & Washington, J. A. (2006). *Malik goes to school: Examining the language skills of African American students from preschool–5th grade.* Mahwah, NJ: Lawrence Erlbaum Associates.

Craig, H. K., Thompson, C. A., Washington, J. A., & Potter, S. L. (2003). Phonological features of child African American English. *Journal of Speech, Language and Hearing Research, 46,* 623–635.

Creel, M. W. (1988). *"A peculiar people": Slave religion and community-culture among the Gullahs.* New York: New York University Press.

Cross, J. B., DeVaney, T., & Jones, G. (2003). Pre-service teacher attitudes toward differing dialects. *Linguistics and Education, 12,* 211–227.

Cunningham, A. E. (1990). Explicit versus implicit instruction in phonemic awareness. *Journal of Experimental Psychology, 50,* 429–444.

Cunningham, A. E. (2005). Vocabulary growth through independent reading and reading aloud to children. In E. H. Hiebert & M. L. Kamil (Eds.). *Teaching and learning vocabulary: Bringing research to practice* (pp. 45–68). Mahwah, NJ: Lawrence Erlbaum Associates.

Cunningham, P. M. (2000). *Phonics they use: Words for reading and writing.* New York: Longman.

Cunningham, P. M., & Cunningham, J. W. (1992). Making words: Enhancing the invented spelling-decoding connection. *The Reading Teacher, 46(2),* 106–115.

Dandy, E. B. (1991). *Black Communications: Breaking down the barriers.* Chicago: African American Images.

Darling-Hammond, L. (1995). Teacher knowledge and student learning: Implications for literacy development. In V. L. Gadsen & D. A. Wagner (Eds.), *Literacy among African American youth: Issues in learning, teaching and schooling* (pp. 177–200). Cresskill, NJ: Hampton Press.

Dash, J. (1992). *Daughters of the dust: The making of an African American woman's film.* New York: The New Press.

Delpit, L. (1988). The silenced dialogue: Power and pedagogy in educating other people's children. *Harvard Educational Review, 58(3),* 280–296.

Delpit, L. (1996). *Other people's children: Cultural conflict in the classroom.* New York: The New Press.

Delpit, L. (1998). What should teachers do? Ebonics and culturally responsive instruction. In T. Perry & L. Delpit (Eds.). *The real Ebonics debate* (pp. 17–26). Boston: Beacon.

Dickinson, D. K., & Smith, M. W. (1994). Long-term effects of preschool teachers' book readings on low-income children's vocabulary and story comprehension. *Reading Research Quarterly, 29,* 104–122.

Dickinson, D. K., & Sprague, K. E. (2001). The nature and impact of early childhood care environments on the language and early literacy development of children from low-income families. In S. B. Neuman & D. K. Dickinson (Eds.), *Handbook of early literacy research* (pp. 263–280). New York: Guilford Publications.

Douglass, F. (1845/1968). *The narrative of the life of Frederick Douglass: An American slave.* New York: Signet.

Doyle, A. C. (1996). *Sherlock Holmes.* New York: Knopf.

Dreeben, R., & Gamoran, A. (1986). Race, instruction, and learning. *American Sociological Review, 51*(5), 660–669.

DuBois, W. E. B. (1982). *Souls of Black folks.* New York: Penguin.

Edwards, W. F. (1992). Sociolinguistic behavior in a Detroit inner-city black neighborhood. *Language in Society, 21,* 93–115.

Elley, W. B. (1989). Vocabulary acquisition from listening to stories. *Reading Research Quarterly, 24*(2), 174–187.

Entwisle, D. R., & Alexander, K. L. (1988). Factors affecting achievement test scores and marks of Black and White first graders. *The Elementary School Journal, 88,* 449–471.

Epstein, J. L. (1985). After the bus arrives: Resegregation in desegregated schools. *Journal of Social Issues, 41,* 23–43.

Ericson, L., & Juliebo, M. F. (1998). *The phonological awareness handbook for kindergarten and primary teachers.* Newark, DE: International Reading Association.

Erikson, E. H. (1968). *Identity, youth and crisis.* New York: Norton.

Etter-Lewis, G. (1985). *Sociolinguistic patterns of code-switching in the language of preschool Black children.* Unpublished doctoral dissertation, University of Michigan, Ann Arbor, MI.

Etter-Lewis, G. (1991). Black women's life stories: Reclaiming self in narrative texts. In S. B. Gluck & D. Patai (Eds.). *Women's words: The feminist practice of oral history* (pp. 43–62). New York: Routledge.

Ewers, C. A., & Brownson, S. M. (1999). Kindergartners' vocabulary acquisition as a function of active vs. passive storybook reading, prior vocabulary, and working memory. *Journal of Reading Psychology, 20,* 11–20.

Fabre, G. (1999). The slave ship dance. In M. Diedrich, H. L. Gates, Jr., & C. Pedersen (Eds.). *Black imagination and the middle passage* (pp. 33–46). New York: Oxford University Press.

Fielding, L., & Pearson, P. D. (1994). Reading comprehension: What works? *Educational Leadership, 51*(5), 62–67.

Fisher, D., Flood, J., Lapp, D., & Frey, N. (2004). Interactive read-alouds: Is there a common set of implementation practices? *The Reading Teacher, 58*(1), 8–17.

Fitzpatrick, J. (1997). *Phonemic awareness: Playing with sounds to strengthen beginning reading skills.* Cypress, CA: Creative Teaching Press.

Foorman, B. R., Francis, D. J., Fletcher, J. M., Schatschneider, C. & Mehta, P. (1998). The role of instruction in learning to read: Preventing reading failure in at-risk children. *Journal of Educational Psychology, 90,* 37–55.

Foster, M. (1987*). 'It's cookin' now': An ethnographic study of a successful Black teacher in an urban community college.* Unpublished doctoral dissertation, Harvard University, Cambridge, MA.

Foster, M. (1989). 'It's cookin' now': A performance analysis of the speech events of a Black teacher in an urban community college. *Language in Society, 18*, 1–29.

Foster, M. (1995a). "Are you with me"?: Power and solidarity in the discourse of African American women. In K. Hall & M. Bucholtz (Eds.). *Gender articulated: Language and the socially constructed self* (pp. 329–350). New York: Routledge.

Foster, M. (1995b). Talking that talk: The language of control, curriculum and critique. *Linguistics and Education, 7*(2), 129–50.

Foster, M. (1997). *Black teachers on teaching.* New York: The New Press.

Foster, M. (2001). Pay Leon, pay Leon, paleontologist: Using call-and-response to facilitate language mastery and literacy acquisition among African American students. In S. L. Lanehart (Ed.). *Sociocultural and historical contexts of African American English* (pp. 281–298). Philadelphia: John Benjamins.

Fought, C. (2003). *Chicano English in context.* New York: Palgrave Macmillan.

Fromkin, V., & Rodman, R. (1998). *An introduction to language*: New York: Harcourt Brace.

Gadsen, V. L. (1993). Literacy, education, and identity among African Americans: The communal nature of learning. *Urban Education, 27*, 352–369.

Gates, H. L. (1988). *The signifying monkey: A theory of African American literary criticism.* New York: Oxford University Press.

Gates, H. L. (1990). The master's pieces: On canon formation and the Afro-American tradition. In C. Moran & E. F. Penfield (Eds.), *Conversation: Contemporary critical theory and the teaching of literature* (pp. 55–75). Urbana, IL: National council of Teachers of English.

Getridge, C. (1998). Oakland superintendent responds to critics of the Ebonics policy. In T. Perry & L. Delpit (Eds.). *The real Ebonics debate: Power, language, and the education of African American children* (pp. 156–159). Boston: Beacon Press.

Gillam, R. B., & van Kleeck, A. (1996). Phonological awareness training and short-term working memory: Clinical implications. *Language Disorders, 17*, 72–81.

Gomez, M. A. (1998). *Exchanging our country marks: The transformation of African identities in the colonial and antebellum South.* Chapel Hill, NC: University of North Carolina Press.

Goodman, K. S., & Buck, C. (1973). Dialect barriers to reading comprehension revisited. *The Reading Teacher, 27*, 219–223.

Goodwin, M. H. (1990). *He-said-she-said: Talk as social organization among Black children.* Bloomington, IN: Indiana University Press.

Green, L. J. (2002). *African American English: A linguistic introduction.* New York: Cambridge University Press.

Griffin, F. J. (1995). *Who set you flowin'? The African American migration narrative.* New York: Oxford University Press.

Griffith, P. L. (1991). Phonemic awareness helps first graders invent spellings and third graders remember correct spellings. *Journal of Reading Behavior, 23*, 215–33.

Griffith, P. L., & Olson, M. W. (1992). Phonemic awareness helps beginning readers to break the code. *Reading Teacher, 45*, 516–22.

Gundaker, G. (1998). *Signs of diaspora/Diaspora of signs: Literacies, creolization, and vernacular practice in African America*. New York: Oxford University Press.

Guthrie, P. (1996). *Catching sense: African American communities on a South Carolina sea island*. Westport, CT: Bergin and Garvey.

Guthrie, P. (2001). "Catching sense" and the meaning of belonging on a South Carolina sea island. In S. S. Walker (Ed.). *African roots/American cultures: Africa in the creation of the Americas* (pp. 275–283). New York: Rowman and Littlefield.

Gutman, H. (1976). *The Black family in slavery and freedom, 1750–1925*. New York: Random House.

Haight, W. L. (2002). *African American children at church: a sociocultural perspective*. New York: Cambridge University Press

Hale, J. E. (1994). *Unbank the fire: Visions for the education of African American children*. Baltimore: Johns Hopkins University Press.

Hammer, C. S. (2001). "Come sit down and let mama read": Book reading interactions between African American mothers and their infants. In J. L. Harris, A. G. Kamhi, & K. E. Pollock (Eds.). *Literacy in African American communities* (pp. 21–43). Mahwah, NJ: Lawrence Erlbaum Associates.

Hammond, B., Hoover, M. E. R., & McPhail, I. P. (2005). *Teaching African American learners to read: Perspectives and practices*. Newark, DE: International Reading Association.

Hansen, J. (1981). The effects of inference training and practice on young children's reading comprehension. *Reading Research Quarterly, 16*, 391–417.

Harris, V. J. (Ed.). (1993). *Teaching multicultural literature in grades K–8*. Norwood, MA: Christopher-Gordon Publishers.

Harris-Lacewell, M. V. (2004). *Barbershops, bibles and BET: Everyday thought and Black political thought*. Princeton, NJ: Princeton University Press.

Harris-Wright, K. (1999). Enhancing bidialectalism in urban African American students. In C. T. Adger, D. Christian, & O. Taylor (Eds.). *Making the connection: Language and academic achievement among African American students* (pp. 53–59). McHenry, IL: Delta Systems.

Harris-Wright, K. (2005). Building blocks for literacy development: Oral language. In B. Hammond, M. E. R. Hoover, & I. P. McPhail (Eds.). *Teaching African American learners to read* (pp. 173–188). Newark, DE: International Reading Association.

Harvey, S., & Goudvis, A. (2000). *Strategies that work: Teaching comprehension to enhance understanding*. Portland, ME: Stenhouse.

Heath, S. B. (1983). *Ways with words: Language, life, and work in communities and classrooms*. Cambridge: Cambridge University Press.

Hedges, L., & Nowell, A. (1998). Black-White test score convergence since 1965. In C. Jencks & M. Phillips (Eds.). *The Black-White test score gap* (pp. 149–181). Washington, DC: Brookings Institution Press.

Hester, E. J. (1996). Narratives of young African American children. In A. G. Kamhi, K. E. Pollock & J. L. Harris (Eds.). *Communication development and disorders in African American children* (pp. 227–245). Baltimore: Brookes.

Hoffman, P. A. (1997). Phonological intervention with storybook reading. *Topics in Language Disorders, 17,* 69–88.

Hohn, W., & Ehri, L. (1983). Do alphabet letters help prereaders acquire phonemic segmentation skill? *Journal of Educational Psychology, 75,* 752–762.

Hollins, E. R. (1982). The Marva Collins story revisited: Implications for regular classroom instruction. *Journal of Teacher Education, 31*(1), 37–40.

Hollins, E. R., McIntyre, L. R., DeBose, C. E., Hollins, K. S., & Towner, A. G. (2005). Literacy development in the primary grades: Promoting a self-sustaining learning community among teachers. In B. Hammond, M. E. R. Hoover & I. P. McPhail (Eds.). *Teaching African American learners to read* (pp. 233–252). Newark, DE: International Reading Association.

Honig, B. (1996). *Teaching our children to read: The role of skills in a comprehensive reading program.* Thousand Oaks, CA: Corwin Press.

Hoover, M. R. (2005). Characteristics of Black schools at grade level revisited. In B. Hammond, M. R. Hoover, & I. P. McPhail (Eds.). *Teaching African American children to read: Perspectives and practices* (pp. 66–78). Newark, DE: International Reading Association.

Hull, M. A., & Fox, B. J. (1998). *Phonics for the teacher of reading.* Upper Saddle River, NJ: Merrill.

Hurmence, B. (Ed.). (1984/2001). *My folks don't want me to talk about slavery.* Winston-Salem, NC: John F. Blair.

Hurmence, B. (1989). (Ed.). *Before freedom: When I just can remember.* Winston-Salem, NC: John F. Blair.

Hurston, Z. N. (1937/1990). *Their eyes were watching God.* New York: Harper & Row.

Hurston, Z. N. (1942/1995). *Dust tracks on a road.* New York: HarperCollins.

Irvine, J. J. (1991). Black students and school failure: Policies, practices and prescriptions. Westport, CT: Praeger Publishers.

Irvine, J. J. (2002). *In search of wholeness: African American teachers and their culturally specific classroom practices.* New York: Palgrave.

Jacobs, H. (1861/1987). *Incidents in the life of a slave girl* (J.F. Yellin, Ed.): Cambridge, MA: Harvard University Press.

Jackendoff, R. (1994). *Patterns in the mind: Language and human nature.* New York: Basic Books.

Jackson-Lowman, H. (1997). Using Afrikan proverbs to provide an Afrikan-centered narrative for contemporary Afrikan-American parental values. In J. K. Adjaye & A. R. Andrews (Eds.). *Language, rhythm, and sound: Black popular cultures into the twenty-first century* (pp. 74–89). Pittsburgh, PA: University of Pittsburgh Press.

Jemie, O. (Ed.). (2003). *Yo' mama! New raps, toasts, dozens, jokes and children's rhymes from urban Black America.* Philadelphia: Temple University Press.

Jencks, C., & Phillips, M. (1998). *The Black-White Test Score Gap.* Washington, DC: Brookings Institution Press.

Johnson, D. (2001). *Break any woman down.* New York: Random House.

Jones, A. C. (1993). *Wade in the water: The wisdom of the spirituals.* Maryknoll, NY: Orbis Books.

Jones, B., & Hawes, B. L. (1972). (Eds.). *Step it down: Games, plays, songs, and stories from the Afro-American heritage.* New York: Harper & Row.

Jones, W. A., Sr. (1976). Introduction. In J. A. Smith, Jr. (Ed.). *Outstanding Black sermons* (pp. 6–7). Valley Forge, PA: Judson Press.

Jones-Jackson, P. (1987). *When roots die: Endangered traditions on the Sea Islands.* Athens, GA: The University of Georgia Press.

Juel, C. (1988). Learning to read and write: A longitudinal study of 54 children from first through fourth grades. *Journal of Educational Psychology, 80*(4), 437–447.

Keene, E. O., & Zimmermann, S. (1997). *Mosaic of thought: Teaching comprehension in a reader's workshop.* Portsmouth, NH: Heinemann.

King, W. (1995). *Stolen childhood: Slave youth in nineteenth-century America.* Bloomington, IN: Indiana University Press.

Kochman, T. (1981). *Black and White styles in conflict.* Chicago: University of Chicago Press.

Kovac, C. (1980). *Children's acquisition of variable features.* Unpublished doctoral dissertation, Georgetown University, Washington, DC.

Labov, W. (1969). Some sources of reading problems for Negro speakers of nonstandard English. In J. C. Baratz & R. W. Shuy (Eds.). *Teaching Black children to read* (pp. 29–67). Washington, DC: Center for Applied Linguistics.

Labov, W. (1972). *Language in the inner city: Studies in the Black English vernacular.* Philadelphia: University of Pennsylvania Press.

Labov, W. (1995). Can reading failure be reversed: A linguistic approach to the question. In V. L. Gadsden & D. A. Wagner (Eds.). *Literacy among African American youth* (pp. 39–68). Cresskill, NJ: Hampton Press.

Labov, W. (1999). Foreword. In J. R. Rickford. *African American vernacular English* (pp. xxiv–xxvi). Malden, MA: Blackwell.

Labov, W. (2001). Applying our knowledge of African American English to the problem of raising reading levels in inner-city schools. In S. L. Lanehart (Ed.). *Sociocultural and historical contexts of African American English* (pp. 299–317). Philadelphia: John Benjamins.

Labov, W., Baker, B., Bullock, S. Ross, L., & Brown, M. (1998). *A graphemic-phonemic analysis of the reading errors of inner city children.* Unpublished manuscript, University of Pennsylvania. Available at: http://www.ling.upenn.edu/~labov/home.html

Labov, W., Cohen, P., Robbins, C., & Lewis, J. (1968). *A study of non-standard English of Negro and Puerto Rican speakers in New York City,* 2 vols. Philadelphia: U.S. Regional Survey.

Ladson-Billings, G. (1994). *The dreamkeepers.* San Francisco: Jossey-Bass.

Lareau, A. (1987). Social class differences in family-school relationships: The importance of cultural capital. *Sociology of Education, 60*(2), 73–85.

LeClair, T. (1981, March 21). "The language must not sweat": A conversation with Toni Morrison. *The New Republic,* 27.

Lee, C. (1993). *Signifying as a scaffold for literary interpretation: The pedagogical implications of an African American discourse genre.* Urbana, IL: National Council of Teachers of English.

LeMoine, N. (1999). *English for your success: A language development program for African American children grades Pre-K–8.* Maywood, NJ: The People's Publishing Group.

Leung, C. B. (1992). Effects of word-related variables on vocabulary growth through repeated read-aloud events. In C. K. Kinzer & D. J. Leu (Eds.). *Literacy research, theory, and practice: Views from many perspectives. Forty-first yearbook of the National Reading conference* (pp. 491–498). Chicago: National Reading Conference.

Levine, L. W. (1977). *Black culture and Black consciousness: Afro-American folk thought from slavery to freedom.* New York: Oxford University Press.

Lewkowicz, N. (1980). Phonemic awareness training: What to teach and how to teach it. *Journal of Educational Psychology, 72,* 686–700.

Lewis, S. A. R. (1980). Teacher attitude change: Does informing make a difference? In M. F. Whiteman (Ed.). *Reactions to Ann Arbor: Vernacular Black English and education* (pp. 85–92). Washington, DC: Center for Applied Linguistics.

Lewis, S. A. R. (1981). Practical aspects of teaching composition to bidialectal students: The Nairobi method. In M. F. Whiteman (Ed.). *Writing: The nature, development, and teaching of written composition* (pp. 189–196). Hillsdale, NJ: Lawrence Erlbaum Associates.

Lincoln, C. E., & Mamiya, L. H. (1990). *The Black church in the African American experience.* Durham, NC: Duke University Press.

Lippi-Green, R. (1997). *English with an accent: Language, ideology and discrimination in the United States.* New York: Routledge.

Lischer, R. (1995). *The preacher king: Martin Luther King Jr. and the word that moved America.* New York: Oxford University Press.

Lundberg, I., Frost, J., & Peterson, O. (1988). Effects of an extensive program for stimulating phonological awareness in preschool children. *Reading Research Quarterly, 23,* 263–284.

Mahiri, J. (1998). *Shooting for excellence: African American and youth culture in new century schools.* Urbana, IL: National Council of Teachers of English.

Major, C. (1994). *Juba to jive: A dictionary of African American slang.* New York: Penguin Books.

Malcolm X. (1965). *The autobiography of Malcolm X.* New York: Ballantine Books.

Manzo, A., & Manzo, U. (1993). *Literacy disorders: Holistic diagnosis and remediation.* New York: Harcourt.

Marshall, P. (1983). *From the poets in the kitchen.* New York: Feminist Press.

Mbiti, J. (1990). *African religions and philosophy.* Portsmouth, NH: Heinemann.

McHenry, E. (2002). *Forgotten readers: Recovering the lost history of African American literary societies.* Durham, NC: Duke University Press.

Meier, T. (1998). Teaching teachers about Black Communications. In T. Perry & L. Delpit (Eds.). *The real Ebonics debate: Power, language and the education of African American children* (pp. 117–125). Boston: Beacon.

Meier, T. (1999). The case for Ebonics as part of exemplary teacher preparation. In C. T. Adger, D. Christian, & O. Taylor (Eds.). *Making the connection: Language and academic achievement among African American students* (pp. 97–114). McHenry, IL: Delta Systems.

Mitchell, A. (1999). African American teachers: Unique roles and universal lessons. *Education and Urban Society, 31*(1), 104–122.

Mitchell, H. (1970). *Black preaching.* Philadelphia: Lippincott.

Mitchell-Kernan, C. (1972). Signifying, loud-talking and marking. In T. Kochman (Ed.). *Rappin' and stylin' out* (pp. 315–335). Urbana, IL: University of Illinois Press.

Mitchell-Kernan, C. (1990). Signifying. In A. Dundes (Ed.). *Mother wit from the laughing barrel: Readings in the interpretation of Afro-American folklore* (pp. 310–328). Jackson, MS: University Press of Mississippi.

Moats, L. C. (1995). The missing foundation in teacher education. *American Federation of Teachers* (Summer).

Morgan, M. (1993). The Africanness of counterlanguage among Afro-Americans. In S. S. Mufwene (Ed.). *Africanisms in Afro-American language varieties* (pp. 423–435). Athens, GA: The University of Georgia Press.

Morgan, M. (2002). *Language, discourse, and power in African American culture.* New York: Cambridge University Press.

Morgan, P. D. (1998). *Slave counterpoint: Black culture in the eighteenth-century Chesapeake and lowcountry.* Chapel Hill, NC: University of North Carolina Press.

Morrison, T. (1970/1993) *The bluest eye.* New York: Alfred Knopf.

Morrison, T. (1973/2002). *Sula.* New York: Alfred Knopf.

Morrison, T. (1977/1987). *Song of Solomon.* New York: Alfred Knopf.

Moss, B. (2003). *A community text arises: A literate text and a literacy tradition in African American churches.* Cresskill, NJ: Hampton Press.

Murray, B. A., Stahl, S. A., & Ivey, M. G. (1996). Developing phonemic awareness through alphabet books. *Reading & Writing: An Interdisciplinary Journal, 8*, 307–22.

NAEP (1997). The NAEP 1997 Arts Report Card: Eighth-Grade Findings From the National Assessment of Educational Progress. Retrieved April 16, 2006, from http://nces.ed.gov/programs/quarterly/Vol_1/1_1/4-esql1-b.asp

Nagy, W. (2005). Why vocabulary instruction needs to be long-term and comprehensive. In E. H. Hiebert & M. L. Kamil (Eds.). *Teaching and learning vocabulary: Bridging research to practice* (pp. 27–44). Mahwah, NJ: Lawrence Erlbaum Associates.

Naylor, G. (1988/1993). *Mama day.* New York: Vintage Books.

Neuman, S. (1999). Books make a difference. *Reading Research Quarterly, 34*, 283–319.

Nichols, P. C. (1989). Storytelling in Carolina: Continuities and contrasts. *Anthropology and Education Quarterly, 20*, 232–245.

Nielsen, A. L. (1997). *Black chant: Languages of African American postmodernism.* New York: Cambridge University Press.

Nobles, W. W. (1991). African philosophy: Foundations of Black psychology. In R. L. Jones (Ed.). *Black psychology.* Berkeley, CA: Cobb and Henry.

Oakes, J. (1985). *Keeping track: How schools structure inequality.* New Haven, CT: Yale University Press.

Oetting, J. B., & McDonald, J. L. (2001). Nonmainstream dialect use and specific language impairment. *Journal of Speech, Language, and Hearing Research, 44*, 207–223.

O'Neil, W. (1998). If Ebonics isn't a language, then tell me, what is? (*pace* James Baldwin, 1979). In T. Perry & L. Delpit (Eds.). *The real Ebonics debate: Power, language, and the education of African American children* (pp. 38–47). Boston: Beacon.

Palincsar, A. S., & Brown, A. L. (1984). Reciprocal teaching of comprehension-fostering and monitoring activities. *Cognition and Instruction, 1*, 117–175.

Paris, S. G., & Myers, M. (1981). Comprehension monitoring, memory and study strategies of good and poor readers. *Journal of Reading Behavior, 13*, 5–22.

Pearson, P. D., & Gallagher, M. C. (1983). The instruction of reading comprehension. *Contemporary Educational Psychology, 8*, 317–344.

Perry, I. (2004). *Prophets of the hood: Politics and poetics in hip hop*. Durham, NC: Duke University Press.

Perry, T. (2003). Up from the parched earth: Toward a theory of African American achievement. In T. Perry, C. Steele, & A. G. Hilliard. *Young, gifted, and Black: Promoting high achievement among African American students* (pp. 1–108). Boston: Beacon.

Perry, T., & Delpit, L. (Eds.). (1998). *The real Ebonics debate: Power, language, and the education of African American children*. Boston: Beacon Press.

Peterson, C. L. (1995). *"Doers of the word": African American women speakers and writers in the North (1830–1880)*. New Brunswick, NJ: Rutgers University Press.

Piestrup, A. M. (1973). Black dialect interference and accommodation of reading instruction in the first grade. Monograph of the Language Behavior Research Lab. Berkeley, CA: University of California.

Pietras, T. P. (1980). Lawyers, linguists, and language arts: From the school administrator's viewpoint. In M. F. Whiteman (Ed.). *Reactions to Ann Arbor: Vernacular Black English and education* (pp. 55–60). Washington, DC: Center for Applied Linguistics.

Pinker, S. (1994). *The language instinct*. New York: William Morrow and Company.

Pitts, W. F., Jr. (1993). *Old ship of Zion: The Afro-Baptist ritual in the African diaspora*. New York: Oxford University Press.

Raboteau, A. J. (1978). *Slave religion: The "invisible institution" in the antebellum South*. New York: Oxford University Press.

Randall, A. (2004). *Pushkin and the queen of spades*. New York: Houghton Mifflin.

Rawick, G. P. (1972). *From sundown to sunup: The making of the Black community*. Westport, CT: Greenwood Publishing.

Read, C. (1975). *Children's categorization of speech sounds in English*. Urbana, IL: NCTE Research Report No. 17.

Reveron, W. W. (1978). *The acquisition of four Black English morphological rules by Black preschool children*. Unpublished doctoral dissertation, Ohio State University, Columbus, OH.

Richardson, E. (2003). *African American literacies*. New York: Routledge.

Richardson, W. F., Jr. (2002). Holding on to your song. In J. Haskins (Ed.). *Keeping the faith: African American sermons of liberation* (pp. 65–74). New York: Welcome Rain Publishers.

Rickford, A. M. (1999). *I can fly*. Lanham, MD: University Press of America.

Rickford, J. R. (1999). *African American vernacular English*. Malden, MA: Blackwell.

Rickford, J. R., & McNair-Knox, F. (1994). Addressee- and topic-influenced style shift: A quantitative sociolinguistic study. In D. Biber & E. Finegan (Eds.). *Perspectives on register: Situating register variation within sociolinguistics* (pp. 235–276). New York: Oxford University Press.

Rickford, J. R., & Rickford, A. E. (1995). Dialect readers revisited. *Linguistics and Education, 7*(2), 107–28.

Rickford, J. R., & Rickford, R. J. (2000). *Spoken soul: The story of Black English*. New York: John Wiley.

Roberts, P. A. (1988). *West Indians and their language*. New York: Cambridge University Press.

Robbins, C., & Ehri, L. C. (1994). Reading storybooks to kindergartners helps them learn new vocabulary words. *Journal of Educational Psychology, 86*(1), 54–64.

Rogoff, B. (2003). *The cultural nature of human development*. New York: Oxford University Press.

Rosenthal, R., & Jacobson, L. (1968). *Pygmalion in the classroom: Teacher expectations and pupils' intellectual achievement*. New York: Holt, Rinehart and Winston.

Royster, J. J. (2000). *Traces of a stream: Literacy and social change among African American women*. Pittsburgh, PA: University of Pittsburgh Press.

Schwartz, M. J. (2000). *Born in bondage: Growing up enslaved in the antebellum South*. Cambridge, MA: Harvard University Press.

Scott, J. H. (1998). Official language, Unofficial reality: Acquiring bilingual/bicultural fluency in a segregated Southern community. In T. Perry & L. Delpit (Eds.). *The real Ebonics debate: Power, language, and the education of African American children* (pp. 189–195). Boston: Beacon.

Secret, C. (1998). Embracing Ebonics and teaching standard English. In T. Perry & L. Delpit (Eds.). *The real Ebonics debate: Power, language, and the education of African American children* (pp. 79–88). Boston: Beacon.

Senechal, M. (1997). The differential effects of storybook reading on preschoolers' acquisition of expressive and receptive vocabulary. *Journal of Child Language, 24*, 123–138.

Senechal, M., & Cornell, E. H. (1993). Vocabulary acquisition through shared reading experiences. *Reading Research Quarterly, 28*(4), 361–374.

Seymour, H. N., & Ralabate, P. K. (1985). The acquisition of a phonologic feature of Black English. *Journal of Communication Disorders, 18*, 139–148.

Simpkins, G. A., Holt, G., & Simpkins, C. (1977). *Bridge: A cross-cultural reading program*. Boston: Houghton Mifflin.

Simpkins, G. A., & Simpkins, C. (1981). Cross cultural approach to curriculum development. In G. Smitherman (Ed.), *Black English and the education of Black children and youth: Proceedings of the National Invitational Symposium on the King Decision*. Detroit: Wayne State University, Center for Black Studies.

Singham, M. (1998). The canary in the mine: The achievement gap between Black and White students. *Phi Delta Kappan, 80*, 8–15.

Slavin, R. E. (1987). Ability grouping and student achievement in elementary schools: A best evidence synthesis. *Review of Educational Research, 57*, 213–236.

Slavin, R. E. (1989). *Effects of ability grouping on Black, Latino, and White students.* Baltimore, MD: Johns Hopkins University, Center for Research on Effective Schooling for Disadvantaged Students.

Smith, E. (1998). What is Black English? What is Ebonics? In T. Perry & L. Delpit (Eds.), *The real Ebonics debate* (pp. 49–59). Boston: Beacon.

Smitherman, G. (1977/1986). *Talkin and testifyin: The language of Black America.* Boston: Houghton Mifflin; reissued, with revisions, Detroit: Wayne State University Press.

Smitherman, G. (1998). Word from the hood: The lexicon of African American vernacular English. In S. S. Mufwene, J. R. Rickford, G. Bailey, & J. Baugh (Eds.). *African American English: Structure, history and use* (pp. 203–225). New York: Routledge.

Smitherman, G. (1999). Language policy and classroom practices. In C. T. Adger, D. Christian, & O. Taylor (Eds.). *Making the connection: Language and academic achievement among African American students* (pp. 115–124). McHenry, IL: Delta Systems.

Smitherman, G. (2000a). *Talkin that talk: Language, culture and education in African America.* New York: Routledge.

Smitherman, G. (2000b). *Black talk: Words and phrases from the hood to the amen corner.* Boston: Houghton Mifflin.

Smitherman, G. (2003). Introduction. In E. Richardson. *African American Literacies.* New York: Routledge.

Snow, C. E., Burns, M. S., & Griffin, P. (1998). *Preventing reading difficulties in young children.* Washington, DC: National Academy Press.

Spears, A. K. (1982). The Black English semi-auxiliary *come. Language, 58,* 850–872.

Spears, A. K. (1988). Black American English. In J. P. Cole (Ed.). *Anthropology for the nineties* (pp. 96–113). New York: The Free Press.

Spears, A. K. (1998). African American language use: Ideology and so-called obscenity. In S. S. Mufwene, J. R. Rickford, G. Bailey, & J. Baugh (Eds.). *African American English: Structure, history and use* (pp. 226–250). New York: Routledge.

Spears, A. K. (2001). Directness in the use of African American English. In S. L. Lanehart (Ed.). *Sociocultural and historical contexts of African American English* (pp. 239–2590. Philadelphia: John Benjamins.

Sperry, L., & Sperry, D. (1996). Early development of narrative skills. *Cognitive Development, 11,* 443–465.

Stallings, J., Robbins, P., & Presbrey, L. (1986). Effects of instruction based on the Madeline Hunter model on students' achievement: Findings from a follow-through project. *The Elementary School Journal, 86,* 571–587.

Stanovich, K. E. (1986). Matthew effects in reading: Some consequences of individual differences in the acquisition of literacy. *Reading Research Quarterly, 21,* 360–407.

Stebbins, L. B., St. Pierre, R. G., Proper, E. C., Anderson, R. B., & Cerva, T. R. (1977). *Education as experimentation: A planned variation model (Vol. IV-A), An evaluation of Project Follow Through.* Cambridge, MA: Abt Associates.

Steele, C. (1992). Race and the schooling of Black Americans. *Atlantic Monthly, 269*, 68–78.

Stockman, I. J. (1996). Phonological development and disorders in African American children. In A. G. Kamhi, K. E. Pollock, & J. L. Harris (Eds.). *Communication development and disorders in African American children* (pp. 117–153). Baltimore: Brookes.

Stockman, I. J., & Vaughn-Cooke, F. B. (1982). Semantic categories in the language of working-class Black children. In C. Johnson & C. Thew (Eds.). *Proceedings from the Second International Congress for the Study of Child Language* (Vol. 1, pp. 312–327). Washington, DC: University Press of America.

Strickland, D. S. (2005). Educating African American learners at risk: Finding a better way. In B. Hammond, M. E. R. Hoover, & I. P. McPhail (Eds.). *Teaching African American learners to read* (pp. 147–160). Newark, DE: International Reading Association.

Stubbs, M. (1983). *Discourse analysis: The sociolinguistic analysis of natural language*. Chicago: University of Chicago Press.

Stuckey, S. (1987). *Slave culture: Nationalist theory and the foundations of Black America*. New York: Oxford University Press.

Sutcliffe, A. (Ed.). (2000). *Mighty rough times, I tell you*. Winston-Salem, NC: John F. Blair.

Taylor, D., & Dorsey-Gaines, C. (1988). *Growing up literate: Learning from inner-city families*. Portsmouth, NH: Heineman.

Taylor, H. U. (1989). *Standard English, Black English, and bidialectalism*. New York: Peter Lang.

Taylor, O. (1971). Response to social dialects and the field of speech. In R. Shuy (Ed.). *Sociolinguistic theory: Materials and practice* (pp. 13–20). Washington, DC: Center for Applied Linguistics.

Teale, W. H., & Sulzby, E. (1991). Emergent literacy. In R. Barr, M. Kamil, P. Mosenthal, & P. D. Pearson (Eds.). *Handbook of reading research* (Vol. 2, pp. 418–452). New York: Longman.

Tomasello, M. (1999). *The cultural origins of human cognition*. Cambridge, MA: Harvard University Press.

Towner, A. G., Hollins, E. R., & Labov, W. (2000). *African American literacy and culture research project: Executive summary* (U.S. Department of Education, Office of Educational Research and Improvement Award No. R215R980014-98). Hayward, CA: California State University, Hayward.

Trask, R. L. (1999). *Key concepts in language and linguistics*. New York: Routledge.

Troutman, D. (2001). African American women: Talking that talk. In S. L. Lanehart (Ed.). *Sociocultural and historical contexts of African American English* (pp. 211–237). Philadelphia: John Benjamins.

Tunmer, W. E., & Hoover, W. A. (1992). Cognitive and linguistic factors in learning to read. In P. B. Gough, L. C. Ehri, & R. Treiman (Eds.). *Reading acquisition* (pp. 175–214). Hillsdale, NJ: Lawrence Erlbaum Associates.

Vaughn-Cooke, A. F. (1999). Lessons learned from the Ebonics controversy: Implications for assessment. In C. T. Adger, D. Christian, & O. Taylor (Eds.). *Making the connection: Language and academic achievement among African American students* (pp. 137–168). McHenry, IL: Delta Systems.

Van Keulen, J. E., Weddington, G. T., & DeBose, C. E. (1998). *Speech, language, learning and the African American child.* Boston: Allyn & Bacon.

Vernon-Feagans, L. (1996). *Children's talk in communities and classrooms.* Cambridge, MA: Blackwell.

Vogt, L. A., Jordan, C., & Tharp, R. G. (1987). Explaining school failure, producing school success: Two cases. *Anthropology & Education Quarterly, 18*(2), 276–286.

Vygotsky, L. S. (1978). *Mind in society: The development of higher psychological processes.* Cambridge, MA: Harvard University Press.

Waters, A. (Ed.). (2002). *Prayin' to be set free.* Winston-Salem, NC: John F. Blair.

Whatley, E. M. (1980). Black English: Implications of the Ann Arbor decision for the classroom. In M. F. Whiteman (Ed.). *Reaction to Ann Arbor: Vernacular Black English and education* (pp. 61–76). Washington, DC: Center for Applied Linguistics.

Wilde, S. (1997). *What's a schwa sound anyway? A holistic guide to phonetics, phonics, and spelling.* Portsmouth, NH: Heineman.

Whiteman, M. F. (Ed.). (1980). *Reactions to Ann Arbor: Vernacular Black English and education.* Washington, DC: Center for Applied Linguistics.

Wolf, S. A. (2004). *Interpreting literature with children.* Mahwah, NJ: Lawrence Erlbaum Associates.

Wolfram, W. (1969). *A sociolinguistic description of Detroit Negro speech.* Washington, DC: Center for Applied Linguistics.

Wolfram, W. (1980). Beyond Black English: Implications of the Ann Arbor decision for other non-mainstream varieties. In M. F. Whiteman (Ed.). *Reactions to Ann Arbor: Vernacular Black English and education* (pp. 10–23). Washington, DC: Center for Applied Linguistics.

Wolfram, W. (1999). Repercussions from the Oakland Ebonics controversy—The critical role of dialect awareness programs. In C. T. Adger, D. Christian, & O. Taylor (Eds.). *Making the connection: Language and academic achievement among African American students* (pp. 61–80). McHenry, IL: Delta Systems.

Wolfram, W., Adger, C. T., & Christian, D. (1999). *Dialects in schools and communities.* Mahwah, NJ: Lawrence Erlbaum Associates.

Wolfram, W., & Schilling-Estes, N. (1998). *American English.* Malden, MA: Blackwell.

Wyatt, T. (1995). Language development in African American English child speech. *Linguistics and Education, 7,* 7–22.

Wyatt, T. (2001). The role of family, community, and school in children's acquisition and maintenance of African American English. In S. J. Lanehart (Ed.). *Sociocultural and historical contexts of African American English.* (pp. 261–280). Philadelphia: John Benjamins.

Wyatt, T., & Seymour, H. N. (1990). The implications of code-switching in Black English speakers. *Equity and Excellence, 24,* 17–18.

Yellin, J. F. (2004). *Harriet Jacobs: A life.* New York: Basic Civitas Books.

Yopp, H. (1988). The validity and reliability of phonemic awareness tests. *Reading Research Quarterly, 23,* 159–177.

Zentella, A. C. (1997). *Growing up bilingual.* Malden, MA: Blackwell.

Zeuli, J. S., & Floden, R. E. (1987). *Cultural incongruities and inequities in schooling: Implications for Practice from Ethnographic Research.* Occasional Paper No. 117, Institute for Research on Teaching, College of Education, Michigan State University, East Lansing, MI.

List of Children's Literature Cited

Adedjouma, D. (1996). *The palm of my heart: Poetry by African American children.* New York: Lee & Low Books.

Adoff, A. (1973/2002). *Black is brown is tan.* New York: HarperCollins/Amistad.

Arkhurst, J. C. (1964). *The adventures of Spider: West African folk tales.* Boston: Hyperion.

Banks, S. H. (1997). *A net to catch time.* New York: Knopf.

Barber, B. E. (1994). *Saturday at the New You.* New York: Lee & Low Books.

Barber, B. E. (1996). *Allie's basketball dream.* New York: Lee & Low Books.

Barrett, J. D. (1989). *Willie's not the hugging kind.* New York: Harper & Row.

Battle-Lavert, G. (1994). *The barber's cutting edge.* San Francisco: Children's Book Press.

Battle-Lavert, G. (1995). *Off to school.* New York: Holiday House.

Belton, S. (2004). *Beauty, her basket.* New York: Greenwillow Books/Amistad.

Belton, S. (1993). *From Miss Ida's porch.* New York: Simon Schuster.

Berry, J. (1997). *First palm trees: An Anancy spiderman story.* New York: Simon & Schuster.

Bolden, T. (2004). *The champ: The story of Muhammad Ali.* New York: Knopf.

Bolden, T. (2001). *Rock of ages: A tribute to the Black church.* New York: Alfred A. Knopf.

Boling, K. (2002). *New year be coming!* Morton Grove, IL: Albert Whitman.

Bradby, M. (1995). *More than anything else.* New York: Orchard Books.

Bridges, R. (1999). *Through my eyes.* New York: Scholastic.

Caines, J. (1988). *I need a lunch box.* New York: HarperTrophy.

Cameron, A. (1981). *The stories Julian tells.* New York: Knopf.

Cameron, A. (1986). *More stories Julian tells.* New York: Knopf.

Cameron, A. (1987). *Julian's glorious summer.* New York: Random House.

Cameron, A. (1988). *Julian, secret agent.* New York: Random House.

Cameron, A. (1990). *Julian, dream doctor.* New York: Random House.

Cameron, A. (1995). *The stories Huey tells.* New York: Knopf.

Cameron, A. (1999). *More stories Huey tells.* New York: Knopf.

Cameron, A. (2001). *Gloria's way.* New York: Puffin Books.

Cameron, A. (2004). *Gloria rising.* New York: Dell Yearling.

Cameron, P. (1961). *"I can't," said the ant.* New York: Scholastic.

Campbell, B. M. (2003). *Sometimes my mommy gets angry.* New York: Putnam.

Chambers, V. (2002). *Double dutch: A celebration of jump rope, rhyme, and sister hood.* New York: Hyperion Books.

Chambers, V. (2005). *Celia Cruz: Queen of Salsa.* New York: Dial.

Clifton, L. (1970). *Some of the days of Everett Anderson.* New York: Henry Holt.

Clifton, L. (1971/1991). *Everett Anderson's Christmas coming.* New York: Henry Holt.

Clifton, L. (1974/1992). *Everett Anderson's year.* New York: Henry Holt.

Clifton, L. (1976/1992). *Everett Anderson's friend.* New York: Henry Holt.

Clifton, L. (1977/2002). *Everett Anderson's 1 2 3.* New York: Henry Holt.

Clifton, L. (1978). *Everett Anderson's nine month long.* New York: Holt, Rinehart and Winston.

Clifton, L. (1983/1988). *Everett Anderson's goodbye.* New York: Henry Holt.

Clifton, L. (2001). *One of the problems of Everett Anderson.* New York: Henry Holt.

Cole, K. (2001). *No bad news.* Morton Grove, IL: Albert Whitman.

Coles, R. (1995). *The story of Ruby Bridges.* New York: Scholastic.

Collier, B. *Uptown* (2000). New York: Henry Holt.

Cooke, T. (1994). *So much.* Boston: Candlewick Press.

Cooke, T. (2003). *Full, full, full of love.* Boston: Candlewick Press.

Cooper, F. (1994). *Coming home: From the life of Langston Hughes.* New York: Philomel Books.

Cooper, F. (2004). *Jump: From the life of Michael Jordan.* New York: Philomel Books.

Cosby, B. (1997). *The best way to play.* New York: Scholastic.

Cosby, B. (1997). *The meanest thing to say.* New York: Scholastic.

Cosby, B. (1997). *The treasure hunt.* New York: Scholastic.

Cosby, B. (1998). *Money troubles.* New York: Scholastic.

Cosby, B. (1998). *Shipwreck Saturday.* New York: Scholastic.

Cosby, B. (1998). *Super-fine valentine.* New York: Scholastic.

Cosby, B. (1999). *Hooray for the Dandelion Warriors!* New York: Scholastic.

Cosby, B. (1999). *My big lie.* New York: Scholastic.

Cosby, B. (1999). *One dark and scary night.* New York: Scholastic.

Cosby, B. (1999). *The day I was rich.* New York: Scholastic.

Cosby, B. (1999). *The worst day of my life.* New York: Scholastic.

Cosby, B. (2000). *The day I saw my father cry.* New York: Scholastic.

Crews, D. (1991). *Bigmama's.* New York: Greenwillow Books.

Crews, D. (1992). *Shortcut.* New York: Greenwillow Books.

Crews, N. (1998). *You are here.* New York: Greenwillow Books.

Cummings, P. (1994). *Clean your room, Harvey Moon!* New York: Aladdin.

Curtis. G. (1998). *The bat boy and his violin.* New York: Simon & Schuster.

Daise, R. (1997). *Little Muddy Waters: A Gullah folk tale.* Beaufort, SC: G. O. G. Enterprises.

DeGross, M. (1998). *Donavan's word jar.* New York: HarperTrophy.

DeGross, M. (1999). *Granddaddy's street songs.* New York: Hyperion.

Diakite, B. W. (2003). *The magic gourd.* New York: Scholastic.

Doyle, A. C. (1996). *Sherlock Holmes.* New York: Knopf.

Evans, F. W. (2001). *A bus of our own*. Morton Grove, IL: Albert Whitman.

Falwell, C. (1993). *Feast for ten*. New York: Clarion Books.

Falwell, C. (2001). *David's drawings*. New York: Lee & Low Books.

Farris, K. C. (2003). *My brother Martin: A sister remembers growing up with the Rev. Dr. Martin Luther King, Jr.* New York: Simon & Schuster.

Feelings, T. (Ed.) (1993). *Soul looks back in wonder*. New York: Puffin Books.

Flournoy, V. (1985). *The patchwork quilt*. New York: Dial.

Flournoy, V. (1995). *Tanya's reunion*. New York: Dial.

Giovanni, N. (1971/1985). *Spin a soft Black song: Poems for children*. New York: Hill and Wang.

Giovanni, N. (2005). *Rosa*. New York: Henry Holt.

Greenfield, E. (1978). *Honey, I love, and other love poems*. New York: Harper Collins.

Greenfield, E. (1996). *Night on Neighborhood Street*. New York: Puffin.

Greenfield, E. (1983). *Grandmama's joy*. New York: Philomel Books.

Greenfield, E. (1974, 1993). *She come bringing me that little baby girl*. New York: HarperTrophy.

Greenfield, E. (1976/1991). *First pink light*. New York: Black Butterfly Children's Books.

Greenfield, E. (1978). *Honey, I love and other love poems*. New York: HarperCollins.

Greenfield, E. (1988). *Grandpa's face*. New York: Philomel Books.

Greenfield, E. (1988). *Nathaniel talking*. New York: Black Butterfly Children's Books.

Greenfield, E. (1988). *Under the Sunday tree*. New York: HarperTrophy.

Greenfield, E. (1991). *Night on neighborhood street*. New York: Dial.

Greenfield, E. (1995). *Rosa Parks*. New York: HarperCollins.

Greenfield, E. (1997). *For the love of the game: Michael Jordan and me*. New York: HarperCollins.

Grimes, N. (1994). *Meet Danitra Brown*. New York: Lothrap, Lee, & Shepard.

Grimes, N. (1997). *Come Sunday*. Cambridge, UK: Eerdman's Books for Young Readers.

Grimes, N. (1997). *It's raining laughter*. New York. Dial.

Grimes, N. (1997). *Wild, wild hair*. New York: Scholastic.

Grimes, N. (1999). *My man Blue*. New York: Puffin.

Grimes, N. (2001). *Stepping out with Grandma Mac*. New York: Orchard Books.

Grimes, N. (2002). *Danitra Brown leaves town*. New York: HarperCollins/Amistad.

Grimes, N. (2005). *Danitra Brown, class clown*. New York: HarperCollins/Amistad.

Hamilton, V. (2003). *Bruh Rabbit and the tar baby girl*. New York: Blue Sky Press/Scholastic.

Harrington, J. N. (2004). *Going north*. New York: Farrar, Straus and Giroux.

Haskins, J. (2002). *Champion: The story of Muhammad Ali*. New York: Walker.

Haskins, J. (2005). *Delivering justice: W. W. Law and the fight for civil rights*. Boston: Candlewick Press.

Havill, J. (1986). *Jamaica's find*. Boston: Houghton Mifflin.

Havill, J. (1989). *Jamaica tag-along*. Boston: Houghton Mifflin.

Havill, J. (1993). *Jamaica and Brianna*. Boston: Houghton Mifflin.

Havill, J. (1995). *Jamaica's blue marker.* Boston: Houghton Mifflin.

Havill, J. (1999). *Jamaica and the substitute teacher.* Boston: Houghton Mifflin.

Havill, J. (2002). *Brianna, Jamaica, and the dance of spring.* Boston: Houghton Mifflin.

Hilliard-Nunn, N. P. (1997). *Foluke: The Afro queen.* Gainesville, FL: Makara.

hooks, b. (2002). *Homemade love.* New York: Jump at the Sun/Hyperion.

hooks, b. (2004). *Skin again.* New York: Jump at the Sun/Hyperion.

Hopkinson, D. (1993). *Sweet Clara and the freedom quilt.* New York: Knopf.

Hopkinson, D. (1999). *A band of angels: A story inspired by the Jubilee Singers.* New York: Atheneum.

Hopkinson, D. (2001). *Under the quilt of night.* New York: Atheneum.

Hort, L. (1991). *How many stars in the sky?* New York: Tambourine Books.

Howard, E. F. (1988). *The train to LuLu's.* New York: Bradbury Press.

Howard, E. F. (1991). *Aunt Flossie's hats (and crab cakes later).* New York: Clarion Books.

Howard, E. F. (1993). *Mac and Marie and the train toss surprise.* New York: Four Winds Press.

Howard, E. F. (1996). *What's in Aunt Mary's room?* New York: Houghton Mifflin Company.

Howard, E. F. (1999). *When will Sarah come?* New York: Greenwillow Books.

Howard, E. F. (2000). *Virgie goes to school with us boys.* New York: Simon & Schuster.

Hru, D. (1993). *Joshua's Masai mask.* New York: Lee & Low Books.

Hudson, C. W., & Ford, B. G. (1990). *Bright eyes, brown skin.* East Orange, NJ: Just Us Books.

Hudson, W. (1993). *I love my family.* New York: Scholastic.

Igus, T. (1992). *When I was little.* East Orange, NJ: Just Us Books.

Igus, T. (1996). *Two Mrs. Gibsons.* San Francisco: Children's Book Press.

Johnson, A. (1989). *Tell me a story, Mama.* New York: Orchard Books.

Johnson, A. (1990). *Do like Kyla.* New York: Orchard Books.

Johnson, A. (1990). *When I am old with you.* New York: Orchard Books.

Johnson, A. (1997). *Daddy calls me man.* New York: Orchard Books.

Johnson, A. (1997). *The rolling store.* New York: Orchard Books.

Johnson, A. (2003). *I dream of trains.* New York: Simon & Schuster.

Johnson, A. (2004). *Just like Josh Gibson.* New York: Simon & Schuster.

Johnson, A. (2004). *Violet's music.* New York: Dial.

Johnson, A. (2005). *A sweet smell of roses.* New York: Simon & Schuster.

Johnson, D. (1992). *The best bug to be.* New York: Macmillan.

Johnson, D. (1998). *What will Mommy do when I'm at school?* New York: Aladdin.

Johnson, D. (2000). *Quinnie blue.* New York: Henry Holt.

Jonas, A. (1984). *The quilt.* New York: Greenwillow Books.

Jones, R. C. (1991). *Matthew and Tilly.* New York: Dutton.

Jordan, D. (2000). *Salt in his shoes. Michael Jordan in pursuit of a dream.* New York: Simon & Schuster.

Joseph, L. (1998). *Fly, Bessie, fly.* New York: Simon & Schuster.

King, C., & Osborne, L. B. (1997). *Oh, freedom!: Kids talk about the Civil Rights Movement with the people who made it happen.* New York: Knopf.

Lauture, D. (1992). *Father and son.* New York: Philomel Books.

Lawrence, J. (1993). *Harriet and the promised land.* New York: Simon & Schuster.

Lester, J. (1994). *John Henry.* New York: Dial.

Lester, J. (2005). *Let's talk about race.* New York: HarperCollins.

Marzollo, J. (2001). *I am a star.* New York: Scholastic.

Mattox, C. W. (Ed.). (1989). *Shake it to the one that you love the best: Play songs and lullabies from Black musical traditions.* Nashville, TN: Warren-Mattox Productions.

McKissack, P. C. (1986). *Flossie and the fox.* New York: Dial.

McKissack, P. C. (1988). *Mirandy and brother wind.* New York: Knopf.

McKissack, P. C. (1989). *Nettie Jo's friends.* New York: Knopf.

McKissack, P. C. (1992). *A million fish . . . more or less.* New York: Knopf.

McKissack, P. C. (1997). *Ma Dear's aprons.* New York: Atheneum.

McKissack, P. C. (2000). *The honest-to-goodness truth.* New York: Atheneum.

McKissack, P. C. (2001). *Goin' someplace special.* New York: Atheneum.

McKissack, P. C. (2005). *Abby takes a stand.* New York: Viking.

McKissack, P. C., & Onawumi, J. M. (2005). *Precious and the Boo Hag.* New York: Atheneum.

Mead, A. (1995). *Junebug.* New York: Farrar, Straus and Giroux.

Mead, A. (1998). *Junebug and the reverend.* New York: Farrar, Straus and Giroux.

Medearis, A. S. (1994). *Annie's gifts.* East Orange, NJ: Just Us Books.

Medearis, A. S. (1994). *Our people.* New York: Atheneum.

Medearis, A. S. (1995). *Poppa's new pants.* New York: Holiday House.

Medearis, A. S. (1995). *The Adventures of Sugar and Junior.* New York: Holiday House.

Medearis, A. S. (1997). *Rum-a-tum-tum.* New York: Holiday House.

Medearis, M., & Medearis, A. S. (2000). *Daisy and the doll.* Middlebury, VT: University Press of New England.

Medina, T. (2002). *Love to Langston.* New York: Lee & Low Books.

Miller, T. (1996). *Can a coal scuttle fly?* Baltimore: Maryland Historical Society.

Mitchell, M. K. (1993). *Uncle Jed's barbershop.* New York: Simon & Schuster.

Mitchell, M. K. (1997). *Granddaddy's gift.* Mahwah, NJ: BridgeWater Books.

Mitton, J. (1998). *Zoo in the sky: A book of animal constellations.* Washington, DC: National Geographic Society.

Morrison, T. (2004). *Remember: The journey to school integration.* Boston: Houghton Mifflin.

Myers, C. (2005). *Lies and other tall tales* (collected by Zora Neale Hurston) New York: HarperCollins.

Myers, W. D. (1997). *Harlem: A poem.* New York: Scholastic.

Myers, W. D. (2000). *Malcolm X: A fire burning brightly.* New York: HarperCollins.

Myers, W. D. (2004). *I've seen the promised land: The life of Dr. Martin Luther King, Jr.* New York: HarperCollins.

Myers, W. D. (1993). *Brown angels: An album of pictures and verse.* New York: HarperCollins.

Nelson, V. M. (2003). *Almost to freedom.* Minneapolis, MN: Carolrhoda Books.

Nolen, J. (1999). *In my momma's kitchen.* New York: Lothrop, Lee, & Shepard.

Norman, L. (2006). *My feet are laughing.* New York: Farrar, Straus and Giroux.

Patrick, D. L. (2004). *Ma Dear's old green house*. East Orange, NJ: Just Us Books.

Paye, W., & Lippert, M. (2002). *Head, body, legs: A story from Liberia*. New York: Henry Holt.

Perdomo, W. (2002). *Visiting Langston*. New York: Henry Holt.

Picó, F. (1994). *The red comb*. Mahwah, NJ: BridgeWater Books.

Pinkney, A. D. (1996). *Bill Pickett: Rodeo-ridin' cowboy*. San Diego: Harcourt.

Pinkney, A. D. (1998). *Duke Ellington: The piano prince and his orchestra*. New York: Hyperion.

Pinkney, A. D. (2000). *Let it shine: Stories of Black women freedom fighters*. San Diego: Harcourt.

Pinkney, A. D. (2002). *Ella Fitzgerald: The tale of a vocal virtuosa*. New York: Jump at the Sun/Hyperion.

Pinkney, A. D. (2003). *Fishing day*. New York: Jump at the Sun/Hyperion.

Pinkney, A. D. (2004). *Sleeping cutie*. Orlando: Gulliver Books/Harcourt.

Pinkney, B. (1994). *Max found two sticks*. New York: Simon & Schuster.

Pinkney, B. (1995). *JoJo's flying side kick*. Boston: Houghton Mifflin.

Pinkney, G. J. (1992). *Back home*. New York: Dial.

Pinkney, G. J. (1994). *The Sunday outing*. New York: Dial.

Pinkney, S. L. (2000). *Shades of Black: A celebration of our children*. New York: Scholastic.

Ransom, C. (2003). *Liberty Street*. New York: Walker.

Rappaport, D. (2001). *Martin's big words: The life of Dr. Martin Luther King, Jr.* New York: Jump at the Sun/Hyperion.

Rashka, C. (1992). *Charlie Parker played be bop*. New York: Orchard Books.

Raven, M. T. (2004). *Circle unbroken: The story of a basket and its people*. New York: Farrar, Straus and Giroux.

Ringgold, F. (1991). *Tar beach*. New York: Crown.

Ringgold, F. (1992). *Aunt Harriet's underground railroad in the sky*. New York: Knopf.

Ringgold, F. (1995). *My dream of Martin Luther King*. New York: Crown.

Ringgold, F. (1999). *If a bus could talk: The story of Rosa Parks*. New York: Simon & Schuster.

Rochelle, B. (1994). *When Jo Louis won the title*. Boston: Houghton Mifflin.

Rochelle, B. (1998). *Jewels*. New York: Lodestar Books/Dutton.

Rockwell, A. (2002). *Our stars*. San Diego: Voyager Books.

Rodman, M. A. (2005). *My best friend*. New York: Viking.

Rosales, M. B. (1999). *Leola and the honeybears*. New York: Scholastic.

San Souci, R. D. (1989). *The talking eggs: A folktale from the American South*. New York: Dial.

San Souci, R. D. (1992). *Sukey and the mermaid*. New York: Four Winds Press.

San Souci, R. D. (1996). *The house in the sky*. New York: Dial.

San Souci, R. D. (1998). *Cendrillon: A Caribbean Cinderella*. New York: Simon & Schuster.

Sendak, Maurice. (1970). *In the night kitchen*. New York: Harper & Row.

Shange, N. (1994). *I live in music*. New York: Welcome Enterprises.

Shange, N. (2002). *Float like a butterfly*. New York: Hyperion.

Shange, N. (2004). *ellington was not a street*. New York: Simon & Schuster.

Smalls, I. (1991). *Irene and the big, fine nickel*. Boston: Little, Brown.

Smalls, I. (1992). *Jonathan and his mommy*. Boston: Little, Brown.

Smalls, I. (1996). *Irene Jennie and the Christmas masquerade*. Boston: Little, Brown.

Smalls, I. (1996). *Louise's gift*. Boston: Little, Brown.

Smalls, I. (1997). *Because you're lucky*. Boston: Little, Brown.

Smalls, I. (1999). *Kevin and his dad*. Boston: Little, Brown.

Smalls, I. (2005). *My Nana and me*. Boston: Little, Brown.

Smalls, I. (2006). *My Pop Pop and me*. Boston: Little, Brown.

Smith, C., Jr. (2000). *Brown sugar babies*. New York: Jump at the Sun/Hyperion.

Smith, E. B. (1994). *A lullaby for Daddy*. Trenton, NJ: Africa World Press.

Smith, P. (2003). *Janna and the kings*. New York: Lee & Low Books, Inc.

Smothers, E. F. (2003). *The hard-times jar*. New York: Farrar, Straus and Giroux.

Steptoe, J. (1987). *Mufaro's beautiful daughters: An African tale*. New York: Amistad.

Steptoe, J. (1997). *Creativity*. New York: Clarion.

Steptoe, J. (2003). *The Jones family express*. New York: Lee & Low Books.

Tarpley, N. A. (1998). *I love my hair!* Boston: Little, Brown.

Tarpley, N. A. (2002). *Bippity Bop barbershop*. Boston: Little, Brown.

Tarpley, N. A. (2003). *Joe-Joe's first flight*. New York: Knopf.

Tarpley, N. A. (2004). *Destiny's gift*. New York: Lee & Low Books.

Taulbert, C. L. (1999). *Little Cliff and the porch people*. New York: Dial.

Taulbert, C. L. (2001). *Little Cliff's first day of school*. New York: Dial.

Taylor, M. D. (1976). *Roll of thunder, hear my cry*. New York: Puffin Books.

Taylor, M. D. (1992). *Mississippi bridge*. New York: Bantam.

Velasquez, E. (2001). *Grandma's records*. New York: Walker.

Walker, A. (2002). *Langston Hughes: American poet*. New York: Amistad.

Walter, M. P. (1980). *Ty's one-man band*. New York: Scholastic.

Walter, M. P. (1999). *Suitcase*. New York: Lothrop, Lee & Shepard.

Walvoord, L. (2004). *Rosetta, Rosetta, sit by me!* New York: Marshall Cavendish.

Weatherford, C. (2005). *Freedom on the menu*. New York: Dial.

Wesley, V. (1997). *Freedom's gifts: A Juneteenth story*. New York: Simon & Schuster.

Wiles, D. (2001). *Freedom summer*. New York: Atheneum.

Wood, M., & Igus, T. (1996). *Going back home: An artist returns to the South*. San Francisco: Children's Book Press.

Woodson, J. (1998). *We had a picnic this Sunday past*. New York: Hyperion.

Woodson, J. (2001). *The other side*. New York: Putnam.

Woodson, J. (2002). *Our Gracie Aunt*. New York: Jump at the Sun/Hyperion.

Woodson, J. (2002). *Visiting day*. New York: Scholastic.

Woodson, J. (2005). *Show way*. New York: Putnam.

Woodtor, D. P. (1996). *Big meeting*. New York: Atheneum.

Wyeth, S. D. (1995). *Always my Dad*. New York: Knopf.

Wyeth, S. D. (1998). *Something beautiful*. New York: Bantam Doubleday Dell.

Yarbrough, C. (1979). *Cornrows*. New York: Coward, McCann & Geoghegan.

Author Index

Subject Index

W

Y

Z